Early Film HISTORY

William R. Foster
Pasadena City College

Kendall Hunt
publishing company
4050 Westmark Drive • P O Box 1840 • Dubuque IA 52004-1840

Cover and title page images:
Mary Pickford © 2009 JupiterImages Corporation
Lumiere brothers © 2009 JupiterImages Corporation

Copyright © 2009 by Kendall/Hunt Publishing Company

ISBN 978-0-7575-5837-5

Printed in the United States of America
10 9 8 7 6 5 4 3 2 1

DEDICATION

To my beautiful wife, Donna Carolan, who makes life a joy and who helped immeasurably in the creation of this book.

To our son, Vincent, who makes me proud every day that I am his father.

CONTENTS

Foreword.. ix

CHAPTER 1 — INVENTING MOTION PICTURES

Prehistory 1
Photography 1
Persistence of Vision 2
Series Photographs, Motion Studies: Muybridge and Stanford...................... 2
Eadweard Muybridge (1830–1904) 3
Edison, Dickson, and the Advent of the
      American Commercial Film Industry............................. 4
August Lumiére (1862–1954) and Louis Lumiére (1864–1948)................... 6
Film Inventors Give Way to Film Makers................................. 7
The Edison Patent Trust 11
The Era of Film Invention Comes to an End........................... 12

CHAPTER 2 — FILM PIONEERS

Moguls, Movie Makers and Movie Stars 13
David Wark Griffith (1875–1948)... 13

CHAPTER 3 — PIONEERS CONTINUED:

Movie Makers, Movie Stars and the Movie Business

Mack Sennett.. 27
Mabel Normand... 32
Fatty Arbuckle 34
The Men Who Made Paramount: Adolph Zukor, Jesse Lasky,
      Cecil B. DeMille, and Others 37
Charlie Chaplin.. 39
Carl Laemmle.. 44
William Fox 46
Samuel Goldwyn... 48
Mary Pickford and Douglas Fairbanks...................................... 50

THE STUDIOS:
Majors and Minors

Thomas Ince and the Industrial Model of Motion Picture Production 55

Paramount and the Advent of the Major Motion Picture Studios.................. 57

MGM: Marcus Loew, Louis B. Mayer, and Irving Thalberg........................... 58

Fox and Twentieth Century 62

Darryl Zanuck.. 62

Warner Brothers 64

Warners Acquires Vitagraph.. 65

RKO 65

Minor Studios.. 67

THE SOUND REVOLUTION

Early Sound Experiments.. 73

The Warner Brothers and the Western Electric Company............................. 74

1928: The Sound Revolution Begins 77

1929: Sound Becomes the Norm 79

The Stars Plan and Make Their Talking Debuts... 81

EUROPE BETWEEN THE WARS:
German Expressionism, Soviet Montage, Surrealism, and National Film Movements

German Expressionism and UFA Studios 85

The Russian Revolution and Soviet Filmmaking... 90

France Between the World Wars... 97

England Between the World Wars... 101

CHAPTER 7 — HOLLYWOOD AND THE GREAT DEPRESSION

The Crash 105
Comedy: Vaudevillians, Romantics and Screwballs 111
Capra, Hawks, and the Screwball Comedy 122
Musicals 128
Horror and Fantasy 132
Mob Rule, G-Men, and Women of the Streets 135
Great Directors of the Thirties 139
Great Movie Stars of the Thirties 143
1939: The Greatest Year 161

CHAPTER 8 — HOLLYWOOD GOES TO WAR

1940–40: Before the Storm 169
Gearing Up the Propaganda 177
The War Comes to America 178
The Paramount Consent Decree (Part One) 179
The Movie Stars Go to War 180
Other Filmmakers Serve by Making Films 183
The Stars Find Other Ways to Serve 185
Important Films from War Time 188
War's End 192

CHAPTER 9 — POST-WAR WORLD CINEMA

The End of World War II and the Beginning of the Cold War 199
The Anti-Communist Witch Hunt and the Motion Picture Industry 200
The Method 202
Film Noir 204
"B" Movies 205
A New Generation of Stars 208
New Directors 213
Paramount Consent Decree: The Resolution 216
Post-War European Cinema 217
Post-War British Cinema 221

Afterword 223
Index 225

FOREWORD

Phineas T. Barnum, the son of a Connecticut innkeeper, rose from the ordinary world of small businessmen to become a crusading newspaperman. His cause was the liberalization of drinking and gambling laws until his editorials against local church leaders landed him in jail for two months for committing libel. After that unfortunate experience Barnum went into the entertainment business, first with a variety troupe he called "Barnum's Grand Scientific and Musical Theater."

In 1841 he opened Barnum's American Museum at Broadway and Ann Street in Manhattan. His collection of freaks and oddities quickly became popular attraction. He publicized his business by performing a never ending string of hoaxes, the first being "FeJee" mermaid, with the head of a monkey and the tail of a fish. His next attraction was a dwarf whom he named General Tom Thumb. The two traveled over the world, even giving a performance for Queen Victoria.

In 1846 Barnum's museum drew four hundred thousand visitors as he was developing his next attraction, Jenny Lind, "The Swedish Nightingale." His preparations for her European tour were so good that she was greeted by forty thousand fans when her ship docked in England.

In 1860 Barnum presented one of his most successful attractions, Chang and Eng, the Siamese Twins. Throughout the Civil War and early post war period, Barnum continued to present new attractions, all the while investing the profits in real estate schemes. In 1865 his museum burned to the ground and the rebuilt museum met the same fate three years later. It was too much for Barnum who went into retirement. The pull of show business was too strong on him. In 1871 he put together a new attraction, "P.T. Barnum's Grand Traveling Museum, Menagerie, Caravan and Hippodrome." It was a combination circus and freak show which was later renamed "The Greatest Show on Earth." In 1881 he teamed up with another circus man, James Bailey. Their combined circuses were truely great shows. The were the first to buy a private train and travel exclusively by rail, making the circus the most efficient and best known in the world. Barnum died in his sleep in 1891, four years before Edison's first kinetoscopes would begin to appear on Broadway. Although he never made a movie, there is no doubt he would have made great spectacles. His spirit of anything goes hucksterism and showmanship did become the blueprint for the way the new medium of the twentieth century would go about capturing the public's imagination.

The penny arcades where movies got their start were in the same neighborhood as Barnum's museum. Arcade men like Marcus Loew would certainly have witnessed the sheer audaciousness of the master showman's ability to make the smallest attraction an imperative experience for the working class and tourist hoards that gathered daily on Broadway. Barnum proved to these movie pioneers that bigger is better, especially when it comes to promotion. As the movies moved out of the arcades and into the nickleodeons they were still just a curiosity, something to do to pass the time. For immigrant factory workers, the movies also served the function of teaching language and customs to an audience eager to jump into the American melting pot and assimilate.

Gradually during the first decade of the twentieth century the movies started to get bigger. Driven by pioneers like Ince and Griffith the flickering curiosities of the nickelodeon were being transformed into something grander. Griffith always claimed to be inspired by David Belasco, the great stage impresario of the nineteenth century. But as Griffith's dreams grew he became increasingly imbued with the spirit of Barnum. He began to fall in love with the idea of the spectacle. But to create such films he would need to put his dreams into the heads of the men who wrote the checks and the people who bought the tickets. Like Barnum, Griffith became a super salesman. Motion pictures had a quality that Barnum would have envied. Through the use of the lens and the projection screen, images could actually be made bigger than life. The selling of the medium would need to also become stupendous. The first entrepreneurs all were salesmen. Goldwyn nee Goldfish sold gloves. Loew and Zukor sold furs. Laemmle sold menswear. Mayer's family was in the junk trade. All of these men understood the power of Barnum to take an attraction, almost ordinary by nature, and to make it seem awesome in the imaginations of the audience. They did the same with motion pictures. They sold dreams. They built picture palaces and movie factories and transformed the flickering curiosities of the nickelodeon into the new greatest show on earth.

Many in the first generation of performers and filmmakers came from sketchy backgrounds such as circuses, carnivals, vaudeville, and traveling theater companies. They were rootless and nomadic. Many were escaping troubled pasts. It's no wonder that they tended to make up their own back stories. It was good for business if the audience believed that a glamorous young actress was the daughter of an Arab sheik or a dashing young actor had been a soldier of fortune. It added to the allure of the movies. When the studios came into existence so did the press agents and publicity departments, people whose only job was to add to the legend of the stars, directors and studio bosses. Film history gets a little tangled as a result. For people and events there are often conflicting accounts. For this book wherever that has been the case the choice has been to discount the sensational and report the most logical account of who people were and what they did.

In the 1920s movies became the fashion and trend setter for the growing middle class. Society was changing fast and motion pictures were both leading and reflecting the change. The studios began to lose their temporary feel and became solid industrial establishments with world wide distribution networks. Talent became capital and the motion picture companies became adept at developing new stars and filmmakers. But it was still a risk taking enterprise populated by people like William Fox who risked and lost everything in his attempt to control the industry. The Warner brothers won their big gamble with sound and newcomers like Walt Disney saw the possibilities, not only in sound, but in color and in making animation an art.

The thirties and the great depression posed a huge threat to the industry. Virtually all of the studios fell into bankruptcy. But, through perseverance and imagination they emerged in tact. They survived through making better movies and by giving the audience value. Another thing the movies did during that dark time was to give people optimism and hope for a better tomorrow. When the even greater threat of world war two emerged, the movies were prepared to respond. The great salesmanship that had developed over the course of movie history became invaluable in keeping American spirits high during the war. The selflessness of many stars and filmmakers also set an example for the rest of the country. When the war was over, the movies were still there to help the country digest and understand what it had been through and to look to the future, rather than dwelling on the past. Of course it was all good business. But there was a real sincerity to the efforts of the immigrant fathers of the movie industry to do the right thing. Most of them had come to America penniless and became wealthy beyond their wildest dreams. They were grateful and cared deeply about their adopted homeland.

In many ways movie history is the story of America growing up as a country and a society. Motion pictures begin as simple stories, told in pantomime. They matured into an industry that has the power to entertain the entire population and create a common social experience that cuts through class lines, ages and geography. The New York banker saw the same movies the Montana farmer saw. The movies taught Americans how to dream and imagine the unimaginable. Today they continue to amuse us and touch us. They continue to evolve with technological change and changing portrayals of the human experience. And the history of movies continues to add new chapters to its story.

INVENTING MOTION PICTURES

PREHISTORY

Virtually all civilizations have depicted people, events, places, and conceptions of spiritual subjects. Stone-age cave dwellers in France adorned the walls of their caves with images of hunting for the woolly mammoth. Some of these scenes even appear to depict the animals in motion. There must be some hard-wired, innate need among humans to record images. For centuries, in both eastern and western civilizations, images have been regarded as treasures, whether they hang in palaces, places of worship, or museums. As the industrial revolution unfolded in the early 1800s humankind's relationship to images began to change. Industrial processes such as mechanized printing and photography made images and image making accessible to the new working and middle classes. The end of the nineteenth century introduced a larger-than-life medium: the motion picture. At first, audiences were astounded by the power and excitement of the projected moving image. Artists and storytellers were inspired by the seemingly limitless possibilities. Likewise, astute businessmen instinctively understood the motion picture's potential to create vast wealth. Today, we also understand the profound role the motion picture plays in the creation of human mythology, style, and attitudes.

PHOTOGRAPHY

The word photography means literally "painting with light." Photographic technology combines optics systems with photo-sensitive chemicals and emulsions that change when exposed to light. Crude optic systems existed long before the Renaissance. Leonardo da Vinci had access to the camera obscura, a device that used pinhole optics to project images on a wall where it could be easily traced.

In 1802 Thomas Wedgewood discovered that images could be created by exposing plates of leather treated with silver nitrate to light. However the image record lasted for only an impracticable few minutes. In 1816 Nicéphore Niépce successfully combined the camera obscura with photosensitive paper to make and capture images. However, not only did this process require up to eight hours of exposure time to make a recognizable image, it began to fade away as soon as it was exposed to light. It would take Niépce an additional eleven years to create images that did not fade.

In 1829 Niépce formed a partnership with Louis Daguerre in the pursuit of practical photography. Four years later Neipce died, leaving Daguerre to continue. During the next ten years Daguerre improved on the technology, finally achieving exposure times of less than half an hour. This made posing for a "daguerreotype" portrait possible and affordable for middle-class Frenchmen. In 1839, the French government bought the rights to the process and publicized them in the public domain for all to use. The popularity of photography swept around the world.

- 1853—The first commercial photography studios begin operation in Paris.
- 1861— New York photographer, Matthew Brady, and his staff document the American Civil War with photographs.
- 1861—James Clerk-Maxwell creates color photographic lantern slides.
- 1888—George Eastman markets the first "do it yourself" consumer home camera system.

PERSISTENCE OF VISION

The ability to see a series of still images in motion is dependent on the fact that the retina, the light-receiving part of our eyes, retains light information for an instant after the image is gone. When a succeeding image with the next step of a motion progression is exposed to the retina, the two images overlap for an instant. At the same time the images are sent to the viewer's iconic memory, which stores and compares them. When a series of related still images are shown to the viewer at a sufficient speed, the result is the experience of motion. The iconic memory makes the connections, and the retina's persistence of vision smoothes out the sense of flicker. The discovery of this principle in the early 1800s led to the development of toys and more serious devices for scientific study such as the zoetrope and the praxinoscope.

SERIES PHOTOGRAPHS, MOTION STUDIES: MUYBRIDGE AND STANFORD

More than any other, the event that sparked the quest for the motion picture was the result of a $25,000 bet Leland Stanford legendarily made with his horse racing pals, that "a galloping horse could fly," and leap forward with his four hooves off the ground.

LELAND STANFORD (1824–1893)

Leland Stanford followed his older brothers to the California gold rush of 1849. Stanford didn't arrive until 1852—and as far as gold was concerned, this was too late to stake a successful mining claim. But Stanford was armed with his upbringing as the son of a prosperous New York farming family replete with a privileged secondary and university education, resulting in his membership in a distinguished Wisconsin law firm in 1848. When Stanford arrived in California, it wasn't to dig for gold, but to sell supplies to those who did. This turned out to be a vastly more profitable business.

Stanford grew his wealth through acquiring land and staking out a role for himself in the developmental politics of early California. He ran unsuccessfully for State Treasurer in 1857 and for Governor in 1859. He won the Governor's office on the Republican, Pro-Union ticket of 1861, effectively keeping California out of the American Civil War.

While in office, Stanford also took advantage of the business opportunities that came his way. When his term ended in 1863, he left office to join Mark Hopkins, Collis Huntington, and Charles Crocker in a daring business venture. These four men combined forces to build the eastbound section of the transcontinental railway. Stanford served as president of the Central Pacific Railway and as co-owner of the Southern Pacific Railway. The railroads received enormous land grants along their rights of way, making the owners some of the wealthiest men on earth.

Stanford was an avid horseman, preferring to live on his estate in Palo Alto, south of San Francisco. When his 15-year-old son died in 1884, Stanford created a lasting memorial with the establishment of Stanford University, today one of the preeminent universities in the world.

EADWEARD MUYBRIDGE (1830–1904)

Born in Kingston upon Thames, England, Muybridge first came to America in 1851. After moving to San Francisco in 1855 he developed an interest in photography, an interest he furthered upon returning to England in 1860. By 1867 Muybridge was back in America with his reputation growing as he photographed the western frontier from his mobile darkroom dubbed "The Flying Studio."

In 1872, Leland Stanford first approached Muybridge to photograph Stanford's horse, Occident, in an attempt to prove that galloping horses would literally fly by lifting all four hooves off the ground midstride. Muybridge's early attempts were unsuccessful, prompting him to return to his photo expeditions. During one of these trips, Muybridge's wife became pregnant as the result of an affair with Major Harry Larkins. Upon learning of the affair, Muybridge shot Larkins to death. Muybridge was tried for the murder in 1875 and acquitted on the basis that the homicide was justifiable.

EADWEARD MUYBRIDGE

© 2008 JUPITERIMAGES CORPORATION

Undaunted by his notoriety or aided by it, Muybridge perfected a camera shutter by 1877 that could make action freezing exposures in as little as one-one-thousandth of a second. Excited about the potential of his new technology, Muybridge returned to Palo Alto, this time to prove that a galloping horse could fly. The preparations were elaborate. A fifty-foot-long shelter was built to house up to twenty-four cameras. Magnetic camera-shutter triggers were devised, and a carefully scaled background structure was created to produce precise measurements of the horse's movements.

In June 1878, a crowd of racing fans and journalists assembled to witness the photographic feat. Horse trainer Charles Marvin, one of Stanford's prize trotters, sped through the camera trap at the whip. Twenty minutes later, Muybridge emerged from the darkroom with the proof Stanford had sought.

Journalists spread news of the event around the world with the speed of the telegraph. Muybridge became a celebrity, and Stanford made his point. Unintentionally, the two men had also managed to create a technology capable of capturing moving images. By 1880 Muybridge developed a projector, the Zoopraxiscope, which he used to show his motion series photographs to enthusiastic audiences throughout the country. His moving pictures were one of the most popular attractions at the Chicago Exhibition of 1893.

THE BET?

Probably as a result of journalistic invention, a legend grew that Stanford had made a $25,000 bet that "horses could fly." Most historians agree the bet never happened and that Stanford's real motivation was his passionate interest in horses. However, more dramatically, he had spent more than $50,000 to prove his point. Adjusted for inflation, the expense comes to as much as seven million dollars, a sum worthy of the attention the event received. One side effect of Stanford and Muybridge's notoriety was to inspire photographers and inventors worldwide to pursue the development of the moving picture.

EDISON, DICKSON, AND THE ADVENT OF THE AMERICAN COMMERCIAL FILM INDUSTRY

THOMAS EDISON

In 1888 Eadweard Muybridge accepted an invitation to visit Thomas Edison's laboratory where the great photographer discussed the future of the moving image with the wizard of invention and his talented young assistant, W. K. L. Dickson. The hosts were inspired to pursue the development of a new medium. Over the next twenty years, Edison would proceed to completely dominate the early motion picture industry. His passion for invention was exceeded only by his desire to control industries through retaining the patent rights to important technologies.

THOMAS ALVA EDISON (1847–1931)

Born in Milan, Ohio and raised in Port Huron, Michigan, Edison was already showing signs of his restless intellect in his first grade of elementary school. After only twelve weeks, Edison's teacher declared him too ill-behaved for the classroom. His parents decided on home schooling. Edison's mother taught the basics: reading, writing, and arithmetic. His father guided him in history and literature. By the time he was eleven, Edison discovered the local library, where he began to teach himself the principles of physics and other sciences. One of the keys to his incredible powers of concentration was his severe hearing impairment, which made it possible for him to shut out the outside world almost completely.

At age twelve, Edison started his working life selling newspapers and refreshments on the local railroad trains. Within the next two years he began intercepting news dispatches over the railroad station telegraphs and published a small newspaper that netted him a substantial income. When he was fifteen Edison mastered Morse code and telegraph operation and then left home to seek his fortune. By 1868, he had moved to Boston where he worked as an operator for Western Union. At night, he tinkered with inventions, leading to his first patent for a vote-counting machine. Edison also attended lectures at what would become the Massachusetts Institute of Technology on the theory of transmitting the human voice by wire. Coincidentally, Alexander Graham Bell, inventor of the telephone, was in Boston at the same time and might have attended some of the same lectures.

In search of entrepreneurial opportunities, Edison next moved to New York City where he quickly landed a well-paying job fixing stock tickers (a teletype device designed to transmit stock prices from the exchanges to the brokerages) for a large brokerage. He continued to spend his spare time working on inventions. In 1871, at age twenty-four, Edison sold the rights to an improved stock ticker he had developed for $40,000. He was rich.

Over the next three years, Edison continued to work on an array of inventions (including his own version of the telephone) and proceeded to build a laboratory for developing and testing them. It was at his invention factory in Menlo Park, New Jersey, that he created the first phonograph in 1877. Two years later, Edison created the first commercially practical light bulb. By 1884, he had developed and patented an entire system for generating and distributing electricity. His laboratory, with its first-rate staff of technicians and craftsmen and state-of-the art equipment, was quickly becoming recognized as the greatest research and development center in the world. In 1892, Edison formed the General Electric Company, today one of the largest corporations in the world, and became its major stock holder.

WILLIAM KENNEDY LAURIE (W. K. L.) DICKSON (1860–1935)

By 1879 Edison was becoming an international celebrity, especially among young aspiring inventors such as Dickson. Born in France, Dickson moved to England with the remainder of his family after the death of his father. He wrote Edison that year to apply for a job at Menlo Park. Dickson received a brief rejection. Three months later his family moved to the United States. Undaunted, Dickson became an accomplished amateur photographer and was accepted when he re-applied to work for Edison in 1883.

In 1888 Edison assigned Dickson to begin work on a motion picture system. Edison wanted Dickson to utilize the company's existing cylinder phonograph technology to devise a single-viewer exhibition device that could be coin operated and, of course, to create a system that ran on electricity. Dickson began by exploring a variety of new photographic developments and by forming strategic relationships with George Eastman and other innovators experimenting with early versions of film roll technology. By this time Eastman was enjoying great success with his amateur camera system. His factory in Rochester, New York was producing miles of film rolls for his customers. By 1990 the cylinder approach had proved to be completely impracticable. Dickson changed his focus to concentrate solely on the film roll approach. George Eastman supplied Dickson with 35-millimeter sprocketed film rolls cut from the 70 millimeter film rolls Eastman had developed for his amateur camera system.

The first prototype Kinetograph camera and Kinetoscope viewing device were completed by May 1991. By August the patent applications were done. The system operated at over 40 frames per second (modern systems standardized on 24 frames per second), producing smooth, unflickering moving pictures. In December 1892 Dickson began construction on a studio that was covered with black tar paper and mounted on railroad tracks so that it could be moved to follow the sunlight. It didn't take long for the studio Dickson built for Edison to be compared to the police wagons of the day and acquire the corresponding nickname "Black Maria." A sense of urgency grew around the project when Edison announced that he would introduce his Kinetoscopes at the 1893 Chicago Exposition. Dickson used the drawing power of the Edison reputation to convince some of the most famous entertainers in the world, such as Sandlow the Strong Man and Buffalo Bill's Wild West Show, to come New Jersey to appear in his films. And so Dickson became history's first film director.

In 1893 Dickson was becoming convinced that film projection in an audience setting was superior to the peep-show approach commanded by Edison. He was also aware that time was of the essence because the Lumière brothers in Paris were already close to having a working system of their own. Dickson was increasingly unhappy with his role in the company. In 1894 Edison appointed William E. Gilmore as general manager of the laboratory. One of his first acts was to demand that Dickson sign over his copyrights and patents to Edison. Dickson's relationship with Edison further deteriorated when Edison contradicted himself by deciding to proceed with the development of a projection system and appointing Charles Kayser to take over Dickson's work. Dickson began to work on his own with other inventors on rival projection systems.

Fed up with Gilmore's accusations of disloyalty, Dickson left the Edison Company in April 1895. By June he formed a partnership with other inventors and entrepreneurs to market their new creations, the Mutoscope viewing system and the Biograph camera. In 1896 Dickson produced the fledgling Biograph studio's first film, "The Empire State Express." The next year he returned to London to manage the company's foreign office and remained in England for the rest of his life.

AUGUST LUMIÈRE (1862–1954) AND LOUIS LUMIÈRE (1864–1948)

The Lumière brothers' father, Antoine, was a successful portrait painter in Lyon, France who recognized the potential of photography to put him out of business. He defected from the world of fine art to begin selling and, later, manufacturing photographic supplies and cameras. August and Louis were encouraged to become involved in the family business and attended a technical trade school to prepare. At age seventeen, Louis dropped out of school to work on a new dry plate photo process. A new factory was built to manufacture the plates, and by 1894 it was producing 15 million plates a year. That same year Antoine was invited to Paris to see a demonstration of Edison's Kinetoscope. He returned to Lyon with a strip of Edison film and convinced his sons to manufacture their own version of the product.

The Lumière brothers had two advantages in designing their system. They were able to build upon what Edison had already created, and they were free from the directive to build a camera that operated on electricity. At the outset the brothers decided that their viewing system would be based on projection and not the peep-show design of the Kinetoscope. Instead of electricity the Lumière camera would be powered by a mechanism similar to a clockwork mainspring. What the brothers came up with was ingenious. It was a combination camera, film processor, and, when fitted with a light source, a projector. In February 1895, the Lumières patented their Cinematographe. It weighed eleven pounds, operated at 16 frames per second, incorporated an intermittent movement like a sewing machine and, most important, it was completely portable.

In April the Lumières began showing their system to groups of engineers and tradesmen. They also began to apply for and receive patents outside of France. The first was in England. On December 28, 1895 they conducted the first public demonstration at the Grand Café in Paris. The program of eight short films was an immediate sensation. Due to the portability of their camera, the brothers were able to create films that were much more dynamic than Edison's and Dickson's and the magnification or blowup of the projected image proved to be more dramatic than the diminutive pictures of the Kinetoscope.

Louis Lumière took his camera around the world, documenting scenes that held audiences in awe. By early 1897 the brothers had opened theaters in London, Brussels, and New York. They called their theaters Cinemas. By the end of the year their film catalog contained 358 titles. By the end of 1898 their catalog topped two thousand titles. By 1900 they had constructed a 100-foot-wide screen for the Paris Exposition. By 1904 Louis had developed the first workable process for color motion pictures. In the early 1900s Auguste turned his attention to medical research and became a pioneer in early radiology.

FILM INVENTORS GIVE WAY TO FILM MAKERS

As the twentieth century unfolded, excitement about the new motion picture medium grew exponentially. New studios in Europe, America, Australia, and elsewhere were going into business at a frenetic rate to supply the demand for movies. A new group of entrepreneurs emerged to provide more venues for showing movies. In America these venues took the form of store-front theaters that could seat anywhere from fifty to a few hundred patrons. Theater owners generally charged five cents or one "nickel" for admission to a program that consisted of thirty minutes to an hour of films, lantern slides, and sing-alongs. The theaters were soon referred to as nickleodeons, and they became a favorite haunt of the hoards of young immigrant factory workers pouring into America from Europe.

Edison was rapidly asserting his dominion over the technical side of the industry by acquiring patents and enforcing them. His production company was one of the largest in the country, but others were gaining on him. The audience was hungry for more elaborate films

A Trip to the Moon (1902) aka Le Voyage Dans La Lune, Directed by Georges Melies, Shown: Production drawing by Georges Melies

and inventor-filmmakers such as Dickson and the Lumières were giving way to showmen and storytellers such as Georges Méliès and Edwin S. Porter.

Georges Méliès (1861–1938)

Méliès was the youngest of three sons born to a wealthy Paris shoe manufacturer. Although he was raised to take a place in the family business, he was much more interested in painting and stagecraft. When he was ten years old Melies saw his saw his first magic show, a performance by the greatest French magician of the time, Robert-Houdin. He was hooked. In 1884 Méliès was sent to London by his father to learn English. There he became a regular audience member at The Egyptian Hall where Maskelyne and Cooke, a watchmaker and cabinetmaker by trade, respectively, were performing elaborate theatrical magic illusions.

Upon returning from England Méliès was required to manage one of his father's factories but continued to study puppetry and magic. When his father retired in 1888 Méliès sold

Georges Melies circa later 1800s

his share in the business to his brothers and purchased Theater Robert-Houdin from the owner's heirs and went into business as a magic show impresario. Although Méliès seldom performed himself, devoting his attention to operating the business, he became famous for designing complicated illusions which were performed by other magicians.

Inspired by the Lumière's work, Méliès purchased a movie camera in 1896 and began to experiment. At first he made small film illusions using stop motion in which he would make objects and people seem to magically appear or disappear. These films were incorporated into the programs at the theater he operated. By 1899 Méliès began to make storytelling films. Whereas other filmmakers of the day were satisfied with single-scene films, Méliès began editing together several scenes to tell a story. His 1899 film, *Cinderella*, is seven minutes long and contains twenty separate scenes.

Méliès's most successful film was his 1902 production of *A Trip to the Moon*, history's first science-fiction film based on stories by Jules Verne and H. G. Wells. By this time Méliès had made hundreds of films and was ready to make something more elaborate. The production budget was generous at ten thousand francs. The film's running time is fourteen minutes and contains thirty separate scenes. The film sets are vivid and fanciful, including the workshop where the spacecraft is constructed, the canon that fires it into space, and a mysterious moon grotto containing giant mushrooms. *A Trip to the Moon* also contains several examples of Méliès's trademark film technique. Stop motion is used to depict fight scenes with moon creatures that explode into clouds of smoke upon contact. Talking planets and stars and other heavenly bodies are achieved by using multiple exposures. An early attempt at a dolly shot is used to show the spacecraft's approach to the Moon.

Méliès never received the financial reward he deserved for *A Trip to the Moon* as it became one of the most plagiarized films in movie history. Even the Edison company distributed pirated copies of the film. Part of the problem was that Méliès insisted on being involved in every aspect of the business including starring in, photographing, editing, and distributing them. Other, better-organized film companies such as Pathé were overtaking Méliès in the competition to make more and better films. By 1903 he had ceased making important films, although his filmography lists films he made as late as 1912. By 1923 Méliès was bankrupt and forced to make a living selling toys from a kiosk on the streets of Paris. Many scholars identify Méliès as the first auteur (film author) in motion picture history as well as a pioneer in the art of storytelling. In is indisputable that Méliès is the father of movie magic and of the art of creating worlds on film that could never exist in reality.

EDWIN S. PORTER (1870–1941)

Born in Connellsville, Pennsylvania, Porter developed an early interest in mechanics and left school at age fourteen to work at a variety of odd jobs including a stint as a stagehand. In 1893 he joined the Navy and trained as a mechanic and electrical engineer working on the development of gunnery technology. In 1895 Porter took a job with the Vitascope company which sold Edison film equipment. In 1896 Porter organized the first projected motion picture show in New York. That year he was hired at Edison laboratories to work on the creation of a new film projector. Projectors were becoming his passion and soon Porter left Edison to become a freelance projectionist.

As a projectionist Porter became fascinated with the films of Georges Méliès. He claimed to have shown *A Trip to the Moon* over fifteen hundred times. During this period, Porter tried, unsuccessfully, to develop his own camera and projector system. By 1900 the Edison Company had ceased making short filmstrips for coin-operated Kinetoscopes and began production of longer, projected films. Porter went back to work for Edison as a producer and director. Between 1900 and 1915 he made 165 films. In 1903 Porter made his first great storytelling film, *Life Of An American Fireman*. The film mixed documentary footage of actual fires with staged fictional scenes of a fireman's duties.

Also in 1903 Porter made his most impressive film, *The Great Train Robbery*. Porter was beginning to create a more sophisticated film language than his contemporaries. Méliès, for instance, used scenes as the basic element for his films. He would position the camera relative to the set so that edges of the film frame matched the edges of the set. The action was organized within that frame and the camera's point of view never changed. It was like sitting in the middle of a theater looking at the action on a stage. It was static. Porter instinctively learned that the individual shot, not the whole scene, was the basic film element. He began to use the camera to present a dynamic point of view. In *The Great Train Robbery* Porter positions his camera at oblique angles to create more depth and interest in his photographic compositions. In one scene in which the robbers capture the engineer, the camera views the action from the back of the coal tender car. It is one of history's first moving shots.

THE GREAT TRAIN ROBBERY (1903) THE EDISON COMPANY, DIRECTED BY EDWIN S. PORTER, SHOWN: HAND-TINTED FRAME

PHOTOFEST

The Great Train Robbery also includes examples of early matte photography in which two separate film shots are put together using a matte device to blank out part of the frame so that that space can be exposed in a subsequent shot. The window of the train station is matted out in one scene. The second time the film is run through the camera, the window area contains a shot of the train arriving. Using this technique, Porter is able to mix the action of a real train with the shot taken on a studio set. The same technique is used in the baggage car scene in which the open door of the set contains footage of the passing countryside. The result brings the set to life.

The Great Train Robbery also introduces a revolutionary approach to editing. While other filmmakers regarded editing as the simple act of splicing fully contained scenes together, Porter uses editing to speed up the narrative and add another dynamic element to the motion picture. In one scene we see the robbers escaping on horseback. That is followed by a scene in which a little girl discovers that the train station master has been knocked out and tied up. She revives the station master and unties him. Then Porter cuts to a scene of a group of men and women at a square dance. The audience intuitively understands that three things are happening at the same time. While the robbers are escaping, the station master is going for help and eventually arrives at the square dance, where the law men are in attendance. The compression of time achieved through this editing approach adds a great deal of excitement to the film.

The Great Train Robbery represents the peak of Porter's creativity as a director. Although he made more than a hundred films after 1903, nothing surpassed this achievement. In 1912 Porter formed the Famous Players Film Company with partner Adolph Zukor. The company specialized in purchasing the rights to successful Broadway plays and adapting them to film using the original cast members. By 1915 Porter had lost interest in filmmaking. He returned to his original fascination with projectors and spent the rest of his professional life improving on projection technology.

THE EDISON PATENT TRUST

In 1895 the Edison Company acquired the patent rights to the Vitascope projection system that was developed by two electrical engineers, C. Francis Jenkins and Thomas Armat. Over the next two years, Edison obtained two more patents for improvements on the Vitascope technology. Armed with these patents, Edison aggressively launched a series of patent infringement lawsuits against anyone who dared to compete in the manufacture of projectors. By 1908, he had succeeded in intimidating the other companies to the point that they agreed to join forces with Edison. As a result, the Motion Picture Patents Company (MPPC) was created, consisting of the Vitagraph, Selig, Lubin, Pathé, Méliès, Essanay, Kalem and Edison member companies. A rival patent company was organized by Biograph and the Klein Optical Company, among others. Eventually the two patent companies agreed to pool their resources, thereby achieving complete dominance over the movie business.

January 1909 was set as the deadline for all production companies to join the patent trust or suffer the consequences. The companies that didn't join in referred to themselves as "the Independents." They quickly became the targets of the MPPC's patent-enforcement efforts. Everywhere in America new nickelodeon theaters were established. The demand for new movies was unquenchable, and the incentives for the Independents to work around the MPPC was irresistible. The MPPC established an organization called the General Film Company to quash the Independents. General Film used all manner of coercive tactics ranging from confiscating unlicensed movie equipment and films, to sending out the thuggish Pinkerton Detective Agency to strong-arm and discourage Independents. George Eastman, the major supplier of sprocketed film rolls, joined in with the MPPC and agreed to refuse to sell film stock to the Independents.

At the beginning of the motion picture industry, films were distributed through outright sales. A production company made a film, printed a few hundred copies, and sold them to nickleodeons. But as companies like Edison began to copyright their films, film rental through film-exchange companies proved to be a better business model. This led the General Film Company to extend its stranglehold on the industry through the acquisition of virtually every substantial film exchange in the country. Independent nickleodeon operators were no longer able to acquire films for their theaters. There was no choice but to cooperate.

William Fox, an intrepid Independent, defied the MPPC. He found ways to bypass the trust and demonstrated to others that cooperation was not inevitable. Soon, Fox was joined by Carl Laemmle's Independent Motion Picture Company (later to become Universal Studios) and Adolph Zukor's Famous Players company (later to become part of Paramount). The independents were emboldened enough to launch a public relations attack on the patent trust, and it worked. By 1911, the nickelodeon boom was winding down. The industry was becoming mature and the domination of the trust was becoming indefensible. During this time, the federal government initiated a series of antitrust lawsuits against the MPPC. In 1915, the courts ordered the MPPC to be dissolved, paving the way for an even greater expansion of the motion picture industry than what had already occurred.

THE ERA OF FILM INVENTION COMES TO AN END

One striking fact about the men who created motion pictures is that many of them lived to see their invention mature and become an important entertainment and art form. Edison lived to be eighty-four and witnessed the advent of the studio system and the introduction of sound. Dickson and Méliès lived to the mid-1930s, and the Lumières lived past the end of World War II. August Lumière lived long enough to experience the age of television. What began as a curiosity and diversion in the late nineteenth century was becoming a powerful new medium as the second decade of the twentieth century unfolded. Film inventors, like great explorers, were soon followed by men and women with the pioneering spirit, ready to build something that would be grand and lasting.

FILM PIONEERS

MOGULS, MOVIE MAKERS, AND MOVIE STARS

In the decade between 1903 (the year *The Great Train Robbery* was released) and 1913, the motion picture industry came of age. It was beginning to attract young people with ambition, talent, energy, and the entrepreneurial instincts necessary to take advantage of the limitless opportunities the new medium provided. At first stage actors had been wary of performing in films. They saw movies as a well paid but an unsavory alternative to the live stage. By 1909 the *New York Times* began to use the term stars when referring to featured movie actors. Investors such as Marcus Loew, who established Loews Theaters in 1904, built nickelodeons at a furious pace. In 1910 Carle Laemmle's Independent Motion Picture Company launched a massive publicity campaign for the purpose of making Florence Lawrence the first movie star recognized by name. The following year movie magazines such as Motion Picture News began publication and credits listing the actors and other principals involved started to appear on movies. In 1912 fifteen production companies, including William Fox's Fox Film Foundation, were operating in Hollywood. The first movie palaces were constructed in 1913 as the motion picture industry moved out of makeshift nickleodeons and into luxurious landmark theaters.

DAVID WARK GRIFFITH (1875–1948)

Griffith's movie career parallels the maturation of the movie industry. His family origins were quite humble. Born on a farm outside of Louisville, Kentucky in 1875, he was as much a product of nineteenth-century southern attitudes as he was of twentieth-century Hollywood. Griffith's father, Jake, was somewhat of a vagabond. He went to California for an unsuccessful bid at the gold rush of 1849. Griffith senior also tried his hand at dentistry until his career was interrupted by the American Civil War (1861–1865). After the war he settled into life as a farmer. However, Jake Griffith's love of Kentucky bourbon greatly exceeded his love of farming. As a result the family struggled to survive.

By the time Griffith was fourteen, his family had moved to Louisville and Griffith had left school to work in a bookstore. This was the beginning of his enlightenment. Literature, particularly poetry and drama, became his passion. In 1896 Griffith was already playing small roles with the local theater company. In the fall of that year he joined the farewell tour of the actress Ada Gray and began touring throughout the Midwest. Nine years later Griffith was still touring the country as an actor. In 1905 he made the decision to go to San Francisco, California where opportunities were abundant. There he met and fell in love with a local actress named Linda Arvidson. They were married in May, 1906. Soon thereafter the Griffiths left for New York in the hope that they would find success on Broadway.

Once in New York Griffith decided to write a stage play, *A Fool and a Girl*. In a short time this experience as a playwright would lead him to try and sell his services as a writer to the new movie production companies that were beginning to sprout up around the city. Around this time the Griffiths were fortunate to be cast in a play written by Thomas Dixon whose work, *The Clansman,* would become the source material for Griffith's first major triumph as a film director. Nonetheless, the remainder of 1906 was a struggle for the young couple. Long periods of unemployment were punctuated by small parts in a few plays and the sale of one of Griffith's poems to a literary magazine for six dollars. In early 1907 James Hackett purchased Griffith's play for seven hundred dollars. It was more money than he had ever seen in his life but wasn't enough to survive on until the play was produced. He accepted an offer to go to Norfolk, Virginia to appear in a historical pageant. It wasn't Broadway, but it put food on the table. His wife stayed in New York to work as a seamstress. Eventually *A Fool and a Girl* opened in Washington, D.C. The critics hated it, bringing Griffith's playwriting career to an end.

Back in New York, Griffith began to make the rounds of the studios in search of work either as an actor or writer. Finally, in January, 1908 his luck began to change when he was hired by the Edison Company to play the leading role in a film titled *Rescued from the Eagle's Nest.* Afterward, Griffith was given a letter of introduction to the Biograph Company, where he obtained work as an actor, paid at the rate of five dollars per day. At this time Biograph was attempting to improve the quality of its films by hiring the best writers and actors their budgets would allow. This appealed to Griffith, who still harbored ambitions of creating art. The studio made two films a week, all directed by George McCutcheon. The most skilled filmmaker at the studio was cameraman Billy Bitzer, who helped Griffith hone his acting style. McCutcheon had a drinking problem and was eventually incapacitated by it. His son had been filling in for the father but Henry Marvin, the studio boss, wanted another solution. He offered the director's job to Griffith. Griffith agreed on the condition that he would get his acting job back if he failed. Bitzer took him under his wing and began to teach Griffith the secrets to making movies. Their first project together was *The Adventures of Dolly.* During the next five years Griffith would direct over four hundred films, most of them collaborations with Bitzer.

Griffith's film education began with Bitzer's teaching him the elements of a good story: "Heart, Interest, Drama, Danger, Comedy, Rescue." Griffith learned how to diagram stories and scenarios and to visualize scenes that encompassed these basic elements. Next the challenge was to get them on film. By the time *The Adventures of Dolly* finished shooting, Griffith, according to his wife, was already bitten by the movie bug. He sensed that Biograph was a place where he could innovate and master the art of filmmaking. *Dolly* sold a total of

D. W. GRIFFITH, CIRCA 1910S, SHOWN ON SET: DIRECTOR D. W. GRIFFITH (SEATED, WITH MEGAPHONE)

PHOTOFEST

twenty five prints, ten more than the studio's previous best. Griffith was given a contract for fifty dollars per week.

Griffith threw himself into sixteen-hour workdays. He quickly began to learn the rudiments of editing. While other directors saw editing as the act of pasting together scenes, Griffith understood that creative editing made stories more lively and dynamic. He was inspired by the storytelling approaches of writers such as Charles Dickens to experiment with narratives that strayed from the purely chronological approach. Bitzer was also teaching Griffith how to position the camera to achieve interesting points of view. They abandoned the old approach of organizing a scene so the camera could capture all of the action in one setup. Instead, they broke down scenes into a variety of shots using longer-range shots to establish the action and close range shots to show the emotion on the actors' faces. Griffith also began to experiment with acting styles. He learned that big gestures were unnecessary when the camera was closer, allowing actors to develop more subtle and interesting performances. Soon he was developing a new film language in his quest to find the perfect gesture for each dramatic moment.

In their first six months together Griffith and Bitzer made the first of many contributions to film grammar when they created the fade-out shot. In the final shot of a scene, Bitzer gradually closed the iris of the camera lens. The result was the fading of the light on the screen as if day had turned to night. They found that this technique resulted in a smoother transition from one scene to the next while conveying the passage of time. Whenever a problem in visualizing a story element presented itself, the two filmmakers sought an innovative way to solve it. As a result they continually added new devices for storytelling to their technique. In 1908 Griffith made a total of forty-eight films, all but a few with Bitzer behind the camera. Griffin was also beginning to attract a nucleus of actors who would remain loyal for years to come. Among them were Bobby Heron, who was regularly cast in juvenile roles. Canadian Mack Sennett showed much promise in comedy roles and was soon tutored to direct comedy films, which held little interest for Griffith.

The model Griffith had in mind for his organization was a theatrical stock company in which an actor would play a leading role in one film and a supporting role in another. In the spring of 1909 a sixteen-year old actress from Toronto paid a visit to Biograph in the hope of supplementing her stage income. Griffith was instantly taken by her attractiveness and energy. Thus, future megastar Mary Pickford entered the film business. During this period Griffith and Bitzer's experimentation continued to produce results. Bitzer discovered that a reflector could be used to add to and enhance a lighting setup. When Griffith wanted a way of focusing a scene on a single character, Bitzer adapted another of his inventions, the lens shade, to achieve the purpose. The year ended with the successful release of Griffith's anti-monopoly film, *A Corner In Wheat*.

That following winter Griffith's troupe and crew became the first Edison Patent Trust company to film in Los Angeles. The west coast was attractive to him for several reasons. There was plenty of sunlight and fresh locations that audiences had never seen apart from the films Colonel Selig's company had been making since 1907. The easy going citizens of California were more accepting of the movie people, who were accustomed to being shunned in the east. Perhaps most important to Griffith, Los Angeles was as far away as he could get from the meddling of the studio bosses back in New York. The studio was a rented vacant lot at the intersection of Grand Avenue and Washington near downtown. A crew quickly built a wooden stage and separate women's and men's dressing rooms, and a nearby rented loft served as a laboratory and costume storage space. Griffith flourished in California. He used the Spanish missions at San Gabriel and San Juan Capistrano as locations for films about Old California. Ventura became the setting for the Native American themed film Ramona. Santa Monica was the backdrop for *The Unchanging Sea*. That winter Griffith also became the first to make a film entirely within Hollywood city limits, predating Cecil B. DeMille's *Squaw Man* by three full years. After the three-month stay in Los Angeles, Griffith would continue to avoid studio production whenever possible in favor of shooting on location.

Upon returning to New York Griffith lost the services of Mary Pickford and her brother Jack, also an actor. Pickford's boyfriend, Owen Moore, had stayed behind when his request for a raise was turned down. In the interim Moore had signed with Carl Laemmle's Independent Motion Picture Company. Wishing not to be separated again, Pickford also signed with IMP, which had promised to give her featured billing in the advertisements for her pictures. At this time she and Moore were secretly married. Griffith was displeased with but ultimately unfazed by the young actress' disloyalty. He proceeded to sign an array of new talent for Biograph including Donald Crisp and Blanch Sweet. In just a matter of months Pickford would leave IMP to work for a new company created by Harry Aitken for the sole purpose of making Pickford films. The era of the movie star was about to begin.

The remainder of 1910 was busy with completing an exhaustive slate of small films. Griffith had received a substantial raise that year and was rapidly becoming well known by his audiences. He was also much sought after by ambitious young actresses. During the 1911 winter sojourn in California, Griffith's wife discovered a love letter from one actress. Unable to settle down to a domestic life, Griffith's marriage started to crumble. Griffith wrote his wife a letter confessing that there had been many such romances and asking for his freedom. Later, in divorce court, this self-incriminating letter would prove to be costly. In 1911 Griffith also met Lionel Barrymore, of the great stage family. Barrymore was broke and asked Griffith to put him to work. Griffith was pleased to have in his ensemble an actor of such stature and talent. Around this same time Mabel Normand, a petite and energetic young actress, also joined the group. Near the end of the year Griffith received another substantial raise to three thousand dollars a month and a percentage of the footage revenues from the sale of his films. However, to earn the raise, he had to commit to making one film per week, a pace that would be too hectic to allow for much experimentation with or development of his film technique.

During the winter of 1912 while in California, Griffith began to dream about a grander motion-picture experience than what could be had in the lowly confines of the nickelodeon. A gifted artist, he even sketched designs for a seven-thousand seat theater. His work that year displayed a renewed sense of energy. One film in particular, *A Beast at Bay*, contains the best chase sequence Griffith had ever created. Another, *The Woman of the Species*, is the story of three women stranded, trekking across a hostile desert. They come upon an orphaned Native American child who awakens their maternal instincts. It is a vivid and an emotionally charged effort. That same winter Mary Pickford briefly returned to work with Griffith. A young actress named Mae Marsh joined the troupe, and Mack Sennett was promoted to directing comedy films on his own. Marsh was assigned to work with Sennett, who would help her develop her screen persona. Marsh learned quickly and was rewarded with the leading role in Griffith's most literary film of the year, *Man's Genesis.*

When the company returned to New York in the spring, construction was well under way on Biograph's new production studio. When finished, it was a well lit and spacious work environment. The entire company reacted with renewed vigor. In July Mary Pickford introduced Griffith to two of her friends from the stage, Dorothy (age 16) and Lillian Gish (age 14). Like the Pickfords, the Gishes were Canadian, had been abandoned by their father, and possessed a stage mother who prodded and directed their careers. Griffith was fatally attracted to these fatherless young women, just as he had been with the similarly situated Mae Marsh. Quickly he developed a film project (*An Unseen Enemy*, 1912) in which the two sisters played young girls trapped in a locked apartment next door to the scene of a robbery. In the most dramatic scene one of the robbers becomes aware of the girls' presence, points the gun through a hole in the wall, and begins shooting at random. The effect is riveting. Throughout the summer, Griffith began slowing down the pace of production so that he could devote more attention to detail and rehearsal in his films. In August and September he made only four films, including his best gangster film to date, *Musketeers of Pig Alley.* During this time Pickford was plotting her escape, having been promised an important stage role by the great stage impresario David Belasco.

Throughout 1912 and 1913 Griffith continually experimented with ways to use editing to speed up the pace of the narrative and the action sequences in his films. He was dreaming of larger, more expensive projects and was beginning to feel confined by the limitations of the Biograph Company. When he left for California in January, 1913, he must certainly have known it would be the last such trip for Biograph. Perhaps for sentimental reasons he included Lionel Barrymore in the cast of actors. The company sensed their star director's restlessness and attempted to placate him by hiring a staff of publicists to sing his praises. The trend toward feature films' lasting an hour or longer was becoming established, particularly by Italian filmmakers. Griffith was eager to join the trend. Gradually he began to stretch the length of his films beginning with Lillian Gish's breakthrough performance in *The Mothering Heart.*

Still, in California, between April and July, Griffith made the fewest films he had made during any similar period of time at Biograph. One film from that period, *The Battle of Elderbush Gulch,* is far and away his best. It contains almost ninety scenes at a time when his contemporaries were telling stories of similar duration in thirty scenes and without as much emphasis on editing. The result is that Griffith's films are much more energetic and exciting. *Elderbush* was so well received that it earned Griffith the clout to approach the Biograph management about making a truly epic film. He wanted a budget of $20,000 or more, five times what the company was accustomed to spending. Management took a big gulp and agreed to the project for fear they would lose Griffith otherwise. Immediately work began on a massive set that was to be built in the very rural San Fernando Valley.

The film, *Judith of Bethulia*, was based on a successful stage play, which, in turn had been taken from the Biblical Apocrypha. It is the story of a young woman's fight to save her city from an invading army. Griffith used the argument that since the play was well known the audience would be "pre-sold," an argument meant to sway the Biograph executives. When production began there were many hardships. The cast and crew had to be bussed from downtown Los Angeles over country roads to the San Fernando Valley every day. Accommodations on the set were primitive, and the whole enterprise was a little disorganized. But Griffith's team was loyal and persevered. Everyone on the set sensed that it was their last Biograph film and gave it their all. In 1913 a production as large as *Judith* was certain to draw curiosity seekers. One visitor to the set was 25-year old-screenwriter Anita Loos, who would soon become one of Griffith's closest collaborators. A production accountant had been sent west by the company management as expenses continued to mount. At the end of shooting costs exceeded $36,000, leading to the chilly reception Griffith received from his bosses upon returning to New York. Even though Biograph had entered into a partnership to make more feature films while Griffith's company was in California, he was punished for his excesses by being assigned to supervise other directors' productions while *Judith* was in post production. As the end of 1913 was nearing, Griffith's contract became due for renewal. Neither Biograph nor their star director made more than half-hearted attempts at renewing the relationship.

After five years and approximately 450 films, Griffith was ready to move on. Two suitors were very interested in acquiring Griffith's name and talent for their company. One was Adolph Zukor, a one-time furrier who had become involved in the penny-arcade business around 1903, which, in turn, led him into the nickelodeon business. In 1913 Zukor had made a huge profit distributing the film *Queen Elizabeth*, starring the celebrated stage actress Sarah Bernhardt. He was in the process of reinvesting his profits in a new production company, Famous Plays by Famous Players. The idea of the company was to adapt successful Broadway stage plays into films employing the original casts. Zukor was a small, strange man whose staff referred to him behind his back as "creepy." The other company interested in Griffith was Harry and Roy Aitken's fledgling Mutual Films. The Aitkens were extremely entrepreneurial. They had entered the motion picture business through acquiring and operating dozens of film exchanges in the Midwest. They were involved in financing Thomas Ince, a Broadway stage producer turned film producer. Ince had adapted Henry Ford's assembly-line approach to manufacturing automobiles to the production of films. His Inceville production facility at Sunset Boulevard and Pacific Coast Highway in Los Angeles was successfully pumping out westerns cheaply and efficiently. Soon the Aitkens bankrolled Mack Sennett in his endeavor to establish a studio devoted to making comedies. Furthermore, the Aitkens were actively involved with William Fox and Carl Laemmle's attempts to bring an end to Edison's Patent Trust. Even though Zukor had offered Griffith a generous salary of $50,000 per year, Griffith was more inclined to get into business with the Aitkens, who were far less conservative and were more encouraging of his desire to make larger, epic films. Griffith's salary would be only three hundred dollars per week, but he would be given a percentage of the profits in his pictures and, most important, he would be allowed to make two independent films per year. Also the Aitkens were willing to do everything they could to lure Griffith's cast of actors and key cameraman Billy Bitzer away from Biograph. The Deal was announced on September 29, 1913.

The Aitkens owned two small studios, Reliance in New York and Majestic in Los Angeles. Griffith's group began production on modestly budgeted ($5,000 per film) programmers in New York that December. Griffith was already planning to make his first independent film to be based on Thomas Dixon's inflammatory Civil War novel, *The Clansman*. In early 1914 Griffith and company moved into new headquarters in Los Angeles. The occupied the old Kinemacolor studio at 4500 Sunset Boulevard and renamed it Fine Arts. This would be Griffith's home until 1920. Upon arriving he began to turn out a series of films intended to create a positive cash flow for Mutual so as to realize his grander ambition. A few of the films made during this period stood out, including *Home, Sweet Home* and *The Avenging Conscience*. Griffith's deal with Mutual called for his films to be shown in New York at Mark Strand's elegant new Broadway theater dedicated solely to showing motion pictures. The Strand was history's first "movie palace," the template for hundreds of similar theaters that would spring up across the country and around the world during the next fifteen years.

Later in the spring of 1914, Griffith began rehearsing his actors for *The Clansman*. The work took place in the evenings after the day's work had been done on whatever program film was in production. Griffith insisted on complete secrecy and he would show up for the nighttime rehearsals with his pockets full of notes but with no script in hand. Meanwhile, negotiations were ongoing with Dixon for the rights to his book and the play that had been adapted from it. The Aitkens were also busy trying to put together the $40,000 that Griffith estimated the project would cost. At the same time carpenters were busy in the San Fernando Valley building a large street set to represent the southern hometown location for the film. Eventually Dixon lowered his demand of $25,000 for the film rights to $2,000 and a percentage of the profits.

QUEEN ELIZABETH (1912 FRANCE) AKA LES AMOURS DE LA REINE LISABETH, DIRECTED BY HENRI DESFONTAINES, LOUIS MERCANTON, SHOWN: SARAH BERNHARDT (EXTREME RIGHT, AS QUEEN ELIZABETH)

Dixon's book and play tell the story of the Camerons, a distinguished southern family whose lives are forever changed by the American Civil War and its aftermath, the period of reconstruction wherein northerners installed a political system that was dominated by former slaves. The heroes of the story are the nightriders, a group of hooded Klansmen who terrorize the countryside in an attempt to re-store white rule in the south. There was no arguing the point that the story portrayed a racist attitude, perhaps not from Griffith's point of view as a native son of the south; but African Americans and northerners clearly found it offensive. Griffith paid no heed to the issue of racism. He was swept up in the notion of staging grand battle scenes, historical recreations such as the assassination of Lincoln, and dramatic rides to the rescue by the Klansman. He believed he was creating great art and that everything else was secondary to this purpose. Filming began on Independence Day, July 4, 1914.

The huge and complex battle scenes were the first order of business. Hundreds of extras, an equal number of horses, artillery pieces, all manner of explosives, props, costumes, and an army of assistants assembled on the site of the present day Forest Lawn Cemetery and Warner Bros. Studios. Later the bucolic communities of Ojai and Big Bear Lake would also serve as locations. At times the battle scenes encompassed an area of over four miles. Assistant Directors such as Raoul Walsh (who would become a respected action director in his own right) oversaw camera crews and battalions of actors and horses, coordinating their work with other crews through the use of a system of signal flags. One constant pres-ence on the battlefield location was "Fireworks Wilson," the one-armed munitions expert. Wilson oversaw the discharge of live cannon rounds and a frightening array of other deadly explosives.

Production continued throughout the summer. At one point Griffith had employed so many horses that he caused a local shortage and more had to be imported from California's central valley. The $40,000 budget was quickly exhausted. When Griffith talked Aitken out of an additional $19,000, he was assured the well was dry. Undeterred, Griffith convinced the cast members to forgo their pay so the extras could be paid. At one point Griffith in-vaded the news room at the Los Angeles Herald newspaper, passing the hat for donations to make the day's $250 payroll. Billy Bitzer invested $7,000 of his own money, as did many of Griffith's colleagues and acquaintances. In November the final scene was shot. One hundred fifty thousand feet of film had been shot. By the time prints were made and an orchestral score had been composed, the cost of the film exceeded $100,000. The film was sneak-pre-viewed in Riverside, California on January 1 and 2, 1915. A few last-minute changes were made, and *The Clansman* was ready for its February 8 premiere at Clunes Auditorium in Los Angeles. One last detail needed attention. Griffith created a new company for himself, Epoch Productions, which would hold and protect the copyright for the picture.

Newspapers began to call the film by its subtitle, Birth of a Nation, but Griffith stuck with *The Clansman*. On the night of the premiere the 2,500-seat theater with an accompanying symphony orchestra was sold out and a crowd thronged outside in the streets. The Los Angeles chapter of the NAACP (National Association for the Advancement of Colored People) had already been to court unsuccessfully trying to stop the showing of the film. Regardless of whether the film was good or not, Griffith was certain to receive more at-tention than all of the film directors in the history of the medium had received up to that point. But the audience was stunned and moved by the film's magnificent imagery and scope and by the grandly emotional music. Critically, *The Clansman* was hailed as a great accomplishment and an important work of art. Sociologically, the film was a tinderbox of reaction to its racism. In an attempt to stem the tide of political resistance, Dixon, who was a college friend of Woodrow Wilson, arranged for the President to see the film in the White House. The hope was that Wilson's endorsement would help to calm the reaction of the African American community and their supporters. It did serve to legitimize *The Clansman* to some small extent, but everywhere the picture was shown controversy, sometimes violent, followed.

Not too far into the film's release the *Birth of a Nation* title replaced the original, perhaps as an attempt to deal with negative publicity. The demand for the film was tremendous; every theater in the country was now clamoring for it. Louis B. Mayer, formerly a Boston area junk dealer, secured the rights to distribute *Birth of a Nation* in New England. By the end of the run, Mayer made more than half a million dollars from the film, enough to start his own studio out in California. By the end of 1917 Epoch Productions reported gross income of almost $5 million and profits of $1.8 million on the film with Griffith's share amounting to almost seven hundred thousand dollars. *Birth of a Nation* had demonstrated several business principles to the motion picture industry. The large-scale feature film commanded higher admission prices and a more enthusiastic audience. In the future motion picture companies would need to be capitalized on a scale sufficient to support the production of epic projects like Griffith's. Motion picture theater operators would need to think big as well. The era of the nickelodeon was now officially over and the new epoch of the motion picture "palace" was about to begin. On its own *Birth of a Nation* had served to propel the motion picture business out of its adolescence into full, corporate adulthood.

THE BIRTH OF A NATION (1915) DIRECTED BY D.W. GRIFFITH

Griffith didn't dwell for long on what he had unleashed on the world. By late winter, 1915 he was already busy on his next film, *The Mother and the Law,* which dealt with the issue of intolerance. No doubt one of his motivations was to respond to his critic's charges of racism. The project was planned for completion in early summer. But by that time, Griffith had expanded the original concept into a sprawling exposé on intolerance intertwining four stories and encompassing centuries of human history. For this spectacle he hired the entire construction crew of the 1915 San Francisco Exposition to build the largest movie set in history, including a recreation of the gates to Babylon. As the working title was changed to

Intolerance Griffith was busy filming the greatest race to the rescue in his career. As had been the case with *Birth*, *Intolerance* was shot without a script. Griffith would dream up ideas for a scene and develop them while he was shooting. This made for an expensive and disorganized production, but Griffith saw himself as an artist working in the medium of his own imagination. Besides, given the success of *Birth*, who was to tell the great showman No? During this time Harry Aitken was busy reorganizing his business. He wanted to combine the operations of Thomas Ince, Mack Sennett, and Griffith under one banner, Triangle Productions. Griffith didn't resist, but nor did he particularly acknowledge the existence of Triangle. At the year's end *Intolerance* was still not finished. Production continued into the spring of 1916. By the time of the first preview on August 6 almost $400,000 had been spent, four times the cost of *Birth*. Nonetheless, the finished film was even more grand and spectacular than its predecessor. The critical reaction was enthusiastic. Before its release, Griffith had assumed that *Intolerance* would be a financial disaster. But by fall the box-office receipts were positive enough to ensure the picture's profitability. At the beginning of 1917 Griffith was on top of the world and more than ready to leave Aitken and Triangle.

Zukor again entered the picture. During Griffith's time with Aitken, Zukor had been busy amassing a stable of movie stars for his company, including Mary Pickford, whom he paid $10,000 per week. Zukor's refusal to combine forces with the Aitkens would shortly lead to the bankruptcy of Triangle. Griffith did not have to think very long about Zukor's promise to finance large-scale motion pictures in return for Griffith's agreement to make six smaller films, each not to exceed $175,000. He then left town to supervise the opening of Intolerance in London, where he was immediately recruited by the royal government to make a picture about the war in Europe. Following the opening Griffith toured the war front in France. The purpose was to gather material and to begin to visualize his war film. The title of the picture would be *Hearts of the World*. Griffith was quickly frustrated by the challenge of filming an actual battle scene. There was no way to get the cameras close enough to the action to capture the drama without putting everyone at grave risk. He settled for a firsthand look at the real war from afar. He returned to England to continue to work on the film for a while, eventually heading back the Hollywood, where all of the tools needed to recreate the battle scenes were at hand. One gesture toward verisimilitude involved Griffith's purchase of actual battle footage from a German defector. Otherwise, *Hearts* is pure movie magic. Other than a few exciting scenes, the film was a standard Griffith melodrama with women in peril rescued by their daring suitors. It was a formula that would eventually wear thin.

Hearts of the World was well received when it opened in April 1918 and earned a handsome profit of over $600,000. But there was no time to revel in the success. Griffith's new Artcraft company was obliged to deliver more films to Zukor, and quickly. During the remainder of the year he made six more pictures and supervised the production of an additional six Dorothy Gish comedies. The pace was taking its toll on the 44-year-old director. However, Lillian Gish had introduced Griffith to a collection of atmospheric short stories by Thomas Burke, entitled *Limehouse Nights*. In particular the first story, about a Chinese man who takes in and protects an abused white girl, caught his attention. Work soon began on Griffith's adaptation of the story, *Broken Blossoms*. Meanwhile, the industry was coming of age. Adolph Zukor was developing his company through a series of astute business moves. In 1916 he had acquired a large distribution and theater company, Paramount. He also merged his Famous Players company with vaudeville entrepreneur Jessie Lasky, who had produced Cecil B. DeMille's enormously successful Squaw Man. The following year Thomas Tally formed the First National Company to purchase, distribute, and exhibit independently made pictures. The sheer scale of his company allowed Tally to outbid the competition for the services of stars like Mary Pickford and Charlie Chaplin. He was also actively pursuing Griffith. Zukor responded by proposing a merger. The resulting company would be larger and more powerful that Edison had ever dreamed of his patent trust becoming. However, the federal government was skeptical of the merger, and it was therefore put on hold. Griffith was wary of either Famous Players or First National and certainly was cold to the idea of a merger. He was concerned that big corporations would inevitably destroy his creative independence. As his representatives continued to discuss Griffith's future with Zukor and Tally, he was also in talks with Hiram Abrams and B. P. Schulberg about founding a new distribution company that would be controlled by artists, not businessmen. In late 1918 Abrams approached Charlie Chaplin. He liked the idea and agreed to pitch it to his friend, Douglas Fairbanks, who was in the midst of getting a divorce so he could wed his new love, Mary Pickford. The two actors were also interested. When Griffith agreed to join in the deal was complete, and United Artists was created in January 1919.

MARY PICKFORD, 1919

Claiming he needed the capital to finance his independent productions, Griffith decided to also sign with First National a mere two weeks after the United Artists deal. As a result he owed Zukor two Artcraft films, three films to First National, and an undetermined number to United Artists. He did have *Broken Blossoms* in the vault and ready for distribution. Believing his film represented a new level of artistic accomplishment, Griffith made preparations for a lavish road show production to accompany the release. Zukor rejected the film as being too dark and noncommercial. He allowed Griffith to buy out his interest so that it could become the director's first United Artists release. *Blossoms* turned out to be a great artistic and a modest financial success. In the next few months Griffith completed the final two films he owed to Zukor and Artcraft as he prepared to leave Hollywood to build a combination estate and studio on the Hudson River about an hour north of New York. Construction would require a few months. Griffith left Lillian Gish in charge of finishing construction, after which she was to begin production on her first picture as a director. In the meantime Griffith took most of the company to the tropical climes of Ft. Lauderdale, Florida. The films they made there were forgettable but served to satisfy the demands of First National and United Artists. However, film critics who had fawned over Griffith's work for almost a decade began to turn. Some even dared to ask if Griffith was becoming old-fashioned.

Upon his return Griffith quickly acquired the rights to a popular, long-running stage play, *Way Down East*. He paid the exorbitant sum of $150,000 plus a percentage of the profits. The heart of the film was to be a daring and dramatic rescue of Lillian Gish, trapped on a block of ice rushing downriver toward a menacing waterfall. This scene necessitated long hours of filming outdoors in the frigid New England winter. Having made so many demands of his actors in the past, Griffith was now asking the impossible. The cold was so severe that Bitzer needed to invent a camera heater that kept the gears from freezing. But once again the loyalty of Griffith's company made the impossible possible. The production lasted well into the following spring. Griffith had borrowed a fortune to make his film. He needed the income it would produce to keep his creditors at bay. United Artists was strapped for product. The company desperately needed new films to release. Conflict became inevitable. Reluctantly Griffith honored his commitment to United Artists. But the result was that Griffith received far less income from *Way Down East* than he would have if another company had released the film. He was no longer financially solvent and would need to rely on loans from UA to finance future productions. Thus began the long downward spiral of Griffith's fortunes. *Orphans of the Storm* was Griffith's next major undertaking. Lillian and Dorothy Gish starred. Set against the backdrop of the French Revolution, the plot was full of complications and difficult to follow. Griffith covered most of the acreage at his studio with elaborate sets and, once again, costs were completely out of control. *Orphans* had no chance of making enough money to bail Griffith out of debt. He was desperate but not desperate enough to accept a lucrative offer from William Randolph Hearst to direct his mistress, Marion Davies, in two pictures a year. In early 1922 Griffith quickly turned out four films. They helped stave off bankruptcy but did damage to his already faltering reputation. Grasping the inevitability of the situation, Lillian Gish parted ways with Griffith and continued to have a long and distinguished career.

Over the next two years Griffith would repeat his pattern of making small, undistinguished films so that he could occasionally raise the money to make a larger film. Then, the larger films would get out of control both financially and artistically and force Griffith to

LILLIAN GISH PORTRAIT, WAY DOWN EAST (1920), DIRECTED BY D.W. GRIFFITH, SHOWN: LILLIAN GISH

UNITED ARTISTS/PHOTOFEST

UNITED ARTISTS/PHOTOFEST

ORPHANS OF THE STORM (1921), DIRECTED BY D.W. GRIFFITH, SHOWN FROM LEFT: DOROTHY GISH, LILLIAN GISH

make more small films for the money. In the December 1924 issue of Photoplay an open letter to Griffith appears. It suggests that he withdraw from making any future films for the good of the industry. However, Griffith was back to working for Zukor, who had become the most powerful individual in the movie world. Lasky's Famous Plays by Famous Players would soon begin to use the Paramount name. A new headquarters building was under construction in Manhattan, and Zukor was spending millions on his new country estate. Griffith was reduced to being a director for hire. By the end of 1926 Griffith's irresponsible spending and his films lackluster performances at the box office brought an end to his relationship with Paramount.

Griffith returned to Los Angeles in mid 1927 to work for Joseph Schenck, one of the founders of Paramount. The compensation and proposed film budgets were generous, but time was quickly running out. The Warner Brothers were pushing their company into the age of sound, a direction everyone would eventually have to take. A whole new generation of filmmakers would soon replace pioneers like Griffith. His personal life was faltering, too. His longtime companion, Carole Dempster, was moving on. Griffith was in danger of becoming a joke. He was unable to modernize his style and insisted on making moralistic, sentimental films in a time when nuance was in fashion. His loyal audiences began to desert him. For Schenck a Griffith film had become a break-even proposition at best. For the first time since leaving Biograph, Griffith was put under the supervision of a studio executive. He chafed at the experience. His last film for the company was the biography *Abraham Lincoln.*

Griffith's final film was a 1931 cautionary tale of alcoholism titled *The Struggle*. The critics were savage. Griffith was like an athlete who had stayed in the game too long, falling short of his earlier greatness. His few remaining friends avoided him for fear of saying the wrong thing and adding to the pain of failure. For Griffith there was still the need to extricate himself from the many business entanglements in which he had engaged over the years. His cousin, Woodson Oglesby, came to the rescue. With daring and creativity Oglesby identified huge sums of unpaid back salary from both United Artists and Griffith's own last production company. By carefully trading what was owed to Griffith against what was owed by him, Oglesby managed to lift Griffith out of debt and leave him modestly situated. No more lavish living for Griffith, who had begun to take consolation in drink. For a time he subsidized his income by doing a twice weekly network radio show about the Hollywood of yesteryear. He still kept in contact with Bitzer, who had himself fallen on hard times drinking his days away. Hal Roach, the owner of a modest comedy studio in Culver City, offered Griffith his last job consulting on the production of *One Million B.C.* What Griffith contributed, if anything, is unknown, but Griffith clearly conveyed to his other friends that Roach had hired him "for old times' sake."

In 1948 Griffith had moved to modest rooms in the Hollywood Knickerbocker Hotel. He remained in touch with Lillian Gish and a few loyal old friends. On July 23 he suffered a stroke and died the next day. He was later buried in the graveyard of the Kentucky church where he worshipped as a boy. The man who did more to create the motion picture industry than any other was largely forgotten by it at the time of his death.

CHAPTER 3

PIONEERS CONTINUED
Movie Makers, Movie Stars and the Movie Business

MACK SENNETT

Michael Sinnott was born in Quebec, Canada in 1880. His schooling was somewhat erratic due to his family's practice of moving every few years. At one point Sinnott and his brother attended a French-language boarding school for about a year. While he was still in his teens the family relocated one last time, settling in the area of Northampton, Massachusetts where the parents operated a restaurant and the brothers worked at the local pulp mill. In 1906 Michael announced to his family that he had decided to leave home, change his name to Mack Sennett, and pursue his dream of becoming an opera singer in New York.

Unsurprisingly, the untrained young Mack had little chance of becoming an opera star. He did begin to land small roles on the stage, claiming that his first was as the rear end on a dancing horse. Within weeks of D. W. Griffith's arrival at Biograph in January 1908, Sennett also was employed by the studio. Much of his early work as a screen actor was directed by Griffith, who recognized Sennett's talent for comedy. By September that year, Sennett was assigned his first leading role in *Father Gets Into The Game*. As Griffith and Billy Bitzer were in the process of developing their new film language and technique, Sennett became their most devoted acolyte, soaking up every lesson he could. By the end of the year he starred in two Biograph comedies, playing the recurring character, M. Dupont.

Sennett got his first chance to direct in a film titled *Comrades* in 1910. Griffith had little interest in comedy and soon, all of Biograph's comedy production was assigned to Sennett. He was allowed to recruit a small company of comedians for his films including Del Henderson, and in 1911, Fred Mace and the petite, vivacious Mabel Normand. Sennett knew both Henderson and Mace from his days on stage in burlesque. The pace of production was furious with Sennett credited for directing 47 films that year. As usual, Sennett spent the winter of 1912 in California with Griffith, although for the most part Sennett worked independently. In fact, when the Griffith company returned to New York, Sennett was dispatched to Albuquerque, New Mexico to film a comedy short. Soon after he made his way back to New York, Sennett was pursued by two young movie businessmen, Adam Kessel and Charles Baumann, who had owned theaters since 1908 and built a new production facility in the Edendale neighborhood of Los Angeles. They had recently hired Thomas Ince to apply his assembly-line method to making westerns. Ince imported an entire wild west show including 60 Native American performers and set up shop at the intersection of Sunset Boulevard and Pacific Coast Highway. Kessel and Baumann wanted Sennett to go west to run a company devoted to producing comedies.

Most of the accounts of how the Keystone Company began are contradictory, no less perplexing since the varying accounts are attributed to Sennett himself.. Some time in August 1912 an agreement was reached with Kessel and Baumann. The Keystone name was almost certainly borrowed from the Pennsylvania Railroad that used the trademark "Keystone" on its rolling stock. In the first fifteen months of production the company cranked out more than 140 films. To accomplish this Sennett raided Biograph to sign Mabel Normand, Ford Sterling, and Fred Mace. Normand wasn't difficult to convince as she and Sennett were rumored to be romantically involved. At first the studio in Edendale was used primarily as a storage facility and meeting place for the casts and crews. The films were shot largely on the streets of Los Angeles. The accommodating citizenry thought nothing of emerging from their offices and stores to find themselves in the middle of the madness of a Keystone comedy improvisation.

The Keystone directors roster consisted of three Biograph refugees, Henry Lehrman, Wilfred Lucas, and George Nichols. The early output included Jewish and blackface comedies with Ford Sterling starring in the former as Toplitsky, the Yiddish rogue. During this time Mabel Normand and Sennett appeared in a successful series of domestic comedies also directed by Sennett. In March 1913 the first of the Keystone Kops films, *The Bangville Police*, was completed. With Sterling in the lead as the police captain, the Kops were a ragtag ensemble of burlesque, vaudeville, and circus comedians. Throughout the remainder of the year the Kops appeared in a supporting role in Mabel Normand's films. In October Keystone's rising star Roscoe "Fatty" Arbuckle starred as one of the Kops in *Fatty Joins the Force*. For the movies' predominately immigrant audiences (who often found themselves

PRODUCTION STILL FROM KEYSTONE HOTEL, SHOWN: THE KEYSTONE KOPS

WARNER BROS./PHOTOFEST

on the receiving end of big-city police corruption), the idea of poking fun at law enforcement was a natural. As 1913 drew to a close, Sennett was making plans to withdraw from acting and directing to concentrate his full attention on management.

As Sennett withdrew from acting, Fatty Arbuckle became the replacement suitor for Mabel Normand. The Mabel and Fatty series of films was an instant success. Normand was slightly less than five feet tall. Fatty was three times her size with the grace of a ballet dancer. They just looked funny together. Normand was already immensely popular with film audiences. After Mary Pickford, she was arguably the second biggest female star in the business. The series was so successful that Sennett allowed Arbuckle to direct the films as well as act in them. Eventually he would have the honor of serving in both roles on all of his films.

In September 1913, Charlie Chaplin signed a contract with Kessel and Baumann for $150 a week and was dispatched to Los Angeles and Keystone in December. Sennett was immediately taken by Chaplin's freshness relative to his other star, Arbuckle. It is also likely that Sennett welcomed a competition between the two. Early on, perhaps in the film *Mabel's Strange Predicament*, Chaplin developed his Little Tramp costume and character. Audiences responded enthusiastically to the populism of a lovable tramp underdog who overcomes snobbery and makes fun of the establishment. From the very beginning Chaplin chafed under the direction of the Keystone staff. By April, Sennett gave in to the complaining and allowed Chaplin to direct himself. He appeared with the entire roster of Keystone performers over the next few months including a large, imposing character actor, Mack Swain, who would become a regular in Chaplin movies for years to come.

Chaplin didn't stay long at Keystone. The conventional wisdom of the time was that actors came to the studio to become known and went elsewhere to get rich. This was a reflection of Sennett's belief that the company's films should be forced to adhere to an austere budgetary model to ensure profitability. One notable exception is *Tillie's Punctured Romance*, history's first feature-length comedy starring Normand and Chaplin with stage

Film sales vs. Film rental

The first method of distributing films had been outright sales. A production company would complete a film and order as many prints from the laboratory as the sales staff could sell. Once a print was sold, the producer relinquished control of the film. From the point view of the nickelodeon operator who had to sell enough tickets to pay the high cost of the film print, the sales system didn't work. Films had to be retained for weeks to show a profit. Their programs became stale and fickle audiences would move on.

In 1904 both William Fox and the Warner brothers' Duquesne Amusement & Supply Co. began to experiment with the idea of renting films to theaters rather than selling them. This was preferable to the theater owner, who paid less to rent than to buy films. It made it easy to change programs frequently and offer audiences a fresh program. Rental opened up many possibilities for both film producers and distributors. The producer would continue to receive revenue from a film long after it was completed. Distributors often became investors in film production, bringing a new infusion of cash to the industry. Distributors also got to know the theater territory very well and were soon making shrewd investments in theaters of their own.

actress Marie Dressler as its third lead. The film's $50,000 budget appalled Kessel and Baumann, who thought Sennett was taking leave of his senses, but Dressler's presence mollified them. At the end of 1914 Chaplin moved on to a more lucrative deal at Essanay. Keystone and Sennett were still the kings of comedy, but the smallness of his vision was beginning to discourage the studio's most talented performers.

In early 1915 Keystone remained the busiest of studios. Kessel and Baumann had constructed several stages on the Edendale lot, which made it possible to have four or five films in production at the same time. Along the way Keystone had also acquired another partner, Harry Aitken and his Mutual Pictures distribution company. Aitken was particularly useful because of his relationships with Wall Street investment banks. This meant a steady stream of capital. Mutual had already been successful in luring Mary Pickford and D. W. Griffith away from Biograph. Aitken was building a huge new studio equipped for and dedicated to making feature-length films on a triangular tract of land in Culver City. After entering into partnership with Kessel and Baumann, and company, Sennett formulated his dream: Sennett, Ince, and Griffith would represent the three sides of this new enterprise, Triangle Films.

Through a series of stock sales and other transactions all of the principals of Keystone and its related companies were becoming millionaires several times over. Arbuckle was becoming more independent with each passing day. At the end of 1915 Sennett set up Fatty with his own independent production facility in Fort Lee, New Jersey. Arbuckle was still making successful films with Normand but was also refining his own performances and the quality of his directing. During the early months of 1916 Sennett was overcommitted. Tied down at the Edendale facility managing a challenging slate of productions, he was also expected to begin creating feature projects for Triangle. Something had to give, and it was Triangle. Sennett chose to renege on his commitments for features. Kessel and Baumann, meanwhile, were losing their grip on the business. The cost of operations and the huge salaries the principals received starved their companies for cash. The entire year became a nightmare of juggling one project to raise the money to finish another. Sennett's beloved Keystone was about to go under.

Other industry forces were congealing at the time. The Paramount Company had prospered distributing Adolph Zukor and Jessie Lasky's Famous Players Company films. Paramount had grown large enough to take over weaker businesses such as Triangle and Keystone. At the end of July 1917, Sennett gave over financial control of Keystone to Paramount and its chief executive, Zukor. Triangle would follow suit two years later. Under the terms of the deal Sennett would remain in command of the Keystone Studio with a commitment to deliver a film every two weeks. At that time Mabel Normand made good on her threats to leave Sennett, taking the opportunity to move to Goldwyn, while Arbuckle had already left for Paramount. Around this time, Fred Mace was found dead in his room at the Hotel Astor in New York. The madcap era of Keystone had reached its end. Sennett would have to carry on without his independence and without his biggest stars.

There was no shortage of movie clowns for Sennett to call on. Ben Turpin became Keystone's new star. He was soon joined by the baby-faced Harry Langdon. Even though the product created by the studio wasn't much more sophisticated than it had been in 1912, the popularity of Keystone's films held up through the mid 1920s. The studio's fortunes were further buoyed when Mabel Normand returned in 1921 after Goldwyn went out of business. Eventually, however, Normand departed once again, while Sennett began for the first time to face formidable competition in the field of comedy production from Hal Roach Studios.

Hal Roach

In 1913 a young man from New York named Hal Roach answered a newspaper ad from a Hollywood studio in need of extras–background actors. He soon formed a friendship with another young man starting out in the business, Harold Lloyd. Early on Roach decided he wasn't cut out for a career in front of the cameras. He worked for a little over a year as an assistant director. In 1915 Roach had amassed a fortune of $350, enough to make his own picture. He teamed up with Lloyd to make *Just Nuts*. Roach had no idea how to proceed from there until the film was shown to the Pathe company for possible distribution. Pathe recognized the quality of the film and Roach's and Lloyd's respective talents. They agreed to finance the fledgling filmmakers.

Roach and Lloyd were successful, so much so that Roach was able to acquire ten acres in Culver City in 1919 to serve as the home of his new studio. From the beginning Roach studios were different from Keystone. The films emphasized character as much as pure action and had more depth and sophistication than Sennett's output. Roach believed that his studio should be a fun place to work without undue interference from management and had no trouble attracting the best comedy directing talent in the business. In addition to Lloyd, Roach developed new stars such as Charlie Chase, Zazu Pitts, Stan Laurel, and Oliver Hardy. Another Roach creation was a group of cute funny child actors known interchangeably as The Little Rascals and Our Gang.

By 1921 Roach was permitting Lloyd to experiment with longer films such as *A Sailor-Made Man*. These became an instant hit with audiences. The studio flourished throughout the 1920s. In spite of the fact that Lloyd left in 1923 to make his own films, other Roach performers, especially Laurel and Hardy, kept the studio prosperous. When sound arrived at the end of the decade, Roach Studios was more than ready for it.

The coming of sound to the motion picture industry in 1927 was particularly challenging for Sennett. His pictures had always been defined by nonstop action with a minimum of character development. Keystone's approach wasn't adaptable to sound. Paramount had dropped distribution of Keystone films earlier in the decade, leaving Sennett continually looking for his next distributor. The stock market crash of October 1929 left him with greatly dwindling assets. Keystone made a few talking comedy shorts in the early thirties including films that featured Bing Crosby and W. C. Fields. Sennett's enthusiasm was flagging. Mabel Normand died in 1930, and Fatty Arbuckle followed in 1933. By that time the Edendale lot had been destroyed by a freak storm. There was little left of the Keystone empire. In December 1933 Sennett filed for bankruptcy.

For the next twenty-seven years Sennett lived on the fringes of the movie industry. He continually plotted his comeback, occasionally announcing a new project that never materialized. At the end of his days, Sennett lived in a small apartment above Hollywood Boulevard. He dressed every morning to spend his days in the lobby of the Hollywood Roosevelt Hotel. Over time his clothes became threadbare. He died November 5, 1960, all but forgotten by the town and the industry he had a hand in building.

MABEL NORMAND

Like many film pioneers, Sennett included, Mabel Normand was given to inventing the details of her biography. At various times she claimed to have been born in Atlanta, Boston, and New York. The best evidence suggests that she was born on Staten Island in 1892. In spite of Normand's claims of hardship and being an orphan, she actually grew up comfortably as the daughter of a master carpenter. Still, her three siblings all died of an incurable lung disease, making health and fitness a genuine issue for young Mabel. As a result she became an accomplished swimmer. In 1908 Mabel set out to make her fortune and was soon a regular model for advertising illustrator Charles Dana Gibson. Being a "Gibson Girl" led to other modeling opportunities and by the end of 1909 Normand was hired to work briefly for Griffith at Biograph. The job ended the next year when Griffith and company left to winter in California. ★ *winter of 1909!*

In early 1910 Normand went to work at Vitagraph studios and was immediately cast in comedy roles. When she returned to Biograph the following year, Griffith cast her in a few of his films, but he was unenthusiastic about Normand's spunkiness, preferring actresses with a virginal, ethereal quality. But Mabel was perfect for Sennett, who was beginning to perfect his chaotic comedy style. For him she was the perfect "queen bee" with a hive of activity swarming around her. She was beautiful and could be glamorous when necessary, but she was also funny and athletic. When Sennett announced the formation of the Keystone Company in 1912, Normand did not hesitate to join him.

For years Normand and Sennett were linked by rumors of a romance. At one point he gave her a magnificent engagement ring. But there never was to be a marriage. For his part, Sennett was never linked with anyone else romantically. He preferred to live with his mother for a large part of his life and died without ever having been married or having had children. Normand, on the other hand, was involved with a

SHOWN: MABEL NORMAN, MACK SENNETT, CIRCA **1915**

PHOTOFEST

number of men. Some of her relationships appear to be the inventions of Keystone publicity agents. Others were verifiably real.

Normand was notorious for giving fan magazine writers a generous supply of grist for their mills. She was a practical joker on the movie lot. She was famous for attending wild parties and out-drinking the men. Her seemingly boundless reserves of energy were often attributed to cocaine use. She was fond of giving outrageous quotes to reporters, including referring to Mary Pickford as a "prissy bitch." Professionally Normand was frustrated. While Pickford and Chaplin were nearing the million dollar mark with their yearly incomes, Normand was still toiling at Keystone at the rate of $500 per week. In May, 1916 she demanded that Sennett give her her own production company. Sennett gave in.

Comfortably ensconced in a small studio with luxurious quarters and a Japanese chef, Normand began work on the feature-length film *Mickey*. Production wasn't completed until the next winter, at which time she left Sennett and Keystone to join forces with Samuel Goldwyn. When it was finally released in 1918, *Mickey* was a huge success. Between 1918 and 1920 Normand continued to make more successful films, which, like *Mickey*, usually involved her first appearing as a tomboy dressed in oversized, mannish costumes and later revealing the true nature of her femininity to her love interest. In 1920 the Goldwyn Company collapsed and Normand returned to Keystone.

In the early 1920's scandals involving well known Hollywood players rocked the movie industry and audiences began to tire of the irresponsible behavior of stars like Normand. In early 1922, Paramount director, William Desmond Taylor, was found shot to death in his bungalow on Alvarado Street. Normand was the last person to see him alive. In 1923 Wallace Reid, a star football player at Princeton and strapping leading man at Paramount, died of heroin addiction. The last big scandal occurred on New Years Day, 1924. Normand's chauffeur, Joe Kelly, shot but did

WILLIAM DESMOND TAYLOR, CIRCA **1922**

not kill the playboy Courtland Dines. The investigation revealed that Kelly was a small-time gangster and that the shooting had occurred while Normand and friend Edna Purviance (Chaplin's usual co-star) were changing in Dines's bedroom after a hard night of drinking. This connection was all just too much for the audience to forgive.

Normand made her last film with Sennett, *The Extra Girl,* in 1923. By this time her lifestyle had taken its toll on her looks and ability to perform. She extended her career by signing with Hal Roach studios in 1926. Normand made a total of five pictures with Roach, none

Drugs and Scandal in Hollywood

At midnight, January 16, 1920 the Eighteenth Amendment to the U.S. Constitution and its accompanying Volstead Act became law. For the next thirteen years it would be illegal to own, sell, or consume alcoholic beverages in the United States. The law of Prohibition proved to be largely ineffective, nowhere more so than in Hollywood.

Given the unreasonable physical demands placed on performers in the movie industry, particularly comedians with their slapstick pratfalls, it is no wonder that the movie community routinely sought pain relief and a source of instant energy wherever they could find it. By 1920 Los Angeles and its Hollywood neighborhood had become a company town. Studio detectives and local police worked hand in hand to ensure that the valuable stars stayed out of trouble insofar as the public eye was concerned. Newspapers, especially those associated with the Hearst empire, also cooperated. They were reluctant to lose their highly profitable movie advertising and the glamorous stories studio publicity departments routinely fed them.

Cocaine was an over-the-counter drug, as was laudanum (a tincture of alcohol and opium). Cocaine served as the antidote for a night of hard partying before an early morning cast call. Laudanum and its related substances was an effective mask for the aches and pains that inevitably resulted from working ten- and twelve hours a day, six days a week. Many of the young people who came to Hollywood in the teens and twenties tended to come from troubled backgrounds. It was a rough and tumble environment in which the ability to be the life of the party was much admired. Often the quality of alcohol available was questionable, making the cure worse than the disease.

America was celebrating its Jazz Age prosperity with a wink and a cocktail. The people in Hollywood weren't behaving any differently than everyone else in the country, they just did it more often and intensely. The inevitable result was scandal.

of the particularly noteworthy. On September 17, 1926, she married one of her old drinking buddies, Lew Cody, in the midst of a days'-long binge. Neither spouse was ever faithful to their vows. Normand's last film was the ironically titled *One Hour Married*. As sound was arriving in 1929 Normand was stricken with tuberculosis. She never recovered, dying in a sanitarium in Altadena, California on February 23, 1930.

FATTY ARBUCKLE

As is the case with so many early film personalities, authorities disagree about Roscoe "Fatty" Arbuckle's early story. Most probably, he was born in Smith Center, Kansas in 1887. He was big from the start, weighing 14 pounds at birth. Roscoe's father was convinced that the boy was illegitimate, prompting the constant beatings he administered to the child well into his teens. The family moved to the hub of southern California citrus ranching, Santa Ana, in 1899. About that time Roscoe's mother died, and his father abandoned him. The twelve-year-old orphan survived by washing dishes at a local hotel. There is some evidence that Arbuckle's talent for singing was discovered around this time by musicians performing in the dining room. He was gifted with a beautiful, clear tenor voice.

In 1902 Arbuckle moved to the San Francisco Bay area in an attempt to reunite with his father. The pattern of abuse resumed, and before long the boy was on his own again. Eventually he found work as a singer in a café owned by theater operator Alex Pantages. By 1904 Arbuckle was touring the west coast with the Pantages Company. Vaudeville was an extremely popular form of entertainment in America from the late 1800s through the early 1920s. It consisted of traveling groups of entertainers who presented a show consisting of a variety of performance styles. There were singers (both popular and operatic), dancers, jugglers, acrobats, comedians, pantomimes, animal acts, and any number of specialized and exotic acts as well. The performers were generous with each other. A young singer like Arbuckle would be taken under someone's wing and taught to dance or do comedy. This breadth of performance skill made vaudeville performers very desirable to pioneer filmmakers.

One of the downsides to vaudeville was the constant travel. Performers typically spent a week or two in each town before moving on to the next by train or bus. They lived in hotels and rarely stayed in any one place long enough to send their laundry out, let alone put down roots. In 1906 Arbuckle was performing in San Francisco when the great earthquake and fire hit. At gunpoint he was commandeered into an army of able-bodied young men to clear away the mountains of rubble. Stuck there for six months, he returned to the stage at the first opportunity.

In 1909 Arbuckle married fellow performer Minta Durfee. It was a typical vaudeville marriage, dependent on their careers following the same path. That same year, he appeared in his first film, *Ben's Kid,* for the Selig Company. Arbuckle was embarrassed by the effort and told nobody about it. Instead he and his wife devoted themselves to touring. During the next four years they traveled with the Ferris Hartman Company to Hawaii, Japan, China, the Philippines, and India. They returned to California at the beginning of 1913, just as Keystone was gearing up for action at the Edendale lot. Arbuckle was a natural for Sennett, who hired not only Minta but Arbuckle's nephew, Al St. John, and his dog, Luke.

In the beginning Arbuckle performed with the Keystone Kops and performed in any other film that needed a supremely graceful big man to do a back flip, mug at the camera, and generally cut up. Keystone director, Henry Lehrman was particularly impressed by Arbuckle's abilities and cast him wherever possible. Lehrman was especially interested in the comic possibilities of pairing Arbuckle with Normand. From 1914 through 1916 Mabel and Fatty made twenty films together.

At the end of 1916 Joseph Schenck, one of the principals in Famous Players -Lasky attempted to lure Arbuckle away from Keystone. The offer was generous. Arbuckle would have his own label and studio. He would direct his own films. He would be allowed to bring his wife, nephew, and dog along to the new company, and he would be paid $1,000 per day plus twenty-five percent of the profits from his films. Arbuckle accepted the deal enthusiastically. However, an emergency necessitated a delay. Arbuckle was seriously ill. He had a carbuncle on his leg that doctors thought might require amputation. During his illness he lost eighty pounds and developed a powerful addiction to morphine. Avoiding amputation, he was finally back on his feet by the end of February 1917. At this time he also signed his old vaudeville friend, Buster Keaton, to his new Comique Films label, but separated from Minta. For the next two years Arbuckle worked happily in relative creative freedom. The company moved to New Jersey (possibly to get Arbuckle away from his morphine dealer) and back to California again. Paramount, the new name for Famous Players-Lasky, was pleased with the results–so much so that Adolph Zukor authorized Schenck to offer Arbuckle a new deal. Under the terms Arbuckle would make only feature-length films and would be paid $1 million per year. It was an extraordinary offer that Arbuckle immediately accepted.

There were two big problems with Arbuckle's new deal. It meant his having to give up creative control to studio executives. To earn the million and assure profits for the studio, he would need to make eight feature pictures a year, entailing a superhuman pace of production. Through the remainder of 1920 and the first three quarters of 1921, Arbuckle made good on his end of the deal. He put in twelve-hour days and seven-day work weeks. He stayed relatively sober and behaved well otherwise. However, whispers reverberated in the halls of Paramount that Arbuckle's films weren't doing as well as expected at the box office. Perhaps his popularity was eroding.

Over Labor Day weekend, 1921, Arbuckle decided to blow off some steam. He had just taken delivery of a beautiful, hand-built Pierce Arrow touring car and decided it would be fun to lead a caravan of his pals up to San Francisco for the holiday. The revelers checked in to the elegant St. Francis Hotel on Union Square. Among them were old friends including Henry Lehrman and Fred Fishbach. A woman named Maude Delmont showed up with a group of very young actresses and other girls from the studio. A bootlegger was summoned to bring cases of Champagne and whiskey. The party roared on for two days and nights.

On Monday, Labor Day morning, Arbuckle and his guests got back in their cars and returned to Los Angeles and the next day's work. Maude Delmont and a studio detective were left to clean up. One of the girls, Virginia Rappe, was very ill. The studio arranged for her to be checked in to a discreet private hospital. Two days later she was dead of peritonitis. Maude Delmont immediately claimed Rappe had been raped by Arbuckle with a Champagne bottle. The press circulated other lurid accounts of Arbuckle's depravity. The Hearst papers ran stories on the front page above the fold using Arbuckle's studio publicity photos with jail-cell bars superimposed. Arbuckle was already guilty in the court of public opinion; organizations like the Catholic Legion of Decency de-

ROSCOE 'FATTY' ARBUCKLE

manded he receive the most extreme punishment possible. For its part, Paramount quietly invoked the morals turpitude clause in Arbuckle's contract, relieving them from any further burden of paying or supporting him in any way. Zukor's hand can be seen in the way Paramount refused to defend its star. Perhaps this was an opportunity to rid the company of an expensive, unproductive, embarrassing has-been.

Arbuckle stood trial in San Francisco. The first trial ended in a hung jury and a mistrial. The second time around Arbuckle was acquitted but not exonerated. Word spread around the motion picture industry that he was poison, blacklisted. Even Sennett would not dare to bring Arbuckle back to Keystone. Lawyers fees and his extravagant lifestyle in no time ate up whatever resources he had. By 1925 Arbuckle was virtually penniless. The William Desmond Taylor affair had only served to convince the motion picture industry that it could afford Arbuckle no mercy. Fatty didn't have a friend in the world except for Buster Keaton, who paid his legal bills and sent Arbuckle on a long trip to the Orient to recuperate.

In 1928 Arbuckle opened a nightclub in Hollywood. It was well supported by his old friends, but the great Depression and another divorce caused him to close it. In 1932, on the tenth anniversary of the Virginia Rappe scandal, a group of Arbuckle's friends took out a full-page newspaper ad asking, "Isn't it time that Fatty Arbuckle be forgiven?" The ad was signed by dozens of the biggest names in the business. Jack Warner offered Arbuckle a contract to star in six 2-reel comedy shorts. The films were finished on June 28, 1933. Warner rewarded Arbuckle with a much more generous contract. Fatty celebrated his good fortune well into the night. The next day he died of heart failure. He was forty-six years old.

THE MEN WHO MADE PARAMOUNT: ADOLPH ZUKOR, JESSE LASKY, CECIL B. DEMILLE, AND OTHERS

Adolph Zukor was born in Risce, Hungary in 1873. Both of his parents died by the time he was seven years old. Zukor was placed under the care of an uncle, a rabbi who expected his nephew to follow in his footsteps. Young Zukor had a different ambition. He managed to save for his passage to America, arriving in New York in 1889 at age sixteen. His first job was sweeping floors in a fur store for two dollars a week. Zukor took advantage of night school, where he studied English and business. By the time he was nineteen he and a friend had amassed the resources to open their own fur business in Chicago. The store's success didn't curb Zukor's restlessness. In 1900 he moved back to New York and began investing in penny arcades and nickleodeons.

PHOTOFEST

ADOLPH ZUKOR, CIRCA 1913

Early on Zukor partnered with another furrier interested in the movie theater business, Marcus Loew. The two became very successful at adapting inexpensive, vacant storefronts into nickleodeons. Eventually Zukor grew weary of fighting to get quality motion pictures for his theaters. He became convinced that the only way to deal with the supply shortage was to create his own production company. Zukor and Loew dissolved their partnership, freeing Zukor to form a new production partnership with Broadway stage producer, Daniel Frohman. Their first venture was to import the French produced film *Queen Elizabeth* staring Sarah Bernhardt, the best known stage actress of the day. Zukor and his partner represented the film as their own production and made enough money from it to start their own production company.

Zukor's concept for the new company was to acquire the rights to successful stage plays and adapt them with the original stage actors reprising their stage roles on film. The company was formed in 1912 and named Famous Plays by Famous Players (later shortened to Famous Players). The idea was an instant success. Audiences were intrigued to see the stage stars on film, and the quality of the material was far superior to most films of the day. In 1914 Zukor entered into an exclusive agreement with W. W. Hodkinson, owner of Paramount Pictures, a large successful distribution company. Paramount also represented Jesse Lasky Feature Play Company.

Jesse Lasky was born in San Jose, California in 1880. As a young man Lasky worked a variety of jobs including newspaper reporter and gold miner. Eventually he was attracted to vaudeville, where he began as a performer but quickly switched to the management side of the industry. In 1911 he partnered with Broadway director-producer Cecil B. DeMille and with Lasky's brother-in-law, Samuel Goldfish (later known as Samuel Goldwyn) to produce a stage operetta. The venture was a failure but in 1914 the three teamed up again to produce the motion picture adaptation of the successful Broadway play *The Squaw Man*. Rather than shoot their film in the familiar confines of Fort Lee, New Jersey, the three partners opted to make it in the more realistic locations around Los Angeles. In 1914 they rented a barn in Hollywood, which, with their one truck and one camera, became their makeshift headquarters and studio. (The barn has been moved and carefully preserved at a location across from Hollywood Bowl on Highland Boulevard).

The Squaw Man directed by DeMille was a great critical and financial success, allowing the fledgling Jesse L. Lasky Feature Play Company to attract the best writers and acting talent available to Hollywood. Paramount became Lasky's distributor. Meanwhile, Adolph Zukor had been busy buying stock in Paramount. He was convinced of the importance of owning control of the distribution sector of the new

JESSE L. LASKY & ADOLPH ZUKOR SHORTLY AFTER PARTNERING TO CREATE PARAMOUNT PICTURES, 1916

industry. In 1915 Zukor convinced Lasky and his partners to merge. This would allow them to capitalize their combined companies at a much higher level than would be possible alone. Zukor also wanted to acquire motion picture theater companies, a goal facilitated by the merger. The new company was named Famous Players–Lasky. Zukor served as president, Lasky as first vice president in charge of production, Goldwyn as chairman, and DeMille as director-general. Two years later they changed the name of the company to Paramount Famous Lasky, and in 1920s to Paramount.

With Lasky and DeMille in charge of production in California, Zukor was free to concentrate on the business and finance end of the company in New York. Zukor and Lasky both agreed on the importance of acquiring the best talent possible. Mary Pickford, Rudolph Valentino, Gloria Swanson, Ernst Lubitsch, Joseph von Sternberg, Maurice Chevalier, and Marlene Deitrich were among the company's early acquisitions.

In 1921 Paramount encountered the first legal challenge to the way it did business. Initially the Federal Justice Department investigated the practice of "block booking." By this time the company was producing over sixty films per year, among them some of the best films of the time. Independent theater owners were forced to acquire a block of Paramount films in order to get access to the best and most popular productions. Inevitably, the block of films contained poor-quality pictures nobody wanted, but Paramount had the independents over a barrel. They had to accept the terms of the deal. The Justice Department contended that this was an unfair restraint of free trade, and was therefore prohibited by American antitrust laws. Later the Justice Department also reviewed Paramount's ownership of its many theaters and how that worked to further restrain free trade. The issue would remain in the courts, unresolved for over twenty five years.

In 1932 Lasky was ousted from the company by his personal assistant, Manny Cohen. Lasky was bankrupt. Within the year he was able to emerge from bankruptcy and form his own Lasky Company in partnership with Fox. Zukor remained the man in charge of Paramount's vast theater, production, and distribution resources and was still involved in management until his death in 1976 at age 103.

CHARLIE CHAPLIN

Chaplin was born in London, England in 1889. Both of his parents were music hall entertainers (the British equivalent of American vaudeville) who expected that young Charlie and his older half brother, Sidney, to join in the family business. Chaplin's first professional job was standing in for his ailing mother when he was just five years old. By twelve his father died of alcoholism and his mother was institutionalized with mental illness. The Chaplin boys were initially placed in an orphanage. Eventually their mother was able to take them in again, but it was up to the boys to support the family financially. Chaplin had only two years of formal schooling, but he was already a skilled stage performer appearing in plays and working as a mime.

In 1907 Chaplin joined the internationally known Karno Pantomime Troupe. He toured with Karno until December 1913 when Adam Kessel saw a New York performance of the Troupe and immediately signed Chaplin to a Keystone contract for $150 per week.

Upon arriving in Los Angeles Chaplin began to clash with Mack Sennett. Chaplin didn't get along with most of the Keystone directors. He was especially bothered by Sennett's tendency work in a chaotic environment. Chaplin had ambitions of becoming a star, and Keystone was not a place where he would be sufficiently promoted to achieve his goal. Furthermore, in the eleven months Chaplin worked at the studio, he learned that improvisation and rehearsal were techniques that made his performances more vivid and funny. Sennett resisted this more time-consuming and expensive approach.

In November 1914, Chaplin signed a new contract with Essanay Films for $1,250 per week with a ten thousand dollar signing bonus to make fourteen films during the next year and a half. Although this was still a challenging pace of production, it allowed him enough time to do a little experimentation and to refine his technique. During this year, Chaplin introduced his Little Tramp character, a small man in baggy pants, wearing oversized shoes, and sporting a bowler hat and cane. He was the classic comedy underdog, fighting for dignity and respect. The film industry's working-class audience embraced the diminutive character, and Chaplin was on the fast track to stardom. During his Essanay period Chaplin also gathered around himself a complementary group of performers including the beautiful and graceful Edna Purviance, who would remain his onscreen (and sometimes offscreen) love interest for the next seven years. In this environment his performances and films were becoming more complex and nuanced.

When the Essanay contract expired there was a competition among the studios to sign him. Chaplin films made big money both in America and abroad. His presence on a studio talent roster would inevitably raise overall value of any motion picture company. He chose to sign with Mutual Films in February 1916, which gave him a $150,000 signing bonus and a $1,000 per week. More importantly, he was given his own studio and authority to employ the technical staff and cast of actors he had assembled at Essanay. The contract called for Chaplin to finish a two-reel film each month, which he did, for a time. However, free from the meddling of studio executives, he began to slow down the pace to one two-reel film every three months. The films were so good and so successful Mutual had no choice but to accept the slower pace of production. Looking back years later, Chaplin would regard the "Mutual period" as the happiest time of his professional life.

In June 1917, Chaplin moved once again. This time First National Exhibitors Circuit gave him the opportunity to become his own producer. Under the terms of the contract he would receive a $125,000 advance for each of eight two-reel films to be completed that year. It was a much talked about million dollar deal. However, because Chaplin retained

CHARLES CHAPLIN/PHOTOFEST

THE KID (1921), DIRECTED BY CHARLES CHAPLIN, SHOWN FROM LEFT: CHARLES CHAPLIN (AS TRAMP), JACKIE COOGAN (AS THE KID)

ownership of his films, the deal was worth much more than a million. With his fortune assured he built himself a new studio on La Brea Boulevard, south of Sunset. Many of Chaplin's best short films were made during this period. His 1918 film *Shoulder Arms* succeeded in turning the horrors of the First World War into comedy. In 1921 he made his first recognized feature-length masterpiece, *The Kid*, costarring young Jackie Coogan, a film that recounts the miseries of Chaplin's own dark childhood. In that same year he made the almost perfect *Idle Class*, in which he plays both the Little Tramp character and a rich snob.

In 1919 Chaplin joined Mary Pickford, Douglas Fairbanks, D. W. Griffith, and Samuel Goldwyn in the formation of United Artists. The idea behind the company was to give these major stars more control over their films and more profit from them by creating their own distribution company.

CHAPLIN'S WOMEN

One theme that runs through Chaplin's life is his reckless and notorious relationships with women. At the time he signed his contract with Mutual, Chaplin was one of the wealthiest and most eligible bachelors in the world. He was associated with almost every beautiful actress in Hollywood. In 1918 Chaplin fell in love with a sixteen-year-old actress, Mildred Harris. Chaplin was twenty-nine at the time. They were married after a brief courtship and had a son, Norman, who died three days after birth. The marriage didn't survive the tragedy. Most biog-

DOUGLAS FAIRBANKS, MARY PICKFORD, CHARLIE CHAPLIN, D.W. GRIFFITH (THE FOUNDERS OF UNITED ARTISTS)

raphers agree that the death of his son served as the inspiration for *The Kid*. The couple were divorced in late 1920, two months before the release of *The Kid*.

In 1923, as he was preparing to go into production on *The Gold Rush*, Chaplin was searching for an actress to replace Edna Purviance. Lita Grey caught his eye. She was sixteen and had previously appeared as a child actress in *The Kid*. He was thirty-five at the time and infatuated. Lita Grey was cast in the new production, but announced her pregnancy to the entire cast and crew a few days into production. The two were hastily married in Mexico in November 1924. Their first son, Charles Jr., was born in May 1925. Their second son, Sidney, was born in March 1926. Soon after, the two engaged in a long and nasty public divorce in which Chaplin was accused of many infidelities. The divorce was final in November 1926.

Between 1931 and 1932 Chaplin embarked on a long world tour after completing *City Lights*. Upon returning to Hollywood, he met Paulette Goddard, a recently divorced actress in her early twenties. Chaplin was forty-three. The two quickly became a couple and entertained and traveled together extensively. Goddard was cast in *Modern Times* (1936).

Around that time Chaplin and Goddard traveled to Asia and claimed to have been married during the trip, although there is no documentation of the nuptial. Goddard also appeared in *The Great Dictator*. Their marriage ended in June 1942 with a Mexican divorce.

Scandal struck twice for Chaplin in 1943. Joan Barry, a twenty-two-year-old actress, with whom Chaplin had been involved for the past two years, sued for paternity. As with the Lita Grey divorce, the lawsuit was a circus of mudslinging. At the same time Chaplin was searching for a new leading lady and met Oona O'Neill, daughter of the great American playwright Eugene O'Neill. At the time Oona was eighteen and Chaplin was fifty-four. The two were married in June. Gossip writers such as Hearst newspaper's Hedda Hopper, instantly registered outrage at the difference in their ages. Chaplin's reputation was immeasurably damaged by the resulting backlash to the two affairs. Despite naysayers, Chaplin and O'Neill had eight children and remained together for the rest of his life.

CHAPLIN'S GREAT FEATURE FILMS

As Chaplin became increasingly independent professionally, his focus shifted from quantity to quality. Without studio intervention, he was able to make the films of his choosing at the time of his choosing. From 1922 on, he made only a handful of short films, electing to concentrate on more artistically challenging and rewarding feature-length projects. His personal wealth was so considerable Chaplin no longer needed to view these projects as a source of income, freeing him to spend years developing and producing a single film.

THE GOLD RUSH (1925), DIRECTED BY CHARLES CHAPLIN, SHOWN: CHARLES CHAPLIN (AS THE LONE PROSPECTOR)

The Gold Rush (1925) The Little Tramp character joins the Yukon Gold Rush of 1897. He and his cabin mate are beset by a ferocious blizzard and forced to remain indoors for weeks without food. The cabin mate begins to hallucinate that Chaplin is a roasted chicken. Their Thanksgiving dinner consists of the Tramp's boiled shoes, an ingenious prop made of licorice. The premise of the film gives Chaplin an opportunity to deeply explore the comedy of *pathos* (the ability of a character or situation to evoke sympathy). Many historians consider this to be Chaplin's greatest film.

The Circus (1928) Production on the film was postponed significantly by the Lita Grey divorce trial. When production resumed, Chaplin had become completely gray haired from stress. Thereafter, he was forced to dye his hair to play the Tramp. In this film he falls in love with a horse trainer and becomes the star of the circus through a series of mishaps.

City Lights (1931) This film begins Chaplin's period of resisting the advent of sound. Although the film contains sound effects and a musical score written by Chaplin, the story is told entirely in pantomime. It is also the last film for the Little Tramp character. In the film Chaplin meets and falls in love with a blind girl who supports herself by selling flowers. His challenge is to convince a millionaire to give him the money for an operation that will restore the girl's sight.

Modern Times (1936) As in the case with *City Lights*, this film is clearly set within the context of the Great Depression. In it Chaplin is released from jail and finds work as a factory worker, shipyard worker, night watchman in a department store, and a harried singing waiter. His real goal is to return to the solitude of jail. In one scene he is famously caught up in the machine he operates, becoming a cog in the machine himself. In *Modern Times* Chaplin explores the theme of authority figures in society.

MODERN TIMES (1936), DIRECTED BY CHARLES CHAPLIN SHOWN: CHARLES CHAPLIN (AS A FACTORY WORKER)

UNITED ARTISTS/PHOTOFEST

The Great Dictator (1940) Thirteen years into the era of talking pictures, Chaplin appears in his first dialogue film. The film is a comedic satire on Adolph Hitler and his designs for world domination. It was the first Chaplin film to receive an Oscar nomination for best picture.

Monsieur Verdoux (1947) This film is less a comedy than an expression of Chaplin's darkening view of the human condition. He plays an out-of-work, destitute family man. To support his family he romances, marries, and kills rich women for their fortunes. This project was originally suggested to Chaplin by Orson Welles.

Limelight (1952) This was Chaplin's last American film for reasons that are explained below. He plays an old, downtrodden vaudeville comedian who saves an equally desperate ballet dancer from killing herself. The film is more drama than comedy and is often cited as Chaplin's best talking picture. It features a short and disappointing duet with Buster Keaton.

A King In New York (1957) Chaplin's response to McCarthyism is the story of a king exiled to New York after a revolution in his home country. He is accused of being a communist and forced to defend himself.

Countess from Hong Kong (1967) Written and directed by Chaplin, Marlon Brando and

Sophia Loren star in this light romantic comedy. Chaplin has a small cameo role but stays behind the camera otherwise.

CHAPLIN'S EXILE

Despite his astounding wealth, Chaplin always carried the scars of childhood poverty. The majority of his films feature underdog characters doing battle with authority figures. For his entire life he had great sympathy for the downtrodden underclass. This, combined with his penchant for courting romantic scandal, made Chaplin a target for moralizing demagogues. J. Edgar Hoover, the cross-dressing first head of the Federal Bureau of Investigation (FBI) had Chaplin squarely in his sights from the outset.

During the Depression, Hollywood, and America in general, engaged in labor activism that, inevitably, involved the influences of international socialism and communism. All of this was changed by World War II and the end of the Great Depression. Following the war, American politics turned virulently anticommunist. The fact that Chaplin had never acquired American citizenship was used against him as evidence of his lack of patriotism.

In 1952 Chaplin prepared to take his family with him to promote the distribution of *Limelight* in Europe. He clearly had some notion that his time in America was over as he made a number of financial moves consistent with the notion of moving back to Europe. As Chaplin and his family left New York, he received a telegram from the U.S. State Department revoking his reentry visa. He was still a British citizen, but he could no longer return to America. Eventually, the family settled on a large and beautiful estate near Corsier, Switzerland.

In 1972 the Motion Picture Academy arranged for Chaplin and his family to acquire temporary visitors' visas for the purpose of returning to Hollywood one last time for the Academy Awards. America had changed a great deal in the twenty years of his absence. Joseph McCarthy, the author of the dark anticommunist chapter in American history and one of Chaplin's chief tormentors, had died of alcoholism in an army hospital, discredited in 1957. The Vietnam War had brought a new liberal political sensibility to the country. It was time to heal old wounds.

The Academy Awards ceremonies had, in the few years prior to 1972, become a platform for the motion picture industry leaders to express political as well as artistic opinions. That evening, in a dramatic presentation, the lights went down in the theater. Next a film montage of the greatest moments from Chaplin's eighty-eight films was shown to an audience that was transported by the wonder of those scenes. As the film ended and the lights came back up, Chaplin stood on the stage amidst the greatest and longest ovation in the history of the Oscars. He was presented an award for lifetime achievement. Shortly thereafter he quietly slipped out of the town that he, as much as anyone else, had built. He died peacefully with his family at his bedside just before Christmas in 1977.

CARL LAEMMLE

Among the film pioneers one of Laemmle's greatest contributions to the new industry was in creating the first permanent wholly integrated movie factory. He was a diminutive man, standing only five feet, three inches. Born in Laupheim, Germany in 1867, he enjoyed a relatively comfortable middle-class childhood, attending both elementary and Latin school. At age thirteen he was apprenticed to an uncle in the stationery business. His mother died unexpectedly when Laemmle was seventeen. Her death strengthened his resolve to immigrate to America. After arriving in New York he worked as a messenger boy until the opportunity to move to the Midwest presented itself. He settled in Oshkosh, Wisconsin and worked in a men's clothing store. In short order he was assistant manager and married the store owner's daughter. In 1906 he asked for a raise and was turned down. He decided to move to Chicago, where opportunities were more plentiful.

Chicago presented many possibilities but Laemmle was intrigued with the new nickelodeon businesses sprouting up around the city. He noted how unsuitable they were for anyone but the immigrant factory workers to which they catered. American factory towns of that time teemed with young men sent by their families in Europe to gain a foothold in the new world. For the most part they worked hard and drank hard. The nickleodeons had become a popular after-work entertainment. The combination of poor ventilation, the constant use of tobacco in its many forms, public drunkenness, and poor personal hygiene made the small storefront theaters unbearable for anyone else. Leammle's idea was to create a movie parlor suitable for the middle class, including women and children.

CARL LAEMMLE SR.

In 1906 Laemmle rented a building on Milwaukee Avenue and converted it into a movie theater. To promote the idea of a clean environment, he painted the interior white and named it the White Front Theater. It was so successful, he opened another theater two months later, which he called the Family Theater. Not long after Laemmle became frustrated with the poor service he was receiving from the film sellers and exchanges that served him. Particularly, he was having a hard time finding family-appropriate films. To solve his problem he founded Laemmle Service Company. Because of its superior customer service and efficiency, within three years it was the largest film exchange in the country.

Inevitably Laemmle's new status in the industry, combined with his decision to go into the production business in 1909, put him on a collision course with the Patent Trust and its leader and spokesperson, Jeremiah Kennedy of Biograph. When Laemmle wouldn't sell his film exchange to the Trust, they did everything they could to put him out of business, including hiring thugs to harass his production crews and conspiring with George Eastman to deny him access to raw film stock. Laemmle responded by importing his film stock from the Lumières in Paris and with a massive public relations campaign and a lengthy court battle that resulted in a victory for Laemmle in 1912.

For Laemmle, film production was a means to an end. He needed family films for his own theaters and those of his exchange customers. There weren't enough to go around. The simple answer was to make them himself. His production company IMP began in 1909 with a fifteen-minute version of Henry Wadsworth Longfellow's poem "Hiawatha." Twelve other similarly themed films followed that year. The following year the company made over one hundred films. During that time Laemmle hired away the Biograph woman who had been refused name billing on Biograph pictures. He happily included her name in the titles and advertising for IMP films, thereby making Florence Lawrence the first movie star. However, with the Trust breathing down his neck on the east coast, it became apparent that he could work in relative freedom by following Jesse Lasky's lead and going west to Hollywood. Land there was cheap, and it was too far away for the reach of Edison thugs.

In 1912 Laemmle was operating two studios in Hollywood, the Nestor, and another studio located in the Edendale neighborhood, near Keystone. With significant production operations in Fort Lee, New Jersey, a small studio in Manhattan and two studios in Hollywood, it was clearly time to reorganize and bring all production operations under one roof. The board of directors wanted a new name for their centralized facility. During a meeting Laemmle gazed out the window, daydreaming, when a Universal Pipe Supply truck passed by. Universal Films became the new name for the company.

In 1914 Universal purchased a ranch in Lankershim Township, north of the Hollywood Hills. Laemmle's plan was to borrow on Thomas Ince's concept of assembly-line film production. The new Universal City would have everything he needed to make motion pictures under one roof. The new facility included an executive office building, writers' bungalows, wardrobe shops, carpentry shops, dressing rooms, makeup rooms, a camera shop, a film laboratory, an art department, a publicity department, a school for child actors, a small hospital, police, and transportation departments to ferry studio staff to and from Los Angeles, some ten miles away. Universal City opened in March 1915. It was the first permanent industrial-style film production facility in the world, and it would remain the largest for the next ten years.

In preparation for the studio opening, Laemmle came west for a few months. He brought with him his personal secretary, nineteen-year-old Irving Thalberg. Thalberg had been Laemmle's next-door neighbor back in New York. Too sickly for college, Thalberg had learned to type and take dictation in night school. Chronically disorganized, Laemmle quickly began to depend on the young man. After the opening, Laemmle returned to New York, leaving Thalberg (escorted by his mother) behind to keep an eye on things. Within a matter on months studio personnel were deferring to the young man for many decisions. Before the end of the year Thalberg was officially managing the studio. The only problem was that he was too young to sign checks, a function Thalberg's mother performed.

To raise the capital to build the studio, Laemmle had to sell his film exchange and take on partners. The next challenge was to buy back enough stock to maintain control of his empire. Laemmle remained in the East to attend to the business side of the company while Thalberg began to attract the best talent available. Over the next few years Universal would be the most desirable place to work in the entire industry. Thalberg's taste was impeccable.

Filmmakers were allowed to work in relative freedom, and the quality of the facilities spurred their imaginations.

WILLIAM FOX

William Fox (born Wihelm Fried) was not even a year old when his family immigrated to America from Hungary in 1880. He was the oldest of thirteen children, six of whom died in childhood. As a very young boy he had to work to help support his family by selling newspapers, candy, and sandwiches on the streets of New York. When he was eleven he got a job working in a garment factory for eight dollars per week. When he was still in his teens Fox and a partner started their own garment company. At the same time he and another friend put together a vaudeville act. Fox married his childhood sweetheart in 1901. Three years later he invested his life savings of sixteen hundred dollars in his first penny arcade and movie theater. It was a struggle in the beginning, but before the end of the first year in the business, Fox opened a second nickelodeon. Within two more years he owned fifteen theaters in Brooklyn and Manhattan.

In 1909 William Kennedy of Biograph approached Fox on behalf of the Edison Patent Trust, then in the midst of buying out all of their competition. Kennedy offered Fox $75,000 for his theaters. Fox countered with a price of $750,000. Kennedy was so outraged that he broke off negotiations and denied Fox any further access to Trust produced films, which at the time accounted for 85% of all the films available in America. Fox countered by launching a $6 million law suit against the Trust based on the Sherman Anti-Trust Act of 1890. The law suit dragged on for almost three years with Fox offering to let the Trust settle out of court for a million dollars. During that time he managed to keep his theater company prosperous. Eventually the Trust settled the suit for $300,000. Fox had prevailed and the Trust was all but finished.

In 1914 Fox entered the motion picture production business. On a budget of $4,500 he made *Life's Shop Window.* He thought the finished project was awful and wanted to burn it, but he released it nonetheless. It became very successful. Soon Fox developed a system for film production. Since he was functionally illiterate, Fox's wife, Eve, would spend her days reading novels to find something suitable for film. In the evening she would recite the story to her husband, who sat smoking his omnipresent cigar, asking questions and clarifying the storyline. The next morning Fox would tell the story to one of his directors, who would set about making it into a film.

One of Fox's early successes was *A Fool There Was*, based on the Rudyard Kipling poem "The Vampire." It is the story of a woman who seduces men and destroys them for pleasure. A beautiful, young middle-class woman from Cincinnati named Theodosia Goodman (changed to Theda Bara) starred in the film and was an instant sensation. The title of the poem was shortened to "Vamp" to convey the dangerous sexuality of this new star. The studio made up a new biography for Goodman, claiming that she was born into a nomadic tribe from Egypt. Movie magazines were soon claiming that Theda Bara was an anagram for Arab Death. In the next three years Bara made over forty "Vamp" films. However, she quickly tired of playing the role in public as well as onscreen. Mothers hid their children from her when she passed.

Western actor Tom Mix was Fox's next big star. Like Bara, his on- and offscreen personality was a studio fabrication. He wore outrageous western costumes in public and traveled in a chauffeured limousine with a hand-tooled leather interior that evoked a fancy cowboy saddle. He lived on one of the largest estates in Hollywood, furnished with gaudy western art and memorabilia. During this period of the 1920s Fox was busy building his empire. He had purchased and built an impressive number of theaters, particularly on the West Coast and in New York. He hired inventor Lee De Forest (who had been instrumental in the development of radio) to work on a new motion picture process, which was eventually called Fox Movietone. This made Fox a leader in the newsreel business. He also acquired the American patent rights for the German Tri-Ergon sound process. He polished the image of his studio by hiring the great German Expressionist director, F. W. Murnau, to direct the 1927 silent film classic *Sunrise*.

By 1928 the Fox Companies had grown so large that it became feasible for William Fox to begin to buy out his competition in an attempt to control the entire movie industry. Through a series of canny stock transactions he was able to amass a huge war chest for this purpose. His first target was Paramount, but Zukor was not interested. He also made a failed attempt at controlling the First National Corp. Fox was finally successful in gaining control of the Loews Corp. The founder of the company, Marcus Loew, had died in 1924, leaving control in the hands of several family trusts and an executive, Nicholas Schenck. Schenk convinced the board of directors and the family to sell to Fox. For his part Schenck received a bonus of almost $10 million dollars. Fox borrowed most of the money for the purchase from Wall Street investment bankers and bond traders.

The acquisition of the Loews Corp. would have been the deal of the century but for two events. The first occurred in July 1929 when Fox was badly injured in a traffic accident. He was out of commission for months while recuperating. His business began to spin out of control, as did the entire American economy. On October 24 Fox attended a banquet at which the featured speaker was Secretary of Commerce Robert P. Lamont. Lamont warned of impending disaster in the financial markets. The next day Fox ordered his brokers to sell all of his stock in companies other than his own. Three days later Black Tuesday hit the stock market. Fox was in the process of selling $20 million worth of stock. The following day the stock was worth only $6 million. As the market crash deepened, Fox's stock, which had traded at $119 per share, was down to $1 dollar a share. William Fox was wiped out. Although he maintained a sizable personal fortune, it was drained by lawsuits and the Internal Revenue Service. Eventually Fox was found guilty of obstruction of justice for trying to bribe a judge at his bankruptcy hearing. In 1941 he was sentenced to a year in prison. He served six months. Emerging from prison, he was truly penniless and friendless.

SAMUEL GOLDWYN

Goldwyn was born Schmuel Gelbfisz in the Jewish ghetto of Warsaw, Poland around 1879. His father, Aaron, supported his family of six children by operating a second-hand furniture store. Goldwyn was sixteen when his father died, and the burden of supporting the family shifted to him, the eldest son. He had no intention of staying in Poland, however. He left home later that year and walked the 500 hundred miles to Hamburg, Germany, where he worked in a glove factory to save the price of passage to join relatives in England. He walked the 120 miles from London to Birmingham, where an uncle helped him to become a blacksmith's apprentice and work selling sponges. His dream was to follow in the footsteps of so many other Europeans of the time and immigrate to America. With stolen sponge money he sailed for New York in 1898, where an immigration officer with a bad ear for Polish rewrote his name, changing it to "Samuel Goldfish." Eventually he settled in the upstate town of Gloversville, N.Y. where the locally economy depended entirely on glove manufacturing.

Goldfish quickly got a job in a glove factory and enrolled in night school to improve himself. He wanted to become a salesman but needed to read and write English better to do so. Meanwhile he became a factory foreman and in 1904 was granted citizenship. That same year he convinced the owner of the Elite Glove Co. to make him a traveling glove salesman. Goldfish was a natural at sales and became quite prosperous. During this time he began to pursue Bessie Ginzberg, the beautiful aristocratic daughter of a Boston diamond merchant. She rebuffed his advances and eventually became involved with and married vaudeville producer and performer Jesse Lasky. As consolation she introduced Goldfish to Lasky's sister, and their relationship blossomed into marriage. Goldfish and Lasky became brothers-in-law in 1910.

Goldfish was becoming bored with the glove business. He persistently tried to convince Lasky that their future was in movies, but Lasky wasn't interested. In 1912 Congress eliminated the tariff on gloves. As a result the American glove industry crashed and Goldfish retired on the small fortune he had accumulated. He resumed trying to convince Lasky to enter the motion picture industry. Lasky's best friend and partner was Cecil B. DeMille. DeMille was tiring of vaudeville and the need to constantly travel. He was interested in movies, and Lasky began to come around. The three men partnered to form the Jesse H. Lasky Motion Picture Company. Goldfish was convinced that the future of movies was in feature-length pictures. Lasky's first project would be a feature-length western *The Squaw Man*. Each of the three principals owned a quarter share of the new company, with the remainder going to Dustin Farnum as payment for his services as the film's star. DeMille and company set out for Flagstaff, Arizona to make their picture. However, Flagstaff proved unsuitable, and DeMille continued his journey to Los Angeles, where he rented a barn at Selma and Vine Streets in Hollywood to serve as headquarters. Farnum insisted on being paid $5,000 cash instead of taking a share. Goldfish scraped together the money. Ten years later Farnum's share would have been worth $2 million dollars.

The Company's next feature was *Brewster's Millions*, another success. Goldfish was responsible for selling and distribution, DeMille wrote and directed, and Lasky ran the corporation. Soon Adolph Zukor proposed merging his Players Company with Lasky. Goldfish was odd-man out. His share was purchased for $900,000. The following year he teamed up with Edgar Selwyn, a theatrical producer. They merged their names to call the new company Goldwyn. To prevent a repeat of his ouster from Lasky and to give the impression that it was solely his company, Goldfish changed his name to Goldwyn. The company quickly signed a number of top actors and writers to its talent roster, among them Griffith veteran Mae Marsh. The focus of Goldwyn's output was refined motion pictures for more sophisticated audiences, as promised in an expensive series of advertisements that appeared in the Saturday Evening Post magazine. A series of hit films resulted, and the company grew rapidly–until a playboy swindler, Frank Joseph Godsol, convinced the directors to oust Goldwyn and replace him with Godsol himself. Goldwyn left. By 1924 the company was bankrupt and forced to merge with Metro. Even though the movie studio, Metro Goldwyn Mayer, bears his name, ironically Goldwyn had no other connection to it.

Goldwyn never again had a partner. In 1924 he formed Samuel Goldwyn Pictures Inc. and proceeded to go it alone. This strategy made it possible for him to concentrate on all aspects of the movie-making business. The first production was the 1925 film *The Dark Angel,* starring an actress Goldwyn discovered on a talent hunt in Europe, Vilma Banky. Many successful productions followed. His first sound production was the 1930 musical *Whoopee*, the making of which caused him to assemble and maintain a chorus line of dancers and bathing beauties who were known as "The Goldwyn Girls." The troupes boasted such luminaries as Betty Grable, Jane Wyman, and Lucille Ball. The company became synonymous with quality motion pictures adapted from stage plays including masterpieces such John Ford's *Arrowsmith*; *The Children's Hour*, which dealt with the controversial subject of lesbianism; and *Dead End*, which introduced movie audiences to Humphrey Bogart. Goldwyn also discovered Broadway choreographer Busby Berkeley, who worked on *The Kid from Spain*, and who became an innovator in designing movie dance scenes.

RKO/PHOTOFEST

SAMUEL GOLDWYN (1949)

Goldwyn is remembered for many reasons. He was a creative producer, an exceptional salesman, and a visionary. Another reason he is remembered is his tortured relationship with the English language. His malapropisms and verbal manglings became legendary, to the extent that he might have invented a few to sustain his legend.

"In this business it's dog eat dog, and nobody's going to eat me."

"Our comedies are not to be laughed at."

"I can answer you in two words: im possible."

"I read part of it all the way through."

"You can include me out."

"I write my autobiography? Oh, no. I can't do that until long after I'm dead."

"His verbal contract is worth more than the paper it's written on."

MARY PICKFORD AND DOUGLAS FAIRBANKS

Mary Pickford is the first woman to become a major figure in motion picture history. She managed her image, her career, and her business affairs as astutely as any of the captains of the industry managed their empires. Like Chaplin, she was one of the first actors to achieve star status. When she married Douglas Fairbanks, the two assumed a position of movie royalty. Their lives were charmed, and they were admitted to the lofty ranks of the American upper class. Like so many other film pioneers, Pickford's story is of the rags-to-riches variety. Unlike so many others, she wore her wealth and her celebrity with grace and dignity.

Pickford was one of the many early film figures to hail from Canada. She was born Gladys Smith in Toronto in 1892. Her father was a heavy drinker and his death when Pickford was six left the family destitute. In true stagemother fashion, Mrs. Smith put her two daughters and her son to work at the local Princes Theater. The three young actors were paid as a family at the rate of $8 dollars per week. Young Gladys loved performing and was soon featured in the theater's advertisements. By the time she was nine, Pickford was touring in a play entitled _The Little Red Schoolhouse_. By age fifteen she was allowed to travel to New York to seek her fortune on her own. This strong self-reliance is a quality she would display throughout her life.

David Belasco, the king of New York theater, was suitably impressed when the independent young woman displayed commitment and persistence by calling on him repeatedly in an attempt to get work in his company. He gave her the stage name Mary Pickford and cast her in the long-running play _The Warrens of Virginia_. Her run with Belasco went well, but when the Broadway theaters closed for the summer season (as was the custom due to lack of air conditioning and ventilation), Pickford decided to pursue work in movies.

In April 1909 Pickford visited the Biograph headquarters and encountered D. W. Griffith. He offered her a job at the going rate of $5 dollars per day. She demurred, insisting to Griffith that she was a Belasco actress and worth at least $10 dollars a day with a $25-dollar-per-week guarantee. Griffith met her demand. The director applied her film makeup himself and put her to work in an aptly titled film _Her First Biscuits,_ Pickford had no trouble adjusting to film production's slightly chaotic process. She moved from drama to comedy effortlessly, making forty-two films (one reel in length, eight to twelve minutes) in the remainder of 1909 and thirty-two the following year, mostly in leading roles. She did, however, begin to clash with Griffith's outsized ego and his overly paternalistic attitude toward young female actresses. In retrospect, she was probably too ambitious for Biograph and its star director. She could see film's potential to bring her much greater rewards than the stage and was anxious for her career to progress faster than it would under Griffith. Another reason she desired to move on was that she had fallen in love with another Biograph actor, Owen Moore. They were quickly married but had to keep it a secret for fear of upsetting Griffith.

In 1911 Pickford accepted Carl Laemmle's offer of $175 to work for his Independent Motion Picture Company (IMP). During this time she was developing her signature screen persona of a spunky girl who can stand up to the bullies. By 1912 Pickford had become a star with her name above the title. In spite of the pay and the notoriety, she was frustrated creatively at IMP and broke her contract after thirty-four films. She returned to Biograph for a short time until Belasco offered her a prestigious role and salary to work onstage. After the stage run, the play was adapted for film by Adolph Zukor's company with Edwin S. Porter directing. Once again Pickford was lured back to the movies with an offer of more money. By 1916 Zukor was paying her $2,000 per week with a $10,000 dollar finishing

Jack Pickford

Being the younger brother of "America's Sweetheart" not surprisingly opened a lot of doors for Jack Pickford. However, living in her shadow proved to be too challenging. Like his sisters, Young Jack was pushed onto the stage before he was of school age. Four years younger than Mary, he followed her path into the movie business. He appeared in a crowd scene in his first film in 1909. He made four more films that year and twenty-three the next year, and he stayed equally busy through 1919. When Mary Pickford signed her lucrative contract with First National in 1918, Jack got his own contract with the company as part of the deal. He played the starring role in Mark Twain's *Tom Sawyer* and starred in the adaptation of Dicken's *Great Expectations*. By any measure he had the potential for a successful career, but his life took a different turn.

Pickford's first marriage was to model and actress Olive Thomas, in 1916. By this time he was already a heavy drinker and suffered from syphilis as a result of his womanizing. There were also rumors of his addiction to heroin. Thomas was a confirmed addict and soon contracted her husband's venereal disease. In 1920 Thomas died in Paris as a result of an overdose of the medicine the two took for syphilis. Jack Pickford never really recovered. Although he was married twice more, Thomas had been the love of his life. Between 1920 and the end of his career Pickford made only 14 films. The 1928 film *Gang War* was his last. From that point on, he lived by borrowing money from his mother and sister. He died of the cumulative effect of his bad habits in the American Hospital in Paris in 1932.

bonus for every picture she made. At only twenty-four years old, she had been in the entertainment business for almost two decades and seen her films distributed throughout Europe and Latin America.

In June 1916 Pickford became the first actress to have her own motion picture company, the Pickford Film Corporation, a division of the new Paramount Company. She was now in control of her own artistic and commercial destiny. One of her first hires was writer Frances Marion, who, while working at Pickford, became one of the first female directors. In one of their early collaborations, *The Poor Little Rich Girl,* Pickford played a twelve-year-old girl. Audiences loved the film, and soon the idea of the young star playing younger girls (often in dual roles, playing both adult and child) was repeated many times over the remainder of her career. Around this time she also hired Marshall "Mickey" Neilan to co-star and direct. Her creative team became complete when Charles Rosher, one of the great cinematographers in movie history, was added to the company payroll. Pickford was becoming a hit-making machine and had gained the sobriquet of "America's Sweetheart."

Sometime in late 1918 as Mary Pickford's marriage was foundering, she became involved with Chaplin's close friend, Douglas Fairbanks. He was also a successful star. Nine years older than Pickford, he was the son of a well-to-do New York lawyer. Another born performer, Fairbanks had been onstage since the age of fifteen. He reached star status in the 1906 play *Man of the Hour*. Fairbanks was affable and athletic, a natural comedy and action actor specializing in manly stunts and self-deprecating humor. He exuded confidence. He was married for the first time in 1907 and had had a son, Douglas Fairbanks, Jr., by the time he met Pickford. Both stars were very conscious of the need to keep their new relationship from the public for fear of a career-damaging scandal until divorces could be obtained. However, they did make one major public appearance in the company of Chaplin at a New York event to sell bonds for World War I. Over fifty thousand fans showed up for the occasion, so great was the drawing power of the three motion picture giants. In January 1919, Pickford and Fairbanks were joined by Chaplin and Griffith to found United Artists, a distribution company controlled by them rather than the studios.

In March 1920 Pickford and Fairbanks became husband and wife. After their marriage the style of his films began to change as he turned away from comedies and toward romantic adventure films, becoming the first great *Robin Hood*. Other adventure films included *The Mark of Zorro, The Three Musketeers,* and *The Thief of Bagdad*. These films not only featured well-choreographed action and spectacular stunts, they were also spectacles with jaw-dropping, full-scale sets, elaborate costumes, enormous casts of extras, and special effects. Pickford's films were changing, too. They became more complex and of a higher quality. As the motion picture industry moved out of the nickelodeons and into the picture palaces, audiences became more sophisticated and demanded a better product from their favorite stars. In 1918 Pickford made only five films; the next year she made four; and in 1920 just two films. But the quality of her films was undeniable and her fans responded enthusiastically. In 1923 she imported famed German director Ernst Lubitsch to helm the film *Rosita*, one of Pickford's early attempts at transitioning into more adult roles.

MARY PICKFORD AND DOUGLAS FAIRBANKS

PHOTOFEST

Pickfair

In 1919 Fairbanks purchased a massive, 48-room, Wallace Neff–designed hunting lodge atop one of the Beverly Hills. He gave if to Pickford as a wedding gift. They spent the year before their nuptials remodeling it extensively. They named their home Pickfair. It soon became the Hollywood gathering place for the elite of the motion picture industry and other figures from the arts and society. Regular dinner party guests included Albert Einstein, George Bernard Shaw, Amelia Earhart, F. Scott Fitzgerald, and Lord Mountbatten. In 1932 Pickford purchased a bar from the historic Union Saloon in Auburn, Arizona. She had the bar dismantled and reassembled at Pickfair as a Christmas present so Fairbanks had a place to display his extensive collection of Old West paintings by Frederick Remington and Charles M. Russell. The gift was also an attempt on Pickford's part to repair a rift that had begun to develop in their marriage. Ironically, Fairbanks wasn't a drinker, having promised his mother he would avoid the family disease, alcoholism, by refraining from drinking until he turned forty.

In 1928 the charmed lives of Mary Pickford and Douglas Fairbanks began to unravel. He began to suffer from periods of dark depression and was involved in a series of affairs with other women. She began to drink heavily, hiding her whiskey in cologne bottles to avoid detection. While Pickford remained in Hollywood to tend to business, Fairbanks chose to go on long trips to Europe. When his affair with Lady Silvia Ashley became public in 1933, Pickford and Fairbanks separated and three years later, divorced. Although Pickford made a few successful talking pictures in the late twenties and early thirties, for the most part both actors' film careers had reached an end. In December 1939 Fairbanks died of a heart attack. He was fifty-six. Pickford married a handsome young actor, Charles "Buddy" Rogers. He doted on Pickford and guarded her fading stardom and reputation until her death in 1979.

THE STUDIOS
Majors and Minors

THOMAS INCE AND THE INDUSTRIAL MODEL OF MOTION PICTURE PRODUCTION

Early motion picture production could be a costly and chaotic affair. Much of what was filmed had been based on a mere premise and a few sketchy ideas for scenes that would tell the story. Cameramen dominated the process, relegating directors to the role of devising the actor's gestures and movements. One of Griffith's great contributions to the new medium was to assume the role of storyteller. But even Griffith often worked from hastily scribbled notes on scraps of paper. As a result he often discarded expensive scenes that could not be incorporated into the final cut. It was inevitable that someone would arrive at a better method of organizing production.

Thomas Ince was born into a family of stage performers in 1882. His parents first pushed him onto the stage when he was six. At age fifteen Ince made his debut on Broadway. He met and married Elinor Kershaw while performing in a play with her in 1907. Elinor Ince was already an established leading actress at Biograph. Trading on her connections, Ince began to appear in Biograph films as well and had become a full-time movie actor by 1910. That year he decided to quit acting to become a director. He was hired by Carl Laemmle to direct Mary Pickford films in Cuba, far from the reach of the Edison Patent Trust. The next year Ince left Laemmle to work for New York Motion Pictures (NYMP), owners of the Bison Life Motion Picture studio in Los Angeles. Ince was sent to California to write and direct westerns.

In 1912 NYMP purchased 18,000 acres of land at the intersection of Sunset Boulevard and Pacific Coast Highway. Ince was assigned the task of constructing a facility for the mass production of westerns. Los Angeles was the perfect setting for filming westerns. Many authentic cowboys had gravitated toward the emerging movie production center as the unsettled parts of the west disappeared in the early 1900s. Legendary lawman Wyatt Earp had settled on a small ranch in what is now the south central district of the city. The saloons and boarding houses of Los Angeles were full of men who could ride a horse, shoot a gun, and wield a lasso. The surrounding countryside was unpopulated and presented a variety of terrain. It was perfect for recreating the Old West. On his vast plot of land, Ince built an office building, a film lab, a commissary, dressing rooms, horse barns, and a number of standing sets that could be used interchangeably. It was the first industrial-style studio, but NYMP had not invested in a permanent facility. Inceville, as it was called, had a temporary quality to it, with many of the structures nothing more than tents atop wooden foundations. (The title of first *permanent* studio would be reserved for Universal City two years later.)

Ince reorganized his production staff. He became history's first producer-director with responsibility to oversee the production of a film from start to finish. He hired several other producer-directors to complete the ambitious slate of productions laid out by the head office in New York. He hired an accountant and gave him the title of production manager to keep everyone within budget. Ince also began to emphasize the importance of a well-developed scenario or script that defined all of the scenes needed to complete a film. He would then break down the scenes, planning ahead which sets and locations to use as well as the need-ed actors (both type and number), the costumes and props, and the number of horses. With other pro-ducer-directors working in the same manner, it became possible for Ince to organize several pro-ductions to take place with maxi-mum efficiency. Ince also began to departmentalize the studio. Ward-robe, camera, script, editing, and set design and construction be-came resources to be shared by all of the productions occurring at the studio. Under this system it was possible to turn out many one- and two-reel films each week. To a greater or lesser extent, this be-came the model for all studios that followed.

CHARLES CHAPLIN CIRCA **1915**, SHOWN FROM LEFT, FOREGROUND: THOMAS INCE, CHARLES CHAPLIN, MACK SENNETT, D.W. GRIFFITH (THE FOUNDERS OF TRIANGLE PICTURES)

Once work was completed on the production facility, Ince was free to devote himself to production again. He continued to make westerns but began also to make films in other genres. His 1913 film *Battle of Gettysburg,* was five reels long, making it one of the first feature films made in America. During 1914 and 1915 he continued the frantic pace of pro-duction at Inceville. NYMP was growing rap-idly during this time, branching into three separate production companies with a shared distribution company, Mutual Films. Ince was courted by other companies that were eager for him to apply his organizing techniques to their productions. In 1915 he left NYMP to become a cofounder of the Triangle Film Cor-poration along with Sennett and Griffith. The enterprise was focused on creating prestige films. Ince worked occasionally as a director at Triangle, but his main function was as an executive. The production operation of the company collapsed in 1918 as a result of fi-nancial mismanagement by financier Harry Aitken. However, Triangle continued as a dis-

WILLIAM RANDOLPH HEARST, HEDDA HOPPER

tribution company. The studio lot would eventually become Metro Goldwyn Mayer (MGM).

After his stint at Triangle, Ince attempted to start his own company. He had limited success until he merged it with First National in 1922. Over the next two years he made only a few pictures including his last as a director, *Anna Christie*, in 1923. In November, 1924 Ince was invited to celebrate his forty-second birthday on a weekend cruise aboard newspaper and motion picture magnate William Randolph Hearst's 280-ft. yacht, Oneida. Other passengers included Hearst's movie star mistress Marion Davies, Charlie Chaplin, and a young newspaper columnist, Louella Parsons. What happened that weekend is shrouded in mystery. Hearst was alleged to have invited Chaplin, the notorious womanizer, to observe his behavior with Davies, whom he suspected of having an affair with Chaplin. In one version of the story, Hearst found the two in bed together and went for his gun to kill Chaplin. Somehow Ince got in the way and was shot in the stomach. When the Oneida landed in San Diego, Hearst arranged for the body to be transported to Ince's home in Los Angeles. The next morning two accounts of his death appeared in Southern California newspapers. One claimed that Ince had been shot, and the other that he had died of acute indigestion. By afternoon the shooting story had disappeared altogether. Louella Parsons had written the indigestion story, after which she became Hearst's primary Hollywood gossip writer for the rest of her life. Many historians believe it was her payoff for covering up the crime.

SHOWN FROM LEFT: JESSE L. LASKY, ADOLPH ZUKOR, SAMUEL GOLDWYN, CECIL B. DEMILLE, ALBERT KAUFMAN NB: SHORTLY AFTER PARTNERING TO CREATE PARAMOUNT PICTURES, SEPTEMBER 1916

PARAMOUNT AND THE ADVENT OF THE MAJOR MOTION PICTURE STUDIOS

By 1916 Paramount had become the first distribution company to serve the entire country. Its size gave it tremendous leverage in negotiating with independent theater owners. Adolph Zukor was convinced and soon persuaded his partners that the future of motion pictures was in controlling all three aspects of the industry: production, distribution, and theater ownership. This became the definition of a major studio or motion picture company. Four other corporations would share the designation: Fox, MGM, Warner Brothers, and RKO. By the early 1920s, Paramount would rival Loews with over two thousand theaters in operation.

The major studios were designed to provide as much product as possible for their theater chains and the customers of their distribution divisions. Actors were signed to personal services contracts that bound them to the studio in almost every aspect of their lives. In turn the studios invested in developing their talent. Actors were routinely given makeovers. They were taught how to dress, walk, talk, and groom themselves. The studios even manufactured actors' identities and personal histories. Actors who refused roles to which they had been assigned were often punished by being loaned out to a less desirable studio at a profit or by having time added to the duration of their contract. Morals clauses in the contracts gave the studios control over actors' private lives as well. To a greater or lesser extent this same system was also applied to directors and writers. The contract system served to control the costs of production and to justify the studios' investments in their high-priced personnel.

In 1924 the first double-feature programs began to appear in movie theaters. Given that most big-city theaters changed their programs weekly, the major studios would need to gear up for an annual production schedule of seventy-five or more feature films. The minor studios would supply the remainder of features for studio-owned theaters and independents. Newsreels, weekly or monthly short films depicting the important events of the day, began to appear as early as 1911. By the 1920s theaters were regularly incorporating them into their programs. Fox led the major studios with its Movietone sound newsreels in 1927. By 1929 MGM and Paramount had launched their own units as well. In time the major studios would also launch production units for making animated short films and documentaries.

MGM: MARCUS LOEW, LOUIS B. MAYER, AND IRVING THALBERG

MARCUS LOEW

Loew was born in New York in 1870. His parents were poor and able to afford only a third grade education for their son. Afterward Loew worked as a paper boy and a printer, and he clerked in men's clothing stores until he was presented with an opportunity to be trained in the lucrative fur business. In 1899 he partnered with actor friend David Warfield and entered into the real estate business. In 1903 Loew met another furrier, Adolph Zukor, who began to invest in the new penny arcade industry. Zukor's Automatic Vaudeville Company was a success, and he invited Loew and Warfield to become partners as the business expanded into Boston, Philadelphia, and Newark. In 1905 Loew and Warfield formed their own arcade enterprise under the banner of People's Vaudeville Company. By this time Edison's coin-operated kinetoscope movie viewing machines had become a popular addition to the arcade industry.

As Loew's business expanded into Cincinnati, Ohio, he became interested in converting one of his arcades into a nickelodeon storefront theater. As the theater business expanded he hired Nicholas Schenck to work as treasurer and manager. By 1919 Loew had almost completely withdrawn from the arcade business to invest in theaters, changing the name of his company to Loew's Incorporated. He also purchased a small, struggling production company, Metro Pictures, which produced the hit film *The Four Horsemen of the Apocalypse* in 1921. Two years later Loew built his first picture palace in Times Square, New York. As was common at the time, it was a combination live vaudeville and motion picture theater. It seated 3,000 patrons. He named it the Loew's State and built a 16-story office tower next door to house his corporate offices.

By 1924 Loew owned over one hundred theaters, and three years later, an additional forty-four were operating in the Northeast, Midwest, and Canada. His theaters had a reputation for being large, well run, and opulent. It was a winning formula. The only drawback was that Metro Pictures could not satisfy the company's demand for quality motion pictures. That year Loew acquired Goldwyn Pictures and its small chain of theaters. With a need for someone to run the new West Coast production enterprise, Loew also acquired Louis B. Mayer Productions, including Mayer himself and his creative executive, Irving Thalberg. The newly merged company was called Metro-Goldwyn-Mayer (MGM) despite the fact that Samuel Goldwyn was not involved. The Goldwyn company also possessed the former Triangle Studios facility in Culver City a few miles southwest of Hollywood. Over the next few years the studio would expand to become one of the world's best production studios. Unfortunately Loew did not live to see the greatness of his creation. He died in 1927 and was succeeded by Nicholas Schenk.

LOUIS B. MAYER

Mayer's family hailed from Minsk, Russia, where he was born in 1885. The following year his family fled to eastern Canada to escape the persecution commonly suffered by Russian Jews. Mayer's father became a scrap metal and junk dealer, and his mother sold live chickens door to door to help make ends meet. Mayer helped in his father's business until he departed for Boston in 1904 to seek his own fortune in the scrap business. He was successful enough to get married, and the following year, his first daughter was born. Mayer was restless in the salvage business. When the opportunity presented itself in 1907 he acquired his first combination vaudeville and movie theater in Haverhill, Massachusetts. It prospered and over the next five years Mayer opened a theater in Boston and another in Philadelphia.

In 1915 Mayer purchased the New England distribution rights for D. W. Griffith's *Birth of a Nation*. The blockbuster success of the film provided him with the investment capital to start a production company, Metro Pictures, in partnership with a Philadelphia supplier of theater equipment. Mayer left Metro three years later, having been accused of a conflict of interest. He next moved to California and rented the Selig Studio in the East Los Angeles village, Monterey Park. The studio was notorious for its menagerie of wild animals, which had been collected over the years to perform in their pictures. Mayer inherited the zoo and enticed Vitagraph Studios' star, Anita Stewart, to produce and perform in a slate of films. Stewart's work wasn't memorable, but it was successful enough to sustain Mayer Studios while its founder busily acquired other potential stars and directors for his production company.

Mayer understood his own limitations in terms of conceiving and creating motion pictures. He decided to seek a partner who could attend to creative matters while he focused on business. Twenty-three year old Irving Thalberg was a perfect fit for the job.

IRVING THALBERG

Thalberg represents the second wave of motion picture pioneers. He was born in America—Brooklyn, New York, to be specific. Although his family came from an Old World Jewish background, he was an assimilated product of the new world. Born in 1899, Thalberg was a sickly child with a heart ailment so severe no one expected him to reach adulthood. He adored playing baseball, despite both the protestations of his protective mother and the fact that he would have to spend days recuperating in bed after a hard-fought game. Following elementary school, Thalberg was encouraged to attend high school, rare for the children of immigrants at the time. He became a voracious reader of plays and novels and the writing of pragmatist philosopher William James, who inspired the young man to strive for both physical and intellectual self improvement.

After high school Thalberg worked in a relative's department store to earn enough money to take night classes at New York University and Spanish and typing classes at a business school. He spent part of the summer of 1918 at his grandmother's beach home on Long Island. Here he met a neighbor, Carl Laemmle, who was soon persuaded by Thalberg's mother to give her son a job. He entered the motion picture industry as Laemmle's assistant's assistant for thirty-five dollars per week.

Thalberg was passionate about his work at Universal headquarters on Broadway in the heart of Manhattan. He put in long hours and took the initiative whenever possible. He attended screening sessions with Laemmle, took detailed notes on each film's flaws, and offered suggestions for improvement. He showed a talent for deftly navigating the volatile personalities of actors and directors twice his age. Soon he became Laemmle's personal secretary and was invited to accompany his boss to the coast to check on affairs at the studio. From that time on he would return to New York only as a visitor.

When Laemmle and Thalberg arrived in California they found Universal City in complete disarray. Laemmle's insistence on running the studio from the East meant that no one was in charge. It took four months to achieve some semblance of order, longer than Laemmle cared to stay away from his New York home. Laemmle decamped and ordered Thalberg to stay behind and do the best he could. Just twenty years old, he found a small vacant office and proceeded to observe every facet of production from shooting stages to the accounting department. When Laemmle returned four months later, the young man recommended that he be appointed studio manager. Laemmle granted this request. In true Laemmle fashion, the result of this promotion was that three different people believed themselves to be in charge of the studio: Isadore Bernstein, Samuel Van Runkel, and Thalberg. Six months later only Thalberg remained at Universal, over which he had complete command—ironic given that he was too young to sign the payroll checks.

Thalberg's biggest challenge was the temperamental and extravagant Erich von Stroheim, a Vienna-born actor-director who specialized in portraying Prussian officers in WWI-era films. Von Stroheim had sold Laemmle on his script for a film about a love triangle, *Blind Husbands*. With its sophisticated sexual overtones, the film was a success with audiences and critics alike. The director was highly praised for his attention to detail. Unfortunately such attention to detail inevitably leads to budgetary excess. *The Devil's Passkey* followed and was equally successful. Fed by success, von Stroheim began to lose touch with reality as production began on his next film, *Foolish Wives*. He insisted on having a full-scale replica of Monte Carlo built, including the casino and hotel. Another equally large set was built 350 miles north of Los Angeles in Monterey, California. After a full year in production the film cost $1 million dollars, and it wasn't even complete. Over the director's objections, Thalberg ordered production on the film to cease. When it was released *Foolish Wives* continued von Stroheim's string of successes, but its profit margins were alarmingly slim. Also, some moralizing critics found the material too racy. Still, Thalberg chanced to attempt another project entitled *Merry Go Round*, but when von Stroheim refused to pick up the pace of production, he was fired for good, establishing young Thalberg as a force to be reckoned with.

Among Thalberg's greatest creative accomplishments at Universal was developing a uniquely gifted actor, Lon Chaney. Chaney was the son of deaf-mute parents and had learned to communicate in pantomime. He was an expert makeup artist and had the ability to contort his body into unbelievable positions. Chaney was perfect for playing grotesque roles. Thalberg bet a small fortune that Chaney would be perfect to play the title role in *The Hunchback of Notre Dame*. The film was a huge hit economically and critically. For Thalberg, it was somewhat of a disappointment as he had been campaigning for a salary commensurate with his contributions to the studio. Laemmle had resisted, and after the unquestioned prestige *Hunchback* brought to the studio, Thalberg took personally Laemmle's refusal to acknowledge his work. He resolved to leave Universal as soon as the opportunity presented itself.

PHOTOFEST

SHOWN FROM LEFT: IRVING THALBERG AND LOUIS B. MAYER

Louis B. Mayer presented just that opportunity for Thalberg. Mayer believed that he needed more time to develop his business and attract more and better talent to his studio. He needed someone who could attend to the day-to-day production issues. The negotiations were swift culminating with the twenty-three-year-old Thalberg agreeing on a starting salary of $600 per week to become the Mayer Company's vice president and production assistant. One of Thalberg's first hires was a young New York actress named Norma Shearer. She would eventually become his wife.

MGM

In 1924 the motion picture business was undergoing a period of mergers and consolidation. Marcus Loew had already acquired Metro Pictures to feed movie product to his theaters, but it wasn't enough. He entered into discussions with Joseph Godsol to take over Goldwyn, as well. He also began discussions with Mayer, whom he believed was the best qualified to manage the new enterprise. On April 17, 1924 Metro Goldwyn Mayer was founded. Although Samuel Goldwyn still owned stock in his old company, he was not a party to the negotiations, and his shares were quickly purchased by Loew. Mayer was appointed vice president and general manager of the studio with a $1,500 per week salary. Thalberg was made second vice president and supervisor of production at $650 per week. In New York Nicholas Schenck would serve as president of the corporation, with budget authority over all production and distribution activities. Together they would rule over the renowned MGM label for more than a decade, a period in which the company would come to stand for quality and greatness in the motion picture industry.

FOX AND TWENTIETH CENTURY

Earlier we described the rise and fall of William Fox and his studio in detail. During the 1920s the Fox Company was known for its glamorous theaters and as a studio that gave its young directors such as John Ford and Howard Hawks the chance to learn expressionist film style from the great German director F. W. Murnau. Vamp Theda Bara and Tom Mix, the frontier-lawman-turned–movie actor, provided all the star power the studio needed to grow its fortunes.

The Fox studio was also a leader in the development of sound technology. It was home to Lee DeForrest, the man who had invented the Audion vacuum tube. It was the essential device in the development of broadcast radio. But DeForrest had lost his patent in a protracted court battle with David Sarnoff, the man who led Radio Corporation of America. Afterward DeForrest turned his energies toward the development of optical motion picture sound.

When the 1929 stock market crash loosened William Fox's grasp on his movie empire, the company descended into a free fall. In 1932 the Fox's company was rescued by a group of investors led by Spyros Skouras, who, with his brothers, had built a successful theater empire in the St. Louis area that eventually sold to Warner Brothers in 1929. The new team first took over management of over 500 Fox theaters in the West Coast. Shortly they assumed control of the studio as well. But the Skouras group was inexperienced at moviemaking. They needed a partner to restore the studio's fortunes. Twentieth Century was perfect for the role.

DARRYL ZANUCK

Darryl Zanuck was atypical for Hollywood in two respects. He did not come to America on a wave of Jewish immigration from Europe. Instead, he was born into a middle-class Christian family in Wahoo, Nebraska in 1902. The son of a hotel owner, Zanuck quit the Page Military Academy at age fifteen and lied about his age to enlist in the Nebraska National Guard. His military duties included chasing Pancho Villa around Mexico and shipping over to France during World War I. After satisfying his military commitment in 1917, Zanuck joined his mother, who had divorced and moved to the Los Angeles area.

The second thing that set Zanuck apart from his fellow movie moguls is that he didn't enter the industry through entrepreneurial channels. After the war he tried his hand at a number of odd jobs, including prizefighting, working in a ship yard and a stint as a press agent. His talent for writing led to his career in Hollywood. He began submitting short stories to magazines, with limited success. He had better luck submitting stories to the Fox Film Corporation. In 1924 he finally got a job on the writing staff at Warner Brothers, where he was especially successful writing stories for the studio's most dependable star, the German Shepherd, Rin Tin Tin. In short time he was Warner's most prolific and dynamic writer and was assigned significant responsibilities in the publicity department as well. When Harry Rapf left Warner Brothers in 1928 to produce at MGM, Zanuck was made lead producer. In this role, he was responsible for the studio's most important films and stars.

Zanuck became instrumental in Warner Brothers' transition into the sound
motion-picture era. He was largely responsible for the highly successful series of gangster films the studio made in
the early thirties. The relationship came
to an end over a disagreement about
money. In the early days of the great
depression, Warner executives agreed
to take voluntary reductions in their pay
despite the fact that Harry Warner was
profiting handsomely on legal insider
trading of stock shares. In 1933 the
company had returned to profitability,
and Zanuck demanded restoration of
his pay. When the studio reneged, Zanuck quit in anger.

LITTLE MISS MARKER (1934), DIRECTED BY ALEXANDER HALL,
SHOWN FROM LEFT: ADOLPHE MENJOU, SHIRLEY TEMPLE

PARAMOUNT PICTURES/PHOTOFEST

Other job offers poured in, but Zanuck
had a grander ambition. He teamed up
with Joseph Schenck, who had made a fortune in the early days of the industry. Schenck was well liked and well connected; his brother, Nicholas, had taken control of Loews/MGM after Marcus Loew's death. Zanuk and Schenck announced the launch of their new studio, Twentieth Century Pictures. With Zanuck's talent for making well-paced, tightly scripted films and Schenk's resources, the venture was bound to succeed. When the Skouras broth-ers invited Twentieth Century to merge in 1934, Spyros became the company's president, with Schenk serving as Chairman of the Board and Zanuck as production chief of the new Twentieth Century Fox Corporation.

Twentieth Century had acquired an impressive roster or acting talent in its brief period as a stand-alone studio. The new company continued to sign even more talent. However, the old Fox studio had already signed one of the greatest stars of the thirties, a little girl who could sing and dance—Shirley Temple. Zanuck created the quintessential Shirley Temple formula: surrounding the ultracute little talent with gruff character actors like Adolphe Menjou and Wallace Beery. In film after film she charmed the most imposing costars into submission and the audience loved it.

WARNER BROTHERS

Benjamin and Pearl Warner escaped Poland in 1882 and eventually settled in the area of Youngstown, Ohio. They had twelve children, several of whom died of childhood diseases. Benjamin was a businessman, first working as a shoemaker and later owning a bicycle shop. In 1903 the family started a nickelodeon business and the next year became involved in film distribution, founding the Duquesne Amusement & Supply Company, serving the western Pennsylvania and Ohio region. The four Warner brothers, Harry (born 1881), Al-

bert (1883), Sam (1887), and Jack (1892), were close knit and hard working. They were determined to make their mark in the motion picture industry.

Between 1904 and 1917 the brothers steadily developed their business. They built theaters, expanded their distribution network, and began to venture into the production business. In 1917 the Warners invested in their first significant feature, *My Four Years in Germany*, based on an American Ambassador's tales of his encounters with Kaiser Wihelm. The project was a success and the brothers

THE WARNER BROTHERS (CA. 1920'S), SHOWN FROM LEFT: HARRY M. WARNER, JACK L. WARNER, SAM WARNER, ALBERT WARNER

decided to fully enter the production business by building a studio on Sunset Boulevard in Hollywood. Their first big star was a German shepherd named Rin Tin Tin, who had been brought back from France following World War I. Rin Tin Tin starred in twenty six very successful features, providing a solid foundation for the new studio. The great but unpredictable stage actor John Barrymore was another early Warners star. He specialized in playing the lead in prestigious plays such as *Hamlet* and *The Sea Beast*. The accomplished German director Ernst Lubitsch was brought in to make *The Marriage Circle* and *Lady Windermere's Fan*, adding to the studio's reputation for sophistication.

WARNERS ACQUIRES VITAGRAPH

By 1925 Warners was growing so rapidly that the studio had run out of space at the Sunset Boulevard location. The brothers also knew that they needed to build and acquire more theaters to keep up with the competition. They started to look for avenues for expansion.

The Vitagraph company was founded by film pioneers Albert Smith, J. Stuart Blackton, and Ronald Reader around 1897. The company became well known for its film actualities of historic figures such as Theodore Roosevelt and the Wright Brothers' first flight at Kitty Hawk. The first studio was built in Brooklyn, N.Y. and grew to become one of the most prolific members of the Edison Trust. In 1910 most production activities moved to Los Angeles. In the mid-teens Vitagraph began to purchase and build theaters, financing them with the profits from foreign sales of their films. World War I posed a crisis for the company when foreign distribution ceased. In 1925 Smith, the last living founder of the company, wished to retire. He sold to Warners for a fraction of its true value.

VITAGRAPH BROOKLYN FIRST BUILDING ON STUDIO LOT **1908**

Sam Warner had always been the brother most interested in technology. Jack focused on production, and Harry and Albert were the businessmen. Sam had been tracking the success of a new medium, radio, since KDKA had become the first commercial station in the country in 1922. He instinctively believed that there was a natural connection between film and radio. With a little prodding, his brothers agreed that Sam should pursue acquiring a station license for the company. In 1925 KFWB Los Angeles (K signifies that the station is located west of the Mississippi River, and FWB stands for the four Warner brothers) became the first studio-owned radio station. The Warner Brothers entrance into the broadcasting business would also position the company to be the leader in transition to sound motion pictures.

RKO

RKO (Radio Keith Orpheum) was the last of the major studios to develop. It was the creation of Joseph Kennedy, the father of the American political dynasty, along with David Sarnoff, the man who created the American broadcasting industry. On October 23, 1928 Kennedy sold his interest in Film Booking Offices of America and the Keith-Albee-Orpheum vaudeville company to Sarnoff's Radio Corporation of America (RCA); the newest major was born.

Joseph Kennedy

Kennedy, the son of a Boston tavern owner, was born in 1888. He graduated from Harvard in 1912 and entered into the banking business, and within a year became the twenty-five year-old president of a small, independent bank, Columbia Trust. In 1919 Kennedy joined investment firm Hayden Stone and Company. Kennedy soon began to explore the movie theater business as a possible investment for his company. After reviewing the books and accounts of the Maine and New Hampshire Theaters Company he was convinced that the movie business had the potential for huge profits.

Kennedy believed that the era of the small production company was coming to an end and that only the larger, consolidated companies would survive. His first act on behalf of Hayden Stone was to purchase Hallmark Pictures, which he sold to British-owned Robertson-Cole/Film Booking Offices (RC/FBO) to create a combined production and distribution company. With $60,000 dollars of his own money, Kennedy next founded a distribution company that served the New England region. In 1921 RC/FBO was in desperate need of financing. Instead of arranging for Hayden Stone to provide the capital, Kennedy used the opportunity to have himself appointed president of the company.

Kennedy's first move as the new principal on RC/FBO was to lure the emerging cowboy star Fred Thompson to sign with his new studio. Thompson's pictures made money, but Kennedy was restless. He wanted more control. In 1924 he abruptly resigned as president. Quietly, Kennedy began to arrange bank financing, and the following year he purchased RC/FBO outright. Immediately, he brought in partners from the banking and railroad industries to prop up the company's finances. With that done, Kennedy departed for Los Angeles to inspect his production facilities.

In Hollywood Kennedy befriended industry leaders such as Adolph Zukor and Marcus Loew by arranging for them to make lecture appearances in the hallowed academic halls of Harvard. He made another acquaintance, megastar Gloria Swanson, who became his mistress while he took over management of her tattered financial affairs. Around the same time the Pathe company invited Kennedy to become its chief executive officer. Pathe had extensive European operations and also was well connected with Paramount in Hollywood. Kennedy was now in charge of two sizable motion picture studios.

In October 1927, Kennedy and Sarnoff secretly met at the Grand Central Station Oyster Bar in New York to hatch a plan for their new studio venture. Kennedy had the studios; RCA had a superior new sound technology. While the leaders of the motion picture industry dismissed the Warner Brothers foray into sound, Kennedy and Sarnoff planned a new studio based on the inevitability that the movies would begin to talk. All that was needed was a theater group of sufficient size and prestige.

David Sarnoff

Sarnoff was born in Russia in 1891. His father soon immigrated to America and began to save for passage for the rest of his family members, who arrived in 1900. Upon seeing the poor state of his father's health, the nine-year-old boy helped support the family by becoming a paper boy. At night he went to public school and was able to speak, read, and write English by age thirteen. From a previous odd job Sarnoff had acquired a telegraph key and became proficient in Morse code. He got a job as an office boy at the American Marconi company and developed the habit of reading every document he was given to file. By the time he was promoted to junior telegraph operator at age sixteen, Sarnoff had an excellent grasp of every aspect of the company's business practices. As a result, he was quickly promoted up the ranks to become Marconi's Senior Inspector, in charge of the technical operations of all telegraph centers.

In 1914 Marconi hired a young inventor, Edwin Armstrong, who had created a powerful new type of radio receiver. Sarnoff and Armstrong tested the equipment at a remote telegraph station. The results were astonishing. They were able to receive messages from halfway around the world. Sarnoff was instantly intrigued and worked tirelessly to convince his superiors that broadcast radio should be the company's future direction. He began to demonstrate the new medium's ability to send radio entertainment programs to thousands of homes with a single broadcast. World War I put Sarnoff's idea on hold temporarily until October 1919 when a new corporation (Radio Corporation of America) was formed by Marconi to launch its two new enterprises: broadcasting and the manufacturing and sales of home radio receivers. By 1926 Sarnoff had developed his idea so thoroughly that there was sufficient demand for him to launch a radio entertainment programming network called the National Broadcasting Company (NBC).

By the time the fateful meeting between Sarnoff and Kennedy took place in 1927, both men understood the power of radio to create new entertainment stars. They also saw how radio stars could easily become motion picture stars in the new talking picture medium. It was agreed that Kennedy would try to acquire a theater chain immediately. He set his sights on the Keith-Albee-Orpheum Company with its 700 theaters, many of which were in prime locations and would make perfect picture palaces. Kennedy went behind Albee's back to make a huge $4.2 million purchase of KAO stock. He claimed to be bored with the movie business and said he was turning his interest to vaudeville. Kennedy became chairman of the board. Within weeks Albee was ousted. All that was left was for Kennedy to sell Film Booking Offices and Keith-Albee-Orpheum to RCA. A new studio was born. Kennedy retained his interest in Pathe Pictures so that he could continue to produce Gloria Swanson's films. RCA executives and a group of promising young filmmakers including Merriam C. Cooper and David Selznick would guide RKO Radio Pictures' early fortunes. Finally, in 1930 Kennedy sold his interest in Pathe for $5 million dollars and left the motion picture world for good.

MINOR STUDIOS

If a major studio is defined as a company that encompasses all three aspects of the industry (theaters, distribution and production), then a minor studio is one that is limited to the production role. In order to get their films distributed, minor studios often turned to "states rights exhibitors," companies that represented producers by selling off the distribution rights to smaller, regional, and statewide distributors. Some minor studios existed only long enough to make a few films and then either disappeared or were swallowed up by larger companies. Others, Columbia and Republic among them, grew and flourished over time. Still others, such as Universal and United Artists/Goldwyn, were large-scale producers with their own distribution capabilities but without their own large-scale theater chains.

POVERTY ROW

In the late teens while Paramount, Fox, and Triangle were developing large permanent production facilities, another, less glamorous series of low-rent facilities began to crop up around the intersection of Sunset Boulevard and Gower Street in Hollywood. It was known alternately as Poverty Row and Gower Gulch. Poverty Row comprised a series of small, cheap, and woeful offices for rent in the neighborhood. They would serve as temporary homes for an endless string of hopeful producers trying to strike it rich in the movie business. Adjacent to the offices were sets, stages, and other production facilities producers rented on a short-term basis. Poverty Row became both a business incubator and sinkhole of swindles and misspent money. The term Gower Gulch referred to the string of saloons and casting offices that lined Sunset Boulevard at the time. Many, if not most, of the films made by Poverty Row producers were low-budget westerns. Therefore, the saloons were always brimming with cowboy actors and extras waiting for a casting call. The entire area had a forlorn quality about it and was regarded with disrespect by everyone fortunate to work for a more reputable company.

MONOGRAM-LONESTAR-REPUBLIC

Monogram's founder W. Ray Johnston was a newspaper man who entered the motion picture industry as an executive of the short-lived Thanhouser Company in 1912. In 1914 he left to found his own company, The Arrow Film Corporation, primarily a distribution company. In 1924 he founded Rayart, a Poverty Row company specializing in low-budget westerns for the states rights market. In response to the advent of sound, Rayart merged with two smaller companies to form Monogram Pictures in 1931.

In 1935, Herbert J. Yates, owner of Consolidated Film Labs, took over Monogram and another small producer of westerns, Lonestar. Lonestar was noteworthy as the studio where John Wayne made many of his early westerns

PHOTOFEST

HARRY COHN PRESIDENT OF COLUMBIA PICTURES

and where legendary stunt coordinator Yakima Canutt trained a generation of action stars, including Wayne, on the intricacies of stunt fighting and riding. Both companies were deeply in debt to the film processing company. Yates named his new company Republic Pictures and soon moved it to a former Sennett production facility in the San Fernando Valley, since low-budget westerns could easily be made nearby. During the thirties Republic became a respected studio, serving as home base for the great director, John Ford.

COLUMBIA

Of the minor studios, Columbia stands out as a company that made quality films over a long time. However, its beginnings were as humble as any motion picture company could be. Harry Cohn was born in New York in 1891. His brother Jack was born eight years later. The Cohn household was highly disciplined, and much was expected of the two sons. By 1912 Harry was trying his best to break into vaudeville. However, his enthusiasm and energy surpassed his talent. Over time he settled for a job pitching songs in New York nickleodeons. Theater operators were happy to welcome the young song pitchers who would arrive with a collection of glass lantern slides and sheet music for the theater pianist. The song pitcher would introduce music to the audience and lead them in a sing-along with the words projected from the slides. Afterward the song pitcher stood outside the theater and sold his sheet music the theater patrons.

Jack Cohn's introduction to show business was more conventional. After elementary school he got a job working for the Hamptons advertising agency. Here he met future partner Joe Brandt, who spent his evenings studying law at New York University. The two young men began to dream about going to work for Carl Laemmle's Independent Movie Corporation (IMP). Jack Cohn succeeded in getting hired by IMP, while Brandt proceeded to pass his bar examination and begin practicing law.

At IMP Jack Cohn began to rise through the ranks quickly. One of his early successes was starting the newsreel *Universal Weekly*. He soon became the head of the editing department and distinguished himself by his ability to create more profitable two-reel films out of the one-reel originals the directors had shot. Jack Cohn's big gamble was marked by his decision to team up and collaborate with director George Tucker. The two young men pitched Laemmle on the idea of making a feature film about the business of prostitution, *Traffic in Souls*. Laemmle was cool to the idea, consumed as he was at that time by his battles with the Edison Trust. The two young men commandeered a few thousand dollars' worth of company resources and proceeded to make the film on their own within the disorganized IMP studio environment. At first Laemmle balked at the audacity of the venture but, when *Traffic* became IMP's top moneymaker, all was forgiven.

In the meantime Harry Cohn had discovered a new movie-related enterprise, himself. He had begun to edit together film clips of stock footage under the words for the songs he was selling in the nickleodeons. They were much more popular than the lantern slides and stimulated greater sheet music sales. Cohn soon had a thriving business making these "song shorts" and selling them to music publishers for a few hundred dollars each. When Harry Cohn pitched the idea to Laemmle, the old man was so impressed, he hired him on the spot. Harry was sent to Hollywood in 1918. Inside IMP, the two Cohn brothers were able to learn every aspect on the nascent movie business.

In 1920 Jack Cohn had an idea he called *Screen Snapshots*, short films about the everyday lives of movie stars. He contacted his old friend, Joe Brandt, and convinced him to join in the venture. Harry would lead the sales department. The new company, CBC, secured a $100,000 line of credit from A. P. Giannini of the Bank of Italy (later Bank of America). In addition to *Snapshots*, the group acquired the movie rights to a popular comic strip called *Hall Room Boys*. This fine idea was undermined when the director they hired to make the films embezzled the budgets. It was decided that Harry would go to Hollywood to oversee whatever production could be accomplished with the remainder of the financing. Their only choice was to set up shop on Poverty Row. Harry hired the best director he could afford and went into production. The completed films were good enough to sell.

In short time CBC not only was making *Snapshots* and *Hall Room Boys* films, but the new company was also churning out westerns and comedies by a Chaplin imitator named Billy West. The organizing principle of the company was that all receipts, accounts, and distribution would be handled by Jack Cohn and Brandt in New York and that Harry would be in charge of production in Hollywood. In 1922 CBC made its first feature-length film at a cost of $20,000. Sold on the states-rights market, the film brought in $135,000. By early 1924, the company had outgrown its name and early reputation. The name was changed to Columbia Pictures. Two years later the company opened four film exchanges, leaving the states-rights market for good. There were also discussions of starting to buy a chain of theaters but Brandt opposed this talk, believing that the theater business was too risky. However, Brandt did believe that it was time to lose the stigma of Poverty Row. The company purchased a small, existing studio on Gower Street, and this became the new headquarters of Columbia Pictures.

DISNEY

Walt Disney was born in Chicago in 1901, eight years after his older brother, Roy. Seeking a more sedate environment, the family moved to a small farm in Missouri in 1906. In 1911 when Disney's father almost died of typhoid, the family sold the farm and moved to Kansas City. Walt and Roy helped support the family with newspaper routes. Because of the long working hours, Walt was indifferent about school work. He was passionate, however, about plays and theater. In 1918 he

WALT DISNEY, CIRCA 1926, SHOWN, RIGHT OF CENTER: MARGIE GAY; FAR RIGHT: WALT DISNEY. NB: AMONG CARTOON CHARACTERS DEPICTED, JULIUS: A FELIX THE CAT LOOK-ALIKE

lied about his age to get a job as a driver in the World War I ambulance corps, where he worked for a year. Upon returning to Kansas City, Disney vowed to become an artist.

Disney's first job as an artist was working for a commercial art company drawing horses and cows for farm equipment catalogs. In 1920 he teamed up with another artist, Ub Iwerks, and both went to work for the Kansas City Slide Company making animated commercials. In their spare time the two young men studied books about animation and sharpened their skills. Walt set up a studio in the family garage and worked evenings creating cartoons with a local twist that he sold to the nearby Newman Theater. From this point on, Disney devoted himself entirely to making cartoons.

In 1922 Disney and Iwerks attempted to start an animation company in Kansas City. Their sole client, however, went bankrupt, and all they had to show for their efforts was an uncompleted reel of film. Disney decided to leave for Los Angeles and room with one of his uncles. He set up a studio in the garage and started to work on a combined live action and animation project, *Alice's Wonderland,* in which a live-action Alice encounters a fantastic array of animated characters. He sold the idea to New York film distributor Margaret Winkler, who agreed to pay $1,500 dollars for each animated short. Knowing he wasn't clever with money, Walt convinced his brother Roy to join the business and tend to practical matters. Iwerks also agreed to come to Los Angeles Thus Disney Brothers Studio was launched in 1923.

In time the Alice character began to wear thin. Disney and Iwerks began to work on a new character, *Oswald the Lucky Rabbit*, which was distributed by Winkler's husband, Charlie Mintz. In 1927 unbeknownst to Disney, Mintz had tricked him out of the rights to Oswald and had sold them to Universal, then in the process of hiring away all of Disney's best animators. Disney and Iwerks were undeterred. They began to work on a new mouse character, originally named Mortimer, later to become Mickey.

Disney and Iwerks quickly turned out three *Mickey Mouse*, cartoons but they needed a hook to help sell them. Walt decided to synchronize sound to one of the cartoons titled *Steamboat Willie*. The company took on a partner, Pat Powers, to do the sound work and run the distribution part of the business. The project was a huge success. Between 1929 and 1932 over one million children joined the Mickey Mouse Club. The arrangement with Powers, unfortunately, soured. He withheld Walt and Roy's share of the profits and attempted to take over the company. Eventually Powers convinced Iwerks to leave Disney, and the two men formed their own animation company.

The Disney company was resilient enough to withstand the loss of Iwerks. A new line of cartoons called *Silly Symphonies* was introduced, as were new characters including Donald Duck, Pluto, and Goofy. The company was already on a roll in 1932 when it teamed up with the Kalmus family's Technicolor corporation to produce history's first three color cartoon, *Flowers and Trees*, which won that year's Academy Award. In 1936 work began on the world's first feature-length cartoon, *Snow White and the Seven Dwarfs*.

Many experts in the motion picture industry doubted that an animated feature could succeed. They were wrong. *Snow White* was such a success, it made Walt's dream of building a new studio a reality. With $3 million dollars to invest, Walt Disney studios rose along the bank of the Los Angeles river in Burbank.

UNITED ARTISTS

When it was founded in 1919 by Chaplin, Griffith, Pickford, and Fairbanks, the idea behind United Artists was that each principal would contribute five films per year. By banding together, the four most powerful stars in the industry would have greater control over their films and would be able to counteract the studio's attempts to dictate star's salaries. Since each of the four partners had his or her own production facilities, the first order of business was to form a distribution company. By the time the company was finally underway in late 1920, it was clear that five features per partner was far too ambitious. By 1924 Griffith had completely dropped out.

Joseph Schenck was brought in to expand the talent roster and recruit other producers to help expand UA's output. Among the new producers were Samuel Goldwyn (who was proposed by Chaplin over the objections of Pickford), Alexander Korda, and the young Texas oil millionaire, Howard Hughes. At the same time Schenck entered into an agreement with Pickford and Fairbanks to use the United Artists name in founding his own, separate theater company.

Pickford and Fairbanks owned real estate and a small production facility on Santa Monica Boulevard near La Brea. Goldwyn and Schenck both made large investments in expanding the facility into a full-fledged studio. It was named United Artists Studio, but Goldwyn took great pleasure in the common misconception that it was his studio alone; in fact most of the buildings did belong to him.. But the land remained the property of Pickford and Fairbanks. In 1935 Schenck left UA to devote his time to Twentieth Century Fox. He sold his interest to Goldwyn, making him an equal partner with Pickford and Fairbanks. Goldwyn left the company in 1940 but retained the studio, renaming it Samuel Goldwyn Studios.

Although United Artists ceased to exist as a minor studio in the late forties, the brand name lived on. It was reorganized as a production and distribution company in 1951 and continued to turn out modestly budgeted but generally successful films for decades to come.

THE SOUND REVOLUTION

EARLY SOUND EXPERIMENTS

On December 24, 1877 Thomas Edison filed for a patent on the first great invention to emerge from his laboratory in Menlo Park, New Jersey: the phonograph. It was originally envisioned to be used as a dictation machine for businessmen. However, later iterations of the phonograph achieved far greater success as home and arcade entertainment devices for playing recorded music. While working on the development of Edison motion picture technology, W. K. L. Dickson was conducting his own experiments in recording sound and pictures together. The first of these experiments took place in 1894. By the following spring the Edison Company was offering arcade owners the opportunity to purchase Kinetophones, a model of the Edison coin-operated movie viewer that included a synchronized record player. It was a novelty that never caught on.

In 1904 the Lubin Manufacturing Company produced a sound film titled *The Bold Bank Robbery.* Theater owners were offered free phonographs on which to play the soundtrack—an enticing offer, but there weren't many takers because the phonographs couldn't produce enough sound volume to be heard in a theater. In Europe, Leon Gaumont was also demonstrating films with accompanying record discs. To his disappointment his idea met with little positive reaction in the film community. Despite early interest in sound films, they remained technically impractical until the development of electronic amplification devices.

In 1907 American inventor Lee DeForrest received a patent for a device he called the Audion vacuum tube. This versatile device could be used for detecting weak wireless telegraph signals, transmitting radio signals, and amplifying sound. In 1910 the Audion was sold to telephone companies for improving the quality of long-distance calls. By 1916 DeForrest had adapted his apparatus for broadcasting and receiving radio signals capable of reproducing human speech and music. This ignited the race to develop commercial radio broadcasting.

In 1920 DeForrest began to experiment with photographing sound waves directly on the margins of motion picture film. He used an electric photo sensor attached to the projector to play back the sound. By 1921 he had successfully completed his first experimental synchronized sound film. The advantage of this approach was that once the sound and picture were synchronized, they stayed in sync. At the same time a group of German engineers were at work on the Tri-Ergon sound system, which was eventually acquired by the Fox Motion Picture Company. In 1923 DeForrest introduced his new completed invention, which he called Phonofilm. The following year it was successfully used to add a music track to James Cruze's western *The Covered Wagon.* By the beginning of the sound craze in 1927, he had already produced over one thousand sound films. In 1925 Fox hired Theodore Case and Earl Sponable, both of whom had collaborated with DeForrest on an early version of the Phonofilm system, to develop a sound process for their newsreel division. The following year the completed system was named Fox Movietone. Despite a claim of interest in the new technology, the motion picture industry was reluctant to adopt sound for any number of business and artistic reasons including the belief that the time "just wasn't right."

THE WARNER BROTHERS AND THE WESTERN ELECTRIC COMPANY

Always looking for new business opportunities, the Warner Brothers decided to get into the new business of broadcast radio. KFWB was their first station. Located in Los Angeles, it was the creation of Western Electric's Bell Labs and its West Coast field engineer, Nathan Levinson. In the early days of the radio industry, individuals and businesses interested in acquiring stations would begin by contacting one of the technology companies that manufactured broadcast equipment such as Westinghouse, RCA, and American Telephone & Telegraph's design and manufacturing subsidiary, Western Electric. These companies provided turn-key radio station assistance. Their engineers would scout a given market for an available broadcast frequency, acquire a license, build the broadcast facility, install their own brand of equipment, and train the staff to operate the new radio station. Levinson had supervised the work on KFWB, which began broadcasting in 1925.

Upon returning to Western Electric's design and engineering headquarters at Bell Laboratories in New York City, Levinson was shown the company's new motion picture sound technology. Bell engineers had been working on the system since 1922 and believed that it was ready for the commercial market. Having spent the last few years in Hollywood, Levinson was asked to suggest which studio to approach. He did not hesitate to recommend Warner Brothers. They were relatively young and forward thinking, and they had a line of credit from the Wall Street investment bank Goldman Sachs. Sam Warner, the brother most interested in technology, went to New York for a demonstration. Legend has it that Sam was so impressed with the quality of the sound that he made the engineers show him what was behind the screen to make certain that it wasn't a hoax. When told of the demonstration, Harry Warner immediately concluded that the company could save a great deal of money by eliminating all of the orchestras that were employed in its largest theaters and replacing them with recorded music tracks. In June, 1925 Western Electric and Warner signed a contract to begin the development of the sound motion picture.

Sam Warner decided that the developmental work would be done in Vitagraph's New York studios rather than in Hollywood. He reasoned that such an expensive endeavor should take place as close to the money center of the industry as possible, and that the new generation of talking movie performers was already working onstage on Broadway. The technology center was also in the east. Eventually, this decision would send a chill through the silent film community back in Hollywood. Under the supervision of Jack Warner, the studio was well into production on a silent adaptation of George Bernard Shaw's play *Don Juan* with John Barrymore in the title role. An increased budget accommodated a recorded musical score. In the East, Sam Warner began work on a second sound project, which was to become *The Vitagraph Concert*. The Manhattan Opera House was converted into a sound stage including an isolation booth for the camera to shield the noisy apparatus from the microphones. Eight different acts were filmed with synchronized sound despite problems caused by nearby subway and construction noises. Meanwhile, the New York Philharmonic Orchestra's recording of the score for *Don Juan* was proceeding with relative ease.

By the time they had made all necessary preparations, the Warners had spent three million dollars on production and on equipping their 1,300-seat Broadway theater for sound. They were heavily in debt, and much was riding on the public's reaction to this new medium. The premiere took place August 6, 1926. The initial critical reaction was praiseful but reserved. There were no pronouncements of a new motion picture era dawning. Yet when the receipts were counted, it was clear that audiences were enthusiastic. In the first eight months, the program grossed the robust sum of eight hundred thousand dollars. Audiences greatly preferred *The Vitagraph Concert* film to *Don Juan*. Seeing and hearing their favorite performers magnified and amplified on the movie screen and sound system was exciting. At the end of the first month, Wall Street had bid up the price of Warner's stock from fourteen dollars per share to fifty dollars per share. The program was also released in Chicago to comparably favorable audience reaction. A second *Vitagraph Concert* program was released in October and generated even better economic results. It included performances by such vaudeville stars as Al Jolson and George Jessel. As a result, Warners/Vitagraph moved into full production mode on a series of short films featuring other vaudeville performers.

At the same time that the Warners were launching their new motion picture technology, David Sarnoff was introducing his new National Broadcasting Company radio network. The two enterprises were in heated competition for the services of popular stage performers. For the owners of vaudeville theaters and circuits, the end of their business was in sight. In the future talking motion pictures and radio would bring the greatest performers in the business into even the smallest communities. Out in Hollywood it was becoming clearer by the minute that movie talent and the entire industry would have to adapt or die.

VITAPHONE CAMERA, CIRCA LATE 1920-EARLY 1930S

One of the concessions Western Electric had made to Warner in exchange for its investment in sound was that the studio would have the right to charge other filmmakers a royalty for the use of the Vitaphone sound technology. In December 1926 the other studios responded by entering into an agreement whereby none would adopt sound until all were ready for the transition, and that under any circumstances, they would not do business with

Vitaphone. Meanwhile, Adolph Zukor of Paramount had already betrayed his partners by negotiating to acquire Vitaphone technology. The negotiations eventually fell through, but momentum was rapidly growing for the change to sound.

In the spring of 1927 William Fox released his second Movietone program of short films that included a two-minute recording of Charles Lindbergh taking off for his historic trans-Atlantic flight. Audiences were stirred by the roar of the airplane engines. By October Fox was producing weekly Movietone newsreels. The excitement of the newsreels had been eclipsed in May when Warner announced its intention to produce a full-length sound feature film. Vaudevillian George Jessel was announced to star in it for the princely sum of $2,000 per week. However, negotiations eventually broke down. Since the Vitagraph technology involved recording the songs on discs, Jessel's people believed that he should receive a record royalty in addition to his acting fee. He was replaced by another veteran of Vitagraph music shorts, the equally popular Al Jolson.

By August work was complete on the new sound stage that Warners had built on their Sunset Boulevard lot. Many technical problems had been solved along the way. The walls and doors of the studio had been treated with sound-proofing material to dampen outside noises. An improved camera booth was constructed as well as a glass walled gallery where the sound recording experts would work. The buzzing of the arc lights had been minimized so the microphones wouldn't pick it up. Inside, the lights made the ninety-by–150-foot stage stifling hot. The cameras had to be modified for sound to operate at twenty-four frames per second as opposed to the sixteen-frames rate used in silent films. The entire ambience of the stage changed. The ordinary bustle of the silent stage included the director verbally guiding the actors while they performed. It was also common to have string quartets play mood music during filming. Minimizing sound on set was crucial. The tension on the sound stage was excruciating.

The Jazz Singer is the story of the Jewish son of a rabbi who disappoints his family by becoming an entertainer

THE JAZZ SINGER (1927), DIRECTED BY ALAN CROSLAND, DEPICTED ON POSTER, FROM LEFT: EUGENIE BESSERER, AL JOLSON

WARNER BROS. PICTURES/PHOTOFEST

instead of following in his father's footsteps. It was conceived as a hybrid film. Much of it would be a standard silent feature with a recorded musical track. The scenes in which Jolson sang and performed his customary stage patter were synchronized sound-film recordings. At times the transitions between synchronized and silent scenes were quite awkward. But Jolson's enthusiasm for performing overshadowed any technical deficiencies. The completed film was sentimental and predictable, but the power of the musical performances and the novelty of the dialogued scenes earned it the highest critical praise. It was one of the most expensive films Warner Brothers had ever made at half a million dollars, but the returns would more than justify the expense.

The opening was set to take place at the Warner Brothers' Manhattan Theater on October 6, 1927. Tragically, Sam Warner, the brother who had most steadfastly championed the cause of sound, died of complications from a sinus infection at age forty, the day before the premiere. At the height of its distribution *The Jazz Singer* was attracting a million theater goers per week. A little over a month after the opening Warner announced it would produce twelve more "talkies" in 1928. The announcement gave reassurance to theater owners that the twenty- to forty-thousand dollar cost of wiring their venues for sound would be justified in the future. By the end of its run *The Jazz Singer* earned the studio $3.5 million in profits and untold millions more for theater owners and distributors. With this huge influx of cash, Warner would soon be able to acquire the much larger First National studio facility in Burbank where they could better complete their ambitious new slate of talking pictures.

1928: THE SOUND REVOLUTION BEGINS

At the beginning of 1928 all but a handful of movie productions were silent films. By the end of the year, virtually every production company in the country was making only sound films. During that year the studios found it necessary to stop all production for significant periods to convert their facilities and train technical staff for talking pictures. Even the basic organization of the industry would be changed by the new technology. Coordinating sound production with film production required far more hands-on management of the process. As a result, producers became more powerful in relationship to directors. There had never been a uniform pay scale for actors. Each studio had its own employment rules. But sound production necessitated far more rehearsal time, which some studios paid and others didn't. This led to discontent and the trend toward organized labor in the industry. The unionization movement gained force when projectionists, whose work was greatly complicated by sound, organized and bargained for better working conditions and rights of seniority. Other trades would soon follow.

The careers of actors, directors, and writers were disrupted by uncertainty and doubt about the old guard's ability to adapt. The motion picture industry's leaders assumed that silent picture scenarists couldn't write dialogue; that actors would suffer from "microphone nerves" and become unable to perform; and that directors would be equally challenged by the new medium. For a brief period the entire industry shifted its attention from Hollywood to New York, where a pool of theater and radio talent awaited. For New York stage actors, the higher wages offered by the film industry was a boon. Playwrights accustomed to living on the meager wages paid by the stage suddenly found themselves courted by the studios and offered unheard of sums of money. The cost of screen rights for successful plays also soared.

In Hollywood silent actors began to enroll in voice and diction classes. It was assumed that the voice of talking pictures would sound cultured, imitating the accents of the aristocracy. People with perfectly acceptable speaking voices, perhaps regionally accented or unaccented, were trained to talk as if they had been to college at Oxford or Cambridge. This rejection of naturalism in talking pictures resulted in films that were awkward and sometimes unintentionally comedic. One early technique used in dialogue recording was for each speaker to pause for an instant before beginning their lines in the belief that audiences would need the time to keep up with what was being said. This affect came off sounding slow and ponderous and artificial. Sound engineers declared that the letter "s" could not be properly reproduced by the technology. This caused writers to tear out their hair out trying to avoid the offending letter in dialogue scenes.

Major stars such as Mary Pickford and Douglas Fairbanks began to carefully and strategically plan their talking debuts. Thanks to radio, audiences were already familiar with many stars' voices. In the case of Chaplin, who had already cut back his output to a single film every year or so, the decision was to resist sound and to continue to give his fans the silent version of his Little Tramp character, with whom they were so familiar. Community playhouses began to spring up around Hollywood so that actors could practice and showcase their speaking abilities. Conrad Nagel was one of the first actors to be declared as "ready for sound." In fact he was cast in so many films between 1928 and 1931 that his career went into a sharp decline thereafter due to overexposure.

At the end of July 1928, MGM released its first talking picture, *White Shadows of the South Seas*, directed by W. S. Van Dyke. In August Columbia released its first two sound pictures, *Scarlet Lady* and *Submarine*. That same month RKO/FBO released their first "talkie." During this period Fox announced that, from then on, it would cast all of its films in New York; also, Paramount was moving most of its sound production to its studios on Long Island as a display of its commitment to sound. In October, Warner announced that they would discontinue all silent film production. The tumultuous year of 1928 was one of transition with many false steps that would have to be reversed later on.

The significant increase in the expense of production caused by sound forced the studios to embark on a campaign of cost cutting. An early casualty of the talking era were theater and studio musicians. However, a new opportunity arose for them at the same time: contributing the theme song. Theme songs were used extensively in radio to identify programs as well as to promote films in advance of their release. Paramount instructed directors that they were allowed only the expense of printing two takes or versions of each scene. This put tremendous pressure on everyone, especially camera operators, to get it right the first time. Following the lead of projectionists, cameramen were soon demanding and receiving better pay and working conditions as a result of the greater responsibility they were bearing. Another economizing move was to fire all of the "gag" men, comedy writers who routinely were assigned to movie sets to add little bits of comedy as the film was being shot. Movie producers and supervisors also earned more power because of the increased complexity of their jobs and the new knowledge required. Rank-and-file actors became restless. They weren't customarily paid for rehearsals, but sound necessitated they spend much more time in preparation. In September 1928, the Academy of Motion Picture Arts and Sciences (AMPAS) announced that actors would henceforth be paid for rehearsals on talking films.

Late in 1928 the talking picture medium hit a rough spot in the road. Production was sluggish as the studios quit making silent films before they were completely tooled up for sound. Audiences were getting over the novelty of sound, and the technical crudeness of many talking pictures generated discontent. This trend was reversed in late September when Warner released Al Jolson's follow-up to *The Jazz Singer*, *Singing Fool*. By Jolson's own admission, the new film was better than its predecessor. *Singing Fool* featured songs such as "I'm Sitting on Top of the World," and "Sonny Boy." They become instant radio and record hits, thereby pumping up interest in the film's release. The film produced over two million dollars in profits which Warner used to offset their

The Singing Fool (1928), Directed by Lloyd Bacon, Shown: Al Jolson, Davey Lee

Warner Bros. Pictures/Photofest

losses from the conversion to sound. In December the studio released a film featuring the "female Jolson" Fanny Brice, a veteran of Florence Ziegfeld's very successful Broadway reviews. Brice was fairly well received, but the luster of Broadway talent was beginning to tarnish for film audiences who missed their favorite movie stars. Their longing for the glamour and spectacle of the silent films couldn't be satisfied by the confined style of adapted theatrical productions.

1929: SOUND BECOMES THE NORM

At the end of 1928 a small group of established Hollywood directors started to make their mark on the talking picture revolution. Lloyd Bacon of Warner Brothers had successfully directed *Singing Fool*. John Ford made his sound debut with a short film, *Napoleon's Barber*, that was intended to display the superiority of the Fox optical sound system. Another established Fox director, Raoul Walsh, had seen a Fox Movietone sound newsreel truck in action, realized its potential for outdoor use, and reasoned it could be used for shooting sound on location. In December the studio released the western *In Old Arizona*, directed by Walsh that had been filmed in authentic locations such as Zion National Park, Utah and the Mojave Desert in California. Warner Baxter starred with Edmund Lowe and Dorothy Burgess. The cast spoke in the natural accents of the frontier west, leading one critic to label the film "the finest bit of entertainment" sound had yet produced. The production served to revive interest in the western genre. Finally, sound pictures developed an appeal based on substance rather than mere novelty.

By early 1929 the new Mitchell Hi-Speed Movement cameras were touted as the answer to the problem of camera noise on a sound set. Suddenly the camera was free to move again, restoring a sense of fluidity to motion picture directing and camera work. Gordon Sawyer, a young engineering graduate from UCLA, had invented the movable microphone boom. Actors were now freed from talking into flower vases and were able to move more naturally as the microphone followed. In March Western Electric introduced the Vitaphone version of sound trucks for location production. On the set of *The Wagon Master,* a Universal western, director Harry J. Brown tried another innovation: shooting dialogue without the customary pauses between lines. The result was more natural and sounded realistic.

The financial and business aspect of the motion picture industry was also changing. By 1929 the boards of directors of the movie companies were populated by executives from the big electrical and technology companies and from Eastern banks. Paramount had eight bankers on its board, and RKO nineteen. One of the problems they struggled with was the effect sound had on undermining foreign markets for American films. To stanch the outward flow of profits, the studios tried a number of approaches. MGM announced it would sell "blueprints" of its films to foreign producers, complete with camera set-ups and lighting details. On MGM's big studio-style productions, the sets were used during the day to film in English and at night to film in Spanish. Warner began using their New York stages to produce short films mostly in German and French. Eventually the industry settled on the practice of dubbing. This entailed recording alternative dialogue tracks in multiple languages and editing the tracks to match as well as possible the on-screen movements of the original English-speaking actors.

By January 1929, the studios began to retreat from New York as a production center. First National and Universal closed their East Coast operations altogether. MGM, Warner, and Fox gradually withdrew. Bi-coastal production had proved to be expensive, and the industry was responding to the audience's demand for their favorite Hollywood movie stars versus their tepid response to Broadway talent.

However, this presented a new problem for movie companies. They needed to introduce their stars to audiences in suitable films that would maintain the star's mystique while avoiding negative reactions to their speaking personas. For some foreign-born actors such as MGM's Greta Garbo, the transition was difficult if ultimately successful. For others such as Emil Jannings, Pola Negri and Samuel Goldwyn's protégé, Vilma Banky, it meant the end of a career in Hollywood. For Universal's Lon Chaney, the challenge was different. He had a fine speaking voice but feared he would not able to perform voices to match the many characters he created.

Richard Barthelmess was one of the first established stars to venture into talkies when he appeared as a singing gangster in *Weary River,* released in January 1929. He received positive notices for the naturalism of his performance but was mildly criticized for using a "voice double" for the singing scenes in the picture. In March William Powell appeared as detective Philo Vance in *The Canary Murder.* He was an immediate hit. The revelation that confirmed the wisdom of returning to Hollywood was MGM's first Hollywood-style musical *Broadway Melody.* The original score was written by Arthur Freed and was performed live on the sound stage with the entire orchestra just out of camera range. By today's standards the film lacks the dynamism usually associated with musicals. But the Hollywood stage craft and hard-bitten street feel of the dialogue as performed by Bessie Love and Charles King was a sensation. Finally the talkies were achieving the quality of realism and vitality to which audiences responded enthusiastically. For MGM the profits exceeded a million dollars, thus pointing toward the direction of the studio's future.

THE STARS PLAN AND MAKE THEIR TALKING DEBUTS

Douglas Fairbanks's first talking film a swashbuckler, *The Iron Mask*, was released in February 1929. The project was designed to allow him to engage in his customary athleticism and acrobatics without talking. Fairbanks was concerned that he would be out of breath for his dialogue, so dialogue was simply excluded. Instead the only talking the great star engaged in was at the beginning and end of the film, when he addresses the audience directly. In all, Fairbanks speaks for no more than two minutes, and even then, he was suspected of using a voice double. The accusation was supported by the fact that when the film was re-released at a later date, his son, Douglas Fairbanks, Jr., provided the voice. This did not qualify as an auspicious beginning for the great star.

Mary Pickford was far more courageous in her talking debut. She made the decision to completely shed her former screen persona, the eternal little girl with golden curls. The haircut alone was shocking to her fans, but she also adopted a southern accent for her flirtatious character in the film *Coquette.* The film's story is depressing. Pickford, who was in her mid-thirties at the time, plays a young woman who flirts with a young man beneath her social status. To protect his daughter from disgrace, the girl's father kills the young man and stands trial for the murder. Despite the story's dreariness, Pickford's fans and the critics were enthusiastic with praise for her performance and maturity. Pickford and Fairbanks followed up their debuts with a screen adaptation of Shakespeare's *Taming of the Shrew*. The film was the first occasion for the couple to perform together onscreen, and it gave Pickford the opportunity to showcase a talent for slapstick and broad comedy. For Fairbanks it was a much more respectable attempt at talking than in *Iron Mask.*

Gloria Swanson had been at work on the silent film *Queen Kelly* in 1929 under the direction of Eric von Stroheim. As was typical for von Stroheim films, the project was disorganized and completely over budget. When Joseph Kennedy finally pulled the plug on it, the film was only two-thirds finished, and it had already cost three quarters of a million dollars. This allowed Swanson to begin work on her first talking picture, *The Trespasser*, which opened in November. In it she plays a young woman who marries into a snobbish. wealthy family and is immediately ostracized. The plot is standard melodrama for the times, but Swanson's acting raises it far above the norm. She had also been taking singing lessons to prepare for the part, and her performance of the song "Love, Your Magic Spell Is Everywhere," helped make the film an overwhelming success.

THE TRESPASSER (1929) DIRECTED BY EDMUND GOULDING, SHOWN: PURNELL PRATT, GLORIA SWANSON

John Barrymore had waited until December to appear in his first all-speaking role in *General Crack*. It was a poorly directed film about a mercenary general who sells his services to the Austrian Emperor. It gave Barrymore an opportunity to display his classical stage training and how well his voice recorded. Critics dismissed the film as pedestrian, but it succeeded in launching the great actor's speaking career.

Greta Garbo had been the subject of much discussion and hand ringing at MGM. Her voice was tested several times to determine if audiences would respond positively to her thick Swedish accent. However, she was one of the studio's greatest stars. It wasn't a matter of if but when she would talk. Her talking picture debut, *Anna Christie*, wasn't released until March 1930, but it proved that Garbo would weather the transition to sound quite well. She was a good actress, able to use her accented voice to create a sensual and world-weary attitude that increased her screen magnetism.

ANNA CHRISTIE (1930), DIRECTED BY JACQUES FEYDER, SHOWN FROM LEFT: GRETA GARBO, LEE PHELPS

Lon Chaney finally changed his mind about talking in 1930. His doubts about audience acceptance were dispelled by the positive reaction to other, similar character actors including George Arlis and Paul Muni. *The Unholy Three* is a remake of one of Chaney's most successful silent films in which he plays multiple characters in multiple disguises. One part is of a kindly old grandmother. His voice was more than adequate. It added another dimension to the colorful characters he created. The film was directed by the very experienced Todd Browning, who had a great capacity for bringing grotesque characters to the screen. Chaney's voice work was so good that, for promotional purposes, the studio made him sign an affidavit swearing that no voice doubles were used. The film's success was followed by a cruel tragedy: Chaney died of throat cancer within weeks of *The Unholy Three*'s release.

THE UNHOLY THREE (1930), DIRECTED BY JACK CONWAY, SHOWN: (IN BASKET) HARRY EARLES, LON CHANEY

John Gilbert didn't fare as well as many of his contemporaries. Before sound he had been the greatest screen lover of his time. He was MGM's biggest male star on the strength of his ability to project passion and sensuality. His voice didn't quite match up at first. *His Glorious Night*, released late in 1929, was a disaster. Although audiences had already heard Gilbert speak in *Broadway Review,* his appearance in that film had been brief. He and Norma Shearer had performed a comedy sketch based on the balcony scene from *Romeo and Juliet.* In it Gilbert was perfectly relaxed, and so was his voice, even if it was a little too high pitched. However, when audiences heard the actor protesting the fever of his ardor for the actress playing opposite him in *His Glorious Night,* the response was embarrassed laughter. The embarrassment came partly from the fact that audiences hadn't yet become used to hearing as well as seeing love scenes. It was like witnessing something a little too private. Compounding the problem was the fact that his voice lacked the dusky sensuality the dialogue suggested. Gilbert was humiliated, but he kept working and improving.

John Gilbert's legend is that his career was undone by sound, but that isn't quite what undid him. While MGM president Nicholas Schenck was conspiring with William Fox for his takeover of MGM, the subject of John Gilbert came up. Fox wanted to be certain that the studio would not lose its biggest star during the merger. Schenck took Gilbert into his confidence when he approached the actor about extending his contract. Gilbert was told that Louie B. Mayer was out and the new megastudio would be managed by Fox executives.

The actor agreed to the contract request and was not the least bit concerned about Mayer's imminent ousting. After the Fox/MGM deal fell through, Mayer was still in charge and acutely aware of Gilbert's treachery. The few roles Gilbert landed in films such as *Redemption* and *Fast Workers* (his last for MGM) did nothing to reverse his decline. The only bright spot came when Garbo insisted that her old co-star play opposite her in *Queen Christina*, but the magic was gone. Gilbert's last film was for Columbia in 1934. In *The Captain Hates the Sea* he was a featured actor, not the star, and there was nothing remarkable about his performance. In January 1936, Gilbert had a massive heart attack and died. He was thirty-nine years old.

By the early 1930s the fact of transitioning to sound was fading from memory. Actors such as Gilbert, Norma Talmadge, Clara Bow, and Colleen Moore had passed from the scene either because of their voices or because the types of characters they played were too old-fashioned for a changing audience. There was a new type of romantic leading man emerging in the era of sound. Clark Gable, Gary Cooper, and Cary Grant would dominate the new decade. A few Broadway character actors such as Paul Muni and Edward J. Robinson had come to Hollywood to stay and prosper. The new women included actresses as diverse as Jean Harlow, Carole Lombard, Myrna Loy, and Bette Davis. As the Great Depression descended upon the world after the stock market crash of October 1929, the escapism that movies offered and a new generation of talent helped the industry survive. In response to the Great Depression, David Sarnoff at RCA decided to put off the introduction of his new invention, television. No doubt this fortunate turn of events contributed to the survival of the movie business during the challenging decade of the 1930s.

QUEEN CHRISTINA (1933), DIRECTED BY ROUBEN MAMOULIAN, SHOWN: GRETA GARBO (AS QUEEN CHRISTINA), JOHN GILBERT (AS ANTONIO)

CHAPTER 6

EUROPE BETWEEN THE WARS
German Expressionism, Soviet Montage, Surrealism, and National Film Movements

GERMAN EXPRESSIONISM AND UFA STUDIOS

Expressionism: An art style and movement that developed simultaneously in several countries around 1905. It is characterized by an emphasis on bold colors and exaggerated imagery. Expressionist artists emphasize the subjective point of view, aiming to reflect their interior state of mind rather than representing the external world. *German Expressionism* dwells on the darker side of human nature, often employing horrific and nightmarish imagery. Expressionists were influenced by the psychoanalytic theories of Sigmund Freud, particularly his interest in dream analysis.

In early 1917, as the inconceivable violence of World War I continued unabated, the German Army formed the Picture and Film Office for the purpose of producing propaganda films. Later in the year, General Erich Ludendorff issued an order to consolidate the entire German film industry for the "purpose of better coordination." This newly minted organization was named Universum Film AG, or "UFA" for short. Many production, distribution, and theater companies that were previously in the hands of private ownership merged into the new movie giant. Paul Davidson, owner of one of the merged companies, was appointed head of production. However, Davidson's primary responsibility was the continued acquisition of film companies, making it impossible for him to be involved in the day-to-day aspects of production work. Therefore, directors were given almost complete authority over the projects in which they were engaged. Inadvertently, UFA became a creative paradise with ever-improving facilities and little management interference.

THE CABINET OF DOCTOR CALIGARI (GERMANY 1920) AKA DAS KABINETT DES DOKTOR CALIGARI, DIRECTED BY ROBERT WIENE, SHOWN FROM LEFT: CONRAD VEIDT (AS CESARE), WERNER KRAUSS (AS DR. CALIGARI)

PHOTOFEST

One of the last companies to be merged into UFA was Erich Pommer's Decla Film. One of the last films produced at Decla before the merger was *The Cabinet of Dr. Caligari* (1919).

The film was directed by Robert Wiene, a young Austrian stage and film director. *Caligari* is generally considered the starting point for the very influential German Expressionist cinematic movement. Pommer had brought together a team of young avant-garde artists including Wiene, cinematographer Karl Freund, and a trio of set designers from the Berlin theater. Werner Krauss played the title role of Caligari, the mad doctor and carnival performer who terrorizes the local village in consort with his fellow performer, a somnambulist freak named Cesare, played by Conrad Veidt.

The sets for the film were unlike anything movie audiences had ever seen. Inspired by post-impressionist artist Marc Chagall and by expressionist artists such as Max Beckmann, the sets mark a major departure from conventional movie design. There are no right angles. Windows are gashes in the walls. The doorways appear to be designed to accommodate alien life forms, not humans. Lighting is unnatural with large shadows and areas of blackness where unspeakable horrors hide. The actors project a profound sense of alienation as if lost in their own nightmares. Everything is purposely arranged to put the audience off balance. The story deals with murder, madness, deceit, and dementia. This film style was unlike any preceding style up to this point in early film history.

Pommer understood the power of marketing and worked tirelessly to sell Caligari around the world. His efforts succeeded. By 1920 filmmakers in Hollywood were attempting to apply this new style to their work. While film design had always played an important role in the creation of motion pictures, the boldness of Caligari stimulated a greater emphasis on the look of a film. In 1921 UFA was reinstated as a privately held company with some government oversight and financial support. The Babelsberg Studios outside Berlin had been under construction by the Bioscope Company since 1918. With their completion in 1920, these production facilities were unrivaled by any in the world. At this time Pommer agreed to merge his company to form Decla-Bioscop AG. In 1921 Decla-Bioscope became part of UFA, thereby creating a company of sufficient size to compete with all of Hollywood. Pommer was appointed to direct both the operations and production.

One of Pommer's first challenges was to attract young filmmaking talent to UFA. He looked to the Berlin theater scene for his source. Max Reinhardt had been made the Director of the Deutsches Theater (the German National Theater) in 1905. He infused the institution with a spirit of experimentation and innovation that caught the attention of young actors, directors, and playwrights. Reinhardt was fond of staging plays on a spectacular scale. His critics often accused him of not being sufficiently modern. But over and again he proved his ability to help the younger talent at his theater to add details and flourishes to their work that breathed life into their productions and made them more vivid and satisfying. The Deutsches Theater became known throughout Europe for trend-setting stagecraft and performance. Reinhardt also established a smaller theater to mount minimalist productions and chamber plays that emphasized characterization and acting over stagecraft and production values. This smaller theater was known as Kammerspiel.

Soon UFA studios boasted an exciting new crop of directors whom Reinhardt had discovered. In a very short time Ernst Lubitsch, F. W. Murnau, Fritz Lang, William Dieterle, and Otto Preminger became star filmmakers with worldwide reputations. UFA released over five hundred films in 1921. The studio controlled three thousand theaters in Germany, stu-

NOSFERATU, EINE SYMPHONIE DES GRAUENS (1922 GERMANY) AKA NOSFERATU, DIRECTED BY
F.W. MURNAU, SHOWN: MAX SCHRECK (AS NOSFERATU)

dios that served almost a million ticket buyers a day. The German film industry had become so powerful by 1922 that it was able to impose an import-export policy on America stipulating that for each American film exported to Germany, a German film be imported to America. Not only were German directors becoming international stars, but so were actors such as Marlene Dietrich, Emil Jannings, Pola Negri, and Conrad Veidt.

    F. W. Murnau was born in Bielefeld, Germany in 1888. He attended college at the University of Berlin and graduated from the University of Heidelberg. He studied under Max Reinhardt until the outbreak of World War I. Murnau served in the German military from 1914 to 1917. He crash landed the plane he was flying and was a prisoner of war in Switzerland until his release at the end of the war. Upon returning to Germany he directed his first feature film, *The Boy In Blue* (1919), for Ernst Hoffman-Film. Several of Murnau's early feature films have been lost, with little known about them. Many of his films are surmised to be either dark expressionistic dramas or horror films. In 1920 Murnau made his first significant horror film, an adaptation of Robert Lewis Stevenson's *Dr. Jekyll and Mr. Hyde*, starring Conrad Veidt and Bela Lugosi.

    Murnau made a total of ten features before his 1922 masterpiece, *Nosferatu: A Symphony of Horror.* Based on Bram Stoker's *Dracula,* the film is a textbook on manipulating audience expectations to create a sense of shock and horror. Nosferatu features Max Schreck as the undead Count Orlock who is in need of a new place to call home where victims are more plentiful. Blessed with a naturally frightening appearance, Schreck was able to play the vampire with minimal makeup. The film stands as an example of the use of naturalistic locations and sets to create expressionistic style primarily through lighting and acting.

In 1924 Murnau adopted the Kammerspiel style of expressionism to make *The Last Laugh*. The film is the story of a doorman (played by Emil Jannings) at a Luxury Hotel who loves the prestige of his job and the dignified uniform that goes with it. One day the manager sees that the old doorman can no longer lift the guest's heavy luggage and assigns him to work as a washroom attendant. The old man is humiliated. Murnau uses a constantly moving, fluid camera to capture every little detail of humiliation. The film is done entirely in pantomime without title cards for dialogue. The result of this is intensified emotion. Murnau's last German film, *Faust*, also starred Jannings.

In 1927 both Murnau and Jannings came to Hollywood. The actor went to work on *The Way of All Flesh* at Paramount under the direction of Victor Fleming. Jannings won a best actor Oscar for his performance. Murnau had been heavily recruited by Fox, which allowed him to bring his own writers and cameraman. His first film at Fox, *Sunrise*, is considered one of his greatest and the first American-produced expressionist masterpiece. Fox's two biggest stars, Janet Gaynor and George O'Brien, played the leading roles of a young couple from the country on their

THE LAST LAUGH (1924, GERMANY) AKA DER LETZTE MANN, DIRECTED BY F.W. MURNAU, SHOWN: EMIL JANNINGS

UFA/PHOTOFEST

first trip to the big city. Murnau's use of the roving camera is even more realized in *Sunrise* than in his earlier films. The film and its director became the model for young Fox directors such as John Ford and Howard Hawks. Murnau made two more films for Fox before partnering up with documentary filmmaker Robert Flaherty on the South Seas romance *Tabu*. Shortly after the film's completion Murnau died in a traffic accident at age forty-two.

Fritz Lang was born in Vienna in 1890. His father was an architect, and young Lang was expected in the father's profession. To this end, he spent time at technical school but was not suited for engineering. After leaving school Lang moved to Paris, where he survived by painting postcards and drawing cartoons until he was called for military duty in World War I. He suffered injuries in the war that required a long recuperation. During that down time Lang began to write screenplays and learned to act. In 1918 he was hired by Erich Pommer's Decla Films and moved to Berlin. Lang directed his first film in 1919, *The Half Caste*. He followed this up with a series of expressionistic crime dramas including *The Testament of Dr. Mabuse* (1922). Lang had ambitions of making epic-scale films. In 1924 he made a two-part adaptation of the *Ring of the Nibelung* saga, which had also served as the underlying story for Wagner's "*Ring Cycle*" operas.

In 1925 UFA was involved in negotiations to create a distribution agreement with Paramount and MGM. When the talks fell through, UFA's position with its bankers was considerably weakened, and the studio began to struggle financially. The following year Lang began production on *Metropolis*, a futuristic tale about a city in which the elite, educated class lives above ground in modern glass towers and the working class lives underground and toil in dark, dehumanizing factories. Lang built enormous sets and used intricate models and dramatic

METROPOLIS (1927 GERMANY), DIRECTED BY FRITZ LANG, SHOWN: UNDERGROUND WORKERS

UFA/PHOTOFEST

photography to create a realistic look for his disturbing future world. When *Metropolis* was released, it was hailed as a great cinematic achievement. However, the budget had surpassed 5.3 million Deutsche marks (by far the largest amount ever spent of a UFA film). On top of the studio's already shaky finances, UFO was on the brink of bankruptcy. In 1927 it was sold to Alfred Hugenberg's Deulig media group. Lang moved on to work at Nero Film AG, where he made his first sound motion picture, *M*, starring Peter Lorre as a child murderer who is tracked down and brought to justice by other criminals disgusted by his grotesque crimes. *M* is often considered to be Lang's greatest film.

Lang enjoyed nurturing the legend that he had been invited by Hitler's right-hand man, Joseph Goebbels, to become the official filmmaker of the Third Reich. Supposedly the director packed his bags after the meeting and left Germany so quickly that he wasn't able to withdraw his money form the bank. While such stories are true of other German film personalities, the historical record shows that Lang did get his money out of Germany and even made several return trips until the political environment became too uncomfortable for him. Lang worked

M (1931 GERMANY), DIRECTED BY FRITZ LANG, SHOWN AT LEFT, FOREGROUND: PETER LORRE (AS HANS BECKERT)

NERO-FILM AG/FOREMCO PICTURES COMPANY/PHOTOFEST

in Europe in the early thirties for Twentieth Century Fox. MGM brought him to America in 1936 to direct the film *Fury*. He moved to Fox the next year and remained there until 1943.

During his time in Hollywood, Lang developed a reputation for being a dictatorial and difficult director. He worked mostly as a freelancer, never remaining at a company for very long. Lang's American films were mostly westerns and crime dramas that incorporated expressionist style with the hard-bitten style of Hollywood detective stories of the time. As the decade of the fifties progressed, Lang found it increasingly difficult to find work. He returned to Germany and tried to revive his successful Dr. Mabuse series of films, with little success. He died in 1976.

THE RUSSIAN REVOLUTION AND SOVIET FILMMAKING

The first Russian Revolution took place in 1905 when the people's faith in Tsar Nicholas II had reached a low point after the defeat of the Russian navy by Japan. An uprising occurred in St. Petersburg in late January. The Tsar ordered the military to shoot the demonstrators, killing hundreds of unarmed workers, women, and children. Known throughout Russia as "Bloody Sunday," the uprising served as inspiration for strikes and riots all over the country. The Tsar capitulated by forming a semidemocratic legislative body called the Imperial Duma. The people were placated for the time being.

In 1917 Russia was at war with Germany. It was losing due to a lack of modern industry and an adequate railway system to support the war effort. Conditions in St. Petersburg began to deteriorate. Three hundred and eighty-five thousand workers were on strike. There was no bread, and the citizens were starving. When the military garrison in the city joined the strike, the Tsar realized his situation was hopeless. He stepped down on February 28, leaving the country in the hands of a provisional government that was only slightly more popular than the Tsar.

Bolshevik leader Vladimir Ilyich Lenin was allowed to return from exile, and he immediately began to agitate against the incompetence of the provisional government. On October 24–25, 1917 the Red Guards stormed the Winter Palace headquarters of the provisional government and seized power in a bloodless coup. Lenin became the undisputed leader of the Russia and began to spread word of the revolution

VLADIMIR I. LENIN, 1917, SHOWN CENTER, AT PODIUM: VLADIMIR I. LENIN, NB: ANNOUNCING THAT THE REVOLUTION HAS BEEN SUCCESSFUL

throughout the land. Lenin was a great believer in the power of film to influence people. He used specially equipped railroad trains that functioned as both movie production facilities and makeshift movie theaters. These trains with their teams of newsreel photographers and political propagandists were dispatched all over the Soviet Union to make and show the new agitprop films to peasants in the countryside and factory workers in the cities alike.

The years immediately following the 1917 revolution were a time of artistic flowering for Soviet art. In Leningrad (formerly St. Petersburg) and Moscow new theatrical groups, all of which received government support, sprang up everywhere. Theater tickets and books of literature and poetry were plentiful and free. Lenin believed that film should become the universal language of the people. He encouraged the establishment of film schools to teach stage directors and writers how to work in film. Many revolutionary ideas were explored in these schools and workshops, resulting in a highly theoretical approach to film and theater.

The Kuleshov Workshop was the creation of Lev Kuleshov, who had begun his film career as a set designer for Alexander Khazonkov studios where he worked under director Evgeni Bauer. Kuleshov learned a great deal from Bauer including the belief that the director should have complete control over all aspects of film production, including sets and wardrobe. Kuleshov was also very influenced by American films, particularly the work of D. W. Griffith. After the revolution, Kuleshov established a workshop where he and other young directors could experiment and theorize about film. Workshop members included Vsevolod Pudovkin and Dziga Vertov.

Workshop members had acquired a print of Griffith's epic film *Intolerance*. They were awestruck by its spectacle and the genius of its editing. Lacking the resources to make their own experimental films, the workshop members began to take apart the reels of *Intolerance* and re-edit them. Soon they discovered that through editing the story and the pace of the film could be endlessly changed. Kuleshov's most famous editing experiment consisted of editing diverse images in juxtaposition with the expressionless face of an actor. The result was that viewer's perception of the actor's expression changed according to the images that adjoined it. Audiences who saw the film clips swore that the actor was giving a superb performance, where there hadn't been any performance at all. As a result of the Kuleshov workshops, young Soviet filmmakers began to place a very strong emphasis on film editing as the essential tool in film story telling.

Sergei Eisenstein

Eisenstein was born in 1898 in Riga, part of the Baltic territory of Latvia. His father was an architect and a civil engineer. Eisenstein's parents separated when he was seven resulting in his splitting his childhood between Riga and St. Petersburg. He received an expensive education, learning to speak French, German, and English fluently. Eisenstein followed his father's orders and trained as a civil engineer, but his first love was the theater. When the revolution broke out he joined the Red Army and was assigned as an engineer until he was able to convince his superiors to assign him to one of the Agitprop film trains. Eisenstein loved his new assignment, which he described as going into battle with a gun in one hand and a camera in the other.

After the revolution, Eisenstein applied to and was accepted to the theater school led by Vsevelod Meyerhold. The school was highly experimental. Meyerhold wanted to break completely with traditional theater and its naturalism and realism. He emphasized a technique he called "biomechanics," which consisted of precise stage movement and acrobatics. Most of the first generation of Soviet directors were trained by Meyerhold. While attending school, Eisenstein became involved with the Proletkult Theater group. At first he worked as a set designer, but within a short time he was directing plays. For Eisenstein the theater proved to be confining. In one play he included a live boxing match. In another he introduced a group of circus performers. His production of the play *Gas Masks* was staged entirely in a gas factory.

In 1924 the Prolekult Theater offered Eisenstein the opportunity to direct what was intended to be the first in a series of eight films dealing with the revolution. His first, and the only film that was actually produced in the series, was *Strike*, the story of a bloody labor uprising in Tsarist Russia. In making *Strike*, Eisenstein rejected the documentary approach to filmmaking. Instead he began to explore the idea of dialectical filmmaking. Dialectics was the Marxist process of change through the conflict of opposing forces, summed up by the concept "thesis plus antithesis equals synthesis." For Eisenstein dialectics meant the collision of images through editing to create a heightened emotional and intellectual reaction on the part of the audience. He compared dialectic montage to the small explosions in an internal combustion engine that propel the car forward.

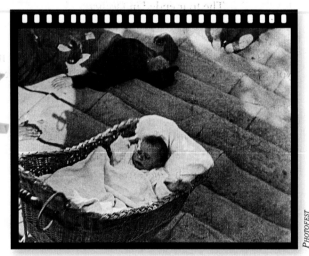

POTEMKIN (1925 U.S.S.R.) AKA BATTLESHIP POTEMKIN, DIRECTED BY SERGEI EISENSTEIN, SHOWN: ODESSA STEPS SEQUENCE

PHOTOFEST

Eisenstein's 1925 film *Battleship Potemkin* was made to celebrate a mutiny and strike aboard the Potemkin as it was moored in the Odessa harbor during the 1905 revolution. The film's most stirring scene takes place on the Odessa steps overlooking the harbor. When the citizens gather there to cheer on the mutineers, the Tsar's mounted Cossack cavalry and infantrymen are sent to wipe out the crowd. In a masterpiece of editing, shots of surging crowds are intercut with marching white boots, slashing sabers, huge closeups of terrified faces, and a motherless baby carriage falling helplessly down the steps. Ironically, *Potemkin* was the last film over which Eisenstein was to have complete artistic control. Lenin had died as a result of a series of strokes in 1924. He was replaced by the iron-fisted Joseph Stalin who exerted complete control over the Soviet film industry.

Eisenstein's next assignment was the film *October: Ten Days That Shook the World,* which was made on the tenth anniversary of the 1917 October revolution. Eisenstein set out to experiment with a new technique he called "intellectual montage." One example of the technique is a scene in which Aleksander Kerensky, the villain of the short-lived provisional government, ascends a flight of stairs. The ascent takes forever as Eisenstein cuts it into twenty separate shots to symbolize Kerensky's unquenchable thirst for power. These shots are, in turn, intercut with shots of a statue holding out a laurel wreath to symbolize Kerensky's vanity. Eisenstein's experiment was poorly received by the party bosses. Furthermore, Stalin insisted that many of the participants in the revolution be deleted from the film as they had fallen into disfavor with the new regime.

Eisenstein's next film, *The General Line,* dealt with the mechanization of Soviet farming. Once again he took an experimental approach in the symbolic use of color and, once again, Stalin was unimpressed, ordering the director to "reshoot a happier ending." In 1929, Eisenstein and his cameraman set off on a tour of Europe and America, giving lectures on his theories. The tour ended in Hollywood, where the director had a contract to make a film for Paramount. He worked on pre-producing two different films that never got made. Hollywood wasn't a good environment for the Marxist filmmaker. At one point Samuel Goldwyn told him, "I've seen your film, *Potemkin*, and admire it very much. What I would like is for you to do something of the same kind, but a little cheaper, for Ronald Coleman."

Next Eisenstein teamed up with the American socialist muckracking author Upton Sinclair. The two set off for Mexico to make a film about the history and the oppression of the Mexican people. It was to do for Mexico what Eisenstein's films had done for the people of the Soviet Union. However the two continually squabbled over money, and the director ultimately returned home with the film unfinished. Later Sinclair hired the producer of the Tarzan films to finish *Que Viva Mexico* in hopes of recouping the investment. Eisenstein returned to the Soviet Union, where he made two successful films, *Alexander Nevsky* and *Ivan the Terrible: Part One*. In order to receive approval for these projects, Eisenstein was forced to renounce his earlier work for its bourgeois style and formalism. *Ivan the Terrible: Part Two* was the director's last project. It became embroiled in an endless series of disagreements with Stalin and his henchmen and was never made. Eisenstein died in 1948 with the project half finished.

VSEVOLOD ILLARIONOVICH PUDOVKIN

Pudovkin was born in 1893 in an industrial city in the south of Russia. He studied physics and chemistry at Moscow University. When World War I began in 1914, he was drafted into the Russian artillery corp. After a year at battle, Pudovkin was wounded and taken prisoner. He escaped and returned to Moscow in 1918. His first job after the war was as a chemist in a laboratory. By chance he met Lev Kuleshov, who helped him enroll in the State Cinema School in 1920. Through the school, Pudovkin got a job writing and directing propaganda films for the government. During this time Pudovkin continued to participate in the Kuleshov workshops where he developed the theory that every film shot has two distinct elements: the visual reality it represents and the meaning it derives from its context through editing. As a demonstration of this principle, Pudovkin made a comedy short, *Chess Fever*

(1925), the story of a wedding gone wrong because of the groom's passion for chess.

Pudovkin is known to history for making four important films:

The Mechanics of the Brain was a 1926 documentary made in collaboration with famed Russian behavioral scientist Ivan Pavlov. The film demonstrates Pavlov's principal of "conditioned reflexes." Working with both animal and human subjects, the film shows the scientist training his subjects to respond in an almost mechanical, subthinking manner to a variety of stimuli.

Mother (1926) is based on a story by Maxim Gorky that is set during the 1905 revolution. A mother becomes distraught over her son's involvement in the anti-tsarist trade-union movement. She accidentally betrays him to the police, and he is imprisoned after a show trial. This radicalizes the mother, who helps lead a political demonstration that ends in her son's escape. In making the film Pudovkin attempted to tone down the performances of the actors who played the mother and the son, in the belief that, through editing, he could add to the emotional intensity better than what would be possible through their acting performances alone. Belief in this theory led Pudovkin to shy away from experienced actors in favor of amateurs.

KONETS SANKT-PETERBURGA (1927) AKA THE END OF ST. PETERSBURG, DIRECTED BY VSEVOLOD PUDOVKIN, MIKHAIL DOLLER (CO-DIRECTOR)

The End of St. Petersburg (1927) commemorates the tenth anniversary of the revolution. It is the story of a young peasant from the countryside who becomes swept up in the monumental events of the time. Pudovkin tested his theory of amateur actors by casting as the film's lead a young man who had shown up intending to be in a crowd scene. Through carefully designed camera work and editing, the director was able to make it appear as if the actor were giving one of the greatest performances in history. *St. Petersburg* was one of the first such films to be seen outside the Soviet Union. Its showing at the Roxy Theater in New York was a sensation. Particularly noteworthy was a montage sequence in which Pudovkin intercuts shots of gleeful stock speculators cavorting on the exchange floor with the lifeless mangled bodies of soldiers on the warfront. *St. Petersburg* was recognized as a cinematic classic and became a subject for study by film students around the world.

Storm Over Asia (1928) is set in outer-Mongolia, the homeland of Genghis Khan. The story is set in 1918, a time when retreating Russian nobles partnered with mercenary soldiers to conquer and claim the territory as their new enclave. Once again, Pudovkin's work was hailed around the world as a great epic film, but he was tiring of the rigors of location filmmaking and announced his semi-retirement, becoming a teacher and mentor to a new generation.

DZIGA VERTOV

Vertov was born Denis Arkadyevitch Kaufman in 1896 in Bialystock, Poland. His father was a Jewish intellectual and book dealer. As a child, Kaufman studied violin and piano and was an accomplished poet by age ten. In 1916 he enrolled in the Petrograd Psychoneurological Institute, where he studied human reactions to sounds he recorded and edited in his Laboratory of Hearing. He was attempting to create new sound effects through the rhythmic grouping of phonetic units. This work caused Kaufman to invent a *nom de guerre* for himself, Dziga Vertov (literally, "spinning top"). He was hired in 1918 to be the assistant to Mikhail Koltstov, the head of the Moscow Film Committee's newsreel division and became a contributing member of the Kuleshov workshops.

In 1919 Vertov and his wife, a film editor, formed a group of young filmmakers who called themselves "Kinoks" or Kino-Eye (cinema eye). They began by publishing a number of theoretical manifestos in avant-garde journals. They rejected "staged" films with their neatly and artificially plotted stories, movie stars, and all the studio approaches to making films. The Kinoks believed that the cinema of the future should be fact based and represent "life caught unaware." They saw the camera lens as a machine that could see and record without bias. Between 1922 and 1925 Vertov directed twenty-three newsreels

THE MAN WITH A MOVIE CAMERA (1929 USSR) AKA CHELOVEK'S KINO-APPARATOM, DIRECTED BY DZIGA VERTOV

VUFKU/PHOTOFEST

that he claimed were "Kino-Pravda," or "cinema truth"; *Pravda* was also the name of the official communist party newspaper. Vertov began to make more elaborate and expressive films by assembling film clips. The result looks very modern today.

The central Soviet film authorities were skeptical of what they saw as Vertov's overly theoretical approach to filmmaking. The establishment's aim was to produce propaganda films that inspired the workers and explained government policies. Vertov's work served neither purpose. In 1926 he made two films, *Stride Soviet* and *A Sixth of the World*, neither of which was well received by the party bosses. Were he not a devoted and vocal Marxist, Vertov might not have received the necessary financing to do his work. When he accepted studio financing to make his long-awaited pet project, *Man with a Movie Camera* (1929), the Kinok group disbanded in protest over its leader's willingness to "sell out" to the studio. *Man with a Movie Camera* was made up of film clips made in a number of cities over an extended time. It is an attempt to show a day in the life of a city, and at the same time, to show how the movie making process works. At one point the film stops for an edit decision to be made. There is a preoccupation with movie theaters and machinery that resembles movie machines. The film succeeds in reminding the audience that what they are engaged in is watching the product of a mechanical process and not in taking a flight of fantasy. Many years later filmmakers from the cinéma vérité and Dogme movements would revisit and modernize Vertov's theories.

In spite of Vertov's sincere attempts to blend Marxist ideology with film theory, the Soviet film establishment had grown impatient with his work. To the establishment, it lacked utilitarian value and was self-indulgent. While he was never renounced nor suppressed as a filmmaker, Vertov was by 1930 no longer making films. He continued to write and explore the theoretical side of cinema until his death in 1954.

KONSTANTIN STANISLAVSKI

Stanislavski created the first system or method for teaching acting. He was born Konstantin Sergeyevich Alexeyev in Moscow in 1863. His family members were wealthy merchants who also dabbled in theater. Throughout his life in the theater Stanislavski was also involved in family business, organizing shareholders meetings and keeping account books. In order not to compromise the family name he took the stage name Stanislavski when he was twenty-five. At that same time he founded his first amateur theater group, the Society of Art and Literature. Through this venture he became skilled in all aspects of stagecraft and began to develop theories about acting. In 1898 he co-founded the Moscow Art Theater, Russia's first ensemble theater, which was devoted to experimentation and unconventional dramatic approaches.

Soon Stanislavski was teaching a method of acting in which the actor would meticulously research the situation created by the script and break down the text according to the character's motivations and emotions. Next the actor would recall a similar experience and emotion in his own life. When performing his role, the actor was to recall and concentrate on what he or she was feeling when they faced the similar situation from their past. Rather than attempting to layer their performance with mannerisms, the actor would trust their emotional context to give the character its form.

Stanislavski's method was particularly well suited for performing the works of new playwrights such as Chekhov, Gorky, Strindberg, and Ibsen. During the 1905 revolution Stanislavski remained oblivious to the changing political environment. When the world-changing events of 1917 occurred, his family history of capitalism nearly resulted in his being declared an enemy of the revolution. This would have certainly resulted in his execution. However, Lenin, who understood Stanislavski's contribution to the arts, intervened and gave him protection. The Stanislavski method was proclaimed the style for the new revolutionary theater, and in 1918 he was put in charge of a school for young actors. He continued to write and teach until his death in 1938. Today the Stanislavski method is still widely seen as a valid approach to acting.

FRANCE BETWEEN THE WORLD WARS

At the end of the First World War in 1919 the French film industry had all but collapsed. Paris, however, was rapidly becoming the center of postwar art movements. The renowned lost generation of would-be artists who had come to Europe for the war now remained in Paris to invent the new art of the twentieth century. Literary masters such as Ernest Hemingway, F. Scott Fitzgerald, Ezra Pound, and T. S. Eliot regularly shared glasses of claret and absinthe with painters such as Pablo Picasso and Salvador Dalí in Gertrude Stein's Parisian salon. They would endlessly discuss the theories of Freud and argue about Dadaism, the meaning of *modernism*, and how the mechanized brutality of the war had changed mankind forever.

Sigmund Freud published his monumental work *The Interpretation of Dreams* in 1900. The First International Congress of Psychoanalysis was held in 1908. In 1900 Max Planck had published his *Theory of Quantum Physics*, and Albert Einstein's theories of relativity were introduced to the world between 1905 and 1915. In July 1917 Tristan Tzara published the first issue of *Dada Magazine*, which proclaimed the stupidity of war and led to the organization of subversive art happenings that were aimed at shocking the art world into consciousness. For the French film community the pursuit of art became the goal of all filmmaking that was not part of the commercial entertainment wing of the industry.

SURREALISM: SALVADOR DALÍ AND LUIS BUÑUEL

During World War I ten million people were killed and another twenty million were injured. Andre Breton was a doctor working at a neurological ward at a hospital in Nantes, when he began to have success treating patients with Freudian therapeutic techniques. When the war ended Breton began to explore the application of those techniques and theories to art. He believed that artists possessed a less pronounced division between their conscious and subconscious minds. He formed a group of young artists for the purpose of exploring the subconscious mind. Their goal was to achieve the state of surrealism, "pure psychic automatism." Their art would be the expression of subconscious thought without interpretation and without adherence to the rules of some art movement.

Dalí's approach was to deconstruct the classical imagery that he had learned in the art academies of Europe and reassemble it with the images from his subconscious. During his time in Paris, Dalí became reacquainted with a fellow art student from Spain, Luis Buñuel. Buñuel was pursuing the artistic possibilities of film at the time and proposed that the two collaborate on a film project. In 1929 they made the first surrealist masterpiece, *Un Chien Andalou*. The short film is an exploration of disturbing images. It begins with a scene in which a woman appears to have her eyeball sliced in two with a straight razor. One recurring image is a new take on the idea of stigmata with ants emerging from the Christ-like wounds on the protagonist's hand. Many repeating motifs recall the strict Roman Catholicism under which the two artists were raised. One scene shows the protagonist attempting to molest his lover, but to reach her he must carry the impossible burden of the stone tablets of the ten commandments, two priests, and two grand pianos with two dead horses oozing gore under the piano lids.

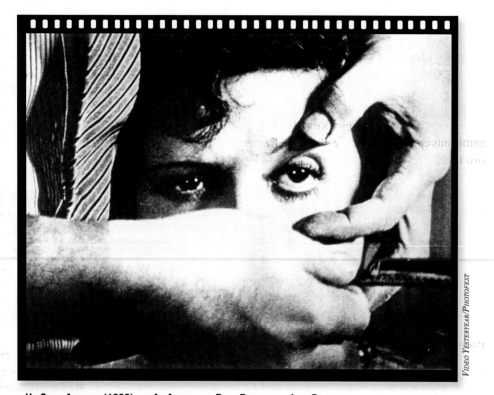

Video Yesteryear/Photofest

Un Chien Andalou (1929) aka An Andalusian Dog, Directed by Luis Bunuel

Un Chien Andalou is meant to be a provocation. It defies the audience to find a narrative that doesn't exist. Its imagery seems to form a mosaiclike jigsaw puzzle, except the parts don't fit together. The film defies reason. The two artists collaborated several more times, but in later life, Buñuel and Dalí focused individually on their respective primary media, film and painting.

Abel Gance was born in Paris in 1889. He was the illegitimate son of a successful physician. Although he took the name of his taxi driver stepfather, Gance's birth father continued to support him throughout his childhood. He was the beneficiary of a first-class education and began law studies after primary school. By age nineteen, Gance had abandoned law in favor of the theater and film. He worked as an actor and scenarist. In 1911 he made his first film. In the years leading up to World War I, Gance developed a reputation as a young filmmaker on the rise. In 1915 he began a life long exploration of cinema technique while working on *La Folie du Docteur Tube* with cameraman Léonce-Henry Burel. The two used mirrors and other photographic effects to create the illusion of characters' appearances being changed by a magical powder.

Over the next few years most of Gance's films were thrillers made in the style of D. W. Griffith. In the waning moments of the war, Gance made his first epic film, an anti-war statement titled *J'accuse* (1919). In the film's climactic scene, the war dead arise from their graves to demand the reason for all of the slaughter. Ironically, many of the actors who appear in the scene were soldiers on leave from the fighting who would return to battle and perish before the Armistice.

La Roue (1920) was Gance's most ambitious epic. Consisting of thirty-two reels, it required three evenings to view. It is the story of the hardships faced by railroad workers. It equates the turning of the wheels in machines to the wheel of life. Given the extraordinary length of the film Gance was able to introduce many fully realized characters and several recurring symbolic motifs. It was extremely well received by figures in the art world as diverse as Pablo Picasso and Akira Kurosawa. However, attempts to distribute the film commercially continually failed because there was no way to edit it down to commercial length.

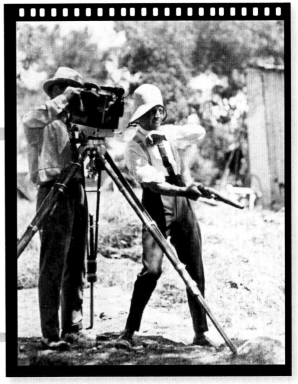

ABEL GANCE, 1927, NB: SHOOTING NAPOLEON (1927)

Gance's greatest achievement is his 1927 film, *Napoleon*. After two years of production the elaborate film premiered at the Paris Opera House. *Napoleon* has a running time of over six hours and required three projectors and a specially fabricated three-section screen for proper showing. The story chronicles the early life of Emperor Napoleon and his rise to power. Gance uses long sequences of rapid montage and handheld camera technique to put the audience members inside the action. At one point scenes of discord and anarchy in the Parliament are intercut with scenes of Napoleon adrift in a small boat on an impossibly stormy sea. To amplify the disorganization of the Parliament, Gance swings the camera back and forth tethered to a rope to create a sense of confusion. The three-screen sequences are used both for creating extremely wide panoramas and triptychs in which three different story lines are followed simultaneously.

Like *La Roue*, *Napoleon* was much too impractical for commercial distribution. MGM had invested a huge some of money in it to acquire the American rights. However, there was little audience interest because of the advent of sound and the craze for talking pictures. The seventy-nine minute version of the film eventually released in America did more to hurt than enhance its reputation. The complete film would not be seen in this country until the late fifties.

Jean Renoir was the second son of the great impressionist painter, Auguste Renoir. His childhood was divided between the family home in Paris and their country estate in the south of France. Young Jean's curiosity was constantly engaged and satisfied. He had an early fascination for puppet theater and the books of Alexandre Dumas. He studied mathematics at the University of Aix-en-Provence before enlisting in the French artillery corps in 1913. He was wounded twice and walked with a limp as a result of a bullet in his thigh. Auguste Renoir died at the war's end in 1919, leaving his sons a small fortune. Jean soon married his father's beautiful model, Catherine Hessling, who wanted to become an actress.

Renoir formed a motion picture production company with his inheritance and directed his first film starring his wife titled *La Fille de L'eau* (1924). He made two other films with his wife, an adaptation of Zola's novel *Nana*, and an erotic fantasy before the advent of sound in 1928. Both films failed miserably and the marriage soon broke up. Renoir's first sound film, *La Chienne*, was made in 1931. He made another film in 1932, *Boudu Sauvé Des Eaux*, the story of a hobo who changes his life. It was remade in America in 1989 as *Down and Out in Beverly Hills*.

La Grande Illusion (1937) is Renoir's anti-war masterpiece. It is the story of French aviators who have been captured and must endure life as German prisoners of war. Their first POW camp is run by a group of captured British officers who exert a very high discipline and organize their own affairs including producing elaborate stage shows for the entertainment of both prisoners and camp guards. Their discipline extends to a very well organized plan for escape. Each inmate's best talent is used to dig an ingenious tunnel to the outside. Several French prisoners are caught during the escape and sent to an isolated castle from which escape is impossible. The camp commandant, played by Erich von Stroheim, is a German nobleman who attempts to befriend the

GRAND ILLUSION (1937 FRANCE) AKA LA GRANDE ILLUSION, DIRECTED BY JEAN RENOIR, SHOWN FROM LEFT: PIERRE FRESNAY, ERICH VON STROHEIM

leader of the French prisoners, a French nobleman, Count Boeldieu. While the German meditates about having more in common with his royal prisoner than with his own men, the Count plots escape.

La Grande Illusion is a beautiful film of naturalistic style. Renoir uses doorways and windows to frame much of the action as if it were a painting brought to life. The characters in the film are realistic, not overly dramatized. They have great depth, and the film avoids stereotypes in favor of examining the human condition. In the last act of the film two escaped Frenchmen (one a rich Jewish banker, the other a mechanic) survive only because of the help of a German widow who has lost her husband and brothers to the war.

La Règle Du Jeu (*The Rules of the Game* 1939) is Renoir's last prewar film. It deals with the silly romances of a group of French aristocrats and the manner in which their childish behavior is mirrored by their servants. It takes place during a weekend party on the country estate of a rich Count. His wife is in love with an aviator, the count is bored with his mistress, and everyone is in the mood for infidelity. The game referred to in the title is the game of adultery. As in *La Grande Illusion,* Renoir uses framing devices extensively. In one scene a stage is constructed in the Count's ballroom, and the guests put on a surreal play that enchants the entire household. A rabbit hunting scene is used to recall the cold bloodedness of both war and adultery.

Unfortunately, by the time *Rules of the Game* was complete, the Germans had occupied France. The film was suppressed by the Nazis, who thought its critique of the decadence of European aristocracy was also a critique of German imperialism. Renoir escaped France to live most of the rest of his life in Hollywood. *Rules of the Game* would not be seen in America until after the Second World War.

ENGLAND BETWEEN THE WORLD WARS

At the end of World War I the British film industry was in a shambles. American films and movie stars, who hadn't been adversely affected by the war, dominated English theaters. The little filmmaking that did take place in Great Britain was mostly the product of American, French, and German companies that had opened branch offices to exploit what little talent existed in the country. When the government mandated that British films appear on British screens, cheaply made "quota quickies" were the best the indigenous industry could muster. The situation called for a complete rebuilding of the British motion picture business.

Alexander Korda was born in Hungary in 1893. His father was the manager of a large country estate where the Korda family lived. Alexander's father died when he was thirteen, leaving the family destitute and forcing Korda to support himself. His first job was at a newspaper. By the time he was sixteen he was a full-time reporter. He was also a voracious reader and student of languages. Blessed with a photographic memory, Korda was fluent in six languages by the time he reached his thirties.

In 1911 Korda began a career in film doing odd jobs at the Pathe studio in Paris, the best production facility in the world at the time. Soon he returned home, where a new generation of filmmakers, including Michael Curtiz and George Cukor, were putting their native

Hungary on the motion picture map. During the First World War, Korda acquired financing to start his own production company named Corvin Films. He both managed the company and produced and directed films. In 1919 Korda left Hungary for Hollywood. He made three films in America, none of which was successful. He convinced Fox to release him from his contract and returned to Europe in 1930 to make several successful films in both France and Germany.

Korda moved to England in 1931. The woeful state of the film industry presented many opportunities for such a talented young man. Korda invested his life savings and everything he could borrow to start his own company, London Film Productions. His first project was the very expensive and very successful *The Private Life of Henry III* (1933), starring the brilliant Charles Laughton. *Henry* was extremely well received in America and won an Oscar for Best Film, which led to a distribution deal with United Artists. Having left Hollywood in disgrace, Korda returned at the top of his game. The deal with UA gave him enough money to build the huge Denham film studio on a 165-acre estate outside of London. Denham's first production was *The Private Life of Don Juan* (1934), notable only for being the last film in which silent film pioneer Douglas Fairbanks appeared.

THE PRIVATE LIFE OF HENRY VIII (1933), DIRECTED BY ALEXANDER KORDA, SHOWN FROM LEFT: CHARLES LAUGHTON, BINNIE BARNES

United Artists/Photofest

Korda teamed up with Laughton again in 1936 to make *Rembrandt*, another very successful collaboration between the two. From this point on Korda withdrew from directing for a time to concentrate on running the business. He had a great eye for talent and managed to attract to his roster excellent directors and an impressive list of actors including Leslie Howard, Merle Oberon, Robert Donat, and Vivien Leigh.

J. Arthur Rank was a far less impressive man than Alexander Korda. He was born in 1888 into a very wealthy British merchant family. For much of his early life, Rank was happy working for his father. His one attempt to break out was to create the Peterkins Self-Raising Flour Company in the late 1920s. When the company failed, Rank went back to work for his father.

Rank was a devout Methodist who believed that film was a good medium for teaching religion in British Sunday Schools. He became the leader of the Religious Film Society to further that interest. The English film industry was in desperate need of investment capital, and the Rank family had plenty of that. During the 1930s he began to acquire both theaters and film production facilities, including the highly respected Odeon Cinema theater company and the historic Gaumont-British production company.

Rank had no pretensions of being a filmmaker himself. His only aspiration was to manage a well-run business. The result of this philosophy was to make his companies attractive to filmmakers who wanted to be free of film executives' interference in the creative process. Many excellent directors did some of their best work for Rank, including Michael Powell, Frank Launder, and David Lean. Lean, the director of many great epic films, once said of Rank, "We can make any subject we wish, with as much money as we think that subject should have spent on it. We can cast whichever actors we choose, and we have no interference with the way the film is made.... Not one of us is bound by any form of contract. We are there because we want to be there."

Alfred Hitchcock represents the awakening of British film invention and creativity. There is much contradicted lore about him, as is true of many early and colorful motion picture personalities. Hitchcock was born in London in 1899. His father was a poultry dealer and produce importer. As a boy Hitch-cock was fond of exploring his city. By the time he was eight he had ridden every bus line and thoroughly explored the waterfront and shipping terminals. The Hitchcock family was part of the Catholic minority in England. They were very devout and saw to it that their son received a proper and challenging Jesuit education. He was also the recipient of strict parenting. One legendary story of Hitchcock's childhood involves a situation in which the boy had misbehaved. His father sent him with a note to the local police station, where he was put in a jail cell for a short time, after which the police

BLACKMAIL (1929, BRITISH), DIRECTED BY ALFRED HITCHCOCK, SHOWN FROM LEFT: JOHN LONGDEN (AS DETECTIVE FRANK WEBBER), ANNY ONDRA (AS ALICE WHITE), DONALD CALTHROP (AS TRACY)

chief told him, "This is what we do to naughty little boys." This gave rise to one of Hitchcock's many phobias, this one related to confinement and uniformed police.

After graduating from St. Ignatius College preparatory school, Hitchcock enrolled at the University of London to study electrical engineering. He was forced to quit school for lack of financial support after his father's untimely death. He began the task of supporting his family by going to work for a cable manufacturing company. Despite the dullness of the work, he advanced to a more creative position in the advertising department. In late 1919 the Famous Players-Lasky Company announced the opening of a London studio. Hitchcock, who had always harbored ambitions of being an artist, saw an opportunity for improving the graphic design of the title cards used to communicate important information and dialogue in silent movies. He made samples of his work and barged through the lines of job seekers to secure an audience with the boss, who recognized the creativeness and quality of the work and hired Hitchcock on the spot.

By 1923 Hitchcock had become a production designer and his taste was well respected within the studio. He was offered a better position at Gainsborough Pictures in Islington and took it. During the next two years he continued to contribute excellent designs while being groomed to direct by filling in when principal directors were unable to show up for work. His big break occurred when he was sent to Munich, Germany to direct his first film, *The Pleasure Garden* (1925). Germany was a place where young directors were taught the expressionist style of filmmaking. It is probable that Hitchcock was exposed to mentors such as F. W. Murnau as part of his German education. His second and last German film was *The Mountain Eagle* (1926).

Upon his return to England, Hitchcock was given the opportunity to direct his first suspense film, *The Lodger* (1926), about a man mistaken for the infamous prostitute killer Jack the Ripper. Following the film's completion, Hitchcock married a screenwriter from Lasky, Alma Reville. The following year he moved to British International Pictures (BIP) and its Elstree studios. His first film was a boxing picture titled *The Ring* (1927), a big success. This was followed by a series of uneven efforts, the quality reflected less Hitchcock's responsibility than the state of the British film industry at the time. His last silent film, *Blackmail* (1929) was also his first sound picture, a film that the studio decided to remake for the new technology. With *Blackmail*, Hitchcock not only proved his technical ability to adapt to sound technology but also his fortitude to deal with the shifting challenges of filmmaking.

A series of mediocre pictures for BIP convinced Hitchcock to return to Gaumont-British, where he was able to pursue his interest in the suspense genre. There he developed many theories, some based on expressionism, about how to manipulate the audience and the narrative to create a sense of tension and anxiety. His developing theories would become the hallmark of Hitchcock's mastery of suspense. He divulged to the audience information he withheld from the characters in the film. The result was immediate anxiety on the part of the audience when they witnessed characters' oblivion to what the audience knew was about to happen. Hitchcock learned to hide the event that sets the plot in motion rather than telegraphing it. This kept the audience searching for the answer to the question, "What happened?"

In the mid thirties Hitchcock made five films that set forth the new rules for movie suspense: *The Man Who Knew Too Much* (1934), *The 39 Steps* (1935), *The Secret Agent* (1936), *Sabotage* (1936), and *The Lady Vanishes* (1938). By this time the winds of World War II were propelling Hitchcock toward Hollywood.

CHAPTER 7

HOLLYWOOD AND THE GREAT DEPRESSION

THE CRASH

Many signs of an economic meltdown preceded the 1929 stock market crash. During the decade of the Roaring Twenties an average of 600 banks failed each year. Farm land decreased in value by forty percent. Union membership in the American Federation of Labor declined from 5.1 million to 3.4 million. By the end of the decade, the richest one percent of Americans owned forty percent of the nation's wealth. For those in the working class, economic conditions were already challenging. The average per-capita income was only $750. The average farmer struggled to get by on $273 per year for each household member.

FRANKLIN DELANO ROOSEVELT, 1930S

PHOTOFEST

Black Tuesday came on October 24, 1929. By the end of the month the total value of stock shares fell by forty percent. A little over two years later one quarter of America's workers found themselves unemployed. Ten thousand banks had failed, and the gross national product had decreased by thirty-one percent. Shares of stock in the industrial companies lost eighty percent of their value. The United States was not alone in this calamity. The rest of the world was also mired in economic despair. In the decade that followed the 1929 crash, cities were brimming with the unemployed standing in breadlines all day to get a free meal. Families were forced to turn out their able-bodied adolescent boys as young as ten years old to reduce the number of mouths to feed. Gangs of hobo boys and men hopped freight trains all over the country in search of jobs or handouts. Society was coming apart at the seams. The only ray of hope came in the form of Franklin Delano Roosevelt, who had defeated Herbert Hoover by an astonishing margin of twenty-two million to fifteen million votes. But even the ebullient FDR was faced with a task more daunting than any president had inherited since the Civil War.

THE ECONOMICS OF THE MOTION PICTURE INDUSTRY

All through 1930's the studios insisted on characterizing the crash as temporary in the belief that a return to "normalcy" was imminent. But the next year it would be impossible to ignore the obvious. In most markets box office receipts fell between ten and thirty-five percent. By the summer of 1932, six thousand American theaters—almost one third the total number—were shuttered. At the peak of the 1920s, weekly ticket sales surpassed 100 million at a time when the total population of the country was only 112 million. At one point in 1933 weekly ticket sales were down to forty million but eventually leveled off at sixty million. At the 1932 Paramount stockholder's meeting, Adolph Zukor wept as he told the audience his heart was broken by the catastrophe that had befallen the company. The next year both Paramount and RKO chose to go into receivership to avoid outright bankruptcy. Accustomed to limitless growth and profits, the motion picture industry had met its first major financial setback in its history.

By the end of 1932 the word from New York to Hollywood was to cut costs and prepare for a long decline. The surviving theaters were forced to cancel the live entertainment portions of their programs and lay off staff. All sorts of gimmicks were employed to lure ticket buyers. Fox Theaters introduced "bank nights" on which audience members participated in drawings for cash prizes. The Rialto Theaters instituted dish night: one night each week theaters handed out a different piece of dinnerware at the door. Persistent theater goers were able to acquire sets of china that they otherwise could not afford. One enterprising theater owner actually employed a doctor who set up shop in the lobby to give psychiatric counseling to downcast ticket holders.

$100 WILL BUY A CAR, **O**NE RESULT OF THE STOCK MARKET CRASH IN **1929.**

All of the cost cutting and ticket selling come-ons worked well, but the strategy most successful at keeping the seats full was to simply make better, more entertaining movies. The people in the creative end of the industry understood how fortunate they were to be working at all, let alone in an industry that still paid better than almost anything else. The depression was a powerful motivator. Everyone did their best to hold on to their jobs. As a result, the thirties became a decade of great inventiveness and creation. New film genres emerged that reflected both the hopes and fears of the country. As counterpoint to the movies' outpouring of imagination was the imposition of a strict code of censorship that served to mollify the industry's critics and ensure that the movies would not become an instrument of social insurrection.

THE GATHERING STORM OF CENSORSHIP

When Will Hays was appointed to "clean up" the movies in December 1921, an expectation of higher morality was planted in the minds of those who objected to the perceived indecency of many films. The Roman Catholic Church and its affiliated Legion of Decency were leaders in the censorship movement. The Legion reviewed the output of the motion picture industry, giving its seal of approval for movies that were morally upright and socially redeeming. Those films that strayed over the line into salaciousness were denied the seal, and it was expected that church goers would steer clear of such unwholesomeness. Church goers were reminded every Sunday that the very high price for seeing unapproved movies was eternal damnation.

Censorship has very deep roots in American culture. Dating back to the pre-revolutionary colonial period, communities regularly exercised their right to remove from their midst and obstruct obscenity in printed material. Anyone possessing offensive documents would be severely punished, ostracized, and ridiculed. After the American Civil War, the country began to experience enormous waves of immigration led by young men from Europe seeking a better life in the cities and factory towns. As a result the streets teemed with young men who had a few nickels in their pockets with which to entertain themselves. Saloons, brothels, and penny arcades sprouted everywhere to separate these young patrons from their spare change. Polite society became apoplectic over the rampant immorality of the streets. One crusader for righteousness was Anthony Comstock, who joined the Young Men's Christian Association in New York to fight for decency. Comstock routinely tipped off the police about where they might arrest someone for lewdness. His campaign even reached the U.S. Congress, which passed what is called the Comstock Act in 1873, outlawing the use of the U.S. Postal Service for transporting obscene material and goods, especially means of contraception, which were found to be particularly objectionable.

When the first movies were shown in penny arcades in the late 1890s, they instantly became the target of reformers. In 1907 the cities of New York and Chicago enacted movie censorship ordinances. In both cases the police were given the responsibility and power to regulate movies in terms of decency. On Christmas Eve, 1908 the New York City Police Commissioner announced the revocation of licenses for 550 film venues. In 1915 the Supreme Court got involved when it handed down the decision in the case of Mutual v. Ohio, stating that the movie industry was a business enterprise and, as such, did not enjoy free-press rights under the First Amendment. In 1916 the heads of the motion picture industry made their own attempt to clean up the movies by forming the National Association of the Motion Picture Industry. However, the attempt was half-hearted and ineffective. By 1921 the movies were trying to appease their critics once again with the appointment of Will Hays to head the new Motion Picture Producers and Distributors of America. Again the organization failed to achieve its purpose. Also in 1921 the State of New York appointed a new, statewide Motion Picture Commission. This commission would eventually become the most activist and powerful censorship body in the country.

Throughout the 1920s religious and social reform organizations followed the leadership of the Legion of Decency in calling for the movie industry to reform itself. But the resistance to lurid movies was surpassed only by the audience's appetite for sexy films. It was clear that the industry would suffer the loss of audience members if it reformed. In the mid twenties, Will Hayes created a list of thirty-six rules for ridding the movies of indecency, but no one in the business seemed to notice. In 1930 the Archbishop of Chicago took matters into his own hands. He appointed a committee of lay church members and Jesuit scholars to create a list of dos and don'ts for movies. When Hays received the final draft he exclaimed it was what he had been seeking for almost a decade. What became known as the Production Code was adopted by the motion picture industry on March 31, 1930. However, no provision was made for enforcement. In fact the most effective censorship body was still the New York Commission.

In 1928 the New York State Motion Picture Commission had excised more than four thousand scenes from the films it reviewed. This presented a business problem for Hollywood that would not be fully resolved until 1934. Filmmakers on the West Coast were in the fog as they tried to second-guess how their product would be received in New York. They were forced to reedit their films and often faced the necessity of calling back the cast and crew and reassembling sets to accomplish costly re-shoots of movies that had been rendered incoherent by the censors. Gradually, the industry began to accept the idea of the Production Code. However, the rewards for skirting its oppressive dictates were still too great to resist. Much of what drew audiences to the theaters in the early years of the depression was forbidden by the code.

THE GANGSTER CYCLE

Gangster films date back to the earliest days of the movies. Audiences have always been attracted to the danger and daringness of the criminal class. Many Americans had become minor criminals themselves as a result of Prohibition. On January 16, 1920 the 18th Amendment to the Constitution went into effect. Backed by the Anti Saloon League and the Women's Christian Temperance Union, the new law made it a federal crime to sell, transport, possess, or consume alcoholic beverages in America. Almost immediately a new kind of criminal appeared on the scene— the bootleggers who trafficked in alcohol. Since many Americans had no intention giving up drinking, an entire underground industry sprang up to serve them. Illegal nightclubs called *speakeasies* served up a lively concoction of jazz and cocktails. It became fash-

LITTLE CAESAR (1931 WARNER BROS), DIRECTED BY MERVYN LEROY, SHOWN: EDWARD G. ROBINSON (AS CESARE ENRICO 'RICO' BANDELLO)

ionable to be seen in the more glamorous clubs. Yet, it was all illegal. The twenties were economic good times for the most part, and the widespread urge to celebrate caused a decade-long slide in American's respect for the law. Real-life gangsters ran organized businesses, and in spite of the violence of the bootlegging industry, were often seen as Robin Hoods engaged in socially acceptable crime. There was no way the storytellers of Hollywood could resist such colorful characters.

Warner Brothers released the first great gangster talkie, Mervyn Leroy's *Little Caesar* in 1930. In it Edward G. Robinson plays Rico, who begins as a small-time thief and rises to the top of the Chicago rackets. It is more of an American success story than a call to lawlessness or a morality play. Depression-era audiences responded to the film's message that the individual can rise to the top through hard work and daring. *Little Caesar* was so successful that fifty more gangster films were brought to the screen the next year. The enthusiasm of the audience for the genre was counterbalanced by increased activism on the part of the New York State Film Commission. In 1931 more than one-fourth of all scenes excised by the Commission were from gangster films. Will Hays issued an edict, warning movie producers not to glorify gangsters and outlaws.

The movie industry was undeterred by the censors' backlash. Warner Brothers released a second gangster classic, *The Public Enemy*, directed by William Wellman in 1931. It stared James Cagney, who excelled at playing brash, tough-guy Irish American outlaws. The film contains the classic scene in which he juices a half grapefruit on the face of his nagging girlfriend. Of course one convention of the genre that filmmakers always observed in deference to public morality was that the protagonist would die at the end, usually in a blaze of gunfire.

THE PUBLIC ENEMY (1931), DIRECTED BY WILLIAM WELLMAN, SHOWN: JAMES CAGNEY, JEAN HARLOW

The last of the great films to emerge from the gangster cycle was *Scarface*, staring Paul Muni, a young New York stage actor who had made quite a splash in Hollywood. The film was the product of millionaire playboy aviator Howard Hughes; brilliant newspaper man turned screenwriter Ben Hecht; and mercurial free-agent director Howard Hawks. Hawks had convinced Hecht to take the project on by describing the story as a modern-day Borgia family living amidst the Chicago underworld, complete with the brother-sister incest plot line.

The resulting film was a dark, expressionistic bloodbath with an astonishing body count and a colorful, mad-dog killer for a protagonist. The censors were certain to hate it, but Hughes was audacious and had limitless resources, and Hawks and Hecht were so in demand by all of the studios that making such a blatantly provocative film didn't seem to faze them at all.

Production began at the end of June in 1931. Newcomer George Raft, who had previously worked as a gigolo, dancer, and mob bodyguard, was cast as the sidekick to Muni's Tony Comonte. Ann Dvorak, Hawks's sometime mistress,

SCARFACE (1932), DIRECTED BY HOWARD HAWKS, SHOWN FROM LEFT: GEORGE RAFT (AS GUINO RINALDO), PAUL MUNI (AS TONY CAMONTE)

played Comonte's sister, with whom he shares an unholy attraction. The censor's first objection was to the way the mother was portrayed as a hideous harpy who is fully aware of her children's wickedness. Photography on the film was completed at the end of October, and Hawks proceeded to his next project, leaving Hughes to oversee editing and negotiations with the Hays Office and the New York Commission. The censors' first demand was to reshoot the ending with Camonte's being hanged for his crimes. But that didn't satisfy Hays, who insisted another scene be added showing indignant citizens wringing their hands over the protagonist's exploits. The back and forth between Hughes and New York was expensive and lasted until March 1932. All of Hollywood took note. In the future, gangster films would need to be greatly toned down, so much so as to render the genre uninteresting.

SHYSTER MOVIES

A shyster is an unscrupulous lawyer, but in depression-era films they take on other forms such as crooked politicians, businessmen, and newspaper men. This type of character fed the mass notion that all of the economic chaos was the result of dirty dealing. Invariably, New York was the setting for these films. It was the financial center of the country and the place where the Great Depression had begun with the Wall Street crash of 1929. The most over-the-top of the newspaper films was *Scandal Sheet* (1931), in which a newspaper editor is such a scandal monger that he kills his unfaithful wife, then writes a story about it before surrendering to the law. Other prominent newspaper films of this type include *Front Page* and *Platinum Bomb*, both of which present an array of sleazy characters from all strata of society.

Shyster lawyer and politician films were equally popular and abundant. The 1932 Warner Brothers film *Lawyer Man* tells the story of an upstanding, small-time attorney who joins an upscale Park Avenue law firm. When he begins to protest the firm's shady practices, the other lawyers frame him in a scandal. As a result the young, idealistic lawyer becomes a shyster himself. Another Warner Brothers film, *The Dark Horse*, represents the unethical political arena. In it a political operative, just out of prison, is hired to manage the campaign of a candidate who is chosen for his dim-wittedness. The idea is to convince the voting public that the candidate is one of them. That the American democracy was being manipulated resonated with audiences, who sensed that somehow they were being cheated out of prosperity and hope.

PARAMOUNT PICTURES/PHOTOFEST

Scandal Sheet (1931), Directed by John Cromwell, Shown: George Bancroft

COMEDY: VAUDEVILLIANS, ROMANTICS, AND SCREWBALLS

The Marx Brothers: Surrealism, Chaos and Farce

The five Marx Brothers—Leonard "Chico" (1887), Adolph "Harpo" (1888), Julius "Groucho" (1890), Milton "Gummo" (1892), and Herbert "Zeppo" (1901)—were born in New York to Jewish immigrant parents from Germany. Their uncle, Al Shean, brother to their mother Minnie, was already a successful stage performer when the boys were born. Minnie thought that show business was a good way to earn a living and encouraged Shean to train the boys to perform. The first thing Shean did was to put Groucho on stage as a soprano with an existing vaudeville act. In 1908 he was joined by Harpo and Gummo. The new act, called "The Three Nightingales," eventually became the "Six Mascots" with all of the brothers performing. Their singing performances were complemented from the beginning by their natural gift for comedy and horsing around on stage. They soon became famous for a comedy skit titled *Fun in Hi Skule*, which was their first all-comedy stage appearance. With extensive coaching from their Uncle Al, the show was a success.

The brothers picked up their famous nicknames and fleshed out their comedy personas during their years on the road in vaudeville. Groucho was the ringleader of the group, with his comical grease-paint moustache and his ability to adlib one-liners with machine-gun rapidity. Harpo was given a red, and later a blonde, fright wig with instructions not to speak but to do his comedy in pantomime with extensive use of props including, car horns, giant scissors, and an assortment of blow torches. Chico was outfitted with a funny hat and ill-fitting clothes and directed to play the part of an Italian immigrant who mangles the English language. Gummo and Zeppo were relegated to playing the straight men, the butt of most jokes. Milton Marx left the act in 1918 to join the army. When he returned he went into business managing his brothers as well as other performers. All of the boys were excellent singers but Chico had a particular talent for playing the piano in a comic manner, which he claimed to have developed working in brothels. Harpo had a talent for coaxing music out of any instrument he encountered, but the harp became part of his identity. Over time he was recognized as a virtuoso on the instrument, and his technique was widely studied by concert musicians.

During the late teens and early 1920s the Marx Brothers toured the country endlessly, performing their ever evolving comedy and music performances. They became famous for comedy improvisations that satirized conventional society. By 1924 they were successful enough to acquire backing to stage a Broadway revue-style show. Vaudeville is a series of performances by different kinds of performers and acts such as singers, dancers, jugglers, acrobats, magicians, and comedians. A revue is a show that is lightly scripted with a continuous storyline and staged to feature one or two main acts. With their multitalented ability to entertain

Paramount Pictures/Photofest

THE COCOANUTS (1929), DIRECTED BY ROBERT FLOREY, JOSEPH SANTLEY, SHOWN FROM LEFT: ZEPPO MARX, GROUCHO MARX, CHICO MARX, HARPO MARX

in many different styles, the Marx Brothers were perfect for this type of stage show. Their first show was primarily a musical revue titled *I'll Say She Is*. It was followed by two comedy shows with some music *Cocoanuts* (1925–26) and *Animal Crackers* (1928–29). Noted playwright George S. Kaufman contributed a great deal of material to the last two shows.

Paramount signed the Marx Brothers to reprise their stage shows for the movie screen in 1929. The deal was engineered by Chico, who had become the business man of the team. *Cocoanuts* was made that same year and, in keeping with the early sound film practices, it was done as a filmed stage play rather than as a play adapted for the motion picture screen. *Animal Crackers* followed in 1930. It was opened up slightly more than the previous film but still had the feel of taking place on a theater stage. After work was completed on the two films, the Marx Brothers were put under studio contract, and they moved their base of operations to Los Angeles.

The studio assigned Herman Mankiewicz to produce the Marx Brothers' Hollywood films. Mankiewicz had a reputation as a prankster, which blended quite well with the brothers' sensibilities. Later in his career Mankiewicz teamed up with Orson Welles to write *Citizen Kane*, perhaps movie history's biggest prank of all. One technique that had made the Marx Brothers' shows and first two films successful was to develop the script on the road, constantly shaping and honing the material until it was as tight as possible. In Hollywood, the brothers needed to adapt to a more cinematic approach. Their first Hollywood film, *Monkey Business*, was written by noted playwright S. J. Perelman, who became quite dismayed when the brothers began to discard his lines and jokes in favor of their own improvisations. From the beginning the studio bosses were wary of such an undisciplined group of jokers, but audiences reacted enthusiastically to the chaotic satire about the frivolous lifestyles of the wealthy. *Horse Feathers* (1932) is a satire based on college life and the role of football on college campuses during the 1930s. The setting provides an excellent platform for the brothers to make fun of stuffed-shirt academics and intellectuals.

Duck Soup was the Marx Brothers' last film for Paramount. It was the end of their five-picture deal. In spite of their profitability, the unconventional Marx team had proven to be a poor fit at the buttoned-down studio. As many put it, Paramount had become "Marxed out." Undoubtedly, *Duck Soup* had contributed to the split. The film had a perfect pedigree. The story was written by veteran comedy writers Bert Kalmer and Harry Ruby. The great Leo McCarey had been assigned to direct. But the subject matter, a satire on the carelessness and incompetence of tyrants who wage war, was problematic in the context of 1933. Mussolini saw the film and instantly banned it in Italy. The Roosevelt administration was insulted by the cynicism of lines like Groucho's "Remember while you're out there risking life and limb through shot and shell, we'll be in here thinking what a sucker you are." When the film failed to connect with audiences, Paramount gave up on the Marx Brothers. Zeppo, who had tired of being the unfunny member of the ensemble, chose this as his time to leave the act. Ironically, when the film was rediscovered in the 1960s, its surrealism, audacity, and rapid-fire jokes made it an instant hit on college campuses and in film schools.

Chico was faced with the problem of finding a proper film home for the Marx Brothers. Eventually he settled on MGM because of Irving Thalberg's reputation and assurances that their future films would be more carefully crafted and their special set of talents most favorably showcased. Their first MGM film was *A Night at the Opera* (1935). As promised, it had a more developed storyline, was less chaotic than their Paramount films, and featured a well-rounded supporting cast, including stalwart Margaret Dumont, who began with the Marx Brothers in 1929 and would appear in her last film with them in 1941.

MGM proved to be a good fit for the Marx Brothers. Thalberg tolerated their antics with surprising aplomb. As an example, Thalberg, always very late for scheduled meetings, arrived at his office over an hour late one day only to find the Marxes sitting in front of his fireplace, naked and roasting potatoes over the fire. Thalberg apologized, promised never to be late again, and sent to the studio commissary for butter for the potatoes. In all the Marx

Brothers made six films for MGM. In 1941 they announced that *The Big Store* would be their last. Although they reprised their team twice more, after leaving MGM the brothers pretty much went their own ways. Groucho stayed busier than the others with nightclub appearances and as a television guest. In 1961 Groucho signed to host a comedy quiz show for the NBC television network. The show, *You Bet Your Life*, was a huge success and stayed in the primetime schedule until 1974. By the time Groucho left television, his career had spanned sixty-six years of vaudeville, stage, movies, radio and television, one of the most remarkable careers in entertainment history.

W. C. Fields

W.C. Fields began his career as a juggler. The exact date of Fields's birth is uncertain but generally given as 1879 or 1880. It is known that he was born William Claude Dunkenfield in Philadelphia, Pennsylvania and that his family was so poor that he was turned out to make his own living at age eleven. For two or three years he lived on the streets until he found a steady job and housing. Thus settled, he entertained himself by playing pool and cards and learning to juggle. By 1893 he was earning his living as a juggler at the Plymouth Park amusement park in Norristown.

At first, Field's act was pure juggling. He wore a tramp costume and he rarely spoke. As he improved, he needed something to distinguish himself from other jugglers. Comedy was the answer. He developed the idea of the intentional mistake. He would appear to have bungled one of his routines only to save it in surprising and remarkable ways. By age nineteen, Fields had joined the prestigious Keith Vaudeville Circuit. This took him to New York. There he jumped to the Orpheum Circuit, which paid a very respectable $125 per week. One of his most famous stunts involved balancing a cigar, top hat, and whisk broom on his foot and kicking them so that the hat landed on his head, the cigar in his mouth and the broom in his pocket. He claimed that it took two years of practice to accomplish the feat.

As his vaudeville career progressed, Fields became known more as a comedian than as a juggler. In 1900 he married his stage assistant, Hattie Hughes. The following year Fields made his first European tour, including a performance before the King and Queen of England at Buckingham Palace. He returned to England in 1913 and entertained the monarchs once more. In 1915 Fields made his first film, a short entitled *Pool Sharks*. That year he also signed to perform with the Ziegfeld Follies in New York. This was the epitome of vaudeville with more luxurious travel arrangements and the princely pay of $800 per week. Fearful of becoming poor again, he was a prodigious saver, known to open a bank account in every city where he performed. He had dropped the tramp makeup, and by 1921, had dropped the juggling to become a full-time comic. Along the way Fields acquired a taste for alcohol. Ever present among his travel trunks was a large piece of luggage that opened up to form a complete cocktail bar, which he used to entertain the young ladies in the chorus line when they visited his dressing room.

In 1923 Fields was cast in the leading role in the Broadway musical *Poppy*. The play was a huge success. (He would reprise the role on screen in 1936.) His character in the play was a curmudgeonly, wisecracking, carnival snake-oil salesman with a soft spot in his heart for his daughter. This was more or less the character he would play for the rest of his life. His stock was rising fast. In 1925 Paramount put Fields under contract as he co-starred in his first major film with D. W. Griffith's mistress, Carol Dempster, in *Sally of the Sawdust*, a circus film. He remained with Paramount until 1938 but was often disappointed in the haphazard way the studio's directors and editors captured his stage act. In 1938 Fields moved to Universal, where he remained until his death.

While filming *Poppy* in 1936 Fields became seriously ill. His alcoholism had caught up with him. He had double pneumonia, two broken vertebrae (the result of too many pratfalls), and acute insomnia. He spent a year in a sanitarium, unable to fulfill his three-films-per-year commitment to Paramount. In January 1937 a radio crew was brought to his bedside so that he could participate in a broadcast commemorating the twenty-fifth anniversary of the studio. The broadcast stirred interest in Fields as a radio performer. Soon he was signed to a $6,500-per-week contract to appear on the NBC Chase and Sanborn Hour in performance with ventriloquist Edgar Bergen and his dummy sidekick, Charlie McCarthy. The radio work completely revived Field's career.

In all, Fields appeared in thirty-eight films, of which twenty-five were talkies. His films were equally split between shorts and features. Among his most successful shorts were *The Golf Specialist* (1930), *The Dentist* (1932), and *The Fatal Glass of Beer* (1933). In 1934 Fields stared in the feature *It's a Gift*. The following year he was cast as Micawber in *David Copperfield*, the only film performance in which he did not improvise or adlib. Among his best features are *You Can't Cheat an Honest Man* (1939), *My Little Chickadee* (With Mae West in 1940), and *Never Give a Sucker an Even Break* (1941). In 1946 Fields developed an untreatable stomach hemorrhage. He died Christmas day in a sanitarium in Pasadena, California. Some of Fields's memorable quotes include the following: "Children should never be seen or heard from---ever again"; "I never vote for anybody. I always vote against"; and "I drink, therefore I am."

MY LITTLE CHICKADEE (1940), DIRECTED BY EDWARD CLINE, SHOWN: MAE WEST, W.C. FIELDS

UNITED ARTISTS/PHOTOFEST

WILL ROGERS

Will Rogers is another colorful vaudeville performer who had a successful movie career. He was born on a large cattle ranch in Oklahoma in 1879. One of the ranch hands, a freed slave, taught him how to use a rope lasso as a tool for herding the longhorn cattle his family raised. As he grew older, Rogers became famous for his ability to do astonishing things with a rope. This led to jobs performing in Wild West shows and onstage in vaudeville where he complemented his rope tricks with a running patter of folksy jokes and observational comedy. He was soon referred to as a "Cowboy Philosopher."

Rogers appeared in his first film, a 1918 western titled *Laughing Bill Hyde*. He appeared in thirty-two silent films in all, most of them for Hal Roach Studios. But it was the talkies that gave Rogers his chance to shine. He made twenty sound films, mostly for Fox, in which he usually played wise-man, folksy roles. He became a major radio star in the late 1920s and was a syndicated newspaper commentator with more than four thousand columns to his name. Rogers became a friend to presidents, particularly Franklin D. Roosevelt, whose New Deal legislative program was the most ambitious attempted in American history. The support of Rogers was politically important in assuring the country that it was finally on the right track.

Among Will Rogers's most successful talking feature films was *A Connecticut Yankee in King Arthur's Court* (1931), *Judge Priest* (1934), and his last film in 1935, In *Old Kentucky*. In addition to Rogers's love of the ranch lifestyle and fast horses was his love of fast airplanes. He died in a plane crash on his way to Alaska with famous aviator Wiley Post in 1935.

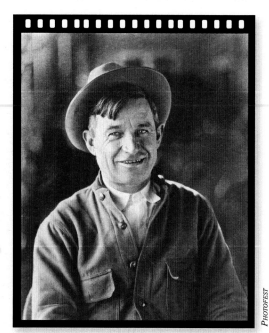

WILL ROGERS

PHOTOFEST

Rogers left a wealth of famous quotations, some of which are still in common use, including, "A remark generally hurts in proportion to its truth"; "Always drink upstream from the herd"; and "Never miss a good chance to shut up."

LAUREL AND HARDY

Both Stan Laurel and Oliver Hardy were successful as individual performers, but in teaming up, they became comedy stars. Laurel was born Arthur Stanley Jefferson in Lancashire, England in 1890. His father was a successful stage performer. Laurel began performing at age sixteen. He rose through the ranks of British music hall performers to become Charlie Chaplin's understudy with the Karno Troupe. Like Chaplin, Laurel immigrated to America in 1912, at which time he changed his name to shorten it for theater posters. His first film was *Nuts* in May (1917). His early film work was undistinguished until he began to appear in a series of spoofs of the day's popular films such as *Mud and Sand* and *Dr. Pyckle and Mr. Pryde*, sendups of Rudolph Valentino's bullfighter in *Blood and Sand*, and the equally successful *Dr. Jekyll and Mr. Hyde*.

Oliver Hardy was born Norvell Hardy in Harlem, Georgia in 1892. As a child, he was recognized for having a beautiful singing voice. At one point he ran away from home to Atlanta to pursue a singing career. Hardy's parents conceded to his ambitions and enrolled him in a music school so that he could receive formal training. It wasn't long before he was skipping classes to perform on the local vaudeville stages. In 1910 the 18-year-old Hardy returned to his family's home in Georgia. Soon he was running the local movie theater, serving as projectionist, manager, and ticket taker. During this period he was inspired to try his hand at movie acting. By 1913 he married and settled in Jacksonville, near the Lubin studios. The following year Hardy appeared in his first film, *Outwitting Dad*. During the next two years he made over fifty-one reel comedies with a Charlie Chaplin imitator, Billy West. Also during this time he divorced and remarried.

In 1917 Hardy moved to Los Angeles. During the next six years he worked steadily at Vitagraph Studios and made over forty pictures, most of which were comedies. In 1924 he was recruited by Hal Roach studios, where Stan Laurel was already working. Hardy continued to work as a single performer, but occasionally he was cast in films in which Laurel also appeared. The great comedy director Leo McCarey was in charge of production at Roach at this time. McCarey began to notice the enthusiastic audience response to films in which the two

WAY OUT WEST (1937), DIRECTED BY JAMES W. HORNE, SHOWN FROM LEFT: OLIVER HARDY, STAN LAUREL

MGM/PHOTOFEST

appeared. In 1927 he approached Hardy and Laurel and convinced them to team up as a comedy duo. Although their comedy was primarily physical, relying on inflicting pain on each other, the timing they developed was unerring. They were a new act at the same time that the motion picture industry was searching for fresh talent for talkies. Hardy was balding and rotund with a slight southern drawl in a high, tenor voice. Laurel was slender and spoke with a British gentlemen's lilt. The two looked and sounded funny together. Their timing was impeccable, and the overall effect was hilarious.

In 1929 the team of Laurel and Hardy made its talking debut in the film *Unaccustomed As We Are*. In all the duo made forty-five comedy shorts and sixteen features during the

1930s. Their 1932 short, *The Music Box,* won the Academy Award for short films. Other excellent short film titles included *Thicker Than Water, Busy Bodies,* and *Them Thar Hills.* Behind the scenes Stan Laurel was the leader of the act. In addition to performing in front of the cameras, he headed up a fairly large staff of writers and was responsible for most of the editing. As a result, Laurel's share of the earnings was fifty percent greater than Hardy's. In the mid-thirties short films became less popular and less lucrative. Laurel and Hardy shifted to making feature-length films. Two of their best were *Sons of the Desert* and *Way Out West.* In 1941 the duo left Hal Roach Studios and struck out on their own. The quality of their work instantly declined. Laurel and Hardy made a total of ten features during the 1940s. Their last true feature was *The Bullfighters.* It was a poorly organized film that suffered from recycled jokes and the advanced age of the two performers.

OUR GANG

In 1922 Hal Roach revived a movie idea that he had originated earlier in the Sunshine Sammy shorts, a series of comedies built around African American child actor Sammy Morrison. The new *Our Gang* concept was based on a diverse cast of child actors. The first group of tykes included a gang leader (Mickey Daniels), a tough boy (Jackie Davis), a cute girl (Peggy Cartwright), the pet bulldog (Pete), and Morrison, as well as another African American actor, one-year-old Allen Clayton "Farina" Hoskins, who would go on to appear in 105 films in the series. The character of a fat boy (Joe Cobb) was added. Roach's inclusion of African American actors and characters was highly unusual in that segregated time. Furthermore, both Morrison and Hoskins were often the central character in episodes. The films were ten to twenty minutes in length, and instead of relying on jokes and slapstick, the humor was derived from the situations in which the children became entangled. In this respect, the films are a forerunner of the situation comedy genre that later became so popular in radio and on television.

OUR GANG AKA THE LITTLE RASCALS, TITLE: DON'T LIE, APRIL 4, 1942, SHOWN: ROBERT "MICKEY" BLAKE, BILLY "BUCKWHEAT" THOMAS, WILLIAM ROBERT "FROGGY" LAUGHLIN, SPANKY MCFARLAND,

HAL ROACH STUDIOS/PHOTOFEST

As the child actors aged or left the series for other reasons, they were replaced by new faces. Jackie Cooper joined the cast in 1929, but would move on to work in feature films by 1931. Roach looked for naturalness rather than acting skills in his casting decisions. In fact, child star Mickey Rooney was turned away when he auditioned in 1928 as being too affected and polished. The settings for the episodes were mundane backyards, alleyways, and playing fields. There was very little adult-child camaraderie, as was the norm for other child stars such as Shirley Temple. In fact adults were usually the enemy, or at the very least, to be avoided. The *Our Gang* world was a kid's world.

In the mid-1930s the strongest cast in the series history came together. George "Spanky" McFarland became the gang spokesman and the informal tough-chubby gang leader form 1932 to 1942. Carl "Alfalfa" Switzer played the freckle-faced kid role with one rogue lock of hair sticking straight up from the middle of his head. He also had a singing voice that mixed equal parts stage-fright and tone deafness. Tommy "Butch" Bond was a daunting tough-guy bully. In 1934 Billie "Buckwheat" Thomas replaced Farina as the gang's African American member. This ensemble was often directed by Leo McCarey's talented and underappreciated brother, Ray. In 1938 MGM purchased Hal Roach Studios, but the production of *Our Gang* episodes continued unabated.

Many great episodes were produced in the late 1930s. In 1938 *Men in Fright* gave Buckwheat a chance to star, and in 1939 Alfalfa was featured in *Clown Princes* and *Time Out for Lessons*. Some of Spanky's best episodes include Arbor Day (1936), *Mail and Female* (1937), and *Men In Fright* 1938). Many Our Gang aficionados believe that *Beginner's Luck* (1935) is the single funniest episode of all time. The series came to an end in 1944 with the production of the last three episodes, *Radio Bugs, Dancing Romero*, and *Tale of a Dog*. In 1955 MGM packaged all of the sound episodes of the *Our Gang* comedies and sold them to television under the title *The Little Rascals*. More than fifty years later the *Our Gang* films can regularly be seen on television.

ROMANTIC AND SCREWBALL COMEDY: LUBITSCH, CAPRA, MCCAREY, AND HAWKS

Comedy films were always an important part of what the movie industry had to offer its audiences, but given the suffering and deprivations of the 1930s, it was essential that Hollywood provide a few laughs and an escape from everyday life. Ironically, the Great Depression was also a high water mark for the comedy film. Sophisticated romantic comedies were a specialty for Paramount's Ernst Lubitsch, while Columbia's Frank Capra and freeagent directors, Howard Hawks and Leo McCarey, grafted new elements onto romantic comedy to create a genre particular to the 1930s: the screwball comedy.

Ernst Lubitsch is usually described by film historians as the most urbane, witty, and respected of the romantic comedy directors of the 1930s. Born in 1892 in Berlin, Germany, he received his dramatic training both as an actor and director at Max Reinhardt's Deutsches Theater, an institution respected throughout the stage world for its cutting-edge experimentation and the outstanding quality of the people who worked there. He began his film career as an actor in 1912. By 1914 he had switched to directing. In all he directed thirty-eight films in his native Germany, most for the Projektions–AG Union company. His German films range from lavish costume dramas such as *Madame Du Barry* (1919) to small comedies such as *Die Bergkatze* (1921). In 1923 Lubitsch was recruited by Mary Pickford to come to America to direct her in *Rosita*, a change of pace from the little-girl roles she had been playing for years. Pickford and Lubitsch did not get along well during the production, and she attempted to keep the film out of circulation for years. Still *Rosita* is a fine example of his talent for making sophisticated light comedies. The film also contributed to Pickford's career in that it represents a step in the direction of maturing her onscreen persona and a step away from her more youthful roles.

In 1924 Lubitsch signed with Warner Brothers, where he would make six films in a little over three years, all silents. His reputation grew rapidly at the studio where he was allowed to explore ideas that interested him, rather than being pushed toward commercial success. The Warner films were small in scale and mostly portrayed women involved in complicated romantic relationships. Lubitsch approached these characters with his customary light touch and sophisticated European attitude toward sex and relationships. One of the most respected films from this period is *The Marriage Circle*. The plot involves two couples, one in a happy relationship and the other less so. The characters toy with the idea of infidelity, but never act on it. Eventually, the experience serves to fortify the original pairings. Although the film follows a morally conventional path, it is the possibility of immorality that makes it spicy.

PRODUCER ADOLPH ZUKOR AND DIRECTOR ERNST LUBITSCH ON THE SET OF THE LOVE PARADE (1929)

In 1927 Paramount lured Lubitsch away from Warner Brothers and MGM (which was also courting him for their slate of talking pictures) as a prelude to making the conversion to talking pictures. His first film at the studio, *The Patriot*, is also the first sound film he directed. Unlike other directors making the transition to talkies, Lubitsch was unfazed by the demands of the new technology and he was upbeat about the possibility of adding the dimension of witty dialogue to his films. During the next ten years he made fourteen films for Paramount and, in so doing, set an example of quality and sophistication that would earn the studio a reputation for films that had "the Lubitsch touch."

There are many different theories as to what the "Lubitsch touch" means. Seven of his films at Paramount were musicals, and he became one of the first directors to attempt to fully integrate songs into story lines and character development rather than stop the action for a song and then resume again. Another aspect of the celebrated touch is his ability to introduce a slight note of sadness into the happiest of scenes. Lubitsch was admired for his ability to suggest much more than was shown on the screen, often using closed doors as a symbol for things that were too private to be seen. His technique included focusing on small details in the midst of grand dramatic scenes, a way of both showing the dramatic action and commenting on it at the same time. Critics generally agree that more than anyone else, Lubitsch advanced movie comedy from slapstick and the pratfall to a genre capable of presenting deep emotional content..

THE LOVE PARADE (1929), DIRECTED BY ERNST LUBITSCH, SHOWN FROM LEFT: JEANETTE MACDONALD, MAURICE CHEVALIER

In 1929 Lubitsch directed Paramount's new star, Jeanette MacDonald, in the musical *Love Parade*. Her love interest in the story is the French star Maurice Chevalier. The film was a critical and commercial sensation. The film's combination of naughtiness and light operatic music was cosmopolitan, a mature film with a hint of European decadence. Over the next few years Lubitsch directed both actors several times in films such as *The Smiling Lieutenant* and *Monte Carlo*. Each film contributed both to the growth of the actors' careers and the studio's fortunes. Furthermore, the director accomplished this without the egotistical outbreaks and tantrums that were often associated with great talent, especially great talent that came from Europe. To the contrary, a Lubitsch set was a fun place to work, very civilized and respectful. It made actors and crew want to give their best, and it elevated the overall quality of the film.

During 1935–36 Paramount promoted Lubitsch to the position of

BLUEBEARD'S EIGHTH WIFE (1938), DIRECTED BY ERNST LUBITSCH, SHOWN FROM LEFT: GARY COOPER, CLAUDETTE COLBERT

head of production at the studio. The hope was that he would teach young directors "the Lubitsch touch," and to some extent, he did so. But his first love was directing, and at the end of one year, he was allowed to resume his passion. His last film for Paramount was *Bluebeard's Eighth Wife* (1938) staring Claudette Colbert and Gary Cooper. It was written by Charles Bracket and young writer—and soon-to-be director—Billy Wilder. Following *Bluebeard*, Lubitsch finally gave in to MGM's attempts sign him. Bracket and Wilder came along as part of the deal.

Lubitsch made two films for MGM, *Ninotchka* (1939), and *The Shop Around the Corner* (1940), both undisputed classics. Ninotchka features the studio's greatest female star, Greta Garbo, playing a Soviet bureaucrat sent to Paris on a government errand. She meets a charming boulevardier, Melvyn Douglas, who melts her icy heart. *Shop* stars Jimmy Stewart and Margaret Sullivan as two shop workers who despise each other on the job but are unaware that they have already been involved as pen pals who slowly fall in love with each other through their letters. Both films are masterpieces of romantic comedy. In 1942 Lubitsch made his last great comedy, an independent production featuring radio star Jack Benny and Carole Lombard, one of the great comedy actresses of her generation. *To Be Or Not To Be* (1942) is a brilliant satire of Hitler's Nazi Germany.

THE SHOP AROUND THE CORNER (1940), DIRECTED BY ERNST LUBITSCH, SHOWN ON THE SET FROM LEFT: MARGARET SULLIVAN, DIRECTOR ERNST LUBITSCH, JAMES STEWART

MGM/PHOTOFEST

In 1947 Lubitch was awarded a Motion Picture Academy Award (Oscar) for his body of work. Over the years he had suffered a series of heart attacks. In November of 1947 he had his sixth and final heart attack while working on a film titled *That Lady in Ermine*. Lubitsch's legacy includes not only the films he made and the sense of style that he brought to Hollywood but also the influence he had on an entire generation of directors and actors. One example of that influence is the famous sign Billy Wilder, who went on to earn a reputation as a great director of classic films in his own right, hung on his office wall. It reads, "What would Lubitsch have done?"

CAPRA, HAWKS, AND THE SCREWBALL COMEDY

The screwball comedy is a genre that grew directly from the social environment of the Great Depression. The role of women was changing rapidly. In 1920 women had won the right to vote with the ratification of the Nineteenth Amendment to the U.S. Constitution. Throughout the decade of the 1920s images of women in film and society changed from sheltered and maternal to sexually independent equals of men. The hardships of the 1930s required women to become economically independent as well. It was natural that motion pictures would reflect a social development of this magnitude.

Frank Capra

It is hard to imagine two more different men that Frank Capra and Howard Hawks. Capra was born in Bisacquino, Sicily in 1897. When he was six, his parents joined the huge wave of Italian immigrants coming to America. Instead of settling in New York, the Capra family chose Los Angeles, where the older brother had already settled. During the cross-country train trip the family lived on bananas and bread, the only words for food they knew in English. Young Frank Capra was enrolled in the excellent Los Angeles public school system of the day. By the time he began high school at Manual Arts, he was supporting himself playing piano in saloons and brothels. In high school Capra also became interested in theater and loved to work backstage on plays and musical productions. During this time he also managed to maintain a very high grade average.

In 1915 Capra was admitted to the Throop College of Technology in Pasadena, California which would later become CalTech. He studied chemical engineering, and although his family thought he was wasting his time with too much schooling, they did supplement his earnings as a night watchman to help him get through college. Capra's father died in 1916, forcing the young man to get a job in the college laundry room to pay for his studies. Capra also joined the campus Reserve Officers Training Corp (ROTC). He graduated in 1918 and immediately joined the army to fight in World War I. However, when he was sent to the Presidio army base in San Francisco for training, Capra fell ill with the deadly Spanish influenza and was quickly discharged from the military at the end of the year.

After his recuperation, Capra got work as an extra on the John Ford film *Outcasts of Poker Flats*. He also attempted, unsuccessfully, to write and sell short stories. Over the next two years he got further involved in the movie business by teaming up with two other

LADIES OF LEISURE (1930), DIRECTED BY FRANK CAPRA, SHOWN FROM LEFT: RALPH GRAVES, BARBARA STANWYCK

COLUMBIA/PHOTOFEST

partners to found the Tri-State Motion Picture Company in Nevada. Capra later returned to Los Angeles and went to work briefly for CBC, the forerunner to Columbia studios, where he was a film editor and sometime director. By 1921 he was a comedy director at the Paul Gerson Picture Corp. He married Helen Howell in 1923 and became a staff writer on the *Our Gang* series at Hal Roach Studios the following year. At Roach, Capra became friendly with comedian Harry Langdon and followed him first to Keystone and then on to First National Pictures. In 1926 Capra directed Langdon in *The Strong Man* for $750 per week. He remained at First National another year.

In 1927 Capra began working for Harry Cohn at Columbia where he would remain for most of his career. Early on he developed a more efficient directing technique, shooting master shots one day, two- shots the next, and closeups the third day. Without having to constantly stop to move lights and camera, the pace of production sped up. At frugal Columbia Studios this was greatly appreciated. By 1929 Capra had become the studio's star director. He and Cohn sought fewer but more prestigious films to direct. In 1930 his film *Ladies of Leisure* starring newcomer Barbara Stanwyck, established both the actress and director as emerging stars of the sound era.

HOWARD HAWKS

Unlike the immigrant Capra, Howard Hawks came from a very privileged background. He was born in Goshen, Indiana in 1896. The Hawks family owned most of Goshen and nearby Neenah as well. The Hawks family also partnered with the Clark family (who would found the Kimberly Clark paper company), investing in industrial properties and paper mills. Hawks' father, Frank, enjoyed escaping the cold winters of the Midwest by taking up residence in the spa town of Pasadena, California. By 1906 Frank Hawks had purchased an interest in several hotels on the West Coast and had acquired an orange ranch west of Los Angeles in Glendora, California. He used these investments as an incentive to move to California and make it his permanent home.

Howard Hawks was enrolled in the first class of the new Polytechnic Elementary School near the Throop Institute in Pasadena. He entered Pasadena High School after graduating from Polytechnic. He was an indifferent student who liked to play tennis and didn't get too involved with school activities. He did like to spend his summers working as a prop man and extra in Hollywood. Most likely through his father's financial contributions, Hawks was admitted for his senior year to the most exclusive preparatory school in the country, the Philips Exeter Academy in New Hampshire. By Easter vacation he had flunked out and returned to Pasadena, where he graduated with his original high school class. Another generous donation earned Hawks admission to Cornell University in 1914.

At Cornell, Hawks maintained his casual attitude toward studies, preferring to drink and gamble and enjoy Greek life among the brothers of Delta Kappa Epsilon. Home for summer vacation, Hawks discovered a new passion, racing, when his grandfather gave him a Mercer race car. Through racing he met two older Pasadenans, Mickey Neilan and Victor Fleming, with whom he became fast friends and later followed into the film business. In April 1917 Hawks's entire junior class at Cornell was drafted into the military for World

War I. Eventually the university awarded degrees to all who had been called up. Hawks waited for his orders in Los Angeles that summer while working on a Cecil B. DeMille film. Hawks also spent time with Neilan, who was already working as a director.

That fall the army sent Hawks to Berkeley, California for basic training and on to Texas to learn how to fly. He spent most of 1918 at flight school and was released from the military in November, when the war ended. He came home to live the life of a rich kid in Hollywood. He played tennis and hobnobbed with the stars. It was a small town and in very little time Hawks knew everyone who mattered. His first postmilitary foray into movies was to make a loan to the Warner brothers, who were perpetually strapped for cash. He befriended Jack Warner, who in exchange for financing the project, put Hawks in charge of producing the *Welcome Comedies*, a new series of one-reel comedy films. When the series was finished, Hawks took his tidy profit and moved on. Next he teamed up with director Alan Dwan and Mickey Neilan to finance feature-length films. Their company was called Associated Films and had a deal with First National, which provided distribution. Between 1920 and 1923 the company made fourteen films, eight of which were directed by Neilan. Eventually the business failed and the partners went their separate ways.

FIRST NATIONAL PICTURES/PHOTOFEST

THE DAWN PATROL (1930), DIRECTED BY HOWARD HAWKS

Hawks's next job was at Paramount, where Jessie Lasky had hired him to be a story editor in charge of purchasing literary works to be adapted into motion pictures. At that time Victor Fleming was also working at Paramount, at times on the very films Hawks developed. At the end of 1925 Hawks jumped ship for a chance to become a director at Fox. The studio was then attempting to double and triple production output. Hawks was one of a group of budding filmmakers who joined more experienced directors at the studio such as John Ford. Hawks's first film was a pedestrian drama, *Road to Glory*, released in 1926. It was followed by *Fig Leaves*, his first comedy. His next three films were all comedies. In all he made eight films for Fox, including his first aviation film, *Air Circus*, in 1928. This film had the additional distinction of being his first talking picture. In 1930 Hawks left Fox to direct his biggest project to date, *Dawn Patrol*, a film about brave pilots fighting in World War I. This was followed by his great gangster film, *Scarface*, made in collaboration with fellow pilot Howard Hughes. This was followed by a motor-racing picture for Warner Brothers,

The Crowd Roars (1932). He made two other films for the studio before moving on to MGM where he made another aviation film, *Today We Live* (1933), his first collaboration with writer and great American novelist William Faulkner. Hawks made one other film and assisted on a third for MGM before moving on to Columbia. Here he directed a film generally accepted as the first screwball comedy, *Twentieth Century* (1934). Throughout this early part of his career Hawks developed a reputation as a director who could work in any film genre, be it action, drama, romance, or comedy. He was also seen as very independent, never truly making a home for himself at a single studio. In his personal life he was known for living the high life and running with a fast crowd of bachelors, among them Victor Fleming.

THE BIRTH OF THE SCREWBALL COMEDY

Screwball comedy reflects many of the social conditions of the 1930s. Because of the growing empowerment of women brought on by the economic conditions of the Great Depression, screwball comedies almost always contained a plot that centered on the battle of the sexes. Women were the equals of the men they fought with, and fighting was often used as a metaphor for romance. Screwball comedies also contain an element of class struggle. Sometimes they involved women and men from different classes learning to overcome those differences in order to succeed in romance. The person from the lower classes most often taught the upper-class character an important life lesson or imparted wisdom. The upper-class characters were usually portrayed as frivolous and completely oblivious to the suffering of the lower classes. The comedy style blended improbable farcical situations, physical slapstick comedy borrowed from the silent era, and very sharp and witty dialogue imported from the New York stage. In fact, a large percentage of screwball comedies were stage plays adapted into motion pictures.

IT HAPPENED ONE NIGHT (1934), DIRECTED BY FRANK CAPRA, SHOWN FROM LEFT: CLAUDETTE COLBERT, CLARK GABLE

COLUMBIA PICTURES/PHOTOFEST

One of Howard Hawks' contributions to the genre was to speed up the pace of the dialogue to create the impression that characters didn't really listen to one another, and to speed up the pace at which the jokes arrived.

Frank Capra's first screwball was *It Happened One Night* (1934). It starred Hollywood's greatest male star at the time, Clark Gable, whom Louis B. Mayer of MGM had loaned out to Columbia as punishment for asking for a raise. Claudette Colbert, Gable's romantic co-star, was a young veteran of 23 films on loan from Paramount. *It Happened One Night* was a welcomed audience success in the deepest throes of the Great Depression. It was such a sensation that it earned the rare sweep of the Academy Awards winning for Best Picture, Best Director, Best Actor, and Best Actress. Colbert went on to have a charmed career in Hollywood, starring in other great screwball comedies such as Ernst Lubitsch's *Bluebeard's Eighth Wife* (1938) and Preston Sturges's *Palm Beach Story* (1942).

Capra proceeded to develop a string of populist screwball comedies for Columbia studios throughout the remainder of the 1930s. In 1936 he made *Mr. Deeds Goes to Town*, written by Capra's steadiest collaborator, Robert Riskin. The film starred Gary Cooper, on loan from Paramount; and Columbia contract player Jean Arthur. Cooper plays a naive country boy who inherits millions and proceeds to New York to claim his fortune and do battle with con artists and shysters. *Deeds* includes a long passage in which the title character experiments with socialism as a strategy for ridding himself of his fortune. Capra's 1938 screwball *You Can't Take it with You* was adapted from a Moss Hart and George S. Kaufman stage play. It teams up Jean Arthur with James Stewart, who was then a relative newcomer. A Princeton graduate, Stewart was on loan from MGM to Columbia. Fellow college man Capra took an instant liking to Stewart, and the two worked together several more times. Their most important collaboration was *Mr. Smith Goes to Washington*. It is the story of a young man appointed to fulfill a vacant term in the U.S. Senate only to discover that everyone is corrupt and wants to manipulate him. This would be Capra's last populist screwball comedy of the thirties.

Howard Hawks also directed two highly respected screwballs after the success of *Twentieth Century* in 1934. His 1938 film *Bringing Up Baby* became an instant classic. An RKO production, it teamed up studio actress Katharine Hepburn with Cary Grant, a former Paramount discovery and one of the first actors to achieve his independence from the studios. Hawks reunited with Grant on the 1940 production of *His Girl Friday*. The film was a remake of the stage play *Front Page*, by Ben Hecht and Charles MacArthur. Hawks gave it his special touch by changing the male character, Hildy, into a woman, played by Rosalind Russell.

Two other practitioners of the screwball comedy were Leo McCarey and Preston Sturges. Veteran comedy director McCarey was comfortable in all comedic styles, but his 1937 screwball *The Awful Truth*, is as good as any in the genre. It stars Cary Grant, Irene Dunne, and Ralph Bellamy. Based on a stage play and made at Columbia, this hysterical romp features a couple who decide to divorce but can't overcome their attraction for each other. McCarey infused the film with improvisational passages of great comedic invention and some of the best reaction comedy ever captured on film. Sturges began his career as a screenwriter of such respected films as *Diamond Jim* (1935), *Easy Living* (1937), and *Never Say Die* (1939). In 1941 he became a hyphenated writer-director with the production of *The Lady Eve*, starring veteran actress Barbara Stanwyck and Henry Fonda. That same year Sturges scored with another screwball, *Sullivan's Travels*, about a spoiled director who wants to make a serious movie but must learn about the serious side of life before he can do so. Joel McCrae plays a feckless director. Rumor had it this character was based on Howard Hawks. Veronica Lake rounds out the cast as a down-on-her-luck actress who helps Sullivan navigate the adversities of the real world. *The Palm Beach Story* (1942) completed the era of the screwball comedy. The Great Depression had, for most purposes, ended in 1939. The onset of World War II led to a new and more serious audience sensibility.

MUSICALS

The advent of sound had inevitably led Hollywood to bring stage musicals, operettas, vaudeville, and radio musical performances to the movie screen. Many of those early examples of motion picture musicals have already been discussed. However, by the mid 1930s, advances in sound and photographic technology, combined with a new generation of talent both in front of and behind the cameras, led to a golden age of the Hollywood musical.

Warner Brothers had a head start in the production of musicals that stemmed from the studio's pioneer work beginning with the *Vitagraph Broadway Review* and *The Jazz Singer*. In fact, every studio with the exception of Columbia made serious commitments to the musical genre at the outset of the 1930s. But it was Warner Brothers that discovered a sure-fire formula for musical success in 1933 that kept the studio at the forefront of musicals for most of the decade.

Busby Berkeley was born in Los Angeles in 1895. His parents sent him to an expensive military academy in New York, after which he enlisted in the army to fight in World War I. His army job was organizing and staging complex precision marching drills for military reviews. After the war he settled in New York and developed a reputation as one of Broadway's best new choreographers. In 1930 Samuel Goldwyn hired Berkeley to come home to Hollywood to direct the dance numbers for the film *Whoopie*, starring Ed-

42ND STREET (1933), DIRECTED BY LLOYD BACON, DANCE DIRECTOR BUSBY BERKELEY. SHOWN: DICK POWELL (AS BILLY LAWLER), RUBY KEELER (AS PEGGY SAWYER)

WARNER BROS./SPRINGER/PHOTOFEST

die Cantor, the studio's answer to Warner's Al Jolson. Soon Berkeley moved on to Warner Brothers, where an ambitious slate of musicals was in the planning stages.

Forty-Second Street (1933) exemplified a new style of musical in a number of ways. Director Lloyd Bacon was working with a new technique in which the music was prerecorded and the performers lip-synced in front of the cameras. This alleviated the need to worry about camera noise and the bulky sound blimps that had to be used to record dialogue and music during filming. The result was freer, more liquid camera work that complemented the flow of the musical numbers. Thus freed, Berkeley was able to design and execute his signature geometric dance numbers and to film them from every imaginable angle, even going so far as to cut a hole in the roof of the stage to get the perfect perspective. Depression-era audiences had never seen anything like it and welcomed the distraction Berkeley's fantasies provided. Another innovation was in casting relative unknowns Ruby Keeler and Dick Powell in the leading roles, lending a refreshing youthfulness to the production. Another young musical star, Ginger Rogers, also emerged from these films.

After *Forty-Second Street* Berkeley both directed and choreographed the films he worked on. He produced a string of hits for Warner Brothers over the next few years; *Footlight Parade* (1933), *The Gold Diggers of 1933*, *The Gold Diggers of 1935* and *Hollywood Hotel* (1937). While audiences never tired of Berkeley's dance designs, they did grow weary of the backstage stories he preferred. As his popularity began to decline, he moved to MGM in hopes of freshening up his reputation. The move did help for a while until it became common knowledge that he was abusive of MGM's younger stars such as Judy Garland. The audience was unforgiving and, although Berkeley did continue to work into the 1960s, he never regained his former success.

Footlight Parade (1933), Directed by Lloyd Bacon, Shown: Busby Berkeley dance sequence

Warner Bros./Photofest

RKO

RKO also had a remarkable run of success with musicals during the 1930s. Unlike Warner Brothers, RKO's success was dependent on two great dance stars, Fred Astaire and Ginger Rogers. In 1933 the two appeared in supporting roles in *Flying Down to Rio*. The two performers seemed to literally jump off the screen. Studio producer Pandro S. Berman, quickly created the 1934 film *The Gay Divorcee* to showcase their talents. Astaire played a devil-may-care playboy; Rogers played a nice girl who could take care of herself. The film's witty dialogue kept things moving until the next dance number was employed to resolve a conflict and express a romantic plot point. Their dancing was fluid and poetic. Some critics said that Astaire gave Rogers class and that she gave him sex appeal. Their next film, *Top Hat* (1935), was an even greater success and spawned a series of follow-ups directed by Mark Sandrich; *Roberta* (1935), *Follow the Fleet* (1936), *Swing Time* (1936), *Shall We Dance* (1937), and *Carefree* (1938). Eventually the two decided it was time to part ways. Astaire wanted to continue his dancing, whereas Rogers wanted to attempt more serious acting. Both were successful, with Rogers winning a Best Actress Oscar in 1940 for her performance in *Kitty Foyle*. One observation about Astaire and Rogers is often repeated: No matter how great he was (and he was very great), she did everything he did except backwards and in high heels.

RKO RADIO PICTURES/PHOTOFEST

THE GAY DIVORCEE (1934). DIRECTED BY MARK SANDRICH, SHOWN: FRED ASTAIRE (AS GUY HOLDEN), GINGER ROGERS (AS MIMI GLOSSOP/MRS. GREEN)

MGM/PHOTOFEST

NAUGHTY MARIETTA (1935), DIRECTED BY ROBERT Z. LEONARD & W.S. VAN DYKE, SHOWN: JEANETTE MACDONALD, NELSON EDDY

Fox

Fox had two musical stars, a little girl named Shirley Temple, and Alice Faye, a former chorus girl who broke through in radio performing with Rudy Vallee's Connecticut Yankees. Temple first appeared on screen in 1932 at age four. She could sing and dance, and she charmed Depression-era America, inspiring a line of dolls and countless Shirley Temple look-alike contests. By the time she reached age twelve in 1940, she had appeared in forty-two films and was largely responsible for Fox surviving the economic calamities of the decade. Alice Faye co-starred with Shirley Temple in *Poor Little Rich Girl* in 1936 and went on to star in twenty-one more Fox musicals. In 1936 Fox also signed Sonja Henie, an Olympic ice skater who could neither sing nor act but could anchor a successful series of musicals built around production numbers that featured her skating.

MGM

MGM had made its first musicals at the beginning of the sound era but didn't get into musical production seriously until the studio teamed established star Jeanette MacDonald with relatively unknown Nelson Eddy. Their first film together, *Naughty Marietta* (1935), was a smash hit. They re-teamed the next year to make *Rose Marie* and proceeded to make four more hit musicals before going their separate ways. Dancer Eleanor Powell's first MGM musical was *Broadway Melody of 1936*. The studio produced six more Powell musicals between 1936 and 1943.

By far MGM's biggest musical star was Judy Garland. She was fourteen when she broke through with *Every Sunday* in

THE WIZARD OF OZ (1939), DIRECTED BY: VICTOR FLEMING, SHOWN FROM LEFT: BERT LAHR (AS THE COWARDLY LION), JACK HALEY (AS THE TIN MAN), RAY BOLGER (AS THE SCARECROW), JUDY GARLAND (AS DOROTHY GALE), TOTO, NICKO, THE FLYING MONKEY, MARGARET HAMILTON (AS THE WICKED WITCH OF THE NORTH)

1936. She made her last musical for the studio, *Summer Stock*, in 1950. In all she made twenty-six films for MGM including the very popular Andy Hardy series of films in which she co-starred with child actor Mickey Rooney. Her three greatest hits were *The Wizard of Oz* (1939), *Meet Me in St. Louis* (1944) and *Easter Parade* (1948).

PARAMOUNT

Paramount was less identified with musicals than were the other major studios with the exception of Paramount's one great musical star, Bing Crosby. Crosby had been a very successful radio performer and recording artist before being signed to appear in *The Big Broadcast* (1932). His performance was so popular with audiences that the studio signed him immediately and proceeded to cast him in over forty more films over the next sixteen years. In 1940 Paramount teamed Crosby with radio comedian Bob Hope in *The Road to Singapore*, which

ROAD TO MOROCCO (1942). DIRECTED BY DAVID BUTLER, SHOWN: BING CROSBY (AS JEFF PETERS), BOB HOPE (AS ORVILLE 'TURKEY' JACKSON)

also starred the exotic Dorothy Lamour. Crosby and Hope played soldiers of fortune continually getting into and out of trouble in the course of their constant travels. The film was so successful that Paramount made four other "road" pictures with *The Road to Morocco* (1942) being the best of the series.

HORROR AND FANTASY

The horror film grows out of the German Expressionist movement of the 1920s. The Expressionists at UFA studios were interested in exploring the darker side of human nature, the impulse to murder, and other perversions of the human spirit such as vampirism. *The Cabinet of Dr. Caligari* (1919), and *Nosferatu* (1922) are early examples of the horror genre. During the 1920s at Universal Studios Lon Chaney created such horrific characters as *The Hunchback of Notre Dame* (1923) and *The Phantom of the Opera* (1925). In the mid 1920s Carl Laemmle actively recruited expressionists from Germany such as Paul Leni to establish Universal as the leader in horror film production.

In 1931 Universal introduced two very successful horror franchises, *Frankenstein* and the vampire film *Dracula*. The following year another German transplant, Karl Freund, added *The Mummy* to the studio's horror linup. Boris Karloff, who played the monster in *Frankenstein*, played an Egyptian priest with has the power to summon the dead back to life. Also in 1932 Universal director Todd Browning, in an attempt to top his success with *Dracula*, created the very disturbing *Freaks*, a film in which most of the principal roles were cast from carnivals and circus sideshows. Performers included dwarfs, conjoined twins, bearded ladies, and pin heads. In 1933 James Whale, who had directed *Frankenstein*, returned to the horror genre with the ingenious screen adaptation of H. G. Wells's story *The*

Invisible Man. In 1935 Whale improved on the original *Frankenstein* with his sequel *The Bride of Frankenstein.* The film's escapism was particularly successful with Depression-era audiences who preferred being scared witless to the reality of economic catastrophe.

In 1933 Merrian C. Cooper and Ernest Schoedsack convinced RKO studio chief David O. Selznick, that they could make a commercial film about a thirty-foot-tall gorilla, King Kong. Known mostly for making documentary films such as *Grass: A Nation's Battle for Life* (1925) and *Chang: A Drama of the Wilderness* (1927), Cooper and Schoedsack were an unlikely choice to mount history's most ambitious special-effects film to date. But they were relentless in developing new rear-screen photographic techniques, using miniatures to create the battle scenes be-

BRIDE OF FRANKENSTEIN (1935), DIRECTED BY JAMES WHALE, SHOWN FROM LEFT: ELSA LANCHESTER (AS THE BRIDE), BORIS KARLOFF) (AS FRANKENSTEIN)

UNIVERSAL PICTURES/PHOTOFEST

tween Kong and prehistoric dinosaurs; and stop-motion animation sequences created by special-effects wizard Willis O'Brien. The result was a remarkable mixture of horror and fantasy that still has the power to mesmerize audiences.

Fantasy films are distinguishable from horror films in that the purpose isn't necessarily to shock or to explore the dark side of human nature. Science fiction is one type of fantasy that dates back to the earliest days of the motion picture industry with Georges Méliès's *Trip to the Moon* (1902). Fairy tales, legends, myths, and comic strips also provide source material for fantasy films. Jules Verne's sea fantasy *Twenty Thousand Leagues Under the Sea* was adapted for film in 1916.

The year 1931 was the 100th anniversary of the great English author Lewis Carroll's birthday. In response that year saw dozens of stage productions of *Alice in Wonderland* mounted. Seizing on the popularity of the idea, Paramount decided to make a film adaptation of the book with an all-star cast. Almost all of the studio's great character actors were cast in the film, including Edward Everett Horton, Jack Oakie, and Ned Sparks. Major stars given cameo roles included Gary Cooper as the White Knight, Cary Grant as the Mock Turtle, and W. C. Fields as Humpty Dumpty. In spite of the care and expense that went into the production, the film was a box-office failure. Many critics explained the failure as the result of the actors' being virtually unrecognizable in the very heavy makeup used for the production.

The fantasy genre was successfully revived in 1937. Walt Disney's first feature-length animated film, *Snow White and the Seven Dwarfs*, was an instant hit with audiences of all ages. The film employed the vivid three-color Technicolor process that Disney had been working with since 1932. The animators effectively utilized the power of color to bring the fairy tale to life. The film's many songs and musical production numbers were as good as or better than anything being done on Broadway. *Snow White* established Disney as the unrivaled leader in animation.

Snow White and the Seven Dwarfs (1937), Directed by David Hand, Shown from left: (at piano) Grumpy, (middle row) Dopey, Sleepy, Doc, (front row) Sneezy, Happy, Snow White, (with cymbals) Bashful

Two other, very different fantasy films were released in 1937. *Topper* is a sophisticated story about a wealthy but stodgy banker haunted by the ghosts of an attractive young couple who were tragically killed in an auto crash. The ghosts take it upon themselves to teach Cosmo Topper how to enjoy the good life, especially a daily cocktail hour. Since Topper is the only person who can see and hear the ghosts, his stuffy family and friends conclude that his new decadent ways are the

Topper (1937), Directed by Norman Z. McLeod, Shown from left: Roland Young (as Cosmo Topper), Constance Bennett, Cary Grant

result of mental illness. Frank Capra's *Lost Horizon* was based on a James Hilton novel of the same title. It is the story of a group of airplane passengers who survive a crash in the remote Himalayan mountains. They are rescued and taken in by a small community of people living in an isolated valley where nature provides for every necessity and many luxuries. The natives live to be well over a hundred years old in this utopia, but the tug of civilization makes the passengers long for home. Both films were economically and critically successful, with *Horizon* regarded as a classic.

Serials are long-form stories that are presented in short, one-reel (eight minute) segments (between ten and thirty episodes were used to tell the whole story) over a period of time. A new episode was included in the weekly theater program. Each episode ends with a cliffhanger in which the protagonist is in mortal danger. Each episode resolved the preceding cliffhanger and built up to a new one. Serials were designed to motivate audiences to go to their local theater every week to keep up with the story, and they were very successful in so doing. The first American serials, the *What Happened to Mary* series, were made by Edison in 1912. Two years later Pearl White starred in the classic *Perils of Pauline*, a twenty-episode serial. White's superb athleticism was employed in constructing hair-raising stunts. The vividness of the action in *Pauline* was imitated by many who followed.

TARZAN ESCAPES (1936), DIRECTED BY RICHARD THORPE, SHOWN FROM LEFT: CHEETAH, JOHNNY WEISSMULLER, MAUREEN O'SULLIVAN

The 1930s begin the golden age of the serials. They were popular with theater owners, who were eager to offer their Depression-era audiences more value for their ticket dollar and who welcomed the fact that audiences got hooked on a serial and returned each week until it was complete. Columbia, Universal, and Republic were the studios most active in serial production. In some respect, all serials were action-driven films. The major serial genres were westerns, jungle adventures, aerial action and stunt movies, and fantasy films.

Westerns were easy and inexpensive to produce because of the abundance of available infrastructure used to produce feature-length westerns. Southern California contained vast open country for recreating the Old West and many studio-operated movie ranches where they maintained horse stables and cattle herds. Buck Jones was one of the biggest stars of the genre. In 1934 he made *Red Rider*, which was so well received Jones made two other serials over the next two years. Johnny Mack Brown was another western star. He appeared in three series with a total of forty-two episodes including *Flaming Frontiers* (1938). Feature star Tim McCoy also made western serials.

Jungle Adventures combined stunt action with animal performances and gave producers an excuse to dress the female actresses in scanty costumes. Famed circus performer and animal trainer Clyde Beatty starred in the 1934 serial *The Lost Jungle. The Jungle Menace* series featured Frank Buck in 1937. By far the most popular jungle serial was the *Tarzan* series, based on the novels of Edgar Rice Burroughs. The first in the series, *Tarzan the Fearless* (1933), starred Olympic athlete Larry "Buster" Crabbe. So popular was the series that it spawned a feature-length series, which starred Olympic medal winner Johnny Weissmuller and Maureen O'Sullivan. Over one hundred Tarzan movies have been made, including Spanish language and animated versions.

Aerial Action serials grow out of the many feature-length films made about flying. Given that Los Angeles was a center of aircraft development and production and given the ready supply of stunt pilots, serials were relatively inexpensive and easy to produce. Two outstanding series were *Mystery Squadron* (1933) and *Ace Drummond* (1936). *Drummond* was based on the popular comic strip of the same name.

Fantasy serials were also popular in the 1930s. Bela Lugosi, who had starred in Universal's *Dracula* and several vampire sequels, starred in the serial *Return of Chandu* (1934). In it he played a mysterious magician. Two more *Chandu* series and a feature film were made by 1939. In 1935 the singing cowboy radio star Gene Autry appeared in a science fiction series titled *The Phantom Empire*. The most popular fantasy series was *Flash Gordon* (1936), based on a 1934 comic strip by Alex Raymond. Larry "Buster" Crabbe was the space traveling star of the series, which featured fanciful sets and imaginative characters and plots. Three sequels were made, totaling forty episodes.

MOB RULE, G-MEN, AND WOMEN OF THE STREETS

Authorities in government and in the film world were concerned with the possibility that the incredible economic suffering so many Americans were experiencing could lead to some form of anarchy or mob rule. There were plenty of examples to draw from elsewhere, as no country in the world completely escaped the Great Depression, and some fared much worse than America. Another fear was that mobs would become an excuse for the imposition of a Fascist dictatorship such as the ones that seemed to be flourishing in Italy and Germany. To reflect these concerns, mobs, mob bosses and demagogues became regular features in thirties film. Some films embraced authoritarianism; some rejected it.

This Day and Age is a 1932 film by Cecil B. DeMille. In it a group of blonde, blue-eyed high school kids decide to take matters into their own hands when a gangster named Garrett (played by Charles Bickford) uses his "million dollar mouthpiece" (shyster lawyer) to get off on a technicality on a murder charge. They kidnap Garrett and take him to a brickyard, where a huge crowd awaits with torches, chanting high school cheers. Garrett is tied up and slowly lowered into a pit teeming with hundreds of rats until he cracks and confesses the murder. The film argues that hoodlums and shysters will take over the country if the people don't take action.

Gabriel Over the Whitehouse was produced by William Randolph Hearst's Cosmopolitan Pictures and very much reflects Hearst's editorials of the time, which called for a strong leader to take over America and get it back "on the right track." Director Gregory La Cava tells the story of a run-of-the mill, hands-off President who experiences a miraculous recovery from a serious automobile accident. Back in office, his outlook has completely changed. He declares a state of national emergency and takes over all government power, branding Congress as "traitorous to the concept of democracy." He enacts laws suspending mortgage payments and sets up an army of the unemployed. He is going to fix what's wrong with the country. The hoodlums have a different outlook. They are making money from the Great Depression and don't want it to stop. They have a leader of a jobless march on Washington assassinated as an example of what happens to do-gooders. The President retaliates by getting the government into the retail liquor business, thus cutting off one of the hood's best revenue streams. The bad guys retaliate gangland style by driving a black limo up to the White House and riddling it with bullets. This gives the newly formed national police the excuse to round up every hoodlum in the country. From there the President goes on to conquer the world and declare peace. Needless to say MGM, the company that distributed Cosmopolitan pictures, was concerned about distributing Hearst's call for a dictatorship and world domination by America.

FURY (1936), DIRECTED BY FRITZ LANG, SHOWN: THE LYNCH MOB

Anti-mob, anti-lynching films presented an opposing view of America. *Fury* is a film Fritz Lang (one of the last expressionist directors to get out of Germany) made at MGM in 1936. It takes place in a small town where a recent kidnapping has put people on edge. Spencer Tracy plays a stranger who just happens to be passing through town. He gets thrown in jail on suspicion, but the sheriff is reluctant to push it any further, believing that Tracy is probably the wrong man. A mob forms and burns down the jail to execute the prisoner. There is an exuberance to the mob that is fueled by Tracy's screams of agony. Smiling mothers hold up their children to see through the jail house windows as the suspected kidnapper is put to death. Eventually the sheriff arrests the ringleaders, and they stand trial for murder. They are about to be convicted when Tracy, who has managed to survive the ordeal, appears in court to save the very people who tried to kill him.

Another film that takes the anti-mob point of view is *They Won't Forget*, directed by Mervyn LeRoy for Warner Brothers in 1937. It depicts a mid-sized southern city in which a student in a secretarial school is murdered. The police arrest one of the teachers, a man from up north. The district attorney seizes the opportunity to gain political favor by getting a conviction and death sentence for the "Yankee" regardless of the truth. The governor realizes what the district attorney has done and pardons the northerner. A mob forms and takes matters into its own hands. Although LeRoy steered the film away from any racial overtones, the National Association for the Advancement of Colored People (NAACP) praised the film for its realistic depiction of the culture of racial lynching in the south.

One of the results of the Great Depression was the changing role of women in American society. Before the economic catastrophe, the archetypal American family consisted of a married couple comprising a breadwinning husband and a decision-making wife who cares for the children and household. With more than twenty-five percent of families losing their breadwinner, women had to become providers. Some women had to learn to take care of themselves however best they could. The movies began to reflect this new, worldlier woman.

Two of the greatest stars of the time, Marlene Dietrich and Greta Garbo, played women who had only one thing to sell and one way to survive. Joseph von Sternberg directed Dietrich in the 1932 Paramount production of *Blonde Venus*. The heroine is a nightclub entertainer in Germany who meets and marries a dashing young American chemist. They re-

BLONDE VENUS (1932), DIRECTED BY JOSEF VON STERNBERG, SHOWN FROM LEFT: MARLENE DIETRICH, CARY GRANT

PARAMOUNT PICTURES/PHOTOFEST

turn to his hometown, have a son, and start a family. Dietrich's husband comes down with a deadly case of radium poisoning. The only cure is at an expensive hospital in Germany. They can't afford it. She goes back to entertaining in a degrading cabaret setting. She comes up with the money to send her husband for the treatments. The money comes not from performing but from the local millionaire (played by Cary Grant) the heroine has seduced to get money for the treatments.

Garbo similarly is forced to use her sexuality to get by in *Susan Lenox, Her Fall and Rise* (1931). She plays a young girl who is little more than a servant to her family. They arrange a marriage for her. When the intended groom shows up, he can't keep his hands off her. She runs away and ends up in a circus, where she becomes the owner's mistress. She moves on to spend time with a rich politician but dreams of reuniting with her one lost love (played by Clark Gable). She tries to follow him to Panama, where she ends up as a bar girl at The Paradise Café.

Women of the world are another archetype that arises in the thirties. Mae West displayed a take-charge bawdiness, a sense of humor about sex that liberates her from the need to even consider the issue of guilt and morality. Jean Harlow characters were often placed in exotic locations and dangerous situations, but these women have a self-confidence and resourcefulness that ensures the audience that they will be all right. She has the same kind of bravery that men are supposed to have and the kind of tenderness that men desire. Joan Crawford's characters often found themselves in desperate circumstances and about to experience something awful. But her characters' wits and quickness get them out of trouble. Bette Davis was just plain tough. Audiences knew that she would do whatever it took to survive and didn't mind if it meant getting into a brawl along the way.

The gangster, shyster, and mob movies painted a picture of an America that was out of control. The Roosevelt administration, the Hays Office, and the leaders of the motion picture industry all agreed that there was a need to present a more orderly and wholesome image of the country. The G-man films are part of that response that deal with issues of honor and morality. Warner Brothers was beginning to become serious about the power of films to effect social consciousness. Jack Warner had become friendly with Roosevelt and used his position as the man in charge of which films got made at the studio to support the aims of the new deal. Three films released by the studio in 1935 and 1936 (*G-Men, Bullets or Ballots*, and *Public Enemy's Wife*) portray federal police like the FBI and Treasury Department as fearless crime fighters who have the numbers, brains, and guns to get the country under control and rid society of its hoodlums.

Paramount came at the same issue in a more oblique manner. Two large-scale westerns, *The Plainsman* (1936) and *The Texas Rangers* (1936), invoke the specter of frontier justice as an allegory for dealing with lawlessness in the 1930s. Cecil B. DeMille's *The Plainsman* stars Gary Cooper as legendary Wild Bill Hickok and Jean Arthur as the equally legendary Calamity Jane. They use their superior skill with guns and their unwavering moral compasses to tame the West and banish outlaws and Native Americans alike. DeMille's formalistic tableau-style of directing gives the heroes a godlike and historical quality that is intended to inspire respect for the law in the present time. King Vidor's *The Texas Rangers* begins with a group of outlaws in the wilds of Texas. They join the Texas Rangers for the sake of a job as well as to give inside information to friends who are still on the wrong side of the law. The Rangers transform the countryside, civilizing it with their no-nonsense approach to criminality. In the process the two former outlaws become civilized themselves. The story is an unabashed advertisement for the power of the law's goodness.

THE WARNER BROTHERS AND SOCIAL CONSCIOUSNESS

Early in the decade of the 1930s Warner Brothers was engaged in making films that dealt with social problems from a position of advocacy. Mervyn LeRoy's 1932 film *I Am a Fugitive from a Chain Gang* wasn't a stock prison movie; it was an attack on the entire chain gang system of prisons.

GREAT DIRECTORS OF THE THIRTIES

John Ford was born John Martin Feeney in Portland, Maine in 1895. His father was an Irish immigrant who worker for many years as a lobsterman until he saved up enough to open a saloon. The Feeneys had eleven children, five of whom died in childhood. John was a distinguished athlete and an adequate student at Portland High School. His greatest school glory came in his senior year, when the school football team won the state championship. John's older brother, Francis, had dropped out of school to join the army in 1898. For several years Francis got in and out of trouble until he was invited to try his lot at acting for the American branch of the Georges Méliès motion picture company in 1907. He changed his name from Feeney to Ford so as not to be an embarrassment to his family. In addition to acting, he also did location scouting and worked toward his goal of directing.

I AM A FUGITIVE FROM A CHAIN GANG (1932), DIRECTED BY MERVYN LEROY, SHOWN: PAUL MUNI (FRONT, AS JAMES ALLEN)

WARNER BROS./PHOTOFEST

By 1912 Francis Ford was working as a director for Thomas Ince, making westerns in the Santa Monica mountains that border Los Angeles. The films they made were very good for the time, but Ince was reluctant to share credit with Ford, so he moved on to Universal the following year. Between 1913 and 1916 Ford produced and directed over eighty films and at least one serial. After graduating from high school in 1914, John Feeney changed his name to John Ford and followed in his brother Francis' footsteps to Hollywood.

In 1914 construction had barely begun on Carl Laemmle's grand design for Universal City. Working conditions were crude but for young John Ford it was a matter of getting into the business on the ground floor. Many legends attach to Ford from this period in his life. He was a prodigious storyteller and was not overly concerned with the truthfulness of his tales. One account of his beginnings had Ford working as an extra on D. W. Griffith's *Birth of a Nation* in 1915. It is certain that Ford did work as a prop boy at Universal at this time, eventually working his way up to more responsible positions. It didn't hurt to have an older brother with some clout within the studio hierarchy. His big break finally did arrive when

Harry Carey, a good friend of Francis, convinced Laemmle to try out young John Ford as a director. The resulting film, *Soul Herder*, was the first of more than twenty films Carey and Ford would make over the next four years. Throughout his life Ford was known as an extremely loyal man. Forty years after *Soul Herder*, Ford was still casting Carey's son, Harry Carey, Jr., in gratitude for Harry Sr.'s help at the beginning of Ford's career.

In December 1920 John Ford left Universal and signed with Fox. It was a step up in quality. At Fox, production budgets were much greater than at Universal. Also the studio was better organized, had better actors under contract, and paid its directors more. The last detail was particularly important to Ford as he had met a girl, Mary McBryde Smith, the previous St. Patrick's Day, and things were getting serious between the two. They were married in July and had their first son, Patrick, nine months later. By 1922 Ford was making over $22,000 per year. Fox was a production wonderland compared to Universal. The great James Wong Howe led a staff of some of the best cinematographers of the day. Ford's directing colleagues included Raoul Walsh, Frank Borzage, and Howard Hawks. Western star Tom Mix was the most important actor on the lot. With his experience directing westerns, Ford fit right in. By 1923 both Fox and Paramount were producing westerns on an epic scale, and audiences were responding enthusiastically.

In 1924 Fox announced that it would make a major motion picture about the construction of the transcontinental railway in the years following the American Civil War. Ford wanted the assignment and campaigned vigorously for it. It was a big responsibility for a director who hadn't yet turned thirty, but Ford already had fifty-two films, mostly westerns, to his credit. The studio executives liked his enthusiasm and gave him the job. Most of the film was shot in Arizona, where the construction department had built a set the size of a small city. Production began with a skeleton crew shooting a cattle drive in Mexico. The work was rugged and Ford loved it. He had also become impressed with his star, George O'Brien, who didn't seem to be fazed by falling off horses and the other discomforts associated with production. For part of the production the company had to live on the trains they were filming. To make matters more difficult, the scenario the studio had prepared for the picture was terrible. Ford had to make it up as he went. Even the assistant editor was forced into action as an actor. In the end the result was spectacular. Ford and crew had captured the drama and excitement of a great historical event in *The Iron Horse*. In the eyes to the Fox executives, the studio had a new star director on its talent roster.

Over the next two years Ford made six more films. They were all successful but none was outstanding. The studio wanted another feature that would be as prestigious as *Iron Horse*. The project was titled *Three Bad Men* and writer John Stone was employed to help with story details while Ford focused on creating large-scale action sequences. Victorville, California was the location for recreating a grand land rush scene. Ford had camera pits dug into the plane where the scene was shot so that horses and wagons could literally roll over the screen. The Teton Mountains near Jackson Hole, Wyoming were also used as a location. The finished film was beautiful to look at, if a little unimaginative in the story department. It was an unmitigated hit, and at the end of the year Fox made Ford the highest paid director in Hollywood with a salary of $2,500 per week.

In 1927 the great German Expressionist director F. W. Murnau was signed by Fox both to produce films for the company and to instruct young directors like Ford and Hawks about expressionist technique. There is no record of discontent with this decision on the part of Ford, who even recycled some of the sets from Murnau's masterpiece, *Sunrise*, for his film *Four Sons* (1928), which was considered another very successful Ford film. Later in the year, Ford was encouraged to get some experience working with Fox's new Movietone sound system. *Napoleon's Barber*, a thirty-two minute comedy short, became his first sound film. Studio executives were sufficiently impressed with Ford's work as to pencil him in as one of the younger directors who would survive the transition to talking pictures in spite of his growing reputation as a serious drinker. Ford's first sound feature, *Strong Boy*, starred Victor McLaglen a big, rugged and burly actor with whom Ford would work for many years to come. In 1929, at a time when directors struggled just to get the dialogue properly recorded on their films, Ford and McLaglen teamed up on a very successful action-sound film, *The Black Watch*. The film follows the adventures of a group of British soldiers trapped in India at the outbreak of World War I.

After the stock market crash in late 1929, the Fox studio was in deep financial trouble and without competent leadership. This condition of near anarchy benefited Ford to some extent; he was perfectly happy working with reduced studio interference, and his films were making money for the cash-strapped company. As far as Ford's finances were concerned, he had lost $76,000 between 1930 and 1932, but he made almost $270,000 during the same time. In 1930 Fox loaned out Ford to Samuel Goldwyn, who had recently acquired the rights to the novel *Arrowsmith*

ARROWSMITH (1931), DIRECTED BY JOHN FORD, SHOWN: RONALD COLMAN, HELEN HAYES

UNITED ARTISTS/PHOTOFEST

by Sinclair Lewis. The film starred two respected stage actors, Ronald Coleman and Helen Hayes. Production proceeded in a businesslike manner and was uneventful except for a few dustups between Ford and Hayes. However, two days after the film had wrapped, Ford was due to begin work with the editor. Ford was a no show. Ten days later Ford finally showed but had obviously been on an alcoholic binge and was unable to work. He disappeared again until October 1, again showing up too hungover to work. Goldwyn took over the reshoots and editing. Two days later Fox announced Ford was fired.

Ford didn't exactly have his choice of studios at this point in his career, and it didn't help that his brother, Francis, had recently bottomed out as a drunk and had been banished from the business. Universal studios came to the rescue. Carl Laemmle had always been grateful for the work Francis and John had done and was willing to be the first to step forward. Ford made *Air Mail*, a perfectly successfully film that encouraged other studios to make him offers. Next came MGM, who wanted Ford to direct Wallace Beery in the wrestling movie *Flesh*. It wasn't a project that particularly interested him, but Ford still needed to prove himself. It worked, and Fox invited Ford back. Ford never signed another long-term contract with the studio but it was enough that he had regained his reputation and stature within the industry.

For the next several years Ford worked mostly for either Fox or for RKO. In 1933 he made two average films at Fox and moved to RKO the next year to make another outstanding adventure film, *The Lost Patrol*, produced by Merrian C. Cooper. Next he was back at Fox to direct Will Rogers in *Judge Priest*. Ford's career was on solid ground again. He decided that it was time to treat himself to a yacht befitting a great director and sailor. He purchased 110-foot long ketch, The Araner. It had two fireplaces, twin-diesel engines, and a poker table in the central salon. It required a crew of six to sail. At the same time Ford registered as a member of the U.S. Navy Reserve, who were glad to have him because of the many films he had made celebrating the Navy's prowess. One of his duties for the Navy was to secretly sail The Araner along military shipping lanes and to photograph the coastline.

The year 1935 was an important year in Ford's career. He made *The Informer* at RKO, which won him his first Oscar for best director, and at the end of the year he became one of the founding members

THE INFORMER (1935), DIRECTED BY JOHN FORD, SHOWN ON-THE-SET IN CENTER: DIRECTOR JOHN FORD (SEATED BACK TO CAMERA), VICTOR MCLAGLAN

RKO RADIO PICTURES/PHOTOFEST

of the new Screen Director's Guild. The following year Ford directed Katharine Hepburn in the RKO picture *Mary of Scotland*. The director and the star spent hours together at her home in the Hollywood Hills. A romance bloomed. Ford's deep Roman Catholic beliefs made it impossible for him to consider leaving his family, and Hepburn would have him on no other terms. The affair ended quietly with the release of the film. Perhaps as atonement, Ford moved back to Fox to direct little Shirley Temple in an adaptation of a Kipling story, *Wee Willie Winkie* (1937). The following year he made two successful adventure films for Fox, but he had something special on his mind that he wanted to discuss with John Wayne.

In late 1938 Ford and Wayne went for a long cruise aboard The Araner. Ford had a script for a western that he wanted Wayne to read. It was unlike any western that had ever been made before. The story was told from several different points of view. The leading man was an escaped convict and a murderer. The leading lady was a prostitute. It was the most adult story ever conceived as a western. Ford thought it just might revive Wayne's moribund career. The director also had a novel idea for shooting the film. Rather than using one of the local studio movie ranches and the usual movie stunt men, Ford wanted to take the production to Monument Valley on the Utah-Arizona boarder. The scenery was majestic, dwarfing the presence of humans the same way the real frontier had done. Part of the territory was an Indian reservation, and there were many Native Americans nearby who could ride and shoot and who were eager to get the work a motion picture would provide. Wayne agreed, and the two set out to make one of the most influential films in movie history, *Stagecoach* (1939). Ford didn't get his second Oscar that year because the competition was the fiercest in Academy history (he did get his statue two years later for How Green Was My Valley.) However, John Wayne's acting career was revived.

GREAT MOVIE STARS OF THE THIRTIES

Clark Gable was born William Clark Gable in 1901. His father was an oil driller, and his mother died before his first birthday. He was sent to live with his grandparents until his father remarried. The three-year-old Gable went back to live with his father and his new step-mother, Jeannie, who doted upon him. Jeannie Gable was an accomplished pianist and made sure that her stepson could play as well. Gable's father was a rough man who taunted his son, calling him a sissy because of his shyness and lack of interest in sports and other typical masculine activities. Gable dropped out of high school to escape his father's house. He moved to Akron, Ohio, where he supported himself working in a factory. Soon he was involved with a local theater group.

GONE WITH THE WIND (1939), DIRECTED BY VICTOR FLEMING, SHOWN FROM LEFT: CLARK GABLE (AS RHETT BUTLER), VIVIEN LEIGH (AS SCARLETT O'HARA)

MGM/PHOTOFEST

Jeannie Gable became seriously ill when her stepson was seventeen. He returned home just in time to be with her when she died. Her death was almost more than Gable could handle. Furthermore, his father insisted that the young man learn the oil drilling business, and the two departed for the oil fields of Oklahoma. Gable hated the work. He took a small amount of money inherited from his grandfather and headed west to Portland, Oregon to pursue an acting career. In Portland he joined an acting group headed by Josephine Dillon, a woman fifteen years his senior. As was the case with his stepmother and other women later in life, Gable was taken in by Dillon, who married him and made him over from a Midwestern farm boy into a handsome, well-dressed actor. She got his teeth straightened, taught him proper manners, and got him to use his middle name, Clark. Next she took him to Hollywood in 1923 to break into acting. By 1926 Gable became impatient that his career wasn't developing quickly enough, and he left Dillon to seek greener pastures in New York.

Once again, Gable became involved with an older woman. Ria Langham was seventeen years older and became the second Mrs. Gable. Langham continued Gable's grooming and introduced him to socially influential people. When he was cast in an important role in the play *The Last Mile*, he caught the attention of MGM talent scouts, who signed him and brought him back to Hollywood in 1931. His first screen appearance for MGM was in *The Easiest Way*. In 1931 he appeared in ten films. The last was *Hell Divers*, in which he co-starred with Wallace Beery. MGM was in need of a new leading man to replace John Gilbert. Gable's tall, rugged masculinity was just the ticket. His looks also appealed to another

MGM star, Joan Crawford. When Louis B. Mayer discovered the two were involved, he threatened to cancel their contracts, effectively ending their relationship, with Gable moving on to an affair with Marion Davies, the mistress of media magnate William Randolph Hearst.

During the early thirties, Gable's star was steadily rising. He was becoming MGM's most valuable actor. In 1934 he approached Mayer to ask for a raise from his $2,000-per-week salary. Mayer decided to teach him a lesson and loaned Gable to Harry Cohn at Columbia. Gable co-starred opposite Claudette Colbert in Frank Capra's screwball comedy, *It Hap-*

THE MISFITS (1961), DIRECTED BY JOHN HUSTON, SHOWN: ESTELLE WINWOOD, MARILYN MONROE, CLARK GABLE

pened One Night. The film swept the Oscars, winning Best Actor, Best Actress, Best Director, and Best Picture. When Gable returned to MGM his salary was doubled to $4,000 per week. Gable continued to work at a fever pitch. In 1934 he appeared in five films. The next year he starred in four, including large-scale adventures such as *China Seas* and *Mutiny on the Bounty*. Once again Gable became involved with an MGM star, Loretta Young, with whom he had worked on *The Call of the Wild*. Young became pregnant, and the studio chose to construct an elaborate cover-up, sending her on an extended European vacation. The baby's paternity never became public until after Young's death in 2000.

1936 was another hectic year for Gable. He made four films including the epic *San Francisco*. Throughout the remainder of the decade MGM continued to create showcase roles for their great star. In 1939 he received his greatest role, Rhett Butler in the Civil War classic *Gone with the Wind*, based on Margaret Mitchell's hugely popular novel. When adjusted for inflation, the domestic box office gross is the highest in American motion picture history. It was also the high point in Gable's career. That year he also married the love of his life, the beautiful comedy actress Carole Lombard. It was one of the legendary Hollywood romances, but it ended tragically in 1942 when she died in a plane crash while touring to sell war bonds. Gable mourned by joining the army air force, where he flew five combat missions before the end of the war in Europe. Gable returned to Hollywood, if not to his former position as number one box office star, in 1945.

In 1949 Gable married for the fourth time to Lady Silvia Ashley. He had an affair with Kay Spreckles, who became the fifth Mrs. Gable in 1955. During the fifties Gable continued to make one or two films each year, but he was growing older and tired of working. In late 1960 Gable suffered a major heart attack while completing work on his last film, *The Misfits*, opposite Marilyn Monroe and Montgomery Clift. Tragically Monroe would make only one more film before her suicide in 1962. On November 16, 1960 Gable suffered a fatal heart attack. His wife was three months pregnant. He never saw his only son.

MYRNA LOY AND WILLIAM POWELL

Myrna Loy was yet another successful screen actress who lost her father at an early age. She was born in Helena, Montana in 1905. Her father was involved in politics, real estate, and banking and was able to provide a comfortable life for his family. Her mother had studied at the American Conservatory of Music in Chicago. In 1918 Loy's father died, and the family relocated to Culver City, a suburb of Los Angeles. The family survived on the income her mother made teaching music. Loy attended Venice High School and excelled in speech competitions and theater. She left school in 1923 to work as a dancer at Sid Grauman's Egyptian Theater, which offered live entertainment to accompany its featured movie programs.

Loy's first movie role was a small part dancing in Cecil B. DeMille's *Ten Commandments*. The experience convinced her to try to break into movies. She tested unsuccessfully for roles in several MGM films before signing a seven-year, $75-per-week contract with Warner Brothers in 1925. Early on she was cast in exotic roles such as the native girl Azuri in the 1929 sound film *The Desert Song*. After the stock market crash of 1929, Warner Brothers let go of many of their contract actors, including Loy. As a free agent, she moved to Goldwyn Studios, where she was cast in her first nonexotic role in *The Devil to Pay*. During the next six years Loy remained a freelance actress, appearing in over sixty films, all in small parts. At the end of 1931, MGM's Irving Thalberg recognized something special in Loy, signed her to a contract, and cast the young actress in her first comedy role in Ruben Mamoulian's Jeanette McDonald musical, *Love Me Tonight*.

In 1934 Loy got her most important role to date, starring in the gangster movie *Manhattan Melodrama*. Shortly thereafter she was cast in *The Thin Man* opposite William Powell. This would become the signature role for both actors. Filmed in only twelve days by W. S. Van Dyke (also known as "one-take Woody"), the film was a stylish adaptation of a Dashiell Hammett Nick and Nora Charles detective novel. Loy played a wealthy heiress married to a private detective. Both are very fond of martinis and solving crimes while maintaining a busy social life. Their small dog, Asta, was their constant companion. In all, Loy and Powell made six *Thin Man Films* and starred together in eight others.

THE THIN MAN (1934), DIRECTED BY W.S. VAN DYKE, SHOWN FROM LEFT: WILLIAM POWELL (AS NICK CHARLES), ASTA, MYRNA LOY (AS NORA CHARLES)

Their screen pairings were a guarantee for box office success. When Loy discovered that her $3,000-per-week salary was half of Powell's, she staged a labor strike by taking an extended vacation to Europe with her husband, production manager Arthur Hornblow. Louis B. Mayer relented, and Loy was given her raise and a $25,000 bonus. It was one of only a few instances in which actors had successfully campaigned against Mayer for more money.

Between 1934 and 1939 Loy appeared in twenty-one films. In 1939 a newspaper reader's poll voted Loy and Clark Gable the queen and king of movies, so great was Loy's popularity. World War II brought a great deal of change to Loy's life. She divorced the controlling Hornblow, dedicated herself to the war effort by joining the naval auxiliary, and became involved in a brief, unhappy marriage with John Hertz, a rich New York advertising executive. At the war's end Loy married for the third time and left MGM, where she had been offered a succession of inferior roles as punishment for her recent lack of productivity. At that time, she extended her career by accepting roles for older women. *The Best Years of Our Lives*, by far the greatest of the films made about soldiers adjusting to life after war, was Loy's first role playing a mother to a teenager. Over the next few years she teamed up with Cary Grant on two very successful comedies, *The Bachelor and The Bobbysoxer* and *Mr. Blandings Builds His Dream House*.

William Powell's movie career began in 1922 when he appeared with John Barrymore in the film version of *Sherlock Holmes*. Powell was born in Pittsburgh, Pennsylvania in 1892. His father, an accountant, moved the family to Kansas City, where Powell grew up. He was expected to become a lawyer but an experience on stage during his high school years convinced him that acting was his true calling. With money he saved from a job at the telephone company and a loan from a wealthy aunt, Powell moved to New York in 1911 and enrolled in the American Academy of Dramatic Arts. One of his classmates was Edward G. Robinson. Powell got his first stage role after a year at the academy and began a period of his life in which he traveled extensively with stock companies presenting the popular plays of the day. He married in 1915 and had one son, William David Powell, ten years later.

Powell's big break came when a movie executive saw him onstage and approached him for the role in *Sherlock Holmes*. He proceeded to make thirty-four silent films over the next seven years, mostly for Paramount. He also worked for William Randolph Hearst's Cosmopolitan Pictures, which was affiliated with MGM. During this period he specialized in playing sophisticated, urbane characters. In 1929 Powell appeared in his first talking picture as private detective Philo Vance in *The Canary Murder Case*. He played Vance in four other films. Powell's voice not only suited his suave image, it enhanced it. He was a natural for talking pictures, and demand for his services increased. In 1931 he moved to Warner Brothers, where

HOW TO MARRY A MILLIONAIRE (1953), DIRECTED BY JEAN NEGULESCO, SHOWN FROM LEFT: WILLIAM POWELL (AS J.D. HANLEY), LAUREN BACALL (AS SCHATZE PAGE)

TWENTIETH CENTURY FOX/PHOTOFEST

he worked exclusively until he was cast by Cosmopolitan alongside Loy and Clark Gable in *Manhattan Melodrama*. The director, W. S. Van Dyke—one of the most respected on the MGM lot—observed the easy chemistry between Powell and Loy on the set. He convinced skeptical studio executives to let him pair up the two on the first *Thin Man* film. MGM was so reluctant about the experiment that it allowed for only twelve shooting days rather than the customary twenty-four. When the result was a smash hit, MGM made plans for many more Powell-Loy films.

Throughout the remainder of his career, Powell appeared in a number of memorable roles including the screwball comedy *My Man Godfrey* (1936). Powell had campaigned for years to get MGM to acquire the rights to the popular stage play *Life with Father*. When Warner Brothers purchased the rights in 1947, Powell jumped at the chance to play the part. In 1953 he appeared in the successful comedy *How to Marry a Millionaire*. Two years later Powell was cast in his last great screen role in *Mr. Roberts*. He had been in the movie business for over thirty years. By that time television was threatening the film industry. Powell made plans to retire to Palm Springs, where he lived until his death in 1984.

Cary Grant began his performing career as a fourteen-year-old member of the Bob Pender Comedy Troupe touring the small towns of England. His birth name was Archibald Leach. His parents were extremely poor, and he was nine when his mother experienced a mental breakdown that left her institutionalized for the remainder of her life. Leach's specialty was acrobatics and pantomime. In 1920 when he was only sixteen, the troupe departed for a two-year tour of America that ended in New York, where young Leach remained to try to make it on his own. He struggled for the next five years doing odd jobs including working as an escort. Finally in 1927 he landed his first significant stage role on Broadway. He did well as a stage actor, but in 1931 he decided that Hollywood would be a better fit. Upon his arrival he did a screen test for Paramount and was signed to a five-year contract. The studio wanted to change his name to Cary Lockwood, but he resisted. He settled on Cary Grant.

In 1932 Grant became a young contract actor on the rise. He appeared in eight films his first year in Hollywood. Starting with small roles, he ended the year costarring in two films opposite major Paramount stars. In *Blonde Venus* he was cast with Marlene Dietrich, and in *Madame Butterfly* with Silvia Sidney. However, at the time Grant was starting his film career, Paramount's biggest star was Mae West—blonde, bawdy, and buxom. The first time she glimpsed the young Englishman, she demanded that he be cast as her leading man. He was suavely handsome and had an obliging British quality that contrasted with and complemented West's brassiness. They made two films together in 1933, *She Done Him Wrong* and *I'm No Angel*. In both films he is the object of West's lusty wisecracking. The pairing probably would have lasted longer but the 1934 imposition of the Production Code put the brakes on West's career when she could no longer get away with her trademark suggestiveness.

In all Grant made six films in 1932. From 1933 through 1936 he starred in four films each year. Paramount kept him busy but he was restless with the shallowness of the roles he was getting. When his contract was fulfilled at the beginning of 1937, Grant decided it was time to move on. His last film for the studio was *Wedding Present*, a screwball comedy with Joan Bennett in which she gets most of the laughs. He was a big enough star by this time that he could determine his own fate without being tied to a single studio. He chose to sign joint contracts with both RKO and Columbia, most likely due to the two studios' reputations for giving talent relative freedom to do their best work without being subservient to the political agendas of the executives.

1937 became Grant's breakthrough year. He made two moderately successful films, *When You're in Love* for Columbia and *The Toast of New York* for RKO. He also made two major hits that year: *Topper,* produced by Hal Roach for MGM, and *The Awful Truth,* directed by Leo McCarey at Columbia. In *Topper*, Grant plays a rich sophisticate killed when he and his wife (played by Constance Bennett) wreck their sports car. They come back as ghosts to do one good thing and help henpecked Cosmo Topper learn how to stand up for himself. Together, Grant and Bennett are the model of glamorous high living and stylishness. It is the first time in his career that Grant is allowed to project the relaxed gracefulness that audiences found so appealing.

In *The Awful Truth* Grant finally became a major star. Going into the production he was wary of McCarey's belief in improvisation, fearing that he would appear more ridiculous than funny. But Grant was equal to the task. Mixing slapstick with farce, witty dialogue and razor-sharp timing, he gives one of the greatest comedy performances the decade. For once his costar doesn't dominate him. He and costar, Irene Dunne, blend like great jazz players, harmonizing their comedic riffs. *The Awful Truth* changed the industry's perception of Grant. He was no longer seen as just arm candy for leading ladies but as a versatile actor who has great charm and magnetism.

Between 1937 and 1940 Grant had one of most amazing strings of successful films in movie history. In 1938 he began his collaboration with Katharine Hepburn in Howard Hawks's *Bringing Up Baby* and George Cukor's *Holiday*. In 1939 Grant demonstrated his ability to play action heroes in director George Stevens's *Gunga Din* and in Hawks'

THE AWFUL TRUTH (1937), DIRECTED BY LEO MCCAREY, SHOWN FROM LEFT: IRENE DUNNE (AS LUCY WARRINER), ASTA (AS MR. SMITH), CARY GRANT (AS JERRY WARRINER)

COLUMBIA/PHOTOFEST

Only Angels Have Wings, in which he costarred with Jean Arthur. In 1940 he returned to comedy roles in Hawks' *His Girl Friday* opposite Rosalind Russell and in *My Favorite Wife* with Irene Dunne. At the end of the year he teamed up with Cukor and Hepburn again in the classic *The Philadelphia Story*. The following year his films weren't as notable, but in 1941 he began his long and fruitful partnership with Alfred Hitchcock in the film *Suspicion*, playing the role of a suspected killer.

Throughout the remainder of the forties and all through the fifties, Grant continued to work at the peak of his game at a time when his contemporaries were beginning to slow down and fall by the wayside. In 1943 he played a gambler with a big heart in *Mr. Lucky*;

and a submarine commander in *Destination Tokyo*. The following year he returned to comedy in *Arsenic and Old Lace*, directed by Frank Capra. In 1946 he worked with Hitchcock again on *Notorious*. In 1949 he starred in Howard Hawks' best post war comedy, *I Was a Male War Bride*. In 1955 and 1959 Grant starred in two of Hitchcock's greatest films, *To Catch a Thief* and *North by Northwest*. The later film required the fifty-five-year-old actor to climb walls and Mt. Rushmore and to romance the much younger Eva Marie Saint, all of which he does beautifully and believably.

Grant's last great romantic part was opposite Audrey Hepburn (who was twenty five years younger than her costar) in the Stanley Donen film *Charade* (1963). He was fifty-nine years old at the time and was beginning to consider the need for a graceful retirement that would leave his reputation intact. He made just two more films after *Charade*, *Father Goose* (1963) and *Walk, Don't Run* (1966), both fluffy comedies that weren't quite up his standards. It was a good time to announce his departure from acting as the film world was about to go through one of its most profound periods of change. Older stars that tried to hang on in the late sixties and seventies often ended up embarrassing themselves. Always the most graceful man in Hollywood, Grant's retirement was as well timed as his many comedy performances. He made seventy-three films in all, a prodigious output considering almost all of his parts were leading roles. During his career Grant worked with most of the great directors and leading ladies of the time. It is no accident that those films were some of their best work.

Gary Cooper was born Frank James Cooper in Helena, Montana on May 7, 1901. His father, Charles, was a prosperous Helena lawyer who rose to become a Montana Supreme Court Justice from 1919 to 1924. The Cooper family split time between life in the state capital and life at their Seven-Bar-Nine Ranch near Yellowstone National Park. In 1910 the doctors told Cooper's mother that she needed the beneficial air of a long sea voyage. She took Cooper and his brother to England, where they settled and didn't return until World War I broke out in Europe in 1917. Cooper attended high school in Montana and college in Montana and Iowa. It was during this time that he became interested in acting.

Cooper came to Hollywood around 1924. He spent his first year working as an extra on westerns, where his ranch skills were a distinct advantage. In 1926 United Artists cast him in *The Winning of Barbara Worth*. His performance in the film drew the attention of Paramount, which signed him in 1927 and cast him in a small role in the hit aerial film *Wings*. From there he was assigned to leading roles in B-picture westerns. He made his last silent film in 1929. That same year he starred in the film that brought him to prominence, *The Virginian*, another western in which he played a man of action and very few words. It was an excellent showcase for his authentically good looks. Cooper became a romantic leading man when he was cast opposite Marlene Dietrich in the exotic *Morocco*.

Throughout the 1930s Cooper continued to demonstrate his versatility appearing in pulp fiction detective roles, romantic leading male roles, and a few notable comedies. In 1936 Paramount loaned him out to Columbia, where he starred in Frank Capra's great *Mr. Deeds Goes to Town*. The role gave Cooper the opportunity to demonstrate his vulnerable side as well as his comic timing. After returning to Paramount he was featured in a series of big-budget epic films, including Cecil B. DeMille's *The Plainsman* (1936).

In 1941 Cooper reunited with Capra to make *Meet John Doe*. This started a string of four of his greatest films: *Sergeant York* (for which he won a best actor Oscar), *Ball of Fire*, *The Pride of the Yankees* (1942), and *For Whom the Bell Tolls* (1943), which was based on the novel by his close friend and hunting partner, Ernest Hemmingway. Cooper received his second Oscar nomination for his work on *For Whom the Bell Tolls*. Throughout the remainder of the 1940s he appeared in a number of successful if not brilliant films. However in 1952 he was given his greatest role as the heroic marshal in *High Noon*, for which he won his second Oscar. Cooper continued to work regularly through the fifties until contracting lung cancer in 1960. He died of the disease in 1961.

Bette Davis was born Ruth Davis in Lowell, Massachusetts in 1908. As was the case with many of Hollywood's leading ladies, Davis's father abandoned the family when she was young. Her mother struggled to raise the money to send her to a proper girls boarding school. After graduation Davis enrolled in a dramatic academy to study acting. She made her Broadway debut in *Broken Dishes* in 1929. This earned her an invitation to Hollywood to screen test for Universal Pictures. She appeared in six small roles for the studio and prepared to return to the stage at the end of her contract. However, Warner Brothers convinced her to sign another contract (for seven years) and remain in Hollywood. Her first major role, *The Man Who Played God* (1932), established Davis as a young star on the rise. She had intensity and intelligence and the drive that all great stars possess. In 1935 she won the first best ac-

SERGEANT YORK (1941), DIRECTED BY HOWARD HAWKS, SHOWN: GARY COOPER

ACADEMY AWARDS, 1936, SHOWN FROM LEFT: BETTE DAVIS (BEST ACTRESS) FOR DANGEROUS, (1935), VICTOR MCLAGLEN (BEST ACTOR) FOR THE INFORMER (1935)

tress Oscar in Warner Brothers' history for her appearance in *Dangerous* (1935).

In 1936 Davis became disenchanted with Warners because she felt that the roles they offered her were inadequate. In 1936 she left to make films in England. The studio sued and forced her return to Hollywood. Davis may have lost the battle, but she won the war. The studio offered her a better contract and the quality roles she had coveted. In 1938 she won her second Oscar for *Jezebel*. In spite of her reputation for being "difficult," Davis was the highest paid woman in America in 1942. During World War II she was instrumental in establishing the Hollywood Canteen, a USO recreation facility where service men could mingle with movie stars. She was later awarded the Distinguished Civilian Service Medal for her work on the Canteen.

ALL ABOUT EVE (1950), DIRECTED BY JOSEPH L. MANKIEWICZ, SHOWN FOREGROUND, FROM LEFT: ANNE BAXTER (AS EVE HARRINGTON), BETTE DAVIS; BACKGROUND: GARY MERRILL, CELESTE HOLM, GEORGE SANDERS, MARILYN MONROE, HUGH MARLOWE

TWENTIETH CENTURY FOX/PHOTOFEST

By 1950 Davis was accepting older female roles. She accomplished a major comeback for her work in *All About Eve*, for which she received her eighth Oscar nomination. She revived her career once again in 1962 with the grotesque *What Ever Happened to Baby Jane?* Davis also led an eventful personal life. She was married four times, all marriages reported to be stormy. She was the first woman to be President of the Motion Picture Academy of Arts and Sciences (the organization that awards Oscars). In her career Davis broke ground for generations of women who followed her into the motion picture industry. She made over one hundred films before her death in 1989.

Spencer Tracy was in most respects the opposite of the classic Hollywood matinee idol. He was handsome but in a rugged and rumpled way at a time when leading men were supposed to have classic good looks. It's no wonder that MGM teamed up Tracy with the studio's other unconventional-looking star, Clark Gable, and in so doing created the classic buddy picture formula. Tracy was also a contradiction. He was a devout Roman Catholic who remained in a loveless marriage for forty-four years rather than offend the church's stricture against divorce. Yet there were many women in his life. He was given to dark moods and monumental bouts of alcoholism, but his friends stood by him. He was a member of Hollywood's "Irish Mafia," a group that included John Ford, Leo McCarey, Pat O'Brien, Mickey Rooney, and Jimmy Cagney, but Tracy could also be a loner, an impulse that grew with age.

Tracy was born in Milwaukee, Wisconsin, in 1900. He was a terror as a child, getting himself kicked out of fifteen different schools before he departed upstate for Ripon College. Ripon is known for its excellence in speech and debate. Tracy proved to be very good at both and thought that he might capitalize on these talents by becoming an actor. He moved to New York and enrolled in the American Academy of Dramatic Arts in 1922. After graduating the next year Tracy knocked around Broadway for several years and developed his reputation as being a thoughtful and naturalistic actor. His break came in 1930 when he was cast as a convicted killer in the crime drama *The Last Mile*. John Ford saw the production and persuaded Fox to sign the thirty-year-old stage actor for Ford's next project, *Up the River*, a prison drama.

From the beginning Tracy was frustrated at Fox. The studio insisted on casting him in gangster and prison films, never giving him a chance to show what he could do. He expressed his frustration with heavy drinking. When he finally got a good role in *The Power and the Glory* (1933), the film did poorly at the box office. About this time Tracy started a relationship with Loretta Young, whom Fox had recently signed at significant expense. Given Tracy's drinking, poor attitude, poor box office, and the possibility of a complicated romance with an actress on the way up, the studio became convinced that he was more trouble than he was worth and did not renew his contract.

LIBELED LADY (1936), DIRECTED BY JACK CONWAY, SHOWN FROM LEFT: WILLIAM POWELL, SPENCER TRACY, JEAN HARLOW

MGM/PHOTOFEST

Louis B. Mayer could not see much of an upside to Tracy but Irving Thalberg's instincts told him that Tracy could be big if he were handled properly. Besides, MGM's star roster was disproportionately female at the time, and they desperately needed leading men. Tracy signed with the studio in 1935 and remained under contract for the next twenty-one years. In 1936 he paid MGM back with two very successful pictures, *San Francisco*, in which he costarred with Gable for the first time and for which he won the first of nine nominations for the best actor Academy Award. The second film, *Libeled Lady*, is an uproarious newspaper comedy with Jean Harlow, Myrna Loy, and William Powell. In 1937 and 1938 Tracy accomplished the rare feat of winning back-to-back Oscars for his performances in *Captains*

Courageous and *Boys Town*. Thalberg was completely vindicated for signing Tracy, who was proving to be the studio's most versatile star.

Tracy teamed up with Gable in two more excellent buddy-picture adventures, *Test Pilot* (1938) and *Boom Town* (1940). But Tracy's destiny was to become known for his pairings with an actress, not Gable. In 1942 he costarred with Katharine Hepburn in *Woman of the Year*. It was one of the few romantic comedies in which he had ever appeared. His looks and style just didn't match up well with MGM's leading ladies. The studio executives were skeptical of putting the two together. However, Hepburn had broken through as a major star in three consecutive films opposite Cary Grant: *Holiday* and *Bringing up Baby* in 1938, and *The Philadelphia Story* in 1940. MGM had just coaxed her away from RKO, where she had begun her career in 1932. Hepburn wanted Tracy for *Woman of the Year* and Hepburn got Tracy—in more ways than one. Not only did 1942 mark the beginning of their on-screen partnership, it was also the start of a romance that would endure for twenty-five years until Tracy's death. During that period they would appear in nine films together with never a false note. They were made for each other.

The Tracy-Hepburn partnership paid big dividends for MGM. They made five more films together in the 1940s including two masterpieces, *State of the Union* (1948) and *Adam's Rib* the following year. As the 1950s unfolded Tracy was still one of MGM's biggest stars, but age was catching up with him. The studio was beginning to see him as suitable only for fatherly roles. In fact his first film of the decade was *Father of the Bride* (1950). The film was commercially successful, but for Tracy it was unchallenging. In 1952 Tracy and Hepburn made their last MGM film together, *Pat and Mike*. The film featured Tracy's studied gruffness contrasted with Hepburn's cosmopolitan sophistication. It was another success. In 1955 Tracy made his last great film for the studio, *Bad Day at Black Rock*, an excellent nourish suspense story with Tracy facing down a whole town with a dark secret. He received another Oscar nomination for his work. The following year things fell apart for Tracy and MGM. On the set of *Tribute to a Bad Man* he began to object to Robert Wise's directing and complained bitterly about the least inconvenience. Eventually Wise had no option but to fire Tracy from the film, bringing to an end his long relationship with the studio.

Tracy's health was declining. He became a near recluse, living alone in a rented house or sharing the guest house at director George Cukor's estate with Hepburn. He saw almost no one and made no effort to find work. During this time he did strike up a relationship with director-producer Stanley Kramer, a man who was developing a reputation for making important issue-oriented films. The two began to make plans for future projects, which seemed to revive Tracy. In 1957 Tracy went back to work with Hepburn on *Desk Set*, a comedy set in the world of business. Next Warner Brothers called to cast Tracy as the solitary fisherman, Santiago, in the screen adaptation of Hemingway's *Old Man and the Sea* (1958). Another Hollywood war horse, the great John Ford, had a perfect part for Tracy as the embattled politician, Frank Skeffington, in *The Last Hurrah*. The two senior members of the "Irish Mafia" made an eloquent and sentimental film about the passing of old-school ward politics that was very well received by audiences and critics.

In 1960 Tracy and Stanley Kramer finally brought one of their projects to the screen, *Inherit the Wind*. The film is the story of the "Scopes Monkey Trial" in which a court was charged with deciding if Darwin's theory of evolution could be taught in public schools. Tracy played the great defense lawyer Clarence Darrow opposite Fredrick March as the great orator William Jennings Bryan. The acting fireworks displayed in the film belied the age of the two stars. Tracy received yet another nomination for Best Actor from the Motion Picture Academy. The following year he received another nomination when he and Kramer reunited on *Judgment at Nuremberg*, the story of the Nazi war crime trials. Again Tracy displayed great power in his performance. But he was

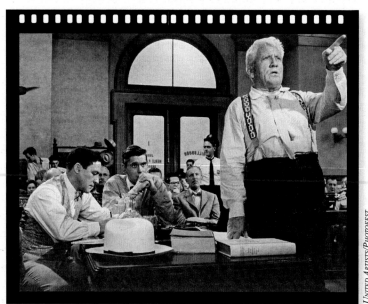

INHERIT THE WIND (1960), DIRECTED BY STANLEY KRAMER, SHOWN FROM LEFT: GENE KELLY (AS E.K. HORNBECK), DICK YORK (AS BERTRAM T. CATES), SPENCER TRACY (AS HENRY DRUMMOND)

UNITED ARTISTS/PHOTOFEST

slowing down noticeably. Next Kramer cast him in a huge, big-budget comedy, *It's a Mad, Mad, Mad, Mad World*. It was typical of the kind of film Hollywood was making to compete with television in 1963. It had a cast list of new and old stars that goes on for several pages. The project definitely took its toll on Tracy, who was dealing with a weak heart. Tracy's last film with Kramer was also his last. Seventeen days after the filming of *Guess Who's Coming to Dinner* wrapped, Tracy died in Hepburn's arms. He had spent his last measure of energy.

Katharine Hepburn always reminded interviewers and biographers that, because of her family's comfortable economic circumstances, she never had to struggle to get her career going as did most other Depression-era actors. She was born in 1907 near Hartford, Connecticut. Her father was a successful surgeon, and in the Hepburn household both Katharine and her older brother, Tom, were encouraged to become individualists and to have strong opinions, however unconventional. Tragedy struck the family in 1921 on a visit to the home of some friends in New York. It is believed that Tom was practicing a magic trick when he was found hanging from the rafters in the attic. This left an indelible mark of young Katharine. She decided that being a girl was "bunk" and cut off her hair and began dressing almost exclusively in pants. She became devoted to athletics, excelling at golf and tennis.

In 1928 Hepburn graduated from Bryn Mawr College, an exclusive school for girls from wealthy New England families. She also got married that year to Ludlow Ogden Smith, from a wealthy Pennsylvania family. In spite of being a new bride, Hepburn began to work in the small stock theater companies that abounded at that time. She was not an instant success. In fact, she was fired more than once, but she retained her supreme self-confidence and continued to plug away. A substantial role in *The Warrior's Husband* got her noticed enough to be invited to Hollywood for a screen test. RKO signed her despite the fact that her facial features were outside the Hollywood norm. She had high cheekbones that gave her face an angular look, but she also displayed an energy and presence that led to her first role in *A Bill of Divorcement* (1932), playing daughter to John Barrymore. The film was directed by George Cukor, who was known as a "woman's director." He had the gift of drawing great performances from the women with whom he worked. Cukor took an instant liking to Hepburn, and the two remained close friends for the rest of his life.

In 1933 Hepburn made three films including her performance as Jo in George Cukor's adaptation of *Little Women*. At RKO Hepburn was directed almost exclusively by Cukor and Pandro S. Berman. It was Berman who directed her in *Morning Glory* (1933), the story of a young actress who struggles to achieve success on Broadway. For this role Hepburn won the first of her four best actress Oscars. Achieving the motion picture industry's highest honor so soon in her career gave Hepburn a degree of freedom that was quite uncommon for the time. She used that freedom to return to the stage in New York whenever Hollywood wasn't sustaining her. In 1933 she sought to capitalize on her movie success and return to the relative comfort of the stage in a Broadway production of *The Lake*. The play was poorly received and proved to be a big disappointment to Hepburn. She returned to Hollywood.

In 1934 Hepburn made only one film. In 1935 she made two; in 1936 she made three films, with two more in 1937. None was very successful and Hepburn was beginning to be perceived as box-office poison. One reason for this lack of success was that compared to other studios, RKO was relatively disorganized at this time. It lacked a visionary executive who knew how to develop and nurture talent. It was a great place for star talent like John Ford and Astaire and Rogers,

BRINGING UP BABY (1938), DIRECTED BY HOWARD HAWKS, SHOWN FROM LEFT: CARY GRANT (AS DR. DAVID HUXLEY), NISSA (AS BABY, THE LEOPARD), KATHARINE HEPBURN (AS SUSAN VANCE)

RKO RADIO PICTURES/PHOTOFEST

who already had an audience following. But a young actress like Hepburn was lost in the shuffle. Furthermore, she was projecting a less-than-feminine image of women in her personal and screen life, choosing to dress in pants and show off her athletic abilities and a time when the norm was much more feminine. She would later be vindicated: In 1986 the Council of Fashion Designers gave Hepburn a lifetime achievement award for this masculine look. In 1938 she made two films, *Bringing up Baby* and *Holiday*. Considered classics today, they were poorly received at the time. Hepburn knew she had reached a crossroads in her career. She had lost momentum as a movie actress and, except for an appearance in a revival of *Jane Eyre*, her stage career was also in the doldrums. It was time to take matters into her own hands.

In 1939 New York playwright Philip Barry wrote a role in the play *Philadelphia Story* especially for Hepburn. The character, Tracy Lord, a high-spirited aristocrat, is about to marry her second husband when her first husband, a newspaper reporter, is assigned to cover the wedding. A series of romantic complications ensue. Hepburn was a hit in the play and became the toast of Broadway. Her boyfriend at the time, Howard Hughes, purchased the film rights for the play and made a gift of them to Hepburn. She had no trouble convincing Louis B. Mayer that MGM should make the picture with her in the leading role. She insisted that Cukor be the director. The resulting motion picture became one of the biggest successes in 1940 and established Hepburn as a major star.

Hepburn's next film was *Woman of the Year* (1942), her first of nine films made with Spencer Tracy. The two were box office magic together and off-screen their romance became the stuff of Hollywood legend. In all, Hepburn remained at MGM for ten years, during which time she worked with Tracy five times. Her departure from the studio preceded his by a few years when she left in 1951 to make *The African Queen* with Humphrey Bogart and directed by John Huston. It was at this point in her career that Hepburn began to play older women, a decision that led to some of her greatest successes. Before her second Oscar came from her last collaboration with Tracy in *Guess Who's Coming to Dinner* (1967), Hepburn had run off a string of great performances including *Summertime* (1955), Suddenly *Last Summer* (1959), and *Long Day's Journey Into Night* (1962).

After Tracy's death, Hepburn commenced one of the most productive periods of her career. In 1968 she won her third Oscar for *Lion in the Winter*, playing Eleanor of Aquitaine opposite Peter O'Toole. In 1973 she starred in the film adaptation on Edward Albee's *A Delicate Balance*. In 1975 she helped John Wayne finish his next-to-last picture, *Rooster Cogburn*, a sequel to Wayne's Oscar-winning *True Grit*. In 1981 Hepburn won her fourth and last Oscar for her role in *On Golden Pond*. The film represents the passing of old Hollywood in several respects. It is not only Hepburn's last great motion picture role but it is also Henry Fonda's last role and the only Oscar Oscar-winning role in his career. The cast also includes Jane Fonda, who received a supporting actress nomination as well. Between 1986 and 1994 Hepburn continued to work in television, starring in a total of five prestigious made-for-television movies. The last was *One Christmas*, based on a Truman Capote story. Thereafter, she retired to her beloved country home in Old Saybrook, Connecticut where she died in 2003.

Errol Flynn just barely lived to age fifty. The doctor who attended to him during his last hours remarked that Flynn had the body of a man twenty years his senior. No wonder; he had crammed more living, glamour, and adventure into those years than most people who live to one hundred. He was born in Hobart, Tasmania in 1909. Flynn's father was a famous biologist who was chagrined by the fact that his son was kicked out of school so many times, that it ceased to make sense to enroll him again. In his late teens Flynn began what he called his years of "roughing it." He worked as a prospector, newspaper reporter, captain of his own commercial schooner, and, allegedly, diamond smuggler. In 1933 he tried his hand at acting in a semi-documentary film, In the *Wake of the Bounty*. Acting interested him enough that Flynn decided to go to England to enroll in the Northampton Repertory Company. He quickly developed a reputation for being equally talented on stage and with the ladies.

In 1934 Flynn was discovered by Irving Asher, who headed Warner Brothers' Teddington Studios in England. Asher cast Flynn in a low-budget suspense film, *Murder at Monte Carlo*. He was so enthusiastic with the results that he signed Flynn to a studio contract and booked his passage to Hollywood. Flynn arrived in early 1935. Almost immediately he became a celebrated member of the local tennis scene and was married to Lili Damita, a film star and close friend of Mrs. Jack Warner. With his charm, good looks, and colorful past, Flynn was instantly accepted into Hollywood society. This led to his big break. British actor Robert Donat had been scheduled to star in an upcoming Warner film, *Captain Blood*. Donat was quarreling with the studio at the time and suggested that he might back out. Jack Warner jumped at the chance to cast his young discovery in the role of the swashbuckling pirate. In director Michael Curtiz's hands, Flynn was a huge success. Critics and audiences both recognized him as the

Captain Blood (1935), Directed by Michael Curtiz, Shown: Errol Flynn (as Dr. Peter Blood)

heir apparent to Douglas Fairbanks. However, whereas Fairbanks had a well deserved image of clean cut, healthy living, there was a more dangerous and sensual dimension to Flynn's performances. Fairbanks was a favorite of the young boys and men who adored the adventurousness of his films. Flynn's sexuality brought women to his pictures as well.

Warner Brothers quickly established the formula for a Flynn picture. Michael Curtiz (who directed Flynn in nine films) or Raoul Walsh (who directed seven Flynn pictures) would be assigned to direct. Both had vast experience in managing the action and crowd scenes that are so essential to successful adventure films. His co-star for *Captain Blood* and seven other films was Olivia De Havilland. Warner had just signed her to a seven-year contract in 1935 when she was teamed up with Flynn. De Havilland was the daughter of a wealthy British patent lawyer. She was well traveled, educated, and beautiful, and she didn't mind taking on subordinate roles in the pictures she did with Flynn. (Her sister Joan Fontaine also had a significant Hollywood career.) Her willingness to be in the background served to increase the power and excitement of the characters Flynn played. Later Warner would pair up Flynn with an actress of similar qualities, Alexis Smith.

After *Captain Blood* came *The Charge of the Light Brigade* (1936). In 1937 Warner made a significant investment in The Adventures of Robin Hood, a film shot in the expensive, three-strip Technicolor process with huge sets and an equally large cast. It was a major success. A World War I film, *Dawn Patrol*, followed and in 1939 Curtiz directed Flynn and

De Havilland in a large scale western, *Dodge City*. Flynn had established himself as the studio's greatest action actor who was equally adept with guns and swords. One of the most challenging roles in Flynn's career came in 1939, when he was cast opposite both Bette Davis and De Havilland in *The Private Lives of Elizabeth and Essex*. Flynn proved he was capable of performing with actresses of Davis's strength. Four more Curtiz films followed: *Virginia City* (1940), *The Sea Hawk* (1940), *Santa Fe Trail* (1940), and *Dive Bomber* (1941). The latter was a World War II film that troubled Flynn. He saw himself as a soldier of fortune, a man who had

GENTLEMAN JIM (1942), DIRECTED BY RAOUL WALSH, SHOWN CENTER: ERROL FLYNN (AS JAMES J. CORBETT AKA GENTLEMAN JIM); RIGHT: WILLIAM FRAWLEY

(vertical, right side of image) WARNER BROS. PICTURES/PHOTOFEST

faced many dangerous situations in his past. Now he was merely acting the part in war films. He was embarrassed. Other actors had left the motion picture industry to fight in the war but, in spite of having recently become a U.S. citizen, Flynn had too many health issues to pass the physical examination required for service. To him being a "make believe" soldier was a blow to his manhood.

1942 was the last peak year of Flynn's career. *Gentleman Jim*, the story of prizefighter "Gentleman Jim" Corbett, was a good as any of his action roles. However, Flynn's private life finally caught up with him. He had always been too fond of his cocktails and had many narrow scrapes with the many women he bedded, but in movie-friendly Los Angeles, the studios could keep his indiscretions out of the headlines. However, in November 1942 the Los Angeles police charged Flynn with two counts of statutory rape for having sex with two underaged girls, Peggy Satterlee and Betty Hansen. Many in the motion picture industry thought that this was the police department's way of reminding Warner Brothers that they hadn't been paying sufficient bribes.

Flynn hired Jerry Geisler, a legendary Hollywood lawyer, who immediately set about packing the jury with nine women. Flynn was eventually acquitted but he was still out of control. During the trial recesses he had constantly flirted with Nora Eddington, an eighteen-year-old girl who worked in the courthouse snack bar. He was thirty-four at the time. To make matters worse her father was a Captain in the county Sheriff's Department. No doubt at the urging of his agents and the studio, Flynn married Eddington in a union that lasted five years. While Flynn wasn't banished from the industry as Roscoe "Fatty" Arbuckle had been twenty years earlier, the quality of the parts he was offered noticeably declined. He remained in the Warner Brothers deep freezer for fifteen years until Darryl Zanuck recruited him for the Twentieth Century Fox production of Ernest Hemingway's *The Sun Also Rises* (1957). Encouraged the success of the Fox film, Warner Brothers finally relented and gave Flynn the lead in the John Barrymore biography *Too Much, Too Soon*. He was excellent playing once heroic, now debauched older men, not unlike himself. However, with the exception of those two roles, Flynn was just barely surviving by working in television and on exploitation films. By mid 1959 he was too ill to work. He died on October 9.

John Wayne was born Marion Morrison in Winterset, Iowa in 1907. His father, Clyde Morrison, was a pharmacist who had a lung illness that forced the family to relocate to the drier climate of the southern California desert. The Morrisons settled on a small ranch in the Antelope Valley where young Marion learned to ride a horse at age four. In 1911 the ranch failed and the family moved to Glendale, California (a suburb of Los Angeles), where Clyde resumed his profession in the pharmacy. Young Marion had a pet dog named Duke who followed him on his rounds delivering prescriptions. Neighbors took to calling Morrison Big Duke (a name he much preferred to Marion) and the dog Little Duke.

In high school Morrison was a gifted athlete and an excellent student. He was a stand-out football player and was recruited heavily by the University of Southern California, where he played from 1925 to 1927. Like many of his teammates (including noted character actor Ward Bond) Morrison got summer work as a prop man carrying heavy scenery and furniture at the Fox studios. Cowboy star Tom Mix befriended Morrison, who was a source of football tickets for Mix and other enthusiastic USC fans including director John Ford. During the summer after his junior year, Morrison injured his shoulder in a surfing accident at Malibu. He was unable to play when the team reported for practice that fall and lost his athletic scholarship. Ford invited him to work as an extra on cowboy movies to pay for rent and food. He also was cast as a football player in a few MGM films. His screen name was usually Duke Morrison, but he also used the name Michael Burn. Ford and fellow Fox director Raoul Walsh took Morrison under their wings and saw to it that he received riding lessons and was taught how to perform in movie fight scenes by legendary stuntman Yakima Canutt. Along the way Walsh gave Morrison his screen name, John Wayne, after the Revolutionary War hero, General Anthony Wayne.

Wayne's first big break came in 1930 when Walsh cast him in the leading role in *The Big Trail*. It was an expensive two million dollar picture intended to be the first sound western extravaganza. Unfortunately the studio had decided to shoot in a large, seventy millimeter, format that few theaters were equipped to handle. The result was box office failure. Wayne's reputation in Hollywood was unfairly damaged by the film's performance, and he spent the next nine years starring in low-budget westerns for Lonestar and Republic Pictures. In 1939 John Ford rescued Wayne from his career rut by casting him as the Ringo Kid, an escaped convict with a heart, in the classic western *Stagecoach.* Ford presented Wayne in such a flattering manner that he instantly became a star. To Wayne's credit, he never forgot the favor and was always willing to appear in Ford films for the rest of their careers.

During World War II Wayne starred in a number of war pictures that portrayed the heroism of the American military. The first was *Flying Tigers* (1942). Four more pictures came, culminating in the well respected *They Were Expendable* (1945), directed by Ford. After the war Wayne's career continued to flourish. He also began to get involved in a number of patriotic and anti-communist organizations including a term as President of the Motion Picture Alliance for the Preservation of American Ideals. In 1949 Wayne received a Best Actor Oscar nomination for his performance in the war movie *The Sands of Iwo Jima*.

REPUBLIC/PHOTOFEST

SANDS OF IWO JIMA (1949), DIRECTED BY ALLAN DWAN, SHOWN FROM LEFT: RICHARD WEBB (AS PFC. DAN SHIPLEY), JAMES BROWN (AS PFC. CHARLIE BASS), JOHN WAYNE (AS SGT. JOHN STRYKER)

During the late 1940s and throughout the1950s Wayne appeared in some of Ford's greatest films, beginning with the "cavalry trilogy," *Fort Apache* (1948), *She Wore a Yellow Ribbon* (1949), and *Rio Grande* (1950). In 1952 the two collaborated on the classic, *The Quiet Man*. Set in Ireland, the film contains one of Wayne's most colorful performances and the best fist fight in movie history. In 1956 Wayne and Ford made *The Searchers*, a western that achieves great visual and dramatic artistry. In 1960 Wayne invested his own fortune to produce, direct, and star in *The Alamo*. Ford won his fourth and last Best Director Oscar for *The Man Who Shot Liberty Valence*, a 1962 film staring Wayne and Jimmy Stewart. In 1969 Wayne finally won a well deserved Oscar for his performance in *True Grit*.

Toward the end of his career Wayne began to experience a series of serious medical ailments. In 1964 a cancer diagnosis resulted in the removal of his lung. Later he needed a heart valve replacement. He contracted stomach cancer in the 1970s. He continued to espouse his conservative political beliefs throughout the turbulent Vietnam War era. He was asked to run for Governor of California twice but declined. He expressed his pro-war feelings in the self-directed 1968 film *The Green Berets*. Wayne spent his last years at his harborfront home in Balboa, California and on his yacht, Pilar, a converted minesweeper. He died in 1979 of stomach cancer. During his career he had appeared in over two hundred films with leading roles in one hundred seventy. His acting career is one of the most prolific in film history.

TRUE GRIT (1969), DIRECTED BY HENRY HATHAWAY, SHOWN: JOHN WAYNE

1939: THE GREATEST YEAR

The Great Depression was clearly at an end as 1939 unfolded. American industry was back in gear. The banks were healthy. Employment was robust and optimism had regained its rightful position at the center of the American spirit. In Europe the picture was far darker. Between 1925 and 1926 Benito Mussolini had established a Fascist dictatorship in Italy, announcing plans for the expansion of the Italian-Roman Empire into North Africa. In 1933 Adolph Hitler became the Chancellor of Germany and began the oppression of Jews, intellectuals, Communists, Gypsies, and homosexuals. In 1936 Germany invaded the French portion of the Rhineland, and the Berlin-Rome axis formed to provide mutual protection. In 1937 Germany announces its plan to occupy much of Eastern Europe. In 1939 Germany captured Czechoslovakia, Austria, and Poland. France, England, and the U.S.S.R. began war preparations.

New York hosted a World's Fair in 1939. It was a demonstration of American industrial and technological might and a celebration of the end of the Great Depression. The most popular attraction at the Fair was the Radio Corporation of America's Television Pavilion. RCA president, David Sarnoff, had been planning the launch of television since 1933 when developmental work on the new medium had been completed, but the economic climate was not right for the venture, so he bided his time until Americans could afford television. Now that time had come and everyone who visited the fair marveled at this new invention that could send and receive both sound and pictures through the air. Hollywood should have been terrified by the prospect of television, but the motion picture industry was too excited about the return of prosperity to notice.

The Oscar nominees for 1939 alone comprise some of the greatest films ever made up to that year.

Gone with the Wind— Based on Margaret Mitchell's best-selling novel of the American Civil War, the film traces the fortunes of Scarlett O'Hara (Vivien Leigh) and Rhett Butler (Clark Gable) with the war and its aftermath as a backdrop. Victor Fleming was loaned out from MGM to direct the spectacle for Selznick International Pictures. It was one of the most expensive productions ever undertaken with massive war battles, including the burning of Atlanta. It swept the Oscars with winners in the Best Actress (Vivien Leigh), Best Supporting Actress (Hattie McDaniel), Art Direction, Director (Victor Fleming), Editing, and Best Picture.

Dark Victory features Bette Davis in one of her most vivid roles as a wealthy socialite who learns she has a fatal brain tumor. She forms a love triangle with her horse trainer, played by Humphrey Bogart, and her surgeon, played by George Brent.

Goodbye Mr. Chips was one of the last films made at MGM's British studio facility before the outbreak of the war. Robert Donat won a best actor Oscar for his performance as an elderly school teacher reflecting on his career and wondering if he made a difference. One by one his former students return to assure him he has been a success. Greer Garson turns in a warm performance as Chips's wife.

Love Affair—Irene Dunne plays an American nightclub singer who meets French heartthrob Charles Boyer, who plays a rich playboy. They have a torrid shipboard romance, but decide to put the brakes on it for a while. They agree that if they still feel strongly for each other, they will meet on the observation deck atop the Empire State Building six months later. This film, directed by Leo McCarey, is such a classic tear jerker that it was remade twice more as *An Affair to Remember* and *Sleepless in Seattle*.

LOVE AFFAIR (1939), DIRECTED BY LEO MCCAREY, SHOWN FROM LEFT: CHARLES BOYER (AS MICHEL MARNET), IRENE DUNNE (AS TERRY MCKAY)

RKO RADIO PICTURES/PHOTOFEST

Mr. Smith Goes to Washington is one of Frank Capra's most respected films. Jimmy Stewart plays a young politician who is elected to the Senate as a reformer. When he gets to Washington, he discovers that the deck is stacked against him and mounts a dramatic filibuster to point out the rampant corruption he has found.

Ninotchka—Under Ernst Lubitsch's deft hand, Greta Garbo gives her best comedic performance. She plays a Soviet bureaucrat who is sent on a low-level mission to Paris, which she finds to be way too bourgeois for her taste. The food is too rich. The art is too gaudy. The music lacks seriousness, and love is just a glandular reaction. Melvyn Douglas plays a French count who changes her mind about everything.

Of Mice and Men is the screen adaptation of John Steinbeck's heartbreaking novella about two Depression-era migrants who dream of a better life. Directed by Lewis Milestone, Lon Chaney, Jr., is convincing as half-wit Lenny, who doesn't know his own strength. Burgess Meredith plays Lenny's caretaker who can't save him from the inhumanity that surrounds them.

NINOTCHKA (1939), DIRECTED BY ERNST LUBITSCH, SHOWN FROM LEFT: GRETA GARBO (AS NINOTCHKA), MELVYN DOUGLAS, UNIDENTIFIED

Stagecoach—John Ford reinvents the western as an adult genre with great complexity and depth. John Wayne becomes a major star as a result of Ford's careful handling.

The Wizard of Oz MGM made a commitment to showcase their young star, Judy Garland, in a musical in which she is required to dance, sing, and act. She pulls it off beautifully. Victor Fleming was the original director but had to leave to start work on *Gone with the Wind*. Mervyn LeRoy and King Vidor filled in admirably. Every scene is a marvel of studio magic with great sets, costumes, and makeup. The stories about the little people who were recruited from carnivals and circuses all over the country to play the Munchkins are the stuff of Hollywood legend. The three-strip Technicolor process never looked better.

OF MICE AND MEN (1939), DIRECTED BY LEWIS MILESTONE, SHOWN FROM LEFT: BETTY FIELD, LON CHANEY JR.

Wuthering Heights is the film adaptation of Emily Bronte's dark gothic novel. Lawrence Olivier plays Heathcliff, the orphan who is taken in by the Earnshaw family. He grows into adulthood with his stepsister Cathy, played by Merle Oberon. As the two become adolescents and adults they share their love for life on the moors and a deep emotional connection develops between them. When Linton, played by David Niven, enters the scene to court Cathy, things begin to go wrong. William Wyler's excellent direction is brought to life by Gregg Toland's brilliant cinematography.

THE LIST OF NON-OSCAR FILMS FROM 1939 IS EVEN MORE REMARKABLE

Beau Gest
Golden Boy
The Hunchback of Notre Dame
Only Angels Have Wings
The Three Musketeers
Union Pacific
Young Mr. Lincoln

WUTHERING HEIGHTS (1939), DIRECTED BY WILLIAM WYLER, SHOWN FROM LEFT: LAURENCE OLIVIER (AS HEATHCLIFF), MERLE OBERON (AS CATHY)

UNITED ARTISTS/PHOTOFEST

1939 also the year that Hollywood finally began to embrace color. Dating back to the earliest days of the motion picture industry there was always an aspiration to make films in color. As early as 1903 projectionists passed the time by hand-tinting copies of *The Great Train Robbery* with translucent paints, one frame at a time. The work was much too tedious to be done on an industrial scale and film prints were often treated roughly, getting scratched, broken, and burnt in the projector. Hand-tinted prints didn't last long enough.

The Kinemacolor system was introduced in 1908. It was an additive color system in that cameras contained color filters to capture the red and green information in the image. When projected red and green color wheels provided the color. In 1913 the Gaumont Chronochrome system was introduced in France using a similar technology. Eastman Kodak introduced the Two Color Kodachrome system in 1915. It was a subtractive color system in which the film was dyed in the processing so that the color was on the film. The major problem with the system was that both sides of the film were dyed, and the film was very prone to scratching. By the mid 1930s there were over nineteen competing color systems. None was considered practical by the motion picture industry.

In 1912 Dr. Herbert Kalmus and two other graduates of the Massachusetts Institute of Technology (M.I.T.) formed the Kalmus, Comstock and Wescott Company to develop a color system. By 1917 they had created a workable two-color additive system (System One). Kalmus took over the company and renamed it Technicolor. The "Tech" in the title was a reference to M.I.T. In 1917 the Technicolor company introduced its System Two, a two-color subtractive system. The method of film dying was superior to anything else. Finally in 1932 System Three, a three-color, three-strip process was introduced. The addition of the third color record (blue) made it much more realistic and pleasing to the eye. But the cameras used three separate rolls of film. They were huge and required much more light than black-and-white photography. Also the laboratory processing was very complicated and expensive, yet there was no getting around the fact that the results were beautiful.

Cinematographers were wary of color photography. They had become very adept at creating amazing lighting effects with black-and-white photography. They saw color as something akin to cheating. The expense was prohibitive at the outset. 1932 was one of the darkest years of the Great Depression. But color had its champions. Color was much more practical in the world of animation. There was no need for three-strip cameras. The animator would create a finished color reel and take three successive exposures using a standard animation camera that had filters added to create the red, blue, and green records. The rest got sorted out at the lab. Walt Disney made the first three-color Technicolor film in 1932, *Flowers and Trees,* an eight-minute animated short. Later that year her made another color short, *The Three Little Pigs.* Both films were a sensation.

At RKO Merrian C. Cooper, the man who would make *King Kong*, and Jock Whitney, a wealthy New York film financier, decided that the time was right for color. In 1934 RKO released *La Cucaracha*, the first live short film to use System Three. In 1935 RKO released *Becky Sharp*, the first feature-length film. In 1936 Paramount produced *The Trail of the Lonesome Pine*, the first Technicolor film to be made outdoors on location. The first feature-length animated film, *Snow White and the Seven Dwarfs* (1937), was the first in Technicolor as well. By the end of 1939, with the obvious artfulness and appeal of both *The Wizard of Oz* and *Gone with the Wind*, there was no question that color would become part of the future of the motion picture industry.

In January 1940 two amazing films appeared on the screen . . . first released on January . . . was Walt Disney's Fantasia . . . 's Mickey Mouse

HOLLYWOOD GOES TO WAR

1940–41: BEFORE THE STORM

America had survived the Great Depression a little worse for wear but with a commonly shared belief that the country had been strengthened by its ordeal. The economy was sound and people were back to work building houses, making automobiles and enjoying a more carefree life. Hollywood continued to add to the great accomplishments of 1939, and although a few filmmakers were turning their attention to events in Europe, most of the industry focused on recapturing the good times and all that came with it.

In January 1940 two amazing films appeared on the scene. The first, released on January 6, was Walt Disney's *Fantasia*. Concerned about the marketability of his Mickey Mouse character and consumed by a desire to create something grand, Disney conceived a project that would mix animation with classical music such as Beethoven's Fifth Symphony and Paul Dukas's "The Sorcerer's Apprentice." Disney sank over two million dollars into *Fantasia* at a time when studio production budgets averaged five hundred thousand. The experimental nature of the film was further emphasized when the decision was made to exclude dialogue and any narrative technique other than that created by the images and music. In addition, Disney included an elaborate new sound system for the road show exhibitions of the film. While *Fantasia* was not an instant success, it showed the lengths

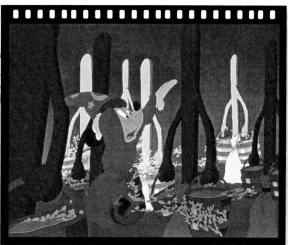

FANTASIA (1940), DIRECTED BY JAMES ALGAR, SAMUEL ARMSTRONG, SHOWN: "SORCEROR'S APPRENTICE" SEGMENT

Walt Disney Pictures/Photofest

Disney was prepared to go to demonstrate his dominance in the world of animation.

Howard Hawks's *His Girl Friday* was released two weeks after *Fantasia*. Returning to the screwball comedy genre, he chose the well traveled stage play *Front Page* as his source material. It is the story of a big-city newspaper editor, Walter Burns, and his star reporter, Hildy Johnson. Hawks had the brainstorm to change the Hildy character. Instead of portraying Hildy as Burns's colleague, Hawks decided Hildy would be a woman, Burns's ex-wife. This was very much in keeping with Hawks' growing interest in developing female characters who could be sexy and also "one of the guys." Rosalind Russell was cast in the Hildy role, with

Cary Grant playing Burns. Ralph Bellamy was once again cast as the hapless and disposable love interest of the heroine. Speeding up the dialogue was another stylistic idea that Hawks had been tinkering with for some time. In *His Girl Friday* Hawks surpasses himself with what might still stand as the fastest dialogue in motion picture history.

In March 1940, Twentieth Century released *The Grapes of Wrath*. Studio chief Daryll Zanuck had concluded that the Great Depression had been over long enough in the minds of audiences and that they were willing to revisit some of its darkest events on screen. John Ford and his writer-collaborator Nunnally Johnson, labored to condense John Steinbeck's epic novel of the Joad family as they are dispossessed of their family farm and forced to take to the road in search of the promised land in California. Henry Fonda acquiesced to Fox Studios' demand for a seven-year contract in order to get the film's prized role of Tom Joad. Jane Darwell, who specialized in playing maternal roles, was cast as Ma Joad. John Carradine, a member of Ford's stock company and an accomplished stage actor in his own right, was cast as the faithless preacher, Casey. The dynamic young cinematographer Gregg Toland photographed the motion picture with a hard-edged focus and moments of breathtaking expressionism. It was the first great film of the year.

THE GRAPES OF WRATH (1940), DIRECTED BY JOHN FORD, SHOWN FROM LEFT: HENRY FONDA, JANE DARWELL

20TH CENTURY FOX/PHOTOFEST

The following month, Selznick International Studios released Alfred Hitchcock's long-awaited first American production, *Rebecca*. The film is based on Daphne du Maurier's book about the second wife of a very wealthy widower. Life on her new husband's estate is a continuing challenge to gain acceptance and to compete with the ghost of her predecessor. Hitchcock had signed with Selznick in late 1938 to escape the war-ravaged British film industry. Upon his arrival in Hollywood, Hitchcock was regarded as a great artist and accorded star treatment by the studio and the press. Accustomed to working with few resources in England, Hitchcock was bemused by the embarrassment of riches he found at Selznick. With *Rebecca*, he successfully guided an insecure young Joan Fontaine though an excellent performance.

ORSON WELLES AND CITIZEN KANE

On May 1, 1941 arguably the most notorious film in movie history was released, *Citizen Kane*. Its director, Orson Welles, was a show-business phenomenon who had never before made a motion picture. Born in Kenosha, Wisconsin in 1915, he was the son of a well-to-do inventor and a concert pianist. By the time he was six, Welles' parents had separated. He was eight when his mother died and thirteen when his father died. Welles' guardian had enrolled him in the Todd boarding school in Woodstock, Illinois, two years earlier. The young orphan seemed mature beyond his years. He was an accomplished pianist by age six. Welles had traveled around the world twice before entering Todd. He counted among his acquaintances many successful actors and actresses. He was blessed with a rich baritone voice perfectly suited for the stage and the microphone. For most of his time at Todd Welles concentrated on studying Shakespeare and organizing dramatic productions. He graduated in 1931 at age sixteen and set out for Ireland.

Welles made his stage debut at the Gate Theater in Dublin and became a member of the Abbey Players theater group. He proceeded to tour on the stage through Spain and Morocco before returning to Chicago in 1932, and he then toured with Katharine Cornell's road company between 1933 and 1934. At age nineteen, with a wealth of stage experience, Welles decided it was time to try his luck in New York. Almost immediately he became the voice of the *March of Time* newsreel series. He also starred as Lamont Cranston in the very popular radio series *The Shadow.*

In 1935 Welles met another stage producer, John Houseman, who was involved with the Federal Theater Project. The Theater Project was a branch of the much more extensive Works Progress Administration, a federal program designed to put people back to work on infrastructure projects. The Theater Project was intended to provide jobs for out-of-work actors, writers, and musicians. One of the aims of the Project was to preserve ethnic traditions and folklore. For Welles and Housman the Theater Project was a playground of creativity. Among their most notable accomplishments was a production of *Macbeth* with an all African American cast from the Negro Theater Project. They received high praise for their modern-dress adaptation of *Julius Caesar,* presented as a cautionary tale about fascism. They broke from the Federal Theater Project in 1937 over a censorship dispute. Welles and Houseman were at work on Marc Blitzstein's anti-capitalist musical *The Cradle Will Rock.* A great deal of political pressure from Nelson Rockefeller and others was brought to bear on the Theater Project's administrators, who were asked to either make changes or stop the production altogether. Wells and Houseman preferred to stop rather than compromise.

In 1938 Welles and Houseman formed the Mercury Theater group, which included actors such as Everett Sloan, Agnes Moorehead, and Joseph Cotton. CBS radio signed the group to produce weekly one-hour radio dramas. At first the audience ratings for the show were disappointing, perhaps because of the highbrow nature of many of the productions. On October 30, 1938 the Mercury Theater of the Air broadcast the most infamous radio program in history, a production of H. G. Wells's *War of the Worlds.* The story of the Martian invasion of Earth was presented as a breaking news story. The result was widespread panic on the part of radio audiences in New Jersey, the fictional landing site of the Martian spacecraft. History may never know for certain if the broadcast was a prank gone wrong or an attempt to draw attention to a program in need of a ratings boost. The result was instant fame for Welles and his group and a new contract from the Campbell Soup Company to sponsor the program's next season as an expanded ninety-minute broadcast. It was such a successful year for the program and its contributors, including writer Howard Koch and composer, Bernard Herrmann, that the production was moved to Hollywood so everyone could simultaneously pursue movie careers. Welles left the Campbell broadcast in 1949 over creative differences.

In July 1939 RKO president George Schaefer reached an agreement with Welles to direct. This was an unprecedented contract for a young man who had never directed a film before. The terms called for two films in two years. Welles would maintain creative control over his films, including the final edited version of the film. Welles' end of the bargain was that he would have to finish on schedule within the standard $500,000 studio budget. Otherwise, all that the studio required was story approval. Immediately there was resentment and envy in the film industry aimed at the twenty-three-year-old first timer.

Ignoring his many critics, Welles got right to work on a screen adaptation of Joseph Conrad's *Heart of Darkness*, which would eventually reach the screen as Francis Coppola's *Apocalypse Now* in 1979. Welles got nowhere with the project, and the studio eventually assigned its most gifted writer, Joseph Mankiewicz, to get the young director on track with a new project. The two hit it off despite the writer's penchant for hard drinking. They began to discuss the idea of telling the story of a great American industrialist from several different points of view. Mankiewicz would later claim that they got the idea from the structure of John Ford's western *Stagecoach*.

Mankiewicz, with his leg in a cast from a traffic accident, sequestered himself in a lodge in the remote high desert near Victorville to begin work. Welles' Mercury Theater partner, John Houseman, was dispatched to assist the writer in getting around and to make sure that his drinking didn't interfere with work. The first draft was a bloated 266 pages that contained the life story of a newspaper magnate, patterned on the enormously powerful and very much alive William Randolph Hearst. Welles announced to the studio bosses that he would be ready to begin filming his project (with the working title *The American*) in three months. After a great deal of revision and after paring down the script to its essentials, Welles was pleased but told the studio it would be impossible to shoot it for less than a million dollars. It was probably a bargaining ploy, and it succeeded in getting the budget increased to $700,000.

It was to Welles's great fortune that cinematographer Gregg Toland was under contract to RKO when production began. Welles knew that he needed all the help he could get and that Toland was the best there was. As for Toland, he was open to the kind of close collaboration the project and the inexperienced director required. The brilliant art director Perry Ferguson signed on and began the sketches and model making for the picture's elaborate and innovative sets. Welles, Toland, and Ferguson wanted to create an entirely new approach to design. They discarded the usual three-wall set approach in favor of very detailed designs that included elaborate ceilings. Toland envisioned shooting from very low angles to give a "larger than life" perspective on the protagonist, Kane. Sometimes this technique required cutting holes in the set floor to make way for the camera.

Casting for *The American* (RKO production 281) was relatively easy. Welles would play the lead, and members of the Mercury Theater would play most of the other roles. This kept down the cost of the cast and ensured greater secrecy once filming began at the studio facility located at Melrose and Gower on the southern edge of Hollywood. Robert Wise was appointed to edit the film. Production began behind locked doors on June 29, 1940 and concluded on October 23. By September word was beginning to leak that the production was about Hearst. Immediately the entire Hearst media empire flew into action to suppress the film. On the RKO sound stages production continued unabated.

Welles and Toland knew they were creating something special. Every challenge led to innovation. The overall visual treatment was the deep focus photography upon which a great deal of the cinematographer's reputation was based. His knowledge of lenses and lighting was unmatched, making it possible to keep foreground objects in equally sharp focus with objects and actors forty feet apart. Single-source lighting and back lighting created deep shadows that contributed to the development and presentation of character elements. Especially prized is Toland's use of the painterly chiaroscuro technique, which is used to create bold contrast within the black-and-white screen compositions. Welles's mastery of radio sound techniques added a layer of artisanship previously missing in sound motion pictures. Furthermore, Welles's performance was a masterpiece of character acting.

CITIZEN KANE (1941), DIRECTED BY ORSON WELLES, SHOWN ON THE SET LOOKING THROUGH CAMERA: ORSON WELLES (AS CHARLES FOSTER KANE); TO THE RIGHT OF HIM: CINEMATOGRAPHER GREG TOLAND

RKO RADIO PICTURES INC./PHOTOFEST

The Hearst newspaper empire continued to inveigh against the film. To punish the studio, all mention of RKO pictures was forbidden in Hearst-owned and affiliated newspapers, which accounted for half the print media in the country. Hearst gossip columnists Louella Parsons and Hedda Hopper were unleashed on Welles and the studio, building a steady drumbeat of criticism. Despite all of this, *Citizen Kane*'s release in May 1941 was mostly positive. Critics appreciated the virtuosity of the film, and it did well in the big cities. But in smaller markets, the Hearst campaign to suppress the film succeeded in keeping attendance very low.

Citizen Kane was nominated for nine Academy Awards including best film, director, actor, cinematography, music, and screenplay. Only Mankiewicz and Welles won, for screenplay. It was a modest success but wasn't recognized as a classic for many years to come, in no small part due to the efforts of Hearst.

Welles's next project for RKO, *The Magnificent Ambersons* (1942), was even more contentious than *Citizen Kane*. Based on Booth Tarkington's 1918 Pulitzer Prize novel, it is the story of a spoiled young heir who interferes with his mother's attempts to reunite with her one true love. Welles had previously produced the story for radio and was able to complete the first draft of the screenplay in nine days. Joseph Cotton played the lead role. At the time of its production, those involved, including Cotton and editor Robert Wise, believed that the *Magnificent Ambersons* was artistically superior to *Citizen Kane*. The studio objected when Welles' final cut ran two hours and eleven minutes. They wanted cuts that the director refused to make. Instead of re-maining to argue over the film and see it to its finish, Welles accepted an assignment from the government to go to Brazil to shoot a wartime documentary. In his absence, Wise did his best to complete the film. RKO previewed *The Magnificent Ambersons* to test audiences several times with negative results. Each time that it was reedited or additional material was added, it seemed to get worse. Wise was in constant contact with Welles in South America, but nothing was working. Finally, in complete frustration, RKO had the film cut down to eighty-eight minutes and destroyed the negative so that it could never

THE MAGNIFICENT AMBERSONS (1942), DIRECTED BY ORSON WELLES, SHOWN FROM LEFT: DOLORES COSTELLO (IN BACKGROUND, AS ISABEL), TIM HOLT (AS GEORGE)

be reconstituted. Welles returned from Brazil before finishing his South American project but was too late to save the *Ambersons* project, or the wartime documentary, for that matter. (The South American film was later released with the title *It's All True*.) Welles had gained a reputation for not finishing what he started, which stuck with him for the remainder of his life. He was never again entrusted with a major studio film.

In September 1941 Twentieth Century Fox released John Ford's *How Green Was My Valley*. The film is the story of a verdant Welsh valley despoiled by coal mining and life and camaraderie among the miners that toil underground. Daryll Zanuck believed deeply in the importance of the project. He supervised the development of the script over a period of two years and polished the final draft himself. William Wyler was scheduled to direct, but the money men in New York objected to the inflated cost of the film and were critical of Wyler's tendency to go over budget. They quashed the project. Zanuck was livid. He insisted that the film go forward. New York finally agreed when Ford was assigned. Ford's reputation for budget discipline soothed the front office anxieties.

How Green Was My Valley starred the distinguished MGM actor Walter Pidgeon, with Maureen O'Hara and young Roddy McDowall as the boy who tells the story. Ford regulars included Donald Crisp and Barry Fitzgerald. The production department ingeniously designed sets on the Fox back lot. Fox veteran Arthur Miller did the cinematography. Ford won his second best director Oscar for the film, and it is considered among his best work.

JOHN HUSTON AND *THE MALTESE FALCON*

Orson Welles wasn't the only director making his debut in 1941. John Huston, a thirty-five year old screen writer, was also making his directorial debut. The son of a stage actor, Walter Huston, and a sports writer, Reah Gore, young Huston divided his time between his divorced parents. He spent his time either following his father around the vaudeville circuits or go-

HOW GREEN WAS MY VALLEY (1941), DIRECTED BY JOHN FORD, SHOWN FROM LEFT: WALTER PIDGEON (AS MR. GRUFFYDD), RODDY McDOWALL (AS HUGH MORGAN)

TWENTIETH CENTURY FOX/PHOTOFEST

ing to the race track with his mother. He was diagnosed with a number of ailments as a child but had outgrown them by the time he became a six-foot, two-inch boxer at Lincoln Heights High School in Los Angeles. Huston dropped out of school for good at age fifteen to box full time and became a successful pugilist. He was also a voracious reader and took painting lessons until turning his attention to acting at age nineteen. He spent two years in Mexico as a young man where he learned to drink and ride horses and was briefly enlisted in the Mexican Calvary.

In 1931 Huston's father arranged for his son to work as a screenwriter on the films in which Huston senior acted. Given the colorful life the young writer had lived thus far, he became an instant celebrity in Hollywood, known for his ability to party hard. This came to an end, however, when Huston was involved in a traffic accident in which a woman was killed. He was absolved from blame, and yet the event shook Huston, who spent the next four years drifting, popping up from time to time in London, Rome, and New York. In 1937 he resumed his career as a screenwriter at Warner Brothers, this time with a sense of purpose and commitment. His work ethic was rewarded with an assignment to direct Dashiell Hammett's 1929 detective story, *The Maltese Falcon.*

Maltese Falcon is generally considered the first example of the film noir genre, as it was described by French movie critics in the 1950s. Humphrey Bogart stars as the hard-bitten, anti-heroic detective, Sam Spade. As opposed to traditional protagonists who adhere to conventional codes of conduct and morality, Spade is a complicated, not altogether nice guy. He is having an affair with his partner's wife. There is a suspicious intimacy with his secretary that hints of past romantic entanglements. Spade becomes sexually involved with a client he greatly distrusts. He plays games with the police, likes money a little too much, and seems to enjoy roughing up weaker men.

Mary Astor costars as Spade's love interest, Brigid O'Shaughnessy, a classic example of the French idea of the *femme fatale* or "deadly woman." She is a compulsive liar who shifts her allegiances depending on who can get her closer to the treasure everyone is chasing. She has no reluctance in using her sexuality to manipulate the men in her path. And, when all else fails, she turns on the water works and lets the tears flow. The other colorful villains include Sydney Greenstreet as Gutman, the mastermind who has been chasing the treasured falcon for seventeen years. He is cultured, witty, and sophisticated but equally capable of ordering his bodyguard to use violence. Peter Lorre plays the third villain, Joel Cairo. He is fey and simpering but also capable of using violence to get his way. Together the three villains are wonderfully colorful.

THE MALTESE FALCON (1941), DIRECTED BY JOHN HUSTON, SHOWN, IN SPADE'S APARTMENT IN THE FINAL SEQUENCE: HUMPHREY BOGART (AS SAM SPADE), MARY ASTOR (AS BRIGID O'SHAUGHNESSY)

Warner Bros./Photofest

As a first-time director, Huston clearly followed the lead of the studio camera department in lighting the film conventionally. However, it is clear that his intent is expressionistic. He uses shadows liberally to indicate Spade's ruthlessness, particularly with the signage on his detective agency. Another wonderful technique is his placement of the camera when photographing the very portly Gutman. He uses very low angles that, in some scenes, fill the entire lower two-thirds of the screen with Greenstreet's ample belly. The last scene in which Mary Astor is led away to her fate is pure expressionism in its suggestions of her well-deserved descent into hell. Huston directed two other films before enlisting in World War II.

PRESTON STURGES AND SULLIVAN'S TRAVELS

Like John Huston, Preston Sturges came from a broken family, saw much of the world as a child, lived a colorful life, and became a screenwriter before he directed. Sturges' father was a member of a prominent and privileged Chicago family. His mother was a bohemian whose closest friend was famed dancer Isadora Duncan. His childhood was spent partly in Chicago but mostly in Europe, constantly touring with his mother, who introduced him to every museum and concert hall on the continent. Eventually, Sturges was parked in a series of boarding schools in Paris and Switzerland. He was fifteen when the First World War erupted in Europe. His mother sent him to Chicago for safety's sake.

In March 1918, Sturges enlisted in the aviation section of the Army Signal Corp and was sent to Tennessee for flight instruction. While on base he began to contribute a weekly cartoon strip to the camp newspaper. He eventually earned his officers wings and was discharged in 1919 at age twenty. For the next few years he drifted around Europe falling in love with a married woman, and at one point, inventing a kiss-proof lipstick. Upon his return to America he married a child-hood sweetheart who soon left him. He drifted some more, trying his hand at songwriting for a while. When he took up with an actress, he decided to become a playwright and succeeded in getting his first play, *The Guinea Pig*, produced on Broadway in 1929. Another successful play followed. Later in the year he married an heir-ess to the Merriweather Post Hutton fortune, built a yacht, and self-financed another failed play that left him in need of finding gainful employment.

SULLIVAN'S TRAVELS (1941), DIRECTED BY PRESTON STURGES, SHOWN FROM LEFT: ERIC BLORE (AS SULLIVAN'S VALET), JOEL MCCREA (AS JOHN L. LLOYD 'SULLY' SULLIVAN)

Once again, his marriage broke up, and Sturges headed for Hollywood.

Sturges was hired as a staff writer at Universal Studios in September 1932. His first assignment was to adapt his hit play, *Strictly Dishonorable*, for the screen. Universal didn't like his work and dropped his contract. Next he wrote a script on speculation, *The Power and the Glory*, and sold it to Jesse Lasky, who was working at Fox at the time. Once again inside the studio, Sturges observed the deferential manner with which directors were treated and decided that he would pursue directing. He didn't find work immediately. Instead, he had a brief stint as a writer at MGM, then moved on to Columbia and back to Universal. Eventually he was offered a short-term contract at Paramount. As he moved from studio to studio, Sturges's pay increased considerably, which made it possible for him to indulge his restlessness again. He opened an engineering company in the state of Washington, refurbished his yacht, sailed in the trans-Pacific yacht race, and, upon his return to Los Angeles, opened a restaurant-saloon on Sunset Boulevard, which became a hangout for songwriters. Sturges's contract with Paramount expired in September 1938 and the studio rewarded him with a new, better paid arrangement. Soon after, he sold the studio a 1932 script, *The Great McGinty*, for ten dollars on the condition that he would direct. He was forty-one when filming began, and for the first time in his life, felt that he was doing what he was born to do.

Paramount was thrilled with Sturges's work. Before long he was made the producer of his own projects which, with his writing, made him an auteur-style director with a level of control over his projects that was equaled by only a handful of directors such as Hitchcock and Hawks. In 1941 *Sullivan's Travels* followed a string of hits including *The Great McGinty, Christmas in July,* and *The Lady Eve. Sullivan's Travels* contains most of the elements of the great screwball comedies of the thirties, to which Sturges added a very sly layer of satire. It is the story of a successful and spoiled young director (possibly based on Howard Hawks) with a series of hit musical comedies but also pretensions of making a "serious film" with the working title of *Oh Brother, Where Art Thou?* When Sullivan announces his intention to the studio bosses, they do everything they can to talk him out of it, including reminding him that he knows nothing about how poor people live. Undaunted, Sullivan goes down to the wardrobe department to get himself a hobo costume and sets out down the road to discover how the other half lives. He is followed in his wanderings by an enormous Airstream motor home full of studio press agents and a private chef.

After an abortive try to see the other side of life, Sullivan returns home, where he meets a down-on-her-luck actress who has given up on Hollywood and decided to go back home. She offers to show Sullivan how to survive on the road, and he accepts. The third act of the film contains a dark, noncomedic passage in which Sullivan learns the value of laughter and light entertainment. Even though *Sullivan's Travels* didn't receive recognition from the Motion Picture Academy, today it is considered a great film.

The Winds of War

World War I was to the people who fought in it the Great War and the War to End All Wars. Yet before the ink was dry on the Treaty of Versailles, the document that set the terms for the war's end, the seeds of the next global war were already being sowed. In July 1921 Adolph Hitler became the leader of the upstart National Socialist (Nazi) Party. Two years later he was imprisoned for attempting to overthrow the government. His prison manifesto, *Mein Kampf,* outlined the basic tenets of the new Aryan Germany. After its publication in 1925, Hitler regained political momentum and was made Chancellor in 1933. Hitler moved quickly to outlaw all opposition parties. This made him the uncontested dictator of Germany.

Benito Mussolini's rise to power in Italy had preceded Hitler's. Mussolini was made the Premier of Italy in 1922. Two years later he disbanded parliament to create his dictatorship.

Both men had ambitions of conquest and world domination. In October 1936 Hitler and Mussolini formed an alliance and began to plot their strategy. In 1938 Germany invaded neighboring Austria. The next year, while American audiences were celebrating the end of the Great Depression and enjoying the fantasy of *Wizard of Oz* and the spectacle of *Gone with the Wind,* the German-Italian Axis was busy invading Czechoslovakia, Albania, and Poland. In September 1939 Britain, France, Australia, New Zealand, and Canada declared war on the Axis. The war was on. 1940 was an even darker year for Europe and the rest of the world. The Axis invaded France, Denmark, Romania, Norway, Belgium, and Egypt. In six short weeks a demoralized France fell under the onslaught of German forces. In September, Japan joined the Axis as all-out war erupted in North Africa.

America was divided. Among isolationists there was a general reluctance to become enmeshed in another bloody war on foreign soil. But internationalists, especially those in the Roosevelt administration, believed that it was inevitable that the United States would be drawn in. It was time to prepare. In mid-1941 Congress passed the Lend Lease Act, giving the President the power to give weapons and supplies to Britain and, later, to Russia (USSR). The policy was to give the allies "all aid short of war" in supporting their struggle against the Axis. America was responding to the gravitational pull of the war.

Through the challenging years of the Great Depression, Hollywood became adept at maintaining its audience base by developing movie genres that were well understood by audiences. The function of this formulaic approach was to ensure that patrons got what they wanted when they purchased a movie ticket. During the Depression the industry had become more organized, bureaucratic, and risk averse. The wars in Europe, North Africa, and Asia presented a challenge to Hollywood's conventional wisdom that audiences wanted escapism and entertainment and not to be reminded of the grim reality that waited outside the theater door. The news media had already essentially chosen sides. Isolationists received little coverage and tended to be portrayed as quaint, old-fashioned, and uninformed. For the motion picture industry the choice wasn't so easy. Foreign film revenues amounted to forty percent of the total and were important to the well being of most major and minor movie companies.

One of the functions the Hays Office had taken on in the thirties was to promote the development of foreign markets. It maintained a division under the direction of Frederick Herron to support this goal. When the Nazis demanded that the American movie companies remove all Jewish employees from Germany, the Hays office complied. In 1938 Joseph Breen actually took a script for the anti-war film, *Idiot's Delight,* with him to Italy so that Mussolini's government could approve it for production. Of course, Breen was known to be an anti-Semitic and anti-communist, with political views not significantly at odds with Mussolini. But that was pretty much the high-water mark for cooperation between Hollywood and the dictators of Europe. Eventually Hitler limited the importation of American films to just twenty per year. At that point there was no longer a profit motive for cooperating with Germany. By 1940 foreign markets comprised an insignificant portion of Hollywood's income. This freed the movie industry to become more interventionist in support of America's involvement in the war.

The First American motion picture to portray events in Europe realistically was Walter Wanger's 1938 film, *Blockade*. The film tells the story of the Spanish Civil War in which Germany and Italy sided with the Royalists; and Russia, liberal Americans, and the British sided with the rebel Loyalists. *Blockade* was made by United Artists, which had already closed its offices in Spain and had nothing to lose financially. Breen warned UA to be cautious in its depiction of the Royalists but the finished project managed to capture the horror and suffering of modern mechanized war. Many theater owners chose to avoid the controversy that surrounded *Blockade* by either declining to book it or choosing to play the film for only one or two weeks. Breen felt vindicated and used the poor reception *Blockade* received to squelch Wanger's next project altogether.

In February, 1938 an Austrian-born U.S. Army deserter, Guenther Rumrich, was arrested in New York City in a clumsy plot to acquire blank American passports for a German secret agent in Hamburg. To receive a more lenient sentence Rumrich informed on three other German spies. When the trial was held that July, Jack Warner dispatched writer Milton Krims to observe the proceedings. Krims's account formed the basis of the script for the very controversial *Confessions of a Nazi Spy*. The German Consul got wind of the project and sent a letter to Joseph Breen demanding that it be terminated. Breen passed the letter on to Jack Warner, who was far from being intimidated by it. Anatole Litvak was assigned to direct, and Edward G. Robinson was cast in

CONFESSIONS OF A NAZI SPY (1939), DIRECTED BY ANATOLE LITVAK, SHOWN FROM LEFT: HENRY O'NEILL, EDWARD G. ROBINSON, SHERWOOD BAILEY

WARNER BROS./PHOTOFEST

the leading role of the FBI agent involved with the case. Breen was powerless to stop it since everything in the script that was the least bit controversial or depicted Germany negatively was a matter of legal fact, taken from the trial transcript. The story is told in a semi-documentary style with long passages of narration. The resulting film was described by the critics as melodramatic, but audiences were stirred by its patriotic message. Warner Brothers had successfully released the first anti-German film of the pre-war era. The very conservative executives at Paramount were appalled. They pleaded with Jack Warner, arguing that the film would be bad for Jews in Europe. Predictably *Confessions of a Nazi Spy* was banned in Germany, Italy, and Spain and in neutral countries such as Switzerland and Ireland.

In the summer of 1940 Charles Chaplin began work on his first talking film, *The Great Dictator*. In spite of complaints and threats about the film's content from United Artists, the company that distributed Chaplin's films, he insisted that he "was determined to go ahead, for Hitler must be laughed at." Chaplin also received criticism from the British Board of Film, the German Consul in Los Angeles, and Joseph Breen. All were concerned that the Lttle Tramp's huge fame and his genius for comedy could combine to create a portrait of Hitler that would provoke a violent reaction from the dictator himself. When the film was released in September, no one could argue that it wasn't a masterpiece. Only one word had been removed by the censors on a technicality. The film was box office magic. It grossed five million dollars, with Chaplin's profits amounting to one and a half million.

Jack Warner and Chaplin had empowered the motion picture community to engage the subject of the brewing war. Soon interventionist films became commonplace. *Pastor Hall*, the story of a World War I German submarine commander–turned anti-war pacifist, was distributed by the President's son, James Roosevelt, of Globe Productions. An emboldened MGM produced *The Mortal Storm*, an examination of the plight of Jews in Germany. Fox was working on a Dudley Nichols script for the interventionist film *The Rogue Male*, and Warner released Fritz Lang's *Man Hunt*, a film which portrays Nazis as evil savages. Films like *A Yank in the RAF* and *International Squadron* depicted Americans enlisting in the British military to get to the war before America was ready to step in. There is no way of knowing for sure what effect these films had on the political decisions relating to the war, but they did prepare the American public for what was to come.

GEARING UP THE PROPAGANDA

PROPAGANDA

The expression of opinions or actions carried out deliberately by individuals or groups with a view to influencing the opinions or actions of other individuals or groups for predetermined ends and through psychological manipulations.

The Roosevelt administration created the basis for a propaganda agency in late 1939, when it authorized the establishment of the Office of Government Reports (OGR). The office was designed to be a clearinghouse for government reports, but suspicious conservatives in congress saw OGR as a possible political operation connected to the reelection campaign of 1940. They refused to fund it. Roosevelt paid for it himself. The director of the agency, Lowell Mellett, a newspaper man, would eventually play a key role in enlisting Hollywood to assist with wartime propaganda.

In August 1940 another agency was created, Office of the Coordinator of Inter-American Affairs (CIAA). Nelson Rockefeller was put in charge of the effort to disseminate the American point of view in Latin America. Another concern was to make certain that any German attack on the United States did not begin in Argentina or Brazil, what with their large German immigrant populations. Rockefeller appointed another New York multimillionaire, John Hay "Jock" Whitney, to head the motion picture division. Whitney was already an experienced Hollywood insider and money-man who had been one of the backers of *Gone with the Wind*.

In March 1941 the Division of Information was established within the existing Office of Emergency Management (OEM). Roosevelt was moving slowly toward total government involvement in the media for wartime purposes. The Federal Communications Commission was already in the process of dismantling the "fairness doctrine" so that broadcasters wouldn't feel compelled to give time to anti-war points of view. In the fall of 1941 the top military command complained of low morale among new recruits. Roosevelt responded by setting up the Office of Facts and Figures (OFF) and put poet and Librarian of Congress, Archibald MacLeish, in charge of quickly refuting negative anti-war stories as they appeared in the print media. In mid December Lowell Mellett was put in charge of coordinating government-produced motion pictures. In a few short weeks, over twelve thousand theaters had signed an agreement to accept and screen any film that was distributed by the War Activities Committee (WAC). Clearly this alphabet soup of federal information agencies needed to be streamlined. The issue was addressed on June 13, 1942 when the Office of Wartime Information was created to oversee all propaganda and information activities. Radio commentator Elmer Davis was appointed chief of the OWI, making him the first information tsar.

THE WAR COMES TO AMERICA

On Sunday morning December 7, 1941 aircraft from a flotilla of Japanese Navy aircraft carriers attacked the army airfield and naval base at Pear Harbor, Honolulu, Hawaii. Much of the American Pacific fleet and air force was destroyed and twenty-four hundred soldiers and sailors were killed. Later in the day Japanese airplanes wiped out the American air forces in the Philippines. The next day the American Congress and Great Britain declared war on Japan. On December 11 Germany and Italy declared war on the United States. World War II had officially begun.

In Hollywood the reaction was swift and reflected an outpouring of patriotism. Paramount changed the title of a film that was already in production from *Midnight Angel* to *Pacific Blackout*. Warner Brothers announced the production of *Spy Swatter,* and Monogram announced *She's in the Army Now*. Republic Pictures registered the title *Remember Pearl Harbor* and rushed the film into production, while Selznick Studios began work on *V for Victory*. The studios instituted an 8:00 A.M, to 5:30 P.M. work schedule so that employees could get home before the evening blackout. Everyone expected that Japan's next attack would be on the west coast of mainland America, most likely Los Angeles, with its many military bases and factories. Squadrons of Japanese submarines had routinely been spotted off the coast from Santa Barbara to San Diego. Many families chose to move their children farther inland to cities such as San Bernardino and Riverside.

During the first few months of the war the outlook for America was grim. General Douglas MacArthur had been forced to retreat from the Philippines, leaving behind thousands of American civilians to deal with the Japanese occupation and life as prisoners of war. Eleven thousand American troops surrendered and were taken prisoner at Bataan and Corregidor. The British Navy was defeated in the South Pacific and the British colony, Singapore, fell in February 1942. In North Africa German Field Marshal Rommel had surrounded Cairo, Egypt with his tank corps. If ever there was a need of uplifting entertainment and positive news, this was it.

One of the problems the major Hollywood studios faced was the length of time it would take from when a film was conceived to when it reached the marketplace. The shortest possible timeline was about four months. This meant that any fictional treatment of the specifics of the war could easily be outdated by the time it was finished. Furthermore there was ongoing confusion about the role that OWI would play in production. Eventually, the situation was clarified with the OWI reviewing all scripts for possible content problems and focusing on producing documentary films with their much shorter production schedules. The studios would produce dramatic films with the overall purpose of uplifting morale both at home and on the warfront. One of the results was that 1942 would become a high-water mark year for the production of movie musicals. Some were patriotic in nature such as Warner Brothers' *Yankee Doodle Dandy*, with Jimmy Cagney starring as songwriter and performer George M. Cohan. Paramount made two war-themed musicals, *The Fleet's In* and *Star Spangled Rhythm* as well as the excellent, *Holiday Inn*, starring crooner Bing Crosby with dancer Fred Astaire. In all more than fourteen musicals were released in 1942.

YANKEE DOODLE DANDY (1942), DIRECTED BY MICHAEL CURTIZ, SHOWN FROM LEFT: FRANCES LANGFORD, JAMES CAGNEY

WARNER BROS. PICTURES/PHOTOFEST

THE PARAMOUNT CONSENT DECREE (PART ONE)

The motion picture industry cooperated with the war effort in a number of ways. One reason for the studios enthusiasm was sincere patriotism but another important motivation was the Roosevelt administration's willingness to suspend anti-trust action against the industry during the course of the war. On June 3, 1940 the United States Justice Department had taken the "big five" studios (Paramount, Warner Brothers, Twentieth Century Fox, Loews-MGM, and RKO) to court for breach of the anti-trust laws. Paramount was the lead defendant, but all five studios were bound by whatever decision the court handed down. Three major issues were identified. The "big five" companies used their ownership of movie theaters to control the marketplace by refusing to rent films to competing independently owned theaters until the studio owned theaters had first run. Another issue was "blind bidding." The independent theater owners were forced to bid on films made by the "big five" without first seeing them. To the Justice Department the most troubling issue was "block booking." In order to rent prestigious pictures from the "big five," the independents were forced to rent a block of twenty or more films, often including a few truly bad movies.

In October the "big five" agreed to enter into a consent decree. This legal maneuver had the effect of stopping the trial while an agreement to change the movie company's business practices was hammered out. From the beginning the three sizable "minor" studios, Universal, Columbia, and United Artists, dissented from this legal approach. Accept for block booking (which United Artists did not employ) the "minors" hadn't engaged in the other prohibited practices and believed that they should not be subject to the decree. After two days of intense closed-door negotiations the parties emerged with the decree. It allowed the "majors" to keep their theaters for the time being. It put an end to blind bidding and it limited block booking to blocks of no more than five films. The decree would expire in 1945, at which time the parties would go back to court. Dissent grew when Charlie Chaplin, Samuel Goldwyn, and others formed the Society of Independent Motion Picture Producers (SIMPP) to protest. Much controversy followed, but the deal held with the war adding pressure on everyone to live up to the decree.

IT'S A WONDERFUL LIFE (1946), DIRECTED BY FRANK CAPRA, SHOWN: DONNA REED, JAMES STEWART

RKO RADIO PICTURES/PHOTOFEST

THE MOVIE STARS GO TO WAR

After the declaration of war, the studios offered to free personnel from their contracts so they could enlist in the military. Almost all actors of any status found a way to be of service to the war effort. Several major stars and directors took up the call to enlist in the military.

James Stewart completed work on *Ziegfeld Girl* in 1942 and announced he was going to war before he had to act in a war movie. He was already an accomplished private pilot when he joined the Army Air Corp. His first assignment was training bombardiers until he was sent to flight school to train to fly B-17 bombers. He eventually flew twenty missions over Europe, and was highly decorated for bravery, including receiving the Distinguished Flying Cross. After the war he stayed in the Air Force Reserve until 1964. He retired from the military as a Brigadier General. His return to Hollywood was in one of his most memorable roles, as George Bailey in Frank Capra's *It's a Wonderful Life* (1946). Coincidentally, the film also marked Capra's return to commercial filmmaking after his own wartime service.

Tyrone Power enlisted in the U.S. Marine Corp in 1942, but Twentieth Century Fox received permission from the Marines to put Power in one last movie, a submarine picture, *Crash Dive*. He entered the military in early 1943. Like Stewart, Power was a private pilot before the war. At age twenty-nine, he was considered too old to fly fighter planes, the Marine's principal combat aircraft. He was trained to fly multi-engine transport airplanes instead. Throughout 1944 he flew missions in the Pacific, including evacuating the wounded from Iwo Jima, one of the bloodiest battles of the war. He returned to Twentieth Century in 1946 to resume his career, starring in the studio's prestigious production of Somerset Maugham's story of a man adrift in the world, *The Razor's Edge.*

The Razor's Edge (1946), Directed by Edmund Goulding, Shown from left: Tyrone Power, Anne Baxter

Photofest

Henry Fonda had left college in 1935 to become a contract actor at Twentieth Century Fox. By the time he appeared as Tom Joad in John Ford's classic adaptation of *The Grapes of Wrath* in 1940, Fonda had become a major star. His last picture for Fox before enlisting in the Navy was the William Wellman western *The Oxbow Incident* (1943). Fonda's first assignment was serving on the navy destroyer, the USS Satterlee. Following sea duty he was promoted to Lieutenant and assigned to an Air Combat Intelligence unit serving in the Pacific. After leaving the navy, his first project at Fox reunited Honda and Ford on the production of *My Darling Clementine* (1946), the story of frontier lawman Wyatt Earp.

Clark Gable was old enough at age forty-two in 1943 to avoid military duty altogether. His studio, MGM, had already lost too many key people to enlistment and the draft and wasn't keen on losing its biggest star as well. Shortly after Pearl Harbor, Gable and his intensely patriotic wife, Carole Lombard, offered their services to the White House. Both were offered symbolic appointments to the military, but Lombard wanted to do something more authentic. She went off on a War Bond tour and Gable and an MGM publicist went to Washington to talk about enlistment with his friend and head of the Army Air Forces, General Henry H. Arnold. On January 16 Lombard died in a plane crash on her way home from a bond tour. Gable sunk into a deep depression, drinking too much and riding his motorcycle too fast. He announced to friends that he was going leave Hollywood and join the army.

Hearing of the tragedy, General Arnold contacted the studio with an offer of a very important assignment for Gable. MGM tried to get control of the situation by reversing course and offering to make Gable's enlistment a studio event. On August 12, 1942 Gable and MGM cinematographer Andrew McIntyre (who would have the job of filming Gable's military life) reported to the Los Angeles Federal Building for a highly publicized swearing-in ceremony. At the request of General Arnold, who was having difficulty getting men to serve as gunners in bomber aircraft, Gable announced that he was signing up for gunner's school.

In late August Gable reported for training at Miami Beach. He was determined to be one of the guys, but the crowds that inevitably formed around him made it difficult. Eventually the Air Force found a more secluded place for training in Pueblo, Colorado. By this time McIntyre had acquired camera equipment from the studio and was busy

CAROLE LOMBARD, CLARK GABLE (MARRIED MARCH 29, 1939), SHOWN SEPT., 1939

documenting everything the star did. Gable's unit arrived in England in April 1943. He flew his first mission over Belgium in May and didn't fly again until July. Skeptics in the military believed that the upper command was purposely choosing "safe" missions for Gable to fly. But there didn't seem to be any envy among the men with whom he directly served. Gable appealed to his commanders to assign him to missions regardless of the danger, and his request was honored. He had a close call on one bombing run when an enemy bullet ripped the heel off of his shoe.

In all, Gable flew about twenty missions and McIntyre exposed about fifty thousand feet of film before being recalled to Washington. He was assigned to the First Motion Picture

Unit and to MGM Studios, where he was to finish a film with the working title of *Combat America.* It was a moderate success upon its release. The film project did serve to help Gable complete the mourning for his wife and restored his interest in filmmaking. After D-Day in June 1944 he asked for and received his release from the Air Force and went back to life as one of the greatest stars in movie history.

Glenn Ford's career was barely under way when the war broke out. At Columbia Pictures Harry Cohn had always resisted signing a large roster of talent to studio contracts, preferring to borrow stars from the other studios. But in 1939 he became convinced of the importance of developing his own talent. He proceeded to sign Rosalind Russell, William Holden, and Glenn Ford. Gradually over the next four years Ford's value to the studio increased. His last film before enlisting in the navy was the war film *Destroyer* (1943). After completing work on the film Ford enlisted in the Marines. His assignment was to build safe houses in German-occupied France for resistance members hiding from the Nazis. He was one of the first Americans to enter the horrific concentration camp and death factory at Dachau. In 1945 he transferred from the Marines to the Navy and ended his war duty in 1946 as a Commander in the Naval reserves.

Ford returned to Columbia in 1946 to play opposite his sometime-girlfriend Rita Hayworth in the film noir classic *Gilda.* Ford's greatest period of stardom stretched from his return from war until 1970, during which time he made sixty-four films. Ford remained in the Navy Reserve until retiring with the rank of Captain in 1990. During the Vietnam war he served two tours of duty with the Marine Amphibious Corp despite being in his midfifties at the time. He also did service as part of the elite Green Berets.

GILDA (1946), DIRECTED BY CHARLES VIDOR, SHOWN: RITA HAYWORTH (AS GILDA), GLENN FORD (AS ?)

COLUMBIA PICTURES/PHOTOFEST

OTHER FILMMAKERS SERVE BY MAKING FILMS

Frank Capra built a reputation during the thirties for making upbeat, populist films that gave hope to the generation mired in grinding poverty during the Great Depression. By 1941, convinced that America would soon become involved in the war, Capra contacted the Army to let it be known that he was available. Before enlisting, though, he needed to make sure that his family would have enough money to make do while he was gone to war. Capra accepted a lucrative offer from Warner Brothers to direct the screen adaptation of *Arsenic* *and Old Lace.* The attack on Pearl Harbor came just as he was completing principal photography on the film. He reported to duty as a Major in the Army Signal Corp.

Prior to World War II the Army Signal Corp was primarily responsible for operating radio equipment and providing photographic support including a very few training films. General George C. Marshall, the Army Chief of Staff, and other top commanders believed that training and indoctrination films could help prepare the coming onslaught of enlistees and draftees for war duty. The Signal Corp was given the assignment and the army purchased a studio facility in Astoria, New York on Long Island. Marshall chose Capra to make a series of films, documentaries in particular, that would explain to soldiers and the civilians back home the principles for which America was fighting the war.

Capra had a team of writers, technicians, researchers and editors under his command. The films were named the *Why We Fight* series. Capra cleverly collected and edited film clips, news reels, the Army archives, and even enemy footage (Capra used extensive clips from Leni Riefenstahl's German propaganda film, *Triumph of the Will*) to weave his stir-

ring messages. Dramatic narration and music, plus a touch of Capra's upbeat style, combined to make films that had the perfect blend of logic and emotion. The *Why We Fight* series consisted of seven films beginning with *Prelude to War* (1942). The other films were: *The Nazis Strike* (1942), *Divide and Conquer* (1943), *The Battle of Britain* (1943), *The Battle of Russia* (1943), *The Battle of China* (1944) and *War Comes to America* (1945). The films were shown on military bases all over the world, on ships at sea, at munitions factories, and in theaters. They were and are considered

FRANK CAPRA, DIRECTOR: WHY WE FIGHT (SERIES, 1943-1945)

the finest example of wartime propaganda ever. Winston Churchill was so impressed with the films that he ordered them shown in all British theaters as well. Ever the humanist, Capra became increasingly disturbed by the needless bloodshed on both sides as the war continued. The diaries he kept during this time show the conflict growing in his conscience. At war's end Capra was happy to leave it behind and to return to making movies that speak to America's best values. His first postwar feature teamed him up with Air Force veteran James Stewart to make *It's a Wonderful Life,* the story of a man who rediscovers the value of family and community.

Darryl Zanuck, the man who ran Twentieth Century Fox Studios since the mid-thirties, felt the call to service in 1942. During World War I he had lied about his age to enlist at the tender age of fifteen. He saw action on both the French and the Belgian fronts. When he enlisted for the Second World War, he was assigned the rank of Lieutenant in the Signal Corp to make training and combat documentaries. Zanuck, accustomed to being the man in charge of the studio, now chafed at military discipline and the need to follow orders and get his work approved by the military command. Although his work for the Signal Corp was of high quality, he was often in trouble with his superiors. Finally he was formally admonished for photographing himself in attitudes of bravery while shooting his Technicolor documentary about the U.S. invasion of North Africa. By mutual agreement he returned, "invigorated," to steer the fortunes of Twentieth Century Fox in 1943.

John Huston, an accomplished writer and director, joined the Army Signal Corp at age thirty-six in 1942. He made two documentaries in 1942, *Winning Your Wings* and *Across the Pacific*. The following year he made *Report from the Aleutians,* the story of B-17 and B-24 bombers striking targets in northern Japan. The film received an Oscar nomination. In 1944 Huston made *Tunisian Victory,* a film about the successful invasion of North Africa.

In 1945 Huston made his finest war documentary, *The Battle of San Pietro*. The film is unflinching in showing the destruction of war. It contains scenes of corpses, maimed children, and American soldiers digging graves for their fallen comrades. *San Pietro* included footage of intense action, leading to two of Huston's crew being killed during the battle. At first the military command attempted to suppress the film, fearing that it was too realistic. But when it was shown to General Marshall, he applauded its

THE BATTLE OF SAN PIETRO (1945) AKA SAN PIETRO DOCUMENTARY, PRODUCED BY: JOHN HUSTON, FRANK CAPRA

realistic treatment of the war and its honest depiction of bravery in the field. He insisted that it be shown to everyone in the service.

Huston's last war documentary was suppressed. *Let There Be Light* (1946) tells the story of shell-shocked soldiers in psychiatric hospitals battling for their sanity. It is the first film to deal with the subject of what we now call term *post-traumatic stress disorder* (PTSD). The military command was not only shocked by the subject matter and the straight-forward manner in which it was explored, they were also upset with the scenes of black and white soldiers fraternally working toward their release from the hospital and playing baseball together in what was then a still-segregated armed forces. *Let There Be Light* was not seen by the public until 1981.

German born **William Wyler** was an unlikely candidate for service in the Signal Corp. As the star director at Samuel Goldwyn Studios, he spent the thirties comfortably turning out one hit classic film after another such as *Dodsworth* (1936), *Dead End* (1937), and *Wuthering Heights* (1939). But duty called him in 1942 when, at age forty, he joined the Corp. He made two particularly remarkable films during his enlistment. The first, *The Fighting Lady*, is the story of the Essex-class aircraft carrier the USS Yorktown, from the day of its commissioning in 1943 to its first battle. The film contains spectacular Kodachrome footage of aerial combat between the Yorktown's fighters and their Japanese foes.

Wyler's other film, *Memphis Belle* (1944), is a wartime classic. It follows the crew of the B-17 bomber on its twenty-fifth and last mission over Germany. The Air Command was anxious to have this flight documented. The bombing runs over northern Europe were so dangerous that crews were promised to be sent home for the duration after twenty-five missions. Almost no one survived that long. The Memphis Belle was poised to be one of the few crews that made it, and Wyler was given the assignment of riding along as the plane attacked the German submarine pens at Wilhelmshaven. The Belle encountered heavy anti-aircraft fire and attacks from German fighter airplanes, but somehow, it managed to return. The dramatic account of the air crew's harrowing flight is one of Wyler's greatest achievements. He returned to Goldwyn and made the greatest postwar film, *The Best Years of Our Lives* in 1946.

THE STARS FIND OTHER WAYS TO SERVE

Not everyone in Hollywood was brave enough or fit enough or young enough or the right sex to serve in the war time military. But most found other ways to assist in the war effort.

War Bonds were one of the strategies the Roosevelt administration used to finance the war. During World War I Liberty Bonds had been instrumental in providing finance at a time when the federal income tax was only two percent. During World War II, the studios and their employees were enthusiastic salespeople for the bonds even before the war began. At the time they were called Defense Bonds. (The name was changed to War Bonds after the Declarations of War.) Other media were also involved. It is estimated that the radio, print, and billboard companies donated $180 million in free advertising for bonds. But Hollywood celebrities were the face of the bond campaigns. Greer Garson and Bette Davis were particularly involved in bond campaigns. But no one did as much as Rita Hayworth, who participated in seven bond campaigns and made personal appearances in over three hundred cities. During 1944 the "Stars Over America" campaign involved 337 motion picture and radio stars and raised $838 million. As mentioned earlier, Clark Gable's wife, Carole Lombard, was killed in a plane crash while returning from a War Bond tour.

The United Services Organizations (USO) was formed in 1940 to promote the welfare of the military. Much of the USO's activity was focused on civilians sending mail and care packages to soldiers in the field. Entertaining the troops was another important function of the organization. Many celebrities and entertainers just getting started in show business enlisted in Uniformed Entertainment Units, which traveled from base to base and to the warfront. Radio and motion picture personality, Bob Hope, traveled hundreds of thousands of miles to entertain troops with his variety show. Mickey Rooney, one of the most successful child actors of the thirties, enlisted in an Army entertainment unit and became famous for putting on shows near the front lines from the back of trucks and jeeps.

In New York the American Theater Wing, a nonprofit organization of people involved in live theater, opened the Stage Door Canteen in 1941. Affiliated with the USO, it provided a facility in New York where troops were fed and entertained by the biggest stars on Broadway. Soldiers passing through the city could spend an evening dancing with beautiful actresses to the music of the best big bands.

One day Warner Brothers star John Garfield mentioned to Bette Davis that it was a shame that with all the soldiers passing through, Los Angeles didn't have a place where they could meet a movie star. Davis ran with the idea. She approached her agent, Jules Stein, co-owner of Music Corporation of America, to put up the seed money for the venture. Cooking celebrity Chef Milani volunteered to be in charge of the kitchen, making the Canteen one of the best restaurants in Hollywood. The chosen location was a former livery stable and night club on Cahuenga Boulevard. Opening night, October 3, 1942, was a star-studded gala. Stein had the idea of selling bleacher seats to the local citizens for a hundred dollars each. This raised ten thousand dollars for the Canteen's operating expenses.

HOLLYWOOD CANTEEN (1944), WRITTEN AND DIRECTED BY DELMER DAVES, SHOWN FOREGROUND, FROM LEFT: JACK CARSON, JANE WYMAN, JOHN GARFIELD, BETTE DAVIS

WARNER BROS./PHOTOFEST

Until the end of the war the Hollywood Canteen was open every evening. Big dance bands such as Jimmy Dorsey's and Woody Herman's provided the music. The vocalists included Judy Garland, the Andrews Sisters, Frank Sinatra, and Bing Crosby. Abbot and Costello, Bob Hope, Jack Benny, and Jimmy Durante did the comedy. For the troops, the main attraction was their dance partners. In addition to Bette Davis, a lucky soldier might get to dance with Katharine Hepburn, Joan Crawford, Veronica Lake, or Betty Grable, who, after a day of working at the studio would drop by the makeup and wardrobe departments to get the glamour treatment before going out to the Canteen.

In 1944 Jules Stein convinced Warner Brothers to make a film about the Canteen featuring the very performers who provided entertainment on a regular basis. Bette Davis was the star, and over forty Canteen regulars appeared in the film. The top stars donated their fifty thousand dollar salaries; Warner donated $1.5 million of their profits to support the Canteen. When it closed at war's end, there was still half a million dollars in the treasury that was donated to various veterans' charities.

Many young actors and actresses destined to become stars in the postwar period were involved in the war effort at home and abroad. Marilyn Monroe (Norma Jean Baker) worked as an inspector in a parachute factory. A crew of army photographers was sent to document public relations images of women working on assembly lines. One of the photographers at the shoot noticed Baker's natural photogenic qualities and contacted her. This led to a modeling career that would include more than thirty magazine covers.

The postwar Truman administration was committed to helping the twelve million Americans who had served in uniform during the war. The GI (Government Issue) Bill of Rights was enacted to give veterans three profound benefits: free college and technical education, small business loans, and affordable home loans. Many took advantage of the educational benefit after leaving the military. Some graduated from colleges such as director Sam Peckinpah (USC-'50). Many attended acting schools such as Actor's Studio in New York. The list of veterans who served represents the elite of the entertainment world's next generation:

- Paul Newman
- Kirk Douglas
- Jack Lemon
- Tony Curtis
- Burt Lancaster
- Lee Marvin

IMPORTANT FILMS FROM WAR TIME

Although the interventionist, propaganda, and morale films of the war period were historically important, a number of films were made during the war that have lasting aesthetic value. Some films succeeded on both levels, and some films were regarded as successful at the time of their release only to become embarrassingly obsolete due to the fast-moving nature of war events. Most of the great fiction films that deal with the battlefield were made after the war. Many of the films made during wartime were aimed at defining the enemy and showing the inherent strength Americans had as a result of fighting for the "right cause" with a diverse military of citizen soldiers. Films about war in the Pacific tended to portray the Japanese as "the beast in the jungle" and contained a great deal of implied and overt racism. Films about war in Europe tended to portray the Germans as being basically good people who were led by evil men. For the most part Hollywood didn't bother to portray the Italians unless they were welcoming the American army liberators.

WAR IN THE PACIFIC

In the early days of the war the Office of Wartime Information (OWI) and its Bureau of Motion Pictures (BMP) struggled to give Hollywood guidance about the nature of the enemy in the Pacific and Europe. One problem the agencies faced was the movie industry's tendency to define the Japanese in racial terms. The Roosevelt administration's decision to send Japanese-Americans to internment camps seemed to institutionalize the racism. Filmmakers, including Frank Capra in his *Know Your Enemy* documentary, saw Italians and Germans as individuals whereas the Japanese were "photographic prints off the same negative." The attack on Pearl Harbor was interpreted as an example of backstabbing treachery as opposed to a brilliant military feat.

Paramount was the first studio to exploit these themes with its 1942 production of *Wake Island*. At the time of its release it was a box office smash. It tells the story of a handful of Marines fighting to the last man against a vastly superior force. It depicts the Japanese bayoneting defenseless Americans as their few remaining comrades wait for death to come while making speeches about the righteousness of the American cause. In truth, the audiences back home were so hungry for word from the warfront they would have found any depiction enlightening.

MGM got into the act with *Bataan* in April 1943. The film portrays an American defeat, with troops fighting while retreating. It shows scenes of Japanese airplanes bombing Red Cross ambulances and indiscriminately killing civilian women and children. Ultimately the OWI was quite pleased with *Bataan*

WAKE ISLAND (1942), DIRECTED BY JOHN FARROW, SHOWN: ROBERT PRESTON

PARAMOUNT PICTURES/PHOTOFEST

because it included an African American private in the combat unit, when in reality, the armed forces were still segregated. The next year Fox released a more mature version of the war in the Pacific, *Guadalcanal Diary*. It is the story of a fierce battle that took place in the Solomon Islands with both sides taking heavy losses and the Americans prevailing. Like many war films it follows a single platoon made up of a cross section of Americana including William Bendix as a New York taxi driver who just wants to get back to his beloved Brooklyn Dodgers. Anthony Quinn appears as the token minority Latino. The men of the platoon describe the enemy as apes and monkeys that use all forms of deceit in battle.

By 1945 depictions of war in the Pacific were becoming much more sophisticated if not less racist. Warner Brothers' film *Objective Burma* stars Errol Flynn as the leader of a group of American paratroopers that destroy an important Japanese radar installation. The film includes a catalog of racial epithets including "dirty yellow rats" and "blasted monkeys." After the Japanese capture and mutilate a group of Americans, one of the characters in the film makes an astonishingly racist speech calling the enemy "degenerate, immoral idiots" and demanding that they should be "wiped off the face of the earth."

One of the issues the OWI and Hollywood faced was distinguishing between the Japanese enemy and the Chinese allies. This was attempted in the MGM film, *Thirty Seconds Over Tokyo*, the story of General Doolittle's daring bombing raid of Tokyo in April 1942. The mission's plan called for the bombers to be launched from a specially equipped aircraft carrier and flown over Japan to land in a friendly region of China. The film contains scenes of friendly peasants helping the downed American

THIRTY SECONDS OVER TOKYO (1944), DIRECTED BY MERVYN LEROY, SHOWN FROM LEFT: DON DEFORE, VAN JOHNSON, ROBERT WALKER

MGM/PHOTOFEST

fliers as a very competent Chinese doctor patches up their wounds. Only one film, RKO's *Behind the Rising Sun* (1943), attempts to show the Japanese as three-dimensional human beings with doubts about the war.

WAR IN EUROPE

Hollywood's treatment of the war in Europe was always destined to be more nuanced and less racist than its depiction of the Japanese. Obviously there are many people of German and Italian ancestry in America and they were not sent to internment camps. Many in Hollywood were born in Europe and more had traveled there. As a result European-themed films were much more diverse. Fox's 1943 film *The Moon Is Down* deals with the issue of what is a good Nazi. It is the story of the German occupation of Norway. A young officer begins to doubt Hitler's sanity and speaks out about it to his superior officer, for which he is punished. In need of human companionship the young German goes to the local pub for a drink, only to be treated as an outcast. Later he falls in love with one of the local girls, who fools him into thinking that she will sleep with him. What he doesn't know is that she has brought to bed a pair of scissors to kill him. The film attempts to make the audience almost feel sorry for the enemy.

Another way of treating the war in Europe was to add war subplots to existing B picture series. In *Enemy Agents Meet Ellery Queen* the popular detective turns his skills on Nazi spies. *Yukon Patrol* shows the Northwest Mounted Police stopping enemy agents from getting a supply of mysterious "Compound X" for their secret weapons program. In *Phantom Plainsman* cowboys out ride and out shoot their German foes. Germans were also the butt of jokes in films like *To Be Or Not To* Be and *The Devil With Hitler*. These films could be very silly, but audiences loved them.

Another example of the sensitive treatment of the European war is Warner Brothers' film adaptation of Lillian Hellman's successful play *Watch on the Rhine* (1943). It is the story of a wealthy American family living in Washington D.C. who play host to two families escaping from Europe. One family is headed by a former Romanian diplomat who longs for the old country and is willing to sell his services to the Nazis. The other is the leader of the resistance movement in Germany who is in America only long enough to make sure his family is

CASABLANCA (1942), DIRECTED BY MICHAEL CURTIZ, SHOWN ON THE SET, FROM LEFT: HUMPHREY BOGART (AS RICK), INGRID BERGMAN (AS ILSA)

safe and to raise money for his cause. Intrigue and murder follow, but the real message of the film is that there are plenty of good Germans willing to do the right thing.

Casablanca (1943) is a great film on its own and by far the best of the wartime films that deal with issue of resistance movements. Over the years it has taken on a mythical reputation. It began as a standard Warner Brothers "A" picture. One early press release listed Ronald Reagan for the lead role, but that was probably the result of a press agent's efforts to get an actor's name in ink. Humphrey Bogart was the studio choice from the beginning. He had played a number of hard-bitten types at Warner, but executive Hal Wallis and others were interested in seeing Bogart branch out into more romantic parts. This one was perfect for him.

The story is based on an unpublished play *Everybody Goes to Rick's*. The screen adaptation was done by Julius and Philip Epstein with additional dialogue by Howard Koch. Hungarian-born Michael Curtiz was chosen to direct. The studio had some of the best character actors in the business under contract. Paul Henreid was chosen to play the resistance leader, Victor Laszlo. Claude Rains played the corrupt police captain and Peter Lorre, Sydney Greenstreet, and Dooley Wilson round out the colorful supporting cast. The only significant effort Wallis made to elevate the project was paying Selznick Studios $25,000 to borrow Ingrid Bergman for the role of Bogart's love interest, Ilsa. One historian claims that thirty different nationalities are represented in the production.

Casablanca is the story of an American expatriate, Rick, who owns a saloon and gambling den in Casablanca, a territory controlled by the Vichy government, which is in collaboration with the Germans. He is pointedly nonpartisan in the affairs of war, but Rick's is known as a place where people on the run might be able to get letters of transit to enable their escape from Nazi Europe. Rick's only trusted friend is the African American piano player, Sam, who has been with him for some time. One evening an old flame, Ilsa, walks into Rick's in need of transit papers for herself and her husband, a resistance leader. She and Rick had been lovers in Paris before the war at a time when Ilsa believed her husband to be dead. Upon discovering he was alive, she left Rick, heartbroken. Now she is willing to come back to Rick if only he will help her husband. In the end Rick's nobility wins out, Ilsa and her husband escape and Rick sets out with "Frenchy" the police captain to join the French Foreign Legion to fight the Germans.

STORY OF **G.I.** JOE (1945), DIRECTED BY WILLIAM A. WELLMAN, SHOWN ON POSTER: BURGESS MEREDITH (AS ERNIE PYLE/NARRATOR)

The one great European combat film to emerge in wartime is *The Story of G.I. Joe*, based on newspaper reporter Ernie Pyle's stories of life among ordinary soldiers during the war. It follows a group of American infantrymen from the time they land in southern Italy all the way north to Rome. It shows the daily rituals of surviving on the warfront and the wretched conditions on the battlefield, where it's always muddy and the food comes out of a can. What makes *The Story of G.I. Joe* special is its realism. Soldiers don't make passionate speeches about the cause for which they are fighting. There is little heroism. The battle scenes are few, but they show not just the death of soldiers but of women and children as collateral damage. Some of the battle footage is documentary borrowed from Huston's *The Battle of San Pietro*. The film contains many human touches. One soldier receives a recording of his son's first words and spends all his time trying to find a record player. Another adopts a puppy and cares for it with extreme kindness. Unlike the films that deal with the war in the Pacific, *G.I. Joe* doesn't bother to vilify the enemy or stoop to racism. It is an honest attempt to capture the war experience.

WAR'S END

On April 30, 1945 Adolph Hitler committed suicide. The war in Europe ended eight days later. The war in the Pacific was still being waged. On August 6 the first atomic bomb was dropped on Hiroshima. Three days later the second was dropped on Nagasaki. On August 14 the Japanese accepted unconditional surrender to end the Second World War. Over thirteen million soldiers had served in the military. The Army suffered over 800,000 dead, wounded, and missing. The Navy and Marines had almost 200,000 casualties combined.

Almost half a million Americans died in the war. For everyone else there was the aftermath of re-entering society with physical and psychological wounds. One great film captures the issue of reentry better than all others.

The Best Years of Our Lives (1946) is the story of three men trying to reconstruct their lives after service in World War II. Samuel Goldwyn studios began to germinate the idea for the film after the publication of a *Time Magazine* article about the difficulty some service men were having adjusting to civilian life after the war. Fredric March plays the oldest veteran whose coping mechanism, alcohol, isn't working. He has a hard time

THE BEST YEARS OF OUR LIVES (1946), DIRECTED BY WILLIAM WYLER, SHOWN: DANA ANDREWS, MYRNA LOY, FREDRIC MARCH, HOAGY CARMICHAEL, HAROLD RUSSELL

RKO/SAMUEL GOLDWYN/PHOTOFEST

relating to his old job as bank manager. Dana Andrews is a handsome former Air Force officer who returns to his old job at the soda fountain. His wife was expecting something more glamorous from her war hero husband and lets him know it. Harold Russell was a real-life Army casualty who lost both hands in an explosion. He essentially plays himself as a disabled veteran whose family has difficulty adjusting to his injuries. (Russell is the only actor to win two Academy awards for a single performance, best supporting actor and a special Oscar for "bringing hope and courage to his fellow veterans.") William Wyler directed, and Gregg Toland photographed. In addition of Russell, Wyler won a Best Director Oscar, March won a Best Actor Oscar, and the film won Best Picture.

CHAPTER 9

POST-WAR WORLD CINEMA

THE END OF WORLD WAR II AND THE BEGINNING OF THE COLD WAR

In February 1945, three years after the United States entered WWII, the three leaders of the allied nations met at the former Black Sea palace of the Russian tsars at Yalta. British Prime Minister Winston Churchill, Soviet dictator Joseph Stalin, and American President Franklin D. Roosevelt convened to draw the map of the post-war world. The Soviet army, twelve million strong, had already occupied Poland and was briefly paused, for the sake of the conference, in its march across the border into eastern Germany. Roosevelt was in failing health but maintained his optimistic belief that the United Nations would provide a civilized forum for dealing with Stalin's ambition to add more European and Asian territory to the Soviet Union. Churchill announced his intention to fire bomb Dresden, the last untouched German city. Stalin agreed to hold free elections in Poland and to help in the defeat of Japan. Despite the alliance the three leaders had formed during the darkest moments of the war, the truce they created seemed shaky and fragile. Most historians point to Yalta as the true beginning of the Cold War. Two months later Roosevelt died of a massive brain hemorrhage and Vice President Harry S. Truman became the thirty-third American President. The war in Europe ended a month later in May 1945. In August, Truman's order to drop the atomic bomb on Japan was carried out. Within six weeks the war in the Pacific was over. Much of the world lay in ruins. Only America was unscathed with its industry and commerce in tact. Stalin did not keep his word to hold free elections in Poland. Instead, he hastened the pace of the development of a Soviet atomic bomb. In a mat-

WWII SHOWN FROM LEFT: WINSTON CHURCHILL, FRANKLIN D. ROOSEVELT, JOSEPH STALIN ON FEBRUARY 9, 1945, AT THE LIVIDIA PALACE, YALTA.

ter of months tensions began to rise between the Soviet Union and its former partners, the United States and Western Europe. World War II was replaced by a new kind of war, a cold war, in which the opposing sides would use threats of unspeakable nuclear destruction and propaganda as bludgeons against each other. America had been skeptical about communism since the 1918 Soviet revolution and the anti-communist "Palmer Raids" when the Department of Justice declared war on left-leaning labor leaders. However, the economic suffering of the Great Depression made the communist critique of capitalism attractive to many American intellectuals, writers and academics. That changed after World War II as America embraced extreme patriotism. Communism became radioactive. It was social and career suicide for anyone in public life to find anything positive in Marxist thought and ideology.

An anti-communist movement arose and began to grow in the political system, the media and the boardrooms of commerce. J. Edgar Hoover, the Director of the Federal Bureau of Investigation, had staked much of his career on rooting out and punishing communists. Influential newspaper columnists such as Walter Winchell and Westbrook Pegler gained huge celebrity and wealth by attacking leftists in government and show business. Congress was cowed by the effectiveness of the anti-communist press in whipping Americans into a lather of hatred toward Marxism. Equally frightening to Washington was the willingness of politicians like Joseph McCarthy to paint their detractors red. In a climate of fear and accusation, Congress became the main stage for the ensuing drama of the communist exorcism.

THE ANTI-COMMUNIST WITCH HUNT AND THE MOTION PICTURE INDUSTRY

In 1938 the House of Representatives created the House Un-American Activities Committee (HUAC) to mollify the American Legion and right-wing politicians' charges that Roosevelt's many New Deal programs had been infiltrated by the communists. The committee's first target was the labor unions. In 1939 Congress passed the Hatch Act which barred communists, Nazis and other political undesirables from working in government service. Other laws followed requiring communists to register as agents of foreign governments and making it a crime to teach or advocate the overthrow of the government. The witch hunt took a holiday for a few years when Germany invaded the U.S.S.R. in the summer of 1941 and the Soviets became military allies of the United States for the purposes of the war. However, the anti-communist right was ready to get back to work once World War II ended.

SHOWN: JOSEPH MCCARTHY

Joseph McCarthy was by far the most opportunistic anti-communist in the immediate postwar period. As a graduate of Roman Catholic Marquette University Law School in Milwaukee, Wisconsin in the mid 1930s, he quickly became involved in politics and won an election for judge in 1939 at age 30. He took a leave of absence from the bench in 1942 to become a Lieutenant in the Marines. He left the military in 1945 to successfully campaign for his old job. The next year he ran for U.S. Senate and was elected as one of the first of many World

War II veterans who would take over Congress in the late 1940s. His Senate career was unremarkable until he made a speech to a group of Republican women in Wheeling, West Virginia in early 1950. He told the luncheon group that Secretary of State, Dean Acheson, had a list of two hundred five communists in the State Department. Later he claimed to have his own list of fifty-seven communists and called for an investigation, thus placing himself in the middle of the hottest political issue of the day. The list proved to be worthless, but McCarthy had become a celebrity.

In 1947, HUAC began to investigate the motion picture industry. This move guaranteed a tidal wave of publicity for Chairman J. Parnell Thomas and all of the committee members (including California Congressman Richard M. Nixon) who delighted in posing as anti-communist warriors defending their country against the evil foe. The Screen Writer's Guild was a ripe target. The committee would show the world how these invisible agents of the U.S.S.R. had subversively planted pro-communist ideas into movie scripts.

The first people to testify before the committee were presented as "friendly witnesses." Jack Warner and Louis B. Mayer spoke on behalf of the captains of the motion picture industry, assuring the committee that no suspected communist would ever find work in Hollywood again. Actors Gary Cooper and Ronald Reagan appeared next and were eager to "name names." Nineteen "unfriendly witnesses" were named

SHOWN: MEMBERS OF THE "HOLLYWOOD 10" SURROUNDED BY THEIR FAMILIES PRIOR TO LEAVING FOR PRISON (CIRCA 1950)

who were believed to be communists. Eleven of these were called to testify. Playwright Bertolt Brecht appeared first, denied being a communist and promptly left America for his native West Germany. The remaining group, who became known as the "Hollywood Ten," included director Edward Dmytryk, and nine screen writers led by Dalton Trumbo, Ring Lardner Jr. and Lester Cole. They were given three undesirable options. They could admit being communists, in which case they would be forced to name other communists or be held in Contempt of Congress. They could deny being communists and be prosecuted for perjury. Or they could invoke their Constitutional right against self incrimination, which they did. The committee ignored the Fifth Amendment and threw them into prison for sentences between six months and a year. Later, Dmytryk lost his nerve and agreed to name other friends and acquaintances who might be communists. After their release from prison, the remaining "Hollywood Nine" found themselves blacklisted and unable to find work. Some used assumed names until a committee of fifty Hollywood executives, afraid the public would turn against the industry, announced that, henceforth, no one would knowingly employ a communist.

In 1951 the HUAC again turned its attention to Hollywood and a second wave of witch hunting was unleashed. A new committee chairman, John S. Wood, compiled a list of three hundred twenty-four names to add to the 1947 black list. Almost two thirds of the people on the list were still working in motion pictures and when their names were released they instantly lost their jobs without appeal. With the assistance of HUAC research director Raphael Nixon, Chairman Wood changed the focus of the hearings from rooting out individuals suspected of communist activities to examining the infiltration of Hollywood's major institutions by the Communist Party itself. This resulted in dramatic mass hearings with as many as ninety witnesses being called at a time.

RONALD REAGAN (1947)
SHOWN: TESTIFYING BEFORE THE
HOUSE UN-AMERICAN ACTIVITIES
COMMITEE (HUAC)

One victim of the 1947 hearings, Robert Rossen, had been a successful writer/director before his encounter with HUAC. After appearing and refusing to cooperate, he found that studios were reluctant to work with him because of suspicions surrounding him. He voluntarily testified when the hearings restarted in 1951. This time Rossen named fifty-seven people, friends and colleagues alike. Even though he was burdened by the fresh stigma of being an informer, his cooperation with HUAC did serve to revive his career, resulting in such film successes as *The Hustler* (1961) and *Lilith* (1964).

Elia Kazan was by far the most famous and powerful director called before HUAC. As a recent Yale Drama School graduate, he began his career at the Group Theater in New York in 1933. The Group was led by Lee Strasberg and was a center for teaching the Stanislavski Method of acting. It was also an organization whose members were intellectually leftist. Some had joined the Communist Party partly in protest of the economic hardships of the Great Depression. Other members of the Group Theater included playwright Clifford Odets and actors John Garfield, Will Geer and Franchot Tone. Kazan quickly distinguished himself as a talented young director who could guide actors through their method-based performances. The Group Theater disbanded in 1941 and Kazan continued to direct on Broadway, forming an important partnership with the rising young playwright Tennessee Williams. Their stage production of "*A Streetcar Named Desire*" brought stardom to both men.

THE METHOD

The Stanislavski method of acting came to America in 1923 as the Moscow Art Theater was performing in New York. Two members, Maria Ouspenskaya and Richard Boleslavski, defected and sustained themselves by teaching at the American Laboratory Theater. In 1924 two young, aspiring actors, Lee Strasberg and Stella Adler, enrolled in the school and immersed themselves in Boleslavski's teaching.

The discipline they were taught begins with the actor performing relaxation exercises to enable a higher degree of concentration. "Sense memory" exercises follow the relaxation technique and are used to engage all five of the actor's senses in creating a character. The actor is taught to constantly ask himself, "What would I do if I were in this situation?" In working on a scene or part, the actor analyzes their character's emotions and recalls a personal situation in which they experienced the same emotion to be used as the basis for their character's behavior. Another form of concentration is to learn to be private on stage, unaware of the audience and in the moment so that if some part of the performance doesn't go as planned, such as dropping a prop, the actor incorporates the mistake into the performance. Method Acting requires the actor to find and define the character they are depicting and to become that character or "get into" that character.

In contrast to Method Acting, the great studio actors of the thirties and forties believed that acting was an acquired professional technique. Often described as naturalistic acting, the studio style focused on working to the camera, creating physical expressions, reactions and gestures that portray the character. Studio actors worked to develop line readings and inflections of dialog that gave emphasis to a situation or an emotion. They would add carefully rehearsed mannerisms to their performances to give more color to the characters they portrayed. Studio style acting is often described as an outside-in technique, while "The Method" is described as an inside-out technique.

In 1947 Kazan founded Actors Studio in New York to continue teaching the Method style of acting. Lee Strasberg joined as artistic director. There was no shortage of students in the post-war era. Early alumni included Marlon Brando, Montgomery Clift, James Dean, Marilyn Monroe and Paul Newman. (A second branch of the school was opened in Hollywood in 1967 to serve actors in the mo-

A STREETCAR NAMED DESIRE (1947–1949 BROADWAY) PLAY BY TENNESSEE WILLIAMS DIRECTED BY ELIA KAZAN, SHOWN: PLAYWRIGHT TENNESSEE WILLIAMS SHOWN BACKSTAGE ON DECEMBER 17, 1947, FROM LEFT: PRODUCER IRENE SELZNICK, DIRECTOR ELIA KAZAN, PLAYWRIGHT TENNESSEE WILLIAMS

PHOTOFEST

tion picture industry.) In the post-war era, Kazan's career was skyrocketing. In addition to his work on Broadway, he was making highly respected films such as *Gentlemen's Agreement*, a portrayal of anti-Semitism in American society, and *A Streetcar Named Desire* with Marlon Brando. But the 1951 revival of HUAC's Hollywood investigations threatened Kazan deeply. At his first appearance before the committee, he admitted his earlier involvement with communism and proceeded to rail against its effects on the entertainment industry. He refrained from naming other communists and left the hearings believing he had gotten away with it. However, the pressure to name names began to mount.

Fellow Greek and president of Twentieth Century Fox Studios, Spyros Skouras, contacted Kazan to share his concern that the director's career would be over if he did not cooperate more fully with the Committee. Kazan asked to testify before HUAC a second time. At this hearing he repeated his belief that Communism must be banished from Hollywood and proceeded to name some of those closest to him as fellow communists including Lee Strasberg and his wife, and Kazan's protégé at the Group Theater, Martin Ritt. While he succeeded in staying off the blacklist, Kazan was the subject of whispers and criticism for the remainder of his days. He continued to make twelve films after his HUAC appearance including *On the Waterfront* (1954) and *East of Eden* (1956). At age eighty-nine, Kazan was awarded a special Motion Picture Academy Award (Oscar) for lifetime achievement. When it was bestowed upon him at the 1999 Academy Awards, many in the audience demonstrated their continuing distaste for Kazan and what he had done forty-five years earlier.

Between 1947 and 1953, HUAC provided data on sixty thousand people to their employers. Of those named, fifteen thousand were federal government employees who were forced from their jobs by government loyalty boards. Loyalty oaths became common. Today in California, school employees are among the twenty million American workers still required to take a loyalty oath as a condition of employment. During the reign of HUAC hundreds of notable celebrities were forced to testify, including Lucille Ball, band leader Artie Shaw, and playwright Arthur Miller. The chilling effect of HUAC's witch hunt lasted well into the 1980s. It also spawned the production of a series of anti-communist motion pictures and a television series that lasted three seasons, "*I Lead Three Lives*."

REPRESENTATIVE ANTI-COMMUNIST FILMS

I Was a Communist for the FBI (1951)
Walk East On Beacon! (1952)
My Son John (1952)
Big Jim McLain 1952)

FILM NOIR

Film noir is a style of film that is derived from pulp fiction literature of the thirties and forties. Literally, pulp fiction refers to books and magazines that were printed on cheap, pulp paper with equally inexpensive, inelegant, covers and bindings. During the Great Depression, pulp fiction magazines and books were aimed at audiences that were interested in inexpensive, entertaining, trashy reading as opposed to fine literature. There were several pulp fiction genres and sub-genres including Westerns, Weird Tales, Spicy Adventure and Weird Menace, a genre mostly associated with the work of writer Hugh Cave. The Hard Bitten Detective and Crime genres were among the most popular of pulp fiction and often crossed over into mainstream literature. Carroll John Daly was the father of the Hard Bitten Detective genre, contributing to magazines such as *Dime Detective Magazine* and *Black Mask*. His detective character, Race Williams, is featured in several novels including, *The Men In Black*, in which a group of rich civic leaders pay him to act as bait for a serial killer. By far the greatest number of Noir detective films has been based on Daschell Hammet's Sam Spade character and Raymond Chandler's Philip Marlow.

"B" MOVIES

Double feature movie programs consisted of a an "A" picture and a "B" picture, as well as newsreels, animated shorts or cartoons, movie trailers, and short subject films that were most often documentaries. This type of theater program began in the 1930s as a strategy for giving depression era audiences more value for their ticket dollar. Around 1960 double feature programs began to fade away as the motion picture industry adapted to the advent of television. Typically, the first half of the program ended with the showing of the "B" picture followed by an intermission, usually fifteen minutes in length, and then the "A" feature film. "B" pictures (also called *programmers*) were inexpensively made and featured lesser known writers, actors and directors. Like the minor leagues in sports, "B" picture production operated within the studio system as a forum for developing talent and experimenting with styles. Minor studios like Republic, Producers Releasing Corporation, and Monogram specialized in producing "B" pictures. Those making films noir in the forties and fifties were unaware that they were creating a new genre. They were only aware of the fact that they were making dark, gritty and pessimistic "B" films. It wasn't until the end of the fifties that the French "new wave" film critics categorized these films as the noir genre.

The visual style for Film Noir is purely expressionistic, capitalizing on cinematographers' love of dramatic lighting set-ups with an abundance of dark corners and menacing shadows. In *The Big Combo* (1955) John Alton makes daring use of large, black, unlit spaces on the screen. His unconventional lighting set-ups elevate the film from a seedy United Artists "B" picture to a great work of visual art.

Sunset Boulevard **(1950)** Directed by Billy Wilder Shown: William Holden (as Joe Gillis), Gloria Swanson (as Norma Desmond)

Directors such as Fritz Lang (*Scarlet Street*, 1945 and *The Big Heat*, 1953) and Billy Wilder (*Double Indemnity*, 1944 and *Sunset Boulevard*, 1950) were instrumental in the creation and development of expressionism in Germany in the 1920s. In the forties and fifties they applied the expressionist style to the grim, pessimistic stories of the film noir genre.

The Film Noir detective hero does not subscribe to society's conventional norms of behavior. He has his own code of conduct and it often skirts the wrong side of the law. He is a loner who expects to be betrayed and only trusts a few intimate insiders. Often he is a former police detective who has become frustrated with the slow methodical ways of the department. He uses more expedient methods, including a little violence from time to time if it will get him what he wants. It's not unusual for the noir detective to become a

THE MALTESE FALCON (1941) DIRECTED BY JOHN HUSTON SHOWN, IN SPADE'S OFFICE: LEE PATRICK (AS EFFIE PERINE), HUMPHREY BOGART (AS SAM SPADE)

suspect in the very crime he is investigating. But he is one step ahead of the cops and does their work for them while they grudgingly express their gratitude.

Women in Film Noir tend to be either pals or killers. In *The Maltese Falcon* (1941), Sam Spade's secretary, Effie, does his errands, lights his cigarettes, helps brush off an unwanted girlfriend and fetches the treasure for which everyone is willing to kill. Spade's client and love interest, Brigid O'Shaughnessy, is a true femme fatale. To get her way, she is willing to offer sex, lie, cheat, cry and grovel. If none of that works, she knows how to use a gun. In *Double Indemnity* (1944), Walter Neff (played by Fred MacMurray) is an ordinary insurance salesman. One day he is seduced by Phyllis Dietrich-

DOUBLE INDEMNITY (1944) DIRECTED BY BILLY WILDER SHOWN FROM LEFT: BARBARA STANWYCK, FRED MACMURRAY, TOM POWERS

son (Barbara Stanwyck), the wife of a client. She convinces him to murder her husband so the two can collect the insurance. Neff allows his life to be ruined by the schemes of a woman who would betray him without a thought.

Noir villains are always more colorful and interesting than the good guys. In Stanley Kubrick's *The Killing* (1956), Sterling Hayden (whose career includes many great films noir) leads a gang of misfits who carefully plot a two million dollar race track heist. The crew includes a cashier at the track whose wife demands more and more money to indulge her affair with an equally greedy lover and a crooked policeman who provides protection and information. The job is financed by an effeminate alcoholic who gets a rush from consorting with gangsters. A Russian gunman and a retired wrestler provide the diversion for the robbery. It is the perfect crime. Or is it?

Another noir convention is the use of narration. Voice-over commentary was a common device in documentary film. In non-fiction film, however, screen writers were discouraged from using the technique because it was seen as literary and not cinematic. Writers were instructed to "show the story" through the character's actions rather than explain it with words. In the "B" picture world of noir, narration often saved the expense of filming scenes that were over budget. Narration was also a writer's device for adding hip, ironic and satirical elements to the story at no expense to the filmmakers. Billy Wilder was a master of narration. His film, *Double Indemnity* opens with protagonist, Walter Neff, in his office late at night, confessing his crimes into a dictating machine as the film unwinds in a series of flashbacks. Wilder's *Sunset Boulevard* begins with a shot of a corpse floating face down in a swimming pool. His nar-

Photofest

THE KILLING (1956) DIRECTED BY STANLEY KUBRICK SHOWN: JAY C. FLIPPEN (AS MARVIN UNGER), STERLING HAYDEN (AS JOHNNY CLAY), ELISHA COOK JR. (AS GEORGE PEATTY), TED DE CORSIA (AS RANDY KENNAN), JOE SAWYER (AS MIKE O'REILLY), ON BED MARIE WINDSOR (AS SHERRY PEATTY)

ration begins to tell the story of how he got there and throughout the film he continues to weave a cynical commentary until the film returns full circle to the body in the pool.

John Huston's *The Maltese Falcon* (1941) is often cited as the first film noir and Orson Welles' *Touch of Evil* (1958) as the last film of the classic period of the genre. The following is a representative list of great noir films and their directors:

Shadow of a Doubt (1943) Alfred Hitchcock
Double Indemnity (1944) Billy Wilder
Murder, My Sweet (1944) Edward Dmytryk
Mildred Pierce (1945) Michael Curtiz
Scarlet Street (1945) Fritz Lang
The Big Sleep (1946) Howard Hawks
The Killers (1946) Robert Siodmak
The Postman Always Rings Twice (1946) Tay Garnett
Dark Passage (1947) Delmer Daves
The Naked City (1948) Jules Dassin
The Lady From Shanghai (1947) Orson Welles
Key Largo (1948) John Huston
The Third Man (1949) Carol Reed
White Heat (1949) Raoul Walsh
Sunset Blvd. (1950) Billy Wilder
D.O.A. (1950) Rudolph Maté
Where the Sidewalk Ends (1950) Otto Preminger
Detective Story (1951) William Wyler
The Big Heat (1953) Fritz Lang
The Big Combo (1955) Joseph H. Lewis
Night of the Hunter (1955) Charles Laughton
Sweet Smell of Success (1957) Alexander Mackendrick

A NEW GENERATION OF STARS

Actors Studio provided a seemingly endless supply of new talent for the motion picture industry and the nascent television medium in the period following the war. Hollywood was looking for new faces to replace the great stars of the thirties. Method Acting was becoming the rage. Motion pictures were becoming more sophisticated to reflect the tastes of a generation that had been exposed to the world through participation in the war. A new generation of playwrights such as Tennessee Williams, Arthur Miller, and Edward Albee were exploring subjects that had been taboo in movies after the introduction of the Production Code. With Will Hays' retirement in 1945 came a trend toward allowing more frankness and emotional reality in films. The men and women who came out of Actors Studio in the late forties were perfectly positioned to take advantage of changing tastes and styles on stage and in the motion picture industry.

Marlon Brando was by far the best known and influential of the post-war Actors Studio alumni. He was born in Omaha, Nebraska in 1924. His abusive father was a traveling sales-man and his mother was an actress in the local community theater. Both were rootless alco-holics. The family moved around a lot and eventually Brando was sent to an expensive mili-tary school in Minnesota where he was expelled for breaking every rule. He left for New York where his two older sisters were trying to start acting careers. Although the Group Theater had disbanded, one of its founders, Stella Adler, was actively teaching "The Method" in New York when Brando arrived in 1943. He credited her for teaching him to "be real" and not act out an emotion he had never experienced. Adler helped Brando land his first significant stage role in a play titled *Truckline Café*. Adler's husband, Har-old Clurman, was the director and Elia Ka-zan was the producer. At first there were doubts about Brando's ability to play the role. He mumbled his way through rehears-als and didn't display the explosiveness the part demanded. But when *Truckline Café* opened, Brando was the whole show. The play closed after just thirteen performances but that was enough to earn him Daily Vari-ety's annual award for Most Promising Young Actor.

A SREETCAR NAMED DESIRE (1951) DIRECTED BY ELIA KAZAN SHOWN: MARLON BRANDO (AS STANLEY KOWALSKI)

PHOTOFEST

Hollywood came calling. MGM of-fered Brando a seven year contract at three thousand dollars per week. He turned it down to remain on stage. His next big break came in the form of Tennessee Williams play, *A Streetcar Named Desire*. Actors Studio had opened in 1947 and Brando was a charter mem-ber. Elia Kazan was one of the teachers and soon took Brando under his wing, helping him improve his method and develop his stage persona. At the time Kazan was also very involved in working with Tennessee Williams. Kazan and Williams maintained an active correspon-dence with the director offering the playwright suggestions for shaping his work into a more commercial product. When Williams presented *A Streetcar Named Desire* to Kazan that year, there were a lot of actors ahead of Brando in line to play the male lead, Stanley Kowalski. John Garfield was everyone's first choice, but he became too expensive for the play's budget. Kazan turned to Brando. Although he was inexperienced and young for the role, when he auditioned for Williams, Brando displayed so much raw sexual energy and power that the playwright was convinced. The role instantly made Brando a star and thousands of people witnessed his jaw-dropping performances during the one and a half year run. When he reprised the role on film in 1950, Brando's movie stardom was also assured.

Montgomery Clift was born in Omaha, Nebraska in 1920. His family was well-to-do and he had traveled extensively in Europe at a young age which helped him acquire fancy manners and an aristocratic demeanor. He began acting in community theater at age twelve. He moved to New York when he was thirteen and began a very successful professional stage career in the play, *Fly Away Home*. An older, wealthy Broadway star, Libby Holman, took an intense romantic interest in him and had a significant role in accelerating his stardom. It would be the only heterosexual relationship in Clift's life.

A Place in the Sun (1951) Directed by George Stevens Shown from left: Shelley Winters (as Alice Tripp), Montgomery Clift (as George Eastman)

Clift's film debut came in a 1948 film, *The Search*, directed by Fred Zinneman. In it, Clift stars as an army private in post-war Berlin who helps a young Czech boy find his family. That same year he appeared in Howard Hawks' western epic, *Red River* where he played opposite John Wayne in a generational tale of struggle to tame the wild west. The film made Clift a movie star. His long experience on stage had made him an accomplished actor and his brooding nature and boyish handsomeness were perfect for the time. In 1948 Clift was offered and accepted an extraordinary contract from Paramount. The terms of the three picture deal gave him script approval and limited the directors with whom he would work to Paramount's best at the time: Billy Wilder, George Stevens and Norman Krasna. He made two films under the deal, *The Heiress* (1949) and *A Place in the Sun* (1951). Tortured over his closeted homosexuality, Clift began to drink excessively and use pharmaceuticals to cope with life in the bright spotlight of Hollywood. After just two pictures Paramount chose to let him out of his deal.

Marilyn Monroe (nee Norma Jean Mortenson) was born in Los Angeles in 1926. Before her birth, Monroe's father purchased a motorcycle and headed for the bay area abandoning his family. Her mother was a film cutter in the laboratory at RKO and was an extremely unstable personality, given to mental illness and alcoholism. She had relationships with a continuous stream of men which confused the little girl about the identity of her father. Eventually Monroe's name was changed to Norma Jean **Baker**, the name of a man her mother had dated earlier in life. From time to time, when her mother's illness made it necessary for her to be institutionalized, Monroe was dumped into foster care homes. In these homes Monroe was horribly mistreated. At six she was nearly raped. One "care giver" attempted to smother her to death. She was sent to the Los Angeles Orphan's Home at age nine where she was forced to work in the kitchen for her keep. At age sixteen, Monroe became legally emancipated, got a job in an aircraft factory and married a man named James Dougherty who she met at the factory. They were divorced four years later in 1946. By that time, Monroe had become a blonde and was beginning to model for swimsuit ads.

MARILYN MONROE (EARLY TO MID **1950S**)

Late in 1946 Monroe signed a contract with Twentieth Century Fox for one hundred twenty-five dollars per week. Her first film was an un-credited appearance in *The Shocking Miss Pilgrim* (1947). The studio assigned Monroe to other small parts in four films over the next two years before casting her in a featured role in *Ladies of the Chorus* (1949). *Ladies* was a "B" picture set in the burlesque business, and Monroe played a chorus girl who becomes a headliner. The film is as close to a "girlie show" as production code allowed the studios to make at that point in time. After *Ladies*, Monroe returned to small parts in better movies, including John Huston's 1950 noir classic, *Asphalt Jungle*, which drew the attention of director Joseph Mankiewicz who would launch her career as a blonde bombshell three years later.

While she was struggling to get her career going at Fox in the late forties, Monroe joined her close friend and roommate, Shelly Winters, in taking classes at the Actor's Laboratory Theater. Founded by Group Theater principals, Madame Maria Ouspenskaya and Richard Boleslavsky, Actor's Laboratory was bringing "The Method" to Hollywood. Because of the success New York actors were enjoying as a result of their method training, young actors like Monroe were eager to learn this new discipline. The one downside of being involved with the

Actors Laboratory was that it was tainted by the communist reputation that had been attached to the Group Theater and Actors Studio in New York. Eventually, Actors' Laboratory would appear on HUAC's radar screen and threaten the careers of the young people who had been involved. Fortunately, Monroe escaped any serious harm to her career.

Other New Actors were emerging in post-war Hollywood. **Elizabeth Taylor** was born in London where her American parents were involved in the art business. The family moved to Los Angeles in 1939 when it became apparent that the Battle of Britain was about to commence. Friends suggested to Taylor's mother who had acted as a young woman, that Elizabeth be screen tested. She was nine years old when Universal signed her in 1941. The studio put her in one film and let her contract lapse at the end of the year. MGM picked her up and began to groom Taylor to become their replacement for Judy Garland who had become too grown up for children's roles. Taylor's first film at the studio was *Lassie Come Home* (1943). She continued to play small parts until she was cast in one of the leading roles in *National Velvet* (1943), the film that made her a child star for the remainder of the forties.

Shelly Winters (nee Shirley Schrift) was born under very humble circumstances in St. Louis in 1920. Her father worked in the garment industry and moved to Brooklyn to seek more steady work when Winters was still a little girl. Her interest in acting began with high school plays. Upon graduation she worked as a store clerk, comedian and singer in Jewish nightclubs and in vaudeville. During this time, she spent all of her earnings on acting lessons. In 1941 she got her first part in a Broadway play and worked on stage for two years before heading to Hollywood. In the 1940s, Winters played a wide variety of parts on screen including the victim of a serial killer and several appearances as a party girl. Her tough New York exterior, mixed with her well-trained ability to act any part that came her way, made Winters popular with casting directors. The most colorful role in her early career was in *South Sea Sinner* (1950) in which she plays a seductress in fishnet stockings opposite the most unlikely male lead in movie history, Liberace.

SOUTH SEA SINNER (1950) DIRECTED BY H. BRUCE HUMBERSTONE SHOWN: SHELLEY WINTERS, LIBERACE

PHOTOFEST

NEW DIRECTORS

For the most part, the great directors of the thirties resumed their careers after the war. For big name directors like John Ford, Alfred Hitchcock and Howard Hawks, the post-war period meant bigger budgets, more control over their films and the prestige of having their names above the title. But a new generation of directors was also making its appearance. Some, like Elia Kazan and Nicholas Ray, had been part of the Method acting revolution and transferred their directing talents from the stage to the screen. Others like Billy Wilder, John Huston and Joseph Mankiewicz made the transition from screen writer to director.

Orson Welles' films, beginning with his first, *Citizen Kane*, were often made in the expressionist style. It was natural for him to become involved with the film noir genre, both because of its appeal to his dark side and because of its heightened sense of drama. His first film noir is *The Lady From Shanghai* (1948), which he directed and starred in opposite his wife at the time, Rita Hayworth.

Billy Wilder was born in Poland in 1906. His father was a successful businessman. His mother had traveled extensively throughout America as a young woman. It left such a lasting impression on her that she named her son after Buffalo Bill Cody of Wild West Show fame. Following high school, Wilder attended university with plans to become a lawyer. However, Europe in the post World War I era was too exciting for him to remain dedicated to his studies. He dropped out and got a job as a newspaper reporter, specializing in stories that involved Americans and all things American. In 1926 he interviewed Paul Whiteman, a famous American jazz band leader. Whiteman was so impressed with Wilder's knowledge, he invited him to join the band for the remainder of its tour to Berlin. Wilder stayed in Berlin and wrote extensively about popular culture.

By 1929, Wilder's contacts landed him with a job writing screenplays for the German film studios. One of his first scripts, *People on Sunday* (1929), a slice of German life, was direct-

Sunset Blvd. (1950) Directed by Billy Wilder Shown from left on set: Director Billy Wilder, Gloria Swanson

ed by Robert Siodmak, who would also eventually immigrate to America. Between 1929 and 1934, Wilder had twenty-three of his scripts produced. During that time he was sending story ideas to American studios in the hope that one would bring him to Hollywood. When Hitler was elected Chancellor of Germany in 1933, Wilder moved to Paris where he had an opportunity to direct one of his scripts, *The Bad Seed* (1933). In 1934 Universal invited Wilder to come to Hollywood to adapt a story he had submitted to the studio. He sailed to New York aboard a British ship so he could work on his English. Although the Universal project fell through, Wilder was in Hollywood to stay.

Other German immigrants helped Wilder get established. He shared an apartment with Peter Lorre, a talented character actor who had starred in Fritz Lang's German noir film, *M* (1931). Wilder sustained himself for the next three years punching up scripts at Twentieth Century Fox. His dark sarcastic sense of humor served him well in sharpening dialog and adding jokes to other people's scripts. Wilder moved to the Paramount writing department in 1937. His first assignment was a rewrite on the script for *Champagne Waltz* (1937).

The next year the studio teamed Wilder with Charles Bracken. The two were complete opposites, Wilder, the liberal German, and Bracken, the conservative Yankee. Bracken had arrived in Hollywood through a circuitous route. He was born in Saratoga Springs, N.Y. and graduated from Williamstown College before serving in the Army during World War I as a Vice Consul in France. Upon his return to America, Brackett attended Harvard Law School and practiced law for three years while writing a novel in his spare time. From 1926 to 1929 he was the drama critic for *The New Yorker* magazine. In 1930 he joined his father's law firm and became a board member of the Adirondacks Trust. He held both of these positions for the remainder of his working life. Brackett's first screenplay was *Enter Madame* for Paramount in 1935.

Wilder and Brackett's first assignment was to write the film adaptation, *Bluebeard's Eighth Wife* (1938). It was a major film project for the studio with Ernst Lubitsch directing and Gary Cooper and Claudette Colbert leading a quality cast of Paramount's best character actors. A string of Wilder and Brackett hits followed, including *Ninotchka* (1939), *Hold Back the Dawn* (1941) and *Ball of Fire* (1942). From the moment he arrived at Paramount, Wilder had begged the studio bosses to let him direct. He got his chance with *The Major and the Minor* (1942) which he co-wrote with Brackett. The film was a light comedy starring Ginger Rogers and Ray Milland. Wilder and his writing partner continued to run off a string of six hit motion pictures including, *Double Indemnity* (1944) and *The Lost Weekend* (1945) and concluding with the magnificent *Sunset Boulevard* (1950). Wilder and Brackett's stormy collaboration ended in 1950. Brackett continued to have success as a writer but nothing on the level of Wilder's. As a director Wilder became one of Hollywood greats during the decades of the fifties and sixties. Wilder also continued to write all of his films with a succession of different co-writers.

Elia Kazan was one of the most controversial figures of his time. He was as great a talent as existed both on the New York stage and in Hollywood. But his breathtaking act of betrayal in naming some of his closest friends before the House Un-American Activities Committee is difficult to understand. It is quite possible that he believed that his friends were inevitably going to become victims of the witch hunt anyway. Or perhaps he harbored some selfish belief that the value of his talent and the value of what he could contribute to culture outweighed the cost paid by his friends.

Kazan was ethnically Greek but was born in Istanbul, Turkey in 1909. In 1913 his father moved the family to New York and became a prosperous rug dealer. Kazan completed his undergraduate work at Williams College and studied drama at Yale as a graduate student. After Yale he returned to New York in the early thirties and joined the Group Theater as an actor and assistant manager. At this time he also became a member of the Communist party. Kazan is representative of a growing trend for stage and motion picture entertainers to begin their dramatic training at universities and colleges. This would be important in the post-war era as audiences became more educated and sophisticated in their tastes.

During the thirties Kazan gained success acting in plays by Clifford Odets such as *Golden Boy*. In 1935, he began directing plays by Thornton Wilder, Arthur Miller and Tennessee Williams. As these men's careers blossomed, so did Kazan's. Kazan was especially close with Williams who as a Southerner was uneducated in the ways of Broadway. Williams was grateful to receive Kazan's aid in shaping his plays for the demands of New York critics and audiences. When Hollywood became interested in the work of these playwrights, it also took notice of Kazan.

Twentieth Century Fox invited Kazan to make his film debut with *A Tree Grows in Brooklyn* in 1945. The modestly made film was a slice of life among the working poor city dwellers in the early 1900s. The acting performances were well directed as would be the case in almost all of Kazan's work. In 1947, MGM hired Kazan to direct Spencer Tracy and Katherine Hepburn in a big budget western, *Sea of Grass*. That same year he made another low budget crime drama for Fox entitled *Boomerang*. Hollywood had shied away from Kazan's ability to deal with controversial subjects. That changed in 1947 with Kazan at the helm of one of Fox' most daring movies of that period, *Gentleman's Agreement*. Gregory Peck, a rising

PANIC IN THE STREETS (1950) DIRECTED BY ELIA KAZAN SHOWN: JACK PALANCE (AS BLACKIE)

young star who had some university training, starred in the film. *Gentlemen's Agreement* is a study of hidden and overt anti-Semitism in American society. The film treats the subject and the audience with intelligence and dignity and was both a critical and financial success. Kazan was awarded the prestigious Best Director Oscar for his work on the film. His next film dealt with another difficult subject, colorism and racism. *Pinky* (1949) is the story of a young light-skinned African American woman from the south who has been to nursing school in the north where she passed as white. Upon returning to her family she announces her intention to marry a young white doctor she met at school. Through many trials and humiliations, the young woman discovers that she needs to be who she is rather than "passing" to escape the burden of racism. Instead, she remains at home to open a clinic to serve her people. In 1950 Kazan made the third of his "message" films for Fox, *Panic in the Streets*. It is the story of an outbreak of the plague in New Orleans and the ensuing panic. Filmgoers understood that Kazan had created an allegory for the communist witch hunt that was infecting the American psyche. At the end of the 1940s and the dawn of the television age, Kazan had put his mark on Hollywood by demonstrating that audiences were just as interested in films that were challenging as well as entertaining. In the next decade he would make history with two unknown young actors and arrival of the method on the big screen, Marlon Brando and James Dean.

PARAMOUNT CONSENT DECREE: THE RESOLUTION

In 1940 the five major studios (Paramount, Fox, MGM, Warner Bros. and RKO) and the three minor studios (Columbia, United Artists and Universal) reached an agreement with the Roosevelt administration's anti-trust lawyers to postpone the resolution of anti-monopoly legal proceedings against the motion picture industry until 1945. In return for the postponement, the studios pledged to fully cooperate with the war effort. The studios made good on their promise but when 1945 arrived it brought with it the moment of reckoning. In October the parties returned to court.

During the five year hiatus, the Society of Independent Motion Picture Producers (SIMPP), led by Samuel Goldwyn, had been busy making the case for punishing the studios. Studio practices such as block booking (forcing independent theater owners to rent blocks of films rather than the specific titles they sought) had caused a powerful backlash among theater owners that weren't affiliated with the powerful studios. In 1939 a series of lawsuits known as the Crescent cases were filed against a group of southern theater chains with interlocking boards of directors. The Crescent group had been found guilty of restraining free trade in the cities where they did business. As a result, they were blocked from acquiring any further theaters. Even though the 1940 consent decree had exempted the studios from any repercussions in the Crescent cases, it became clear that the courts' disposition would not favor the studios when proceedings resumed.

In June 1946, the New York court found both the major and minor studios guilty of conspiracy but allowed the majors to retain their theaters. Ironically, 1946 was the year that motion picture attendance peaked. That year, Paramount alone, reported thirty-nine million dollars in profits. The government lawyers did not believe that the decision went far enough and appealed the case to the U.S. Supreme Court, which heard arguments in February

1948, including those from the SIMPP. In May the decision was handed down. The court affirmed the violations of anti-trust law, outlawed block booking and sent the case back to lower courts with directions to break-up the vertical integration of the major studios. For the majors, this meant the end to ownership of studios, distribution companies and theaters by a single company.

The Justice Department approached the majors with the idea of a consent decree. If the studios so chose, any one of them would be allowed to opt out of any further legal proceedings if they would agree to divorce production from distribution. The studios expressed disinterest in the proposal. The first to break was Howard Hughes who, at the time, owned RKO. No doubt influenced by his other dealings with the government as a military contractor, Hughes agreed to sell RKO Theaters Corporation. The consent decree was signed in November 1948. For the other four studios, the trial date was set for April 1949. Paramount was the next to fall. Management decided that a long court fight would be too disruptive. In February 1949, the most powerful of the majors capitulated and signed a consent decree. The Justice Department allowed Paramount to retain its powerful Canadian chain of the theaters which was three hundred and fifty strong at the time. It was allowed to spin off its American theaters into a separate chain but the size of the new company was limited to one thousand theaters at a time when Paramount controlled almost fifteen hundred theaters. Leonard Goldenson became the president of the new theater company. The remaining three majors vowed to fight on, but it was clearly just a matter of time before it became counterproductive to do so.

Paramount had chosen to withdraw from the battle for a reason unconnected to the motion picture theater business. They were aggressively investing in the television business. In 1938, Paramount had purchased a four hundred thousand dollar stake in the fledgling DuMont Corporation, which manufactured television sets. Paramount also owned four of the nine television stations that were in operation in the early forties and was acquiring interests in as many more as the Federal Communications Commission (FCC) would allow. In the meantime, both Fox and RKO had had their applications for television licenses turned down due to the uncertainty of the anti-trust cases. Clearly Paramount was sacrificing its historic business model for a new one based on the exciting new electronic medium.

POST-WAR EUROPEAN CINEMA

World War II was such a cataclysmic event that much of the world had to be recreated in its wake. Many of Europe's great cities were reduced to rubble. Manufacturing centers and port cities had been the targets of daily air raids for years. Food was in short supply. Hoards of homeless people wandered the countryside foraging for a morsel to eat. Germany and many of the Eastern European countries would take decades to rebuild. For those people and those countries, the restoration of culture, including film production, would have to wait while the basic necessities for living were receiving maximum attention. Two countries, Italy and Great Britain, however, had resilient motion picture industries that were ready and able to depict the immediate aftermath of the war.

Italian Neo-realism grew out of the Fascist Cinema that Benito Mussolini and his culture tsar, Luigi Freddi, had spent so much time and money cultivating during the thirties. Unlike Hitler who insisted on totalitarian thought control over the German people and those he conquered, Mussolini allowed a great deal of cultural pluralism in Italy. Until the war, Fascist propaganda films were usually limited to short documentaries shown in Italian theaters alongside a variety of lighthearted films. "White telephone" films (referring to the upper class homes where stylish telephones were part of the general opulence) were popular with the Italian audiences. The genre consisted of escapist romantic comedies and melodramas in which there was little mention of the political situation in Europe. Mussolini maintained close relationships with the film community. He was drawn to the glamour of the industry and saw himself as a showman in the political arena. His son, Vittorio, made a few films himself and became a producer in the post-war era.

Mussolini's greatest contribution to the Italian Cinema was the construction of Cinecittà (cinema city), a sprawling complex of production facilities, stages and back lots on the outskirts of Rome. He had promised the Italian motion picture community that they would have the best facilities in Europe. He delivered on that promise when the studio opened in April, 1937. Cinecittà inspired filmmakers to want to please Mussolini and they did with a robust fascist cinema.

Political leaders pushed for more realism in films and for more location production which would show off the many monuments and public works that had been constructed under Mussolini. One of the aims of this approach was to stimulate citizens' pride in their country and their patriotism.

During the Second World War, the Italian film industry continued to be prolific while other countries were experiencing a slowdown or complete stop in production. Two filmmakers who worked through the war years, **Roberto Rossellini** and **Vittorio De Sica**, emerged in the post-war period as masters of the new Italian Cinema and its neorealist style. They were, in turn, greatly influenced by the work of an older director, Luchino Visconti, and his 1943 film, Ossessione, which pointed the direction to neorealism. Another strong influence was the work of screenwriter, Cesare Zavattini, who collaborated with De Sica extensively.

Roberto Rossellini was born in Rome in 1906, the son of a wealthy and successful architect who also built and owned one of the largest movie theaters in the city. He began experimenting with amateur films as a young man and developed an especial interest in the technological aspects of film. In 1938 Rossellini made a very competent short film, *Afternoon of a Faun*, which was eventually banned by the Italian censorship board for being indecent. His friend, Vittorio Mussolini, (the son of the Italian dictator) saw the film and thought is was quite good. Over the next three years Rossellini continued to make experimental films and worked at the studios as a sound man. In 1941 young Mussolini offered him a chance to work professionally under the auspices of the Navy Propaganda Center. At age twenty-three Rossellini began work on what was originally planned to be a documentary about a hospital ship, *The White Ship* (1941). As production progressed, the film expanded into a feature length theatrical fiction project. *The White Ship* was entered into the Venice Film Festival and won the award for best propaganda film. This would become the first film in his "fascist trilogy." The next year Rossellini made *A Pilot Returns* (1942) about a downed pilot who is captured and held at a British prisoner of war camp. The third film in the trilogy is *Man of the Cross* (1943), the story of a military chaplain.

The "fascist trilogy" is stylistically important in leading to the development of neorealism. The government film board insisted that filmmakers follow three rules: (1) Documentary film footage is to be included in fictional films. (2) The story lines must focus on the lives and issues of contemporary, ordinary people. (3) Wherever possible, films are to be made on location and sets built for studio shoots should not be glamorized but should reflect the living conditions of contemporary, ordinary people. The government officials believed that following these rules would result in films that appeared to be factual and, therefore, would better sell the propagandistic messages they contained. Neorealist style embraced these rules and added to them: (1) The use of non-professional actors which gives the director more control over the portrayal of a character. (2) Using characters to represent ideas and belief systems such as communism, fascism and Catholicism. This eliminates the need for long dialog passages in which the characters argue about ideology. (3) Choosing stories that contain moral ambiguity in which characters are forced to make choices between two morally undesirable options.

Rossellini's neorealist trilogy begins in 1945 with the film *Rome: Open City*. The title is ironic in that it tells the story of the last days of the brutal Nazi occupation of Rome. During the war years Rossellini had become friendly with a young writer, Federico Fellini (who would become one of Europe's greatest directors in the fifties and sixties), and a young actor, Aldo Fabrizi. In *Open City* Fabrizi plays the part of a Catholic priest who, contrary to his vows, assists the communist freedom fighters in their struggle against the Nazis. The second film in the trilogy is *Paisà* (1946), which consists of a series of vignettes about chance meetings between people from different backgrounds and cultures. The final film in the trilogy, *Germania, Anno Zero* (1948), is about the struggle for survival in

OPEN CITY (1945 ITALY) AKA ROME: OPEN CITY AKA ROMA, CITTÀ APERTA DIRECTED BY ROBERTO ROSSELLINI SHOWN CENTER: ANNA MAGNANI

post-war Germany where everything has been reduced to rubble. All three films in the trilogy were well received around the world. The neorealist style became an inspiration to a new generation of filmmakers who were taken with its honesty and for the uncontrived emotion the style evoked.

Vittorio De Sica was born in Sora, Italy in 1901, but spent most of his childhood in Naples. His family was very poor and it was necessary for De Sica to begin working as an office clerk around age ten. He had a passion for performing in amateur theatrical productions and by the time he was seventeen he had appeared in his first motion picture, *Il Processo Clémenceau* (1918). From that point he continued to work in the movies, developing a very pleasant screen persona that often got him cast as the leading man's best friend. By 1932, De Sica was playing leading roles and building a successful career as a romantic comedy actor. He began directing in 1940 with the adaptation of a successful stage play, *Rose Scarlatti*.

De Sica and screenwriter Cesare Zavattini first collaborated on the 1944 film *The Children Are Watching Us*. Already committed to a style that contained many of the elements of neorealism, the writer exerted a great deal of influence on the director in the making of the film. Wherever possible, amateur actors were cast and the film was shot almost exclusively on location. The collaboration between the two men strengthened over the next few years. *Sciuscià (Shoeshine)* (1946) reveals life in Italy under the Allied Occupation of Italy following the end of the war. The story follows two teenage boys who scrape out an existence by shining shoes on the streets of Rome. De Sica's direction elicits beautiful, heartfelt performances from the young actors while creating an accurate record of life in Rome at that time. The third collaboration between De Sica and Zavattini was *Ladri di Biciclette (The Bicycle Thief)* (1948). The film is the heartbreaking story of a man who provides for his family by doing errands on his bicycle. When it is stolen, the family is faced with the moral dilemma of starving to death or stealing someone else's bicycle to survive. Like *Shoeshine, The Bicycle Thief* captures with unblinking realism the plight of ordinary people trying to survive in the wake of one of history's greatest events. In subsequent years these films would inspire French, British and American filmmakers to strive for greater depth of emotion and truthfulness in their films.

PHOTOFEST

The Bicycle Thief (1948 Italy) aka Ladri di biciclette Directed by Vittorio De Sica Shown: Lamberto Maggiorani (center in hat, as Antonio Ricci)

POST-WAR BRITISH CINEMA

Before World War II, the British film industry suffered from a lack of resources and technology. As early as 1937 Alfred Hitchcock had begun to explore the possibility of moving to Hollywood because of his disappointment with the limitations of British sound recording technology and the poor quality of work done by the film laboratories. Young actors like David Niven, Cary Grant and Laurence Olivier were drawn to Hollywood by its size and the limitless opportunities it presented. The war years resulted in a greater erosion of the British cinema. American companies had comprised a large share of film production in Great Britain since the twenties. When the war came, the American companies shut down, leaving just a few indigenous studios to serve British audiences with homemade films.

At the end of the war, Prime Minister Clement Atlee's Labour Party was swept into office, largely on a wave of enthusiasm for Britain's victory in what was considered "the people's war" by working class Englishmen. People were allowing themselves to believe that British society was about to be remade as a fairer, less class-driven democracy. The thinking was that if Britain could win the war, it could also wipe out poverty, fix education and provide opportunity for the underclass. But in the five years following the war, optimism gave way to the reality that the country was bankrupt and its ambitions would have to wait. By the end of the forties a kind of gloom descended over Britain that would be reflected in the mirror of its cinema during the next decade.

Post-war British filmmakers were attempting to makeover their industry. Wartime films from Britain were known for their stodgy documentary approach. In America they were mostly relegated to the "B" picture slot in theater film programs. Studio owners like J. Arthur Rank were attempting to capitalize on England's cultural resources with films such as *Henry V* (1945) and *Hamlet* (1948) starring Laurence Olivier, who had returned home to demonstrate his unmatched skill in Shakespearian roles. Rank successfully distributed *Henry V* in America as a prestige film but he and the rest of the British film community would soon hit a wall of trade protectionism. In 1947 England was experiencing a financial crisis that led it to place a seventy-five percent import tax on foreign film sales. America was the primary target of the tax and it reacted with a total boycott of British films. Eventually a quota system was arranged, but the event further dampened the financial outlook of the British film industry.

J. Arthur Rank managed to survive this period by making a series of successful adaptations of major literary works which, by virtue of its distribution company, became the outlet for almost all films made in England. Alexander Korda turned his attention from directing to producing. He merged his London Film Production Co. with British Lion Productions (formerly the English branch of MGM). The combined companies were strong enough to survive and were making internationally successful films by the end of the forties. *Anna Karenina* (1948) was recognized for its superior quality. The following year Korda's company produced one of the great films in British cinema history, *The Third Man* (1949). The film was directed by Carol Reed and written by the very colorful Graham Green. Green had been an operative in the British spy service, MI-6, during the war. He and Reed collaborated on three spy films during the next several years. During his film career Green wrote books, plays and screenplays that served as the basis for fifty-five films. The film reunites Mercury Theater alums, Orson Welles and Joseph Cotton, and also stars British actor, Trevor Howard. It was filmed on location in Vienna by the brilliant cinematographer, Robert Krasker. *The Third Man* is one of the movies that defined the spy film genre. It is the story of black market intrigue and treachery in post-war Europe.

The other survivor of the post-war period was Ealing studios. The company produced twenty-three films between the end of the war and the end of the decade. The most successful of these productions is a string of comedies including, *Hue and Cry* (1948), *Passport to Pimlico* (1949) and *Kind Hearts and Coronets* (1949). Ealing's comedies were successful largely because of the talents of three gifted comedy actors, Alec Guinness, Alastair Sim and Margaret Rutherford. The whimsical and understated style of these films became the hallmark of British comedy style. During the fifties British films would undergo a major transformation of style and embrace the worldwide call for social realism. But the formulas for quality adaptations and comedies that were established in the post-war period would remain in demand well into the future.

THE THIRD MAN (1949) DIRECTED BY: CAROL REED SHOWN: ORSON WELLES

AFTERWORD

1950 brought to an end the first half of motion picture history. The entire world was engaged in monumental changes in society, industry, communications and culture. The next half century and more of movie history would occur in the context of a dazzling array of developments in electronic communications. Television would be the first new entertainment medium to successfully challenge the dominance that movies had enjoyed for so long. It wouldn't end there, however. Soon the videocassette, the compact disc, cable television, the internet, the DVD, and other digital products would change the way entertainment products would be made and enjoyed.

Early film history encompasses a colorful time when pioneers and buccaneers created and defined an industry for which no rules existed. Whatever they needed, whether it be technology or any of the other raw materials for a new art and entertainment medium, the challenge was to make it from scratch. Looking back at the early history it is clear that the thrill and satisfaction of inventing something new was a big part of what attracted people to the industry. And what an amazing array of people it attracted—circus clowns and geniuses, artists and imitators, business men and scoundrels, the beautiful and the grotesque—all contributed what talents they had to the delight of the audience.

The next generation of movie makers would be different. They would be at the helm of a mature industry. Moguls would give way to MBAs. Directors would learn their art and craft in film schools rather than the school of hard knocks. The studio system with its paternalism and exploitation would give way to a system of agents, free agents and corporations. Films would get bigger, some so big in fact, that they would require years of advanced planning, involve thousands of people and cost more money than the entire industry made in 1950. Film technology would usher in a world where if it can be imagined, it can be put up on the screen. New generations of movie stars would become as powerful as the men who built the studios.

In the future, the audience and its attitudes would change. It would become more sophisticated and educated. At the behest of the public, the old censorship schemes would be replaced with more liberal and dynamic methods of dealing with the issue of indecency in films. Freed of the old restrictions, movies would be able to put the spotlight on every facet of human nature and behavior, from sex to war. Modern transportation and communications would make it possible to take movie production to the remotest places in the world. Audiences would become open to movie experimentation and films as art. Sometimes the result was laughably far off the mark, but just as often the result was groundbreaking and moved the state of the art.

A new commercialism would be brought to the motion picture industry as studios became divisions of corporations. At its best, this made it possible for mountains of resources to be devoted to achieving the vision of a great filmmaker. At its worst, corporate movies would become imitative and mind numbing. But with corporatization would come the opportunity to create an alternative, independent cinema. New technologies that radically reduced the cost of filmmaking would make it possible for filmmakers to find their financing without sacrificing control over the film. Eventually, the internet would make it possible for anyone to make a film and show it to the world.

In many ways film gave birth to the audio visual world that surrounds us today. Those furriers, glove makers and junk traders that came to America and dreamed up the movie business never allowed it to become static and antique like vaudeville became. They didn't accept boundries. Because of that, the movies never stopped getting better, newer, bigger. The exuberance of the Pioneers of the film industry for movies was so contagious that it still drives filmmakers today. Much of what they created, including the idea of what a movie is and how to go about making one, is still in use today. People in the movie industry still quote the wisdom of the founders and shake their heads wondering "how did they know?"

INDEX

18th Amendment to the Constitution   34, 108

19th Amendment to the Constitution   123

35-millimeter   6

39 Steps, The   104

70-millimeter   6

A Fool There Was   47

Abbey Players Theatre Group   171

Abbot and Costello   191

Abrams, Hiram   23

Academy Awards   44

Academy of Motion Picture Arts and Sciences (AMPAS)   79

Ace Drummond (film series)   136

Acheson, Dean   201

Across the Pacific   189

Actor's Laboratory Theater   211, 212

Actors Studio   192, 203, 208, 209, 212

Adam's Rib   155

Adirondacks Trust   214

Adler, Stella   202, 209

Adventures of Dolly, The   14

Adventures of Robin Hood, The   160

aerial action   135, 136

African Queen, The   158

Afternoon of a Faun   218

agitprop film trains (Russia)   91

agitprop films (Russia)   91

Air Circus   125

Air Mail   143

Aitken Brothers   19

Aitken, Harry   16, 18, 20, 22, 30, 56

Aitken, Roy   18

Alamo, The   162

Albee, Edward   158, 208

Alexander Nevsky   93

Alexeyev, Konstantin Sergeyevich   96

Alice in Wonderland   133

Alice's Wonderland   71

All About Eve   153

Alton, John   205

amateur camera system   6

American Academy of Dramatic Arts   148, 154

American Federation of Labor   105

American Laboratory Theater   202

American Marconi Company   66

American Telephone & Telegraph   74

American Theater Wing   191

American, The (working title)   172, 173

America's Sweetheart (Mary Pickford)   53

An Affair to Remember   164

Andrews Sisters   191

Andrews, Dana   197

Animal Crackers   112

animated shorts, also cartoons   205

Anna Christie   57, 82

Anna Karenina   221

Anthony Comstock   107

Anti Saloon League   108

anti-communist   199

anti-trust laws, breach of   184

Apocalypse Now   172

Araner, The (yacht)   143, 144

Arbuckle, Roscoe Fatty   28, 29, 30, 31, 34, 35, 36, 37, 161

Archbishop of Chicago   108

Arlis, George   83

Armant, Thomas   11

Armstrong, Edwin   66

Army Air Forces   186

Army Chief of Staff   188

Army Signal Corp   177, 188

Arnold, General Henry H.   186

Arrow Film Corporation   68

Arrowsmith (novel)   142

Arrowsmith: The Children's Hour   50

Arsenic and Old Lace   151, 187, 188

Artcraft company   22, 23

Arthur, Jean   127, 139, 150

Arvidson, Linda   13

Asher, Irving   159

Ashley, Lady Sylvia   54, 146

Asphalt Jungle   211

Associated Films   125

Astaire, Fred   130, 157, 183

Astor, Mary   176

Atlee, Clement (Prime Minister)   221

Audion vacuum tube   62, 73

Automatic Vaudeville Company   58

Autry, Gene   136

Avenging Conscience, The   19

Awful Truth, The   127, 149, 150

B Movies, also programmers   205

Babelsberg Studios   86

Bachelor and the Bobbysoxer, The   148

Bacon, Lloyd (director)   79, 129

Bad Day at Black Rock   155

Bad Seed, The   214
Baker, Norma Jean   192, 211
Ball of Fire   152, 214
Ball, Lucille   50, 204
Bangville Police, The   28
bank nights   106
Bank of America   70
Bank of Italy   70
Banky, Vilma   50, 80
Bara, Theda   47, 48, 62
Barry, Joan   42
Barry, Philip   158
Barrymore, John   64, 74, 75, 82, 148, 157, 161
Barrymore, Lionel   16, 17
Barthelmess, Richard   81
Bataan   193
Battle of Britain, The   188
Battle of China, The   188
Battle of Elderbush Gulch, The   17
Battle of Gettysburg   56
Battle of Russia, The   188
Battle of San Pietro, The   189, 196
Battleship Potemkin   92, 93
Bauer, Evgeni   91
Baumann, Charles   27, 29, 30
Baxter, Warner   80
Beast at Bay, A   16
Beatty, Clyde   136
Beau Gest   166
Beckmann, Max   86
Beery, Wallace   64, 143, 145
Beethoven's Fifth Symphony   169
Beginner's Luck   119
Behind The Rising Sun   194
Belasco, David   17, 51, 52
Bell Labs   74
Bell, Alexander Graham   5
Bellamy, Ralph   127, 170
Bendix, William   193
Bennett, Constance   150
Bennett, Joan   149
Benny, Jack   122, 191
Ben's Kid   35
Bergen, Edgar   115
Bergman, Ingrid   196
Berkeley, Busby (choreographer)   50, 128, 129
Berman, Pandro S. (producer at RKO)   130, 157

Bernhardt, Sarah   18, 38
Bernstein, Isadore   60
Best Years of Our Lives, The   147, 190, 197
Bickford, Charles   136
Bicycle Thief, The   220
Big Broadcast, The   132
Big Combo, The   205, 208
Big Heat, The   206, 208
Big Jim McLain   204
Big Sleep, The   208
Big Store, The   114
Big Trail, The   162
Bill of Divorcement, A   157
Biograph   32, 45, 46, 47, 51, 55, 11, 14, 17, 19, 25, 27, 28, 30
Biograph camera   6
Biograph Studio   6
Bioscope Company   86
Birth of A Nation   20, 21, 22, 140, 59
Bison Life Motion Picture Studio   55
Bitzer, Billy   14, 15, 19, 20, 24, 26, 27
Black Maria (studio)   6
Black Mask   204
Black Tuesday (October 24, 1929)   105
Black Watch, The   142
Blackmail   104
Blackton, J. Stuart   65
Blind Husbands   60
Blitzstein, Marc   171
block booking   39, 216
Blockade   180
Blonde Venus   138, 149
Blood and Sand   117
Bluebeard's Eighth Wife   122, 127, 214
Bob Pender Comedy Troupe   149
Bogart, Humphrey   50, 158, 164, 176, 195, 196
Bold Bank Robbery, The   73
Boleslavski, Richard   202, 211
Bond, Tommy Butch   119
Bond, Ward   161
Bondu Sauve Des Eaux   100
Boom Town   155
Boomerang   215
Borzage, Frank (director)   141
Bow, Clara   84
Boy in Blue, The   87
Boyer, Charles   164
Boys Town   155

Brackett, Charles   122, 214
Brady, Matthew   2
Brando, Marlon   43, 203, 209, 210, 216
Brandt, Joe   69, 70
Brecht, Bertolt   201
Breen, Joseph   179, 180, 181
Brent, George   164
Breton, Andre   97
Brewster's Millions   49
Brice, Fanny   79
Bride of Frankenstein, The   133
Bringing Up Baby   127, 150, 155, 158
British Board of Film   181
British film industry   221
British International Pictures (BIP)   104
British Lion Productions   221
Broadway Melody   81
Broadway Melody of 1936   131
Broadway Review   83
Broken Blossoms   22, 23
Broken Dishes (play)   152
Bronte, Emily   166
Brown, Harry J. (director)   80
Brown, Johnny Mack   136
Browning, Todd (director)   83, 132
Bryan, William Jennings   156
Bryn Mawr College   157
Buck, Frank   136
Bullets or Ballots   139
Bullfighters, The   118
Bunuel, Luis   97, 98
Bureau of Motion Pictures (BMP)   193
Burel, Leonce-Henry   98
Burgess, Dorothy   80
Burke, Thomas (writer)   22
Burn, Michael   161
Burroughs, Edgar Rice   136
Busy Bodies   118
Cabinet of Dr. Caligari, The   85, 86, 132
Cagney, James, also Cagney, Jimmy   109, 153, 183
California, used as film setting   16
Call of the Wild, The   145
Cal Tech   123
camera heater, invention of   24
Camera obscura   1
Campbell Soup Company   171
Canary Murder Case, The   81, 148
Cantor, Eddie   129

Canutt, Yakima (stunt coordinator)   69, 161
Capote, Truman   158
Capra, Frank (director)   119, 123, 124, 126, 127, 135, 145, 151, 152, 164, 185, 187, 188, 193
Captain Blood   159, 160
Captain Hates The Sea, The   84
Captains Courageous   154, 155
Carefree   130
Carey Jr., Harry   141
Carey, Harry   141
Carradine, John   170
Carroll, Lewis   133
Cartwright, Peggy   118
Casablanca   195, 196
Case, Hugh   204
Case, Theodore   73
CBC   70, 124
CBS Radio   171
Censorship   107
Central Pacific Railway   2
Chagall, Marc   86
Champagne Waltz   214
Chandler, Raymond   205
Chaney, Jr., Lon   165
Chaney, Lon   61, 81, 83, 132
Chang: A Drama of the Wilderness   133
Chaplin, Charles Jr.   41
Chaplin, Charlie, also Chaplin, Charles   23, 29, 30, 33, 39, 40, 41, 42, 43, 44, 51, 53, 57, 72, 78, 116, 117, 181, 184
Chaplin, Norman   41
Chaplin, Sidney   39, 41
Charade   151
Charge of the Light Brigade, The   160
Chase, Charlie   31
Chef Milani   191
Chekhov, Anton   96
Chess Fever   93
Chevalier, Maurice   39, 121
chiaroscuro technique   173
Children Are Watching Us, The   220
China Seas   145
Christmas in July   178
Churchill, Winston   188, 199
Cinderella   9
Cinecitta (cinema city)   218
cinema verite   96

Cinemas   7
Cinematographe   7
Circus, The   42
Citizen Kane   170, 173, 174, 213
City Lights   41, 43
Clansman, The   19, 20
Clansman, The (novel)   19, 21
Clansman, The (play)   14
Clark family   124
Clerk-Maxwell, James   2
Clift, Montgomery   146, 203, 210
Clown Princes   119
Clurman, Harold   209
Cobb, Joe   118
cocaine   34
Cocoanuts   112
Cody, Buffalo Bill   213
Cody, Lew   34
Cohan, George M.   183
Cohen, Manny   39
Cohn brothers   70
Cohn, Harry   69, 70, 124, 145, 187
Cohn, Jack   69, 70
Colbert, Claudette   122, 127, 145, 214
Cold War   199
Cole, Lester   201
Coleman, Ronald   93, 142
Columbia, also Columbia Pictures   68,
    69, 78, 84, 70, 119, 124, 126, 127,
    128, 135, 145, 149, 151, 177, 184,
    187, 216
Combat America   187
Comique Films   36
commercial radio broadcasting   73
Communism   199, 200
Communist Party   202, 215
Comrades   27
Comstock Act (1873)   107
Confessions of A Nazi Spy   180, 181
*Connecticut Yankee in King Arthur's
    Court, A*   116
Conrad, Joseph   172
Consolidated Film Labs   68
Coogan, Jackie   41
Cooper, Charles   151
Cooper, Frank James   151
Cooper, Gary   84, 133, 139, 122, 127,
    151, 152, 201, 214
Cooper, Jackie   118
Cooper, Merriam C.   67, 133, 143, 167

Coppola, Francis   172
Coquette   81
Corbett, Gentleman Jim   160
Cornell, Katharine   171
Corner in Wheat, A   15
Corvin Films   102
Cosmopolitan Pictures   137, 148
Cotton, Joseph   171, 174, 222
Council of Fashion Designers Lifetime
    Achievement Award   158
Countess from Hong Kong   43
Covered Wagon, The   73
Cowboy Philosopher   116
Crabbe, Larry Buster   136
Cradle Will Rock, The   171
Cranston, Lamont   171
Crash Drive   185
Crawford, Joan   139, 145, 191
Crescent cases   216
Crescent Group   216
Crime   204
Crisp, Donald   16, 175
Crocker, Charles   2
Crosby, Bing   31, 132, 183, 191
Crowd Roars, The   126
Cruze, James   73
Cukor, George   101, 150, 155, 157, 158
Curtis, Tony   192
Curtiz, Michael   101, 159, 160, 196, 208
D.O.A.   208
da Vinci, Leonardo   1
Dada Magazine   97
Dadaism   97
Daguerre, Louis   1
daguerreotype   1
Daily Variety   209
Dali, Salvador   97, 98
Daly, Carroll John   204
Dancing Romero   119
Dangerous   153
Daniels, Mickey   118
Dark Angel, The   50
Dark Horse, The   111
Dark Passage   208
Dark Victory   164
Darrow, Clarence   156
Darwell, Jane   170
Darwin's theory of evolution   156
Dassin, Jules   208
Daves, Delmer   208

David Copperfield   115
Davidson, Paul   85
Davies, Marion   24, 57, 145
Davis, Bette   84, 139, 152, 153, 160, 164, 190, 191, 192
Davis, Elmer   182
Davis, Jackie   118
Davis, Ruth   152
Dawn Patrol   125, 160
D-Day   187
De Havilland, Olivia   160
De Sica, Vittorio   218, 219, 220
Dead End   50, 190
Dean, James   203, 216
Decla Film   85, 88
Decla-Bioscope AG   86
Defense Bonds   190
DeForrest, Lee   48, 62, 73
Deitrich, Marlene   39
Delicate Balance, A   158
Delmont, Maude   36
DeMille, Cecil B.   16, 23, 136, 139, 37, 38, 39, 49, 125, 146, 151
Dempster, Carole   25, 115
Denham film studio   102
Dentist, The   115
Department of Justice   199
Der Bergkatze   119
Desert Song, The   146
Desk Set   155
Destination Tokyo   151
Destroyer   187
Detective Story   208
Deulig media group   89
Deutsches Theater (German National Theater)   86, 119
Devil to Pay, The   146
Devil with Hitler, The   195
Devil's Passkey, The   61
Diamond Jim   127
Dickens, Charles   15, 52
Dickson, W.K.L. (William Kennedy Laurie)   4, 5, 8, 12, 73
Dieterle, William (director)   86
Dietrich, Marlene   87, 138, 149, 151
Dietrichson, Phyllis   206
Dillon, Josephine   145
Dime Detective Magazine   204
Dines, Courtland   33
dish nights   106

Disney Brothers Studio   71
Disney, Roy   70, 71
Disney, Walt   70, 71, 134, 167, 169
Distinguished Civilian Service Medal   153
Dive Bomber   160
Divide and Conquer   188
Division of Information   182
Dixon, Thomas (writer)   14, 19, 21
Dmytryk, Edward   201, 208
documentaries   205
Dodge City   160
Dodsworth   190
Dogme movements   96
Don Juan   74, 75
Donald Duck   71
Donat, Robert   102, 159, 164
Donen, Stanley   151
Dorsey, Jimmy   191
Double Indemnity   206, 207, 208, 214
double-feature programs   58
Dougherty, James   211
Douglas, Kirk   192
Douglas, Melvyn   122, 165
Down and Out in Beverly Hills   100
Dr. Jekyll and Mr. Hyde   87, 117
Dr. Pyckle and Mr. Pryde   117
Dracula   87, 132, 136
dream analysis   85
Dressler, Marie   30
du Maurier, Daphne   170
Duck Soup   113
Dukas, Paul   169
Dumas, Alexandre   100
DuMont Corporation   217
Dumont, Margaret   113
Duncan, Isadora   177
Dunkenfield, William Claude   114
Dunne, Irene   127, 150, 164
Duquesne Amusement & Supply Company   29, 64
Durante, Jimmy   191
Durfee, Minta   35, 36
Dvorak, Ann   110
Dwan, Alan (director)   125
Ealing Studios   222
Earhart, Amelia   54
Earp, Wyatt   55, 185
Easiest Way, The   145
East of Eden   204

Easter Parade   131
Eastman, George   2, 5, 12, 45
Easy Living   127
Eddington, Nora   161
Eddy, Nelson   131
Edison company   6, 9, 10, 11, 12, 14, 46
Edison Laboratories   9
Edison patent trust   15, 18, 23, 47, 55, 65, 69
Edison, Thomas Alva   4, 5, 6, 7, 10, 12, 23, 73
Einstein, Albert   53, 97
Eisenstein, Sergei   91, 92, 93
electricity, system for   5
Eliot, T.S.   97
Elite Glove Co.   49
Elstree studios   104
Empire State Express, The   6
End of St. Petersburg, The   94
Enemy Agents Meets Ellery Queen   195
Enter Madame   214
Epoch Productions   20, 21
Epstein, Julius and Philip   196
Ernst Hoffman-Film   87
Essanay Films   11, 30, 40
Eva Marie Saint   151
Every Sunday   131
Everybody Goes to Rick's (play)   196
Expressionism   85
Extra Girl, The   33
Fabrizi, Aldo   219
fade-out shot   15
Fairbanks, Douglas   23, 41, 51, 53, 54, 72, 78, 81, 102, 159
Fairbanks, Jr., Douglas   53, 81
fairness doctrine   182
Family Theater   45
Famous Players - Lasky   23, 35, 38, 39, 103
Famous Players Film Company   11, 12, 30
Famous Plays by Famous Players   18, 25, 38
Fantasia   169
Fantasy films   133, 134, 135, 136
Farce   111
Farnum, Dustin   49
Fascist cinema (Italy)   217
Fascist propaganda films (Italy)   218
fascist trilogy   218

Fast Workers   84
Fatal Glass of Beer, The   115
Father Gets Into The Game   27
Father Goose   151
Father of the Bride   155
Fatty Joins the Force   28
Faulkner, William   126
Faust   88
Faye, Alice   131
Federal Bureau of Investigation (FBI)   44, 200
Federal Communications Commission (FCC)   182, 217
Federal Theater Project   171
Feeney, John Martin   140
Fellini, Federico   219
femme fatale (deadly woman)   176
Ferguson, Perry   172
Ferris Hartman Company   35
Fields, W. C.   31, 133, 114, 115
Fig Leaves   125
Fighting Lady, The   190
Film Booking Offices of America   65, 67
film distribution   29
film editing   91
film noir   176, 187, 204, 205, 206, 207, 213
film projection, in audience setting   6
film rental   29
film sales   29
first film director   6
First International Congress of Psychoanalysis   97
First Motion Picture Unit   186
First National Exhibitors Circuit   40
First National, also First National Company, also First National Corporation, also First National Pictures   23, 24, 52, 57, 77, 48, 124, 125
first three-color Technical film (Flowers and Trees)   167
Fishbach, Fred   36
Fitzgerald, Barry   175
Fitzgerald, F. Scott   54, 97
Flaherty, Robert   88
Flaming Frontiers (film serial)   136
Flash Gordon (comic strip)   136
Flash Gordon (film series)   136

Fleet's In, The   183
Fleming, Victor (director)   88, 124, 125, 126, 164, 165
Flesh   143
Flowers and Trees   71, 167
Fly Away Home (play)   210
Flying Down to Rio   130
Flying Tigers, The   162
Flynn, Errol   159, 160, 161, 194
Follow the Fleet   130
Fonda, Henry   127, 170, 185
Fonda, Jane   158
Fontaine, Joan   160, 170
Foolish Wives   61
Footlight Parade   129
For Whom the Bell Tolls   152
Ford, Francis (director)   140, 141, 142, 143
Ford, Glenn   187
Ford, John (director)   50, 62, 69, 79, 88, 123, 125, 140, 141, 142, 143, 144, 153, 154, 155, 157, 161, 162, 165, 170, 172, 174, 175, 185, 213
Ford, Patrick   141
Fort Apache   162
Forty-Second Street   129
Four Horsemen of the Apocalypse, The   58
Four Sons   142
Fox   39, 57, 58, 62, 63, 64, 68, 78, 80, 83, 84, 88, 102, 116, 125, 131, 141, 142, 143, 154, 161, 170, 175, 177, 181, 193, 194, 211, 215, 216, 217
Fox Company   48, 62
Fox Film Foundation   13
Fox Motion Picture Company   73
Fox Movietone   48, 58, 73, 76, 142
Fox optical sound system   79
Fox Theaters   106
Fox, Eve   47
Fox, William   12, 13, 18, 29, 47, 48, 62, 76, 83
Frankenstein   132, 133
Freaks   132
Freddi, Luigi   217
Freed, Arthur   81
Freud, Sigmund   85, 97
Freudian   97
Freund, Karl (cinematographer)   86, 132
Fried, Wilhelm   47

Frohman, Daniel   38
Front Page (play)   110, 127, 169
Fun in Hi Skule   111
Fury   90, 137
Gable, Clark   84, 139, 126, 127, 144, 145, 146, 147, 148, 153, 154, 155, 164, 185, 186, 187, 190
Gable, Jeannie   144
Gable, William Clark   144
Gabriel Over the Whitehouse   137
Gainsborough Pictures   104
Gance, Abel   98, 99
Gang War   52
gangster films   63, 108, 139
Garbo, Greta   80, 82, 84, 122, 138, 139, 165
Garfield, John   191, 202, 209
Garland, Judy   129, 131, 165, 191, 212
Garnett, Tay   208
Garson, Greer   164, 190
Gas Masks (play)   92
Gate Theatre (Dublin)   171
Gaumont Chonochrome system   166
Gaumont, Leon   73
Gaumont-British production company   103, 104
Gay Divorcee, The   130
Gaynor, Janet   88
Geer, Will   202
Geisler, Jerry   161
Gelbfisz, Schmuel   48
General Crack   82
General Electric Company   5
General Film Company   12
General Line, The   93
Gentleman Jim   160
Gentlemen's Agreement   203, 215, 216
German Consul   181
German Expressionism   85, 86, 132
German Tri-Ergon sound process   48
Germania, Anno Zero   219
Giannini, A.P.   70
Gibson Girl   32
Gibson, Charles Dana   32
Gilbert, John   83, 84, 145
Gilda   187
Gilmore, William E.   6
Ginzburg, Bessie   49
Gish, Dorothy   17, 22, 24
Gish, Lillian   17, 22, 23, 24, 26

Globe Productions   181
G-man films   139
G-Men   139
Goddard, Paulette   41, 42
Godsol, Frank Joseph   50, 62
Goebbels, Joseph   89
Gold Diggers of 1933, The   129
Gold Diggers of 1935, The   129
Gold Rush, The   41, 42
Golden Boy   166
Golden Boy (play)   215
Goldenson, Leonard   217
Goldfish, Samuel   38, 49
Goldman Sachs   74
Goldwyn   30, 49, 62
Goldwyn Company   33, 59
Goldwyn Girls, The   50
Goldwyn Pictures   59
Goldwyn Studios   146, 190, 197
Goldwyn, Samuel   33, 38, 39, 41, 48,
    50, 59, 62, 72, 80, 93, 128, 142, 184,
    216
Golf Specialist, The   115
Gone With the Wind   146, 164, 165, 167,
    179, 182
Goodbye Mr. Chips   164
Goodman, Theodosia   47
Goofy   71
Gore, Reah   175
Gorky, Maxim   94, 96
Government Issue Bill of Rights (GI
    Bill)   192
Governor of California   163
Gower Gulch   68
Grable, Betty   50, 191
Grant, Cary   84, 127, 133, 138, 148,
    149, 150, 151, 155, 170, 221
Grapes of Wrath, The   170, 185
Grass: A Nation's Battle for Life   133
Grauman, Sid   146
Great Depression, also the
    Depression   122, 127, 169, 170, 179
Great Dictator, The   42, 43, 181
Great Expectations   52
Great McGinty, The   178
Great Train Robbery, The   10, 11, 13,
    166
Green Berets, The   163
Green, Graham   221
Greenstreet, Sydney   176, 196

Grey, Lita   41, 42
Griffith, D.W. (David Wark)   13, 14, 15,
    16, 17, 18, 19, 20, 21, 22, 23, 24, 25,
    26, 27, 30, 41, 51, 53, 55, 56, 59, 72,
    91, 98, 115, 140
Group Theater   202, 204, 209, 211, 212,
    215
Guadacanal Diary   193
Guess Who's Coming to Dinner   156,
    158
Guinea Pig, The (play)   177
Guinnness, Alec   222
Gunga Din   150
Hal Roach Studios   31, 33, 116, 117,
    119, 124
Half Caste, The   88
Hall Room Boys   70
Hallmark Pictures   66
Hamlet   221
Hamlet (play)   64
Hammett, Dashiell   147, 176, 205
Hamptons advertising agency   69
Hansen, Betty   161
Hard Bitten Detective   204
Hardy, Andy (series of films)   131
Hardy, Norvell   117
Hardy, Oliver   31, 116, 117, 118
Harlow, Jean   84, 139, 154
Harris, Mildred   41
Hart, Moss   127
Hatch Act   200
Hawks, Frank   124
Hawks, Howard (director)   62, 141, 142,
    88, 109, 110, 119, 123, 124, 125, 126,
    127, 128, 142, 150, 151, 169, 170,
    178, 208, 210, 213
Hayden, Sterling   207
Hayes, Helen   142
Hays Office   110, 139, 179
Hays, Will   107, 108, 109, 208
Hayworth, Rita   187, 190, 213
Hearst newspapers   34, 36, 42
Hearst, William Randolph   24, 57, 137,
    145, 148, 172, 173, 174
Heart of Darkness   172
Hearts of the World   22
Hecht, Ben   109, 110, 127
Heinreid, Paul   196
Heiress, The   210
Hell Divers   145

Hellman, Lillian   195
Hemingway, Ernest   97, 152, 155, 161
Henderson, Del   27
Henie, Sonja   131
Henry V   221
Hepburn, Audrey   151
Hepburn, Katharine   127, 143, 150, 155, 156, 157, 158, 191, 215
Hepburn, Tom   156
Her First Biscuits   51
Herman, Woody   191
Heron, Bobby   15
Herrmann, Bernard   172
Herron, Frederick   179
Hertz, John   147
Hessling, Catherine   100
Hiawatha   46
High Noon   152
Hilton, James   135
Hiroshima   197
His Girl Friday   127, 150, 169, 170
His Glorious Night   83
Hitchcock, Alfred   103, 104, 150, 151, 170, 178, 208, 213, 221
Hitler, also Hitler, Adolph   43, 89, 122, 163, 178, 179, 181, 195, 197, 214, 218
Hodkinson, W.W.   38
Hold Back The Dawn   214
Holden, William   187
Holiday   150, 155, 158
Holiday Inn   183
Hollywood Canteen   153, 191, 192
Hollywood Hotel   129
Hollywood Ten   201
Holman, Libby   210
home radio receivers   66
Home Sweet Home   19
Hoover, Herbert   105
Hoover, J. Edgar   44, 200
Hope, Bob   132, 191
Hopkins, Mark   2
Hopper, Hedda   42, 173
Hornblow, Arthur   147
horror film   132
Horse Feathers   113
Horton, Edward Everett   133
Hoskins, Allen Clayton Farina   118
House Un-American Activities Committee (HUAC)   200, 201, 202, 203, 204, 212, 214

Houseman, John   171, 172
How Green Was My Valley   144, 174, 175
How To Marry A Millionaire   149
Howard, Leslie   102
Howard, Trevor   222
Howe, James Wong (cinematographer)   141
Howell, Helen   124
Hue and Cry   222
Hugenberg, Alfred   89
Hughes, Hattie   114
Hughes, Howard   72, 109, 110, 125, 158, 217
Hunchback of Notre Dame, The   61, 132, 166
Huntington, Collis   2
Hustler, The   202
Huston, John   158, 175, 176, 177, 189, 208, 211, 213
Huston, Walter   175
I Am A Fugitive From A Chain Gang   140
I Lead Three Lives (TV series)   204
I Was A Communist for the FBI   204
I Was A Male War Bride   151
Ibsen   96
Idiot's Delight   179
Idle Class   41
Il Processo Clemenceau   220
I'll Say She Is   112
I'm No Angel   149
I'm Sitting On Top of the World (song title)   79
In Old Arizona   80
Ince, Elinor   55
Ince, Thomas   18, 22, 27, 30, 46, 55, 56, 57, 140
Inceville   18, 56
Independent Motion Picture Company (IMP)   12, 13, 16, 46, 51, 69
Informer, The   143
Inherit the Wind   156
intellectual montage (technique)   93
International Squadron   181
Interpretation of Dreams, The   97
Intolerance   22, 91
Invisible Man, The   133
Irish Mafia   153, 155
Iron Horse, The   141

Iron Mask, The   81
It Happened One Night   126, 127, 145
It's A Mad, Mad, Mad, Mad World   156
It's All True   174
Italian censorship board   218
Italian Cinema   218
Italian Neo-realism   217, 218, 219, 220
It's A Gift   115
It's A Wonderful Life   185, 188
Ivan The Terrible, Part One   93
Ivan The Terrible, Part Two   93
Iwerks, Ub   71
J'accuse   98
James, William   60
Jane Eyre (play)   158
Jannings, Emil   80, 87, 88
Jazz Singer, The   76, 77, 79, 128
Jefferson, Arthur Stanley   116
Jenkins, C. Francis   11
Jesse H. Lasky Motion Picture
    Company   49
Jessel, George   75, 76
Jessie Lasky Feature Play Company   38
Jezebel   153
Johnson, Nunnally   170
Johnston, W. Ray   68
Jolson, Al   75, 76, 77, 79, 129
Jones, Buck   135
Judge Priest   116, 143
Judgement at Nuremberg   156
Judith of Behulia   18
Julius Caesar   171
jungle adventures   135, 136
Jungle Menace, The (film serial)   136
Just Nuts   31
Justice Department   217
Kalem   11
Kalmer, Bert   113
Kalmus Family   71
Kalmus, Comstock, and Wescott
    Company   166
Kalmus, Dr. Herbert   166
Kammerspiel   86, 88
Kansas City Slide Company   71
Karloff, Boris   132
Karno Pantomime Troupe   39
Karno Troupe   116
Kaufman, Denis Arkadyevitch   95
Kaufman, George S.   112, 127
Kayser, Charles   6

Kazan, Elia   202, 203, 204, 209, 213,
    214, 215
KDKA   65
Keaton, Buster   36, 37, 43
Keeler, Ruby   129
Keith Vaudeville Circuit   114
Keith-Albee-Orpheum Company
    (KAO)   65, 67
Kelly, Joe   33
Kennedy, Jeremiah   45
Kennedy, Joseph   65, 66, 67, 82
Kennedy, Wiliam   47
Kershaw, Elinor   55
Kessel, Adam   27, 29, 30, 39
Key Largo   208
Keystone Company, also Keystone   27,
    28, 29, 30, 31, 32, 33, 35, 37, 39, 40,
    46, 124
Keystone Kops   28, 35
KFWB (radio station)   74
Khan, Genghis   94
Khazonkov, Alexander   91
Kid from Spain, The   50
Kid, The   41
Killers, The   208
Killing, The   207
Kimberly Clark paper company   124
Kind Hearts and Coronets   222
Kinemacolor system   166
kinetograph camera   5
kinetophones   73
kinetoscope   5, 6, 7, 10
kinetoscope viewing device, at the 1893
    Chicago Exhibition   6
kinetoscope, coin-operated   58
King in New York, A   43
King Kong   133, 167
King, Charles   81
kinoks, or kino-eye (cinema eye)   95
Kino-Pravda (cinema truth)   95
Kipling, Rudyard   47, 143
Kitty Foyle   130
Kitty Hawk   65
Klein Optical Company   11
Know Your Enemy   193
Koch, Howard   172, 196
kodachrome footage   190
Koltstov, Mikhail   95
Korda, Alexander   72, 101, 102, 221
Kramer, Stanley   155, 156

Krasker, Robert   222
Krasna, Norma   210
Krauss, Werner   86
Krims, Milton   180
Kubrick, Stanley   207
Kuleshov Workshop   91, 93, 95
Kuleshov, Lev   91, 93
Kurosawa, Akira   99
KWFB Los Angeles   65
La Cava, Gregory   137
La Chienne   100, 101
La Cucaracha   167
La Fille de L'eau   100
La Folie du Docteur Tube   98
La Grande Illusion   100, 101
La Regle Du Jeu   101
La Roue   99
Laboratory of Hearing   95
Labour Party (British)   221
Ladies of Leisure   124
Ladies of the Chorus   211
Ladri di Biciclette (The Bicycle Thief)   220
Lady Eve, The   127, 178
Lady From Shanghai, The   208, 213
Lady Vanishes, The   104
Lady Windermere's Fan   64
Laemmle Service Company   45
Laemmle, Carl   12, 13, 16, 18, 132, 140, 141, 44, 45, 46, 51, 55, 60, 61, 69, 143
Lake, The (play)   157
Lake, Veronica   128, 191
Lamont, Robert P.   48
Lamour, Dorothy   132
Lancaster, Burt   192
Lang, Fritz (director)   86, 88, 89, 90, 137, 181, 206, 208, 214
Langdon, Harry   30, 124
Langham, Ria   145
lantern slides   69
Lardner, Jr., Ring   201
Lasky   104
Lasky Company   39
Lasky, Jessie   23, 25, 30, 37, 38, 39, 46, 49, 125, 177
Lassie Come Home   212
Last Hurrah, The   155
Last Laugh, The   88
Last Mile, The   154
Last Mile, The (play)   145

laudanum   34
Laughing Bill Hyde   116
Laughton, Charles   102, 208
Launder, Frank (director)   103
Laurel and Hardy   31, 116, 117, 118
Laurel, Stan   31, 116, 117, 118
Lawrence, Florence   13, 46
Lawyer Man   111
Leach, Archibald   149
Lean, David (director)   103
Legion of Decency   107
Lehrman, Henry (director)   28, 35, 36
Leigh, Vivien   102, 164
Lemon, Jack   192
Lend Lease Act   179
Leni, Paul   132
Lenin, Vladmir Ilyich   90, 91, 92, 96
LeRoy, Mervyn   109, 138, 140, 165
Let There Be Light   189, 190
Levinson, Nathan   74
Lewis, Joseph H.   208
Lewis, Sinclair   142
Libeled Lady   154
Liberace   212
Liberty Bonds   190
Life of An American Fireman   10
Life With Father   149
Life's Shop Window   47
Lifetime Achievement Award, 1972   44
lightbulb, invention of   5
Lili Damita   159
Lilith   202
Limehouse Nights (short stories)   22
Limelight   43, 44
Lincoln, Abraham   25
Lindbergh, Charles   76
Lion in Winter, A   158
Little Caesar   109
Little Rascals, The   31, 119
Little Red Schoolhouse, The (play)   51
Little Tramp (Chaplin character)   29, 40, 42, 43, 78, 181
Little Women   157
Litvak, Anatole   180
Lloyd, Harold   31
Lockwood, Cary   149
Lodger, The   104
Loew, Marcus   13, 38, 48, 57, 58, 59, 62, 66
Loew's Incorporated   58

Loew's State   58
Loews Theaters   13
Loews-MGM   184
Lombard, Carole   84, 122, 146, 186, 190
London Film Production Co.   102, 221
Lonestar   68, 162
Long Day's Journey Into Night   158
Longfellow, Henry Wadsworth   46
Loos, Anita   18
Loren, Sophia   44
Lorre, Peter   89, 176, 196, 214
Los Angeles Herald (newspaper)   20
Lost Horizon   135
Lost Jungle, The (film serial)   136
Lost Patrol, The   143
Lost Weekend, The   214
Louis B. Mayer Productions   59
Love Affair   164
Love Me Tonight   147
Love Parade   121
Love, Bessie   81
Love, Your Magic Spell is Everywhere
   (song)   82
Lowe, Edmund   80
Loy, Myrna   84, 146, 147, 148, 154
Lubin   11
Lubin Manufacturing Company   73
Lubitsch touch, the   120, 122
Lubitsch, Ernst   39, 53, 64, 86, 119,
   120, 121, 127, 165, 214
Lucas, Wilfred (director)   28
Ludendorff, General Erich   85
Lugosi, Bela   87, 136
Luke   35
Lumiere brothers, also Lumieres   6, 7,
   8, 12, 46
Lumiere, August   6, 12
Lumiere, Louis   6, 7
M   89, 214
Mabel's Strange Predicament   29
MacArthur, Charles   127
MacArthur, General Douglas   182
Macbeth   171
MacDonald, Jeanette   121, 131
Mace, Fred   27, 28, 30
Mackendrick, Alexander   208
MacLeish, Archibald   182
MacMurray, Fred   206
Madame Butter   149
Madame Du Barry   119

Magnificent Ambersons, The   174
Mail and Female   119
Maine and New Hampshire Theaters
   Company   65
Majestic studio   19
Major and the Minor, The   214
major studio (theaters, distribution,
   production)   67
Maltese Falcon, The   176, 206, 208
Mamoulian, Ruben   147
Man Hunt   181
Man of the Cross   219
Man of the Hour (play)   53
Man Who Knew Too Much, The   104
Man Who Played God, The   152
Man Who Shot Liberty Valence, The   162
Man with a Movie Camera   95, 96
Manhattan Melodrama   147, 148
Mankiewicz, Herman   113
Mankiewicz, Joseph   172, 173, 211, 213
Man's Genesis   17
March of Time newsreel (series)   171
March, Frederick   156, 197
Marion, Frances (director)   52
Mark of Zorro, The   53
Marriage Circle, The   64, 120
Marsh, Mae   17, 49
Marshall, General George C.   188
Marvin, Henry   14
Marvin, Lee   192
Marx Brothers   111, 112, 113
Marx, Chico (Leonard)   111, 113
Marx, Groucho (Julius)   111, 112, 114
Marx, Gummo (Milton)   111, 112
Marx, Harpo (Adolph)   111, 112
Marx, Zeppo (Herbert)   111, 112, 113
Marx, Milton   112
Marx, Uncle Al   111
Marxism   200
Mary of Scotland   143
Maskelyne and Cooke   8
Massachusetts Institute of Technology
   (M.I.T.)   5, 166
Mate, Rudolph   208
Maugham, Somerset   185
Mayer Company   61
Mayer, Louis B.   21, 58, 59, 59, 61, 62,
   83, 84, 126, 145, 147, 154, 158, 201
McCarey, Leo (director)   113, 117, 119,
   127, 149, 150, 153, 164

McCarey, Ray (director)   119
McCarthy, Charlie   115
McCarthy, Joseph   44, 200, 201
McCarthyism   43
McCoy, Tim   136
McCrae, Joel   128
McCutcheon, George   14
McDaniel, Hattie   164
McDonald, Jeanette   147
McDowell, Roddy   175
McFarland, George Spanky   119
McIntyre, Andrew   186
McLaglen, Victor   142
Mechanics of the Brain, The   94
medical research   7
Meet John Doe   152
Meet Me in St. Louis   131
Mein Kampf   178
Melies, Georges, also Melies Motion
    Picture Company   8, 10, 11, 12, 133,
    140
Mellett, Lowell   181, 182
Memphis Belle   190
Men In Black, The   205
Men In Fright   119
Menjou, Adolphe   64
Mercury Theater Group   171
Mercury Theater of the Air   171, 172,
    173, 222
Meredith, Burgess   165
Merry Go Round   61
Method Acting   203, 208, 213
Method, The   203, 209, 211
Metro Goldwyn Mayer (MGM)   50, 57,
    58, 59, 62, 63, 78, 80, 81, 82, 83, 84,
    89, 90, 99, 113, 119, 120, 122, 126,
    127, 129, 131, 137, 143, 145, 146,
    147, 148, 149, 153, 154, 155, 158,
    161, 164, 175, 177, 181, 185, 186,
    187, 193, 194, 209, 212, 215, 216, 221
Metro, Metro Pictures   50, 58, 59, 62
Metropolis   89
Meyerhold, Vsevolod   92
Mickey   33
Mickey Mouse   71, 169
Mickey Mouse Club   71
microphone nerves   77
Midnight Angel   182
Mildred Pierce   208
Milestone, Lewis   165

Milland, Ray   214
Miller, Arthur   175, 204, 208, 215
minor studio (production)   67
Mintz, Charlie   71
Misfits, The   146
Mitchell Hi-Speed Movement
    camera   80
Mitchell, Margaret   146, 164
Mix, Tom   48, 62, 141, 161
mob movies   139
Modern Times   41, 43
modernism   97
Monkey Business   113
Monogram Pictures   68, 182, 205
Monroe, Marilyn   146, 192, 203, 211
Monte Carlo   121
Moon is Down, The   194
Moore, Colleen   84
Moore, Owen   16, 51
Moorehead, Agnes   171
Morning Glory   157
Morocco   151
Morrison, Clyde   161
Morrison, Duke   161
Morrison, Marion   161
Morrison, Sammy   118
Mortal Storm, The   181
Mortenson, Norma Jean   211
Mortimer (cartoon character)   71
Moscow Art Theater   96, 202
Moscow Film Commission   95
Most Promising Young Actor Award
    (Daily Variety)   209
Mother   94
Mother and the Law, The   21
Mothering Heart, The   17
Motion Picture Academy of Arts and
    Sciences   44, 153, 156
Motion Picture Alliance for the
    Preservation of American Ideals   162
Motion Picture Commission   107
Motion Picture News   13
motion picture palace   21
Motion Picture Patents Company
    (MPCC)   11, 12
Motion Picture Producers and
    Distributors of America   107
motion series photographs   4
Mountain Eagle, The   104
Mountbatten, Lord   54

movable microphone boom   80
movie censorship ordinances   107
movie palaces   13, 19
movie parlor   45
movie theater   58, 59
movie trailers   205
Movietone, also Fox Movietone   76, 79
*Mr. Blandings Builds His Dream
    Home*   148
Mr. Deeds Goes to Town   127, 151
Mr. Lucky   150
Mr. Roberts   149
Mr. Smith Goes to Washington   127, 164
Mud and Sand   117
Mummy, The   132
Muni, Paul   83, 84, 109, 110
Murder at Monte Carlo   159
Murder, My Sweet   208
Murnau, F.W. (director)   48, 62, 142, 86,
    87, 88, 104, 142
Music Box, The   118
Music Corporation of America   191
musical   128
Musketeers of Pig Alley   17
Mussolini, Benito   113, 163, 178, 179,
    217, 218
Mussolini, Vittorio   218
Mutiny on the Bounty   145
Mutoscope viewing system   6
Mutual Pictures, also Mutual Films   18,
    19, 30, 40, 41, 56
Mutual v. Ohio   107
Muybridge, Eadweard   3
My Darling Clementine   185
My Favorite Wife   150
My Four Years in Germany   64
My Little Chickadee   115
My Man Godfrey   148
My Son John   204
Mystery Squadron (film series)   136
Nagasaki   197
Nagel, Conrad   78
Naked City, The   208
Nana   100
Napoleon   99
Napoleon's Barber   79, 142
narration, in film noir   207
National Association for the
    Advancement of Colored People
    (NAACP)   20, 138

National Association of the Motion
    Picture Industry   107
National Broadcasting Company
    (NBC)   66, 75
National Socialist Party, also Nazi
    Party   178
National Velvet   212
Naughty Marietta   131
Navy Propaganda Center (Italy)   218
Nazi Germany   122
Nazis Strike, The   188
NBC Chase and Sanborn Hour   115
NBC Television Network   114
Neff, Wallace   53
Negri, Pola   80, 87
Negro Theater Project   171
Neilan, Marshall Micky   52, 124, 125
neorealist trilogy   219
Nero Film AG   89
*Never Give A Sucker An Even
    Break*   115
Never Say Die   127
new wave (French)   205
New York Motion Pictures (NYMP)   55
New York Philharmonic Orchestra   75
New York State Film Commission   109,
    110
New York State Motion Picture
    Commission   108
New York University   69
New York World's Fair   163
New Yorker, The (magazine)   214
Newman Theater   71
Newman, Paul   192, 203
newspaper films   110
newsreels   58, 205
Nichols, Dudley   181
Nichols, George (director)   28
Nick and Nora Charles (novel)   147
nickelodeon   7, 12, 13, 16, 18, 21, 29,
    37, 38, 45, 47, 53, 58, 64, 69
Niepce, Nicephone   1
Night At The Opera, A   113
Night of the Hunter   208
Ninotchka   122, 165, 214
Niven, David   166, 221
Nixon, Raphael   202
Nixon, Richard M.   201
noir detective   205

Normand, Mabel   16, 27, 28, 29, 30, 31, 32, 33, 35
North By Northwest   151
Northampton Repertory Company   159
Nosferatu: A Symphony of Horror   87, 132
Notorious   151
Nuts   117
Oakie, Jack   133
Oberon, Merle   102, 166
Objective Burma   194
O'Brien, George   88, 141
O'Brien, Pat   153
O'Brien, Willis   133
October: Ten Days That Shook The World   93
Odeon Cinema Theater Company   103
Odets, Clifford   202, 215
Of Mice and Men   165
Office of Emergency Management (OEM)   182
Office of Facts and Figures (OFF)   182
Office of Government Reports (OGR)   181
Office of the Coordinator of Inter-American Affairs (CIAA)   181
Office of Wartime Information (OWI)   182, 183, 193, 194
Oglesby, Woodson   26
O'Hara, Maureen   175
Old Kentucky   116
Old Man and the Sea   155
Olivier, Lawrence   166, 221
On Golden Pond   158
On The Waterfront   204
One Christmas   158
One Hour Married   34
One Million B.C.   26
O'Neill, Eugene   42
O'Neill, Oona   42
one-take Woody   147
Only Angels Have Wings   150, 166
optical motion picture sound   62
Orphans of the Storm   24
Orpheum Circuit   114
Ossessione   218
O'Sullivan, Maureen   136
Oswald the Lucky Rabbit (cartoon)   71
O'Toole, Peter   158
Our Gang (series)   31, 118, 119, 124

Ouspenskaya, Maria   202, 211
Outcasts of Poker Flats   123
Outwitting Dad   117
Oxbow Incident, The   185
Pacific Blackout   182
Paisa   219
Palm Beach Story, The   127, 128
Palmer Raids   199
Panic in the Streets   216
Pantages Company   35
Pantages, Alex   35
Paramount   12, 23, 25, 30, 31, 33, 36, 37, 48, 52, 57, 58, 66, 68, 76, 78, 80, 88, 89, 93, 106, 112, 113, 115, 119, 120, 121, 122, 125, 127, 149, 151, 167, 177, 178, 180, 182, 183, 184, 193, 210, 214, 216, 217
Paramount Consent Decree   183, 216
Paramount Famous Lasky   39
Parsons, Louella   57, 173
Passport to Pimlico   222
Pastor Hall   181
Pat and Mike   155
Patent Trust, also Edison Patent Trust   45, 46
Pathe studio   101
Pathe, also Pathe Pictures, also Pathe company   9, 11, 31, 66, 67
pathos   42
Patriot, The   120
Paul Gerson Picture Corp   124
Pavlov, Ivan   94
Pearl Harbor   182, 186, 188, 193
Peck, Gregory   215
Peckinpah, Sam   192
peep-show   6
Pegler   200
People on Sunday   213
People's Vaudeville Company   58
Perelman, S.J.   113
Perils of Pauline   135
Peterkins Self-Raising Flour Company   102
Petrograd Psychoneurological Institute   95
Phantom Empire, The (film series)   136
Phantom of the Opera, The   132
Phantom Plainsman   195
Philadelphia Story, The   150, 155
Philadelphia Story, The (play)   158

Phonofilm   73
phonograph, invention of   5, 73
Photography, painting with light   1
Photoplay Magazine   25
Picasso, Pablo   97, 99
Pickfair   53
Pickford Film Corporation   52
Pickford, Jack   16, 52
Pickford, Mary   15, 16, 17, 22, 23, 29,
     30, 33, 39, 41, 51, 52, 53, 54, 55, 72,
     78, 81, 119, 120
Picture and Film Office (German
     Army)   85
picture palaces   53, 58
Pidgeon, Walter   175
Pilar (yacht)   163
Pilot Returns, A   218
Pinky   216
Pitts, Zazu   31
Place in the Sun, A   210
Plainsman, The   139, 151
Planck, Max   97
Platinum Bomb   110
Players Company   49
Pleasure Garden, The   104
Pluto   71
Pommers, Erich   85, 86, 88
Pool Sharks   114
Poor Little Rich Girl, The   52, 131
Poppy   114, 115
Porter, Edwin S.   8, 9, 10, 52
Post, Wiley   116
Postman Always Rings Twice, The   208
post-traumatic stress disorder
     (PTSD)   189
Pound, Ezra   97
Poverty Row   68, 70
Powell, Dick   129
Powell, Eleanor   131
Powell, Michael (director)   103
Powell, William, also Powell, William
     David   81, 146, 147, 148, 149, 154
Power and the Glory, The   154, 177
Power, Tyrone   185
Powers, Pat   71
Pravda   95
Praxinoscope   2
Prelude to War   188
Preminger, Otto (director)   86, 208
Pride of the Yankees, The   152

Private Life of Don Juan, The   102
Private Life of Henry III, The   102
*Private Lives of Elizabeth and Essex,
     The*   160
Producers Releasing Corporation   205
Production Code   108, 149, 208, 211
Prohibition, also Prohibition Act   34,
     108
Projektions AG   119
Prolekult Theater Group   92
propaganda (wartime)   188
propaganda films   85
Public Enemy, The   109
Public Enemy's Wife   139
Pudovkin, Vsevolod Illarionovich   91,
     93, 94
pulp fiction   204
Purviance, Edna   33, 40, 41
Pyle, Ernie   196
Que Viva Mexico   93
Queen Christina   84
Queen Elizabeth   18, 38
Queen Kelly   82
Quiet Man, The   162
Quinn, Anthony   193
radio   65
Radio Bugs   119
Radio Corporation of America
     (RCA)   62, 65, 66, 67
Radio Keith Orpheum   65
radiology   7
Raft, George   110
Rains, Claude   196
Ramona   16
Rank, J. Arthur   102, 103, 221
Rapf, Harry   63
Rappe, Virginia   36, 37
Ray, Nicholas   213
Rayart   68
Raymond, Alex   136
Razor's Edge, The   185
RCA   74, 84
RCA Television Pavilion at the New York
     World's Fair   163
Reader, Ronald   65
ready for sound   78
Reagan, Ronald   195, 201
Rebecca   170
Red Rider (film serial)   136
Red River   210

Redemption 84
Reed, Carol 208, 221
Reid, Wallace 33
Reinhardt, Max 86, 87, 119
Reliance studio 19
Religious Film Society 102
Rembrandt 102
Remember Pearl Harbor 182
Renaissance 1
Renoir, Auguste 100
Renoir, Jean 100
Report from the Aleutians 189
Republic, also Republic Pictures 68, 69,
    135, 162, 182, 205
Return of Chandu (film series) 136
Reville, Alma 104
Rialto Theaters 106
Riefenstahl, Leni 188
Rin Tin Tin 63, 64
Ring Cycle (opera) 89
Ring of the Nibelung 88
Ring, The 104
Rio Grande 162
Ripon College 154
Riskin, Robert 127
Ritt, Martin 204
RKO Productions, also RKO
    Pictures 57, 80, 106, 127, 129, 143,
    149, 155, 157, 167, 172, 173, 174,
    184, 194, 211, 216, 217
RKO Radio Pictures 65, 67
RKO Theaters Corporation 217
RKO/FBO 78
Roach, Hal 26, 31, 118, 149
road pictures 132
Road to Glory 125
Road to Morocco, The 132
Road to Singapore, The 132
Roaring Twenties 105
Roberta 130
Robertson-Cole/Film Booking Offices
    (RC/FBO) 66
Robin Hood 53
Robinson, Edward G. 84, 109, 148, 180
Rockefeller, Nelson 171, 181
Rogers, Charles Buddy 54
Rogers, Will 115, 116, 143
Rogue Mole, The 181
Roman Catholic Church 107
Rome: Open City 219

Rooney, Mickey 119, 131, 153, 191
Roosevelt Administration 113, 139,
    179, 181, 183, 190, 193, 216
Roosevelt, Franklin Delano 105, 116,
    139, 182, 199
Roosevelt, James 181
Roosevelt, Theodore 65
Rooster Cogburn 158
Rose Marie 131
Rose Scarlati 220
Rosher, Charles 52
Rosita 53, 119, 120
Rossellini, Roberto 218, 219
Rossen, Robert 202
Ruby, Harry 113
Rules of the Game, The 101
Rumrich, Guenther 180
Russell, Harold 197
Russell, Rosalind 127, 150, 169, 187
Russian Revolution (1905) 90
Rutherford, Margaret 222
Sabotage 104
Sailor-Made Man, A 31
Sally of the Sawdust 115
Samuel Goldwyn Pictures 50
Samuel Goldwyn Studios 72
San Francisco 146, 154
Sandrich, Mark (director at RKO) 130
Sands of Iwo Jima, The 162
Santa Fe Trail 160
Sarnoff, David 62, 65, 66, 67, 75, 84,
    163
Satterlee, Peggy 161
Saturday Evening Post Magazine 50
Sawyer, Gordon 80
Sawyer, Tom 52
Scandal Sheet 110
Scarface 109, 125
Scarlet Lady 78
Scarlet Street 206, 208
Schaefer, George 172
Schenck, Joseph 25, 35, 36, 63, 72
Schenck, Nicholas 48, 58, 59, 62, 63,
    83
Schoedsack, Ernest 133
Schrek, Max 87
Schrift, Shelly 212
Schulberg, B.P. 23
science fiction 133
Sciuscia (Shoeshine) 220

Scopes Monkey Trial   156
Screen Director's Guild   143
Screen Snapshots (short films)   70
Screen Writer's Guild   201
screwball comedy, also romantic
    comedy   119, 122, 126, 128
Sea Beast, The (play)   64
Sea Hawk, The   160
Sea of Grass   215
Search, The   210
Searchers, The   162
Secret Agent, The   104
Selig   11
Selig Company   35
Selig Studio   59
Selwyn, Edgar   49
Selznick International Pictures   164
Selznick International Studios   170
Selznick Studios   182
Selznick, David O.   67, 133
Sennett, Mack   15, 17, 18, 22, 27, 28,
    29, 30, 31, 32, 33, 35, 37, 40, 56, 69
Sergeant York   152
serials (episodic long-form stories)   135
Shadow of A Doubt   208
Shadow, The (radio series)   171
Shakespeare, William   81, 171
Shall We Dance   130
Shaw, Artie   204
Shaw, George Bernard   54, 74
She Done Him Wrong   149
She Wore A Yellow Ribbon   162
Shearer, Norma   61, 83
sheet music   69
Sherlock Holmes   148
She's In The Army Now   182
Shocking Miss Pilgrim, The   211
Shop Around the Corner, The   122
short subject films   205
Shoulder Arms   41
shyster lawyer   110
shyster movies   139
Sid Grauman's Egyptian Theater   146
Sidney, Sylvia   149
Silly Symphonies   71
Sim, Alastair   222
Sinatra, Frank   191
Sinclair, Upton   93
Singing Fool   79
Sinnott, Michael   27

Siodmak, Robert   208, 214
Six Mascots   111
Sixth of the World, A   95
Skouras brothers   63
Skouras, Spyros   62, 63, 204
Sleepless in Seattle   164
Sloan, Everett   171
Smiling Lieutenant, The   121
Smith, Albert   65
Smith, Alexis   160
Smith, Gladys   51
Smith, Ludlow Ogden   157
Smith, Mary McBryde   141
Snow White and the Seven Dwarfs   71,
    134, 167
Society of Art and Literature   96
Society of Independent Motion Picture
    Producers (SIMPP)   184, 216, 217
Sonny Boy (song title)   79
Sons of the Desert   118
Sorceror's Apprentice, The   169
Soul Herder   141
sound motion picture, development
    of   74
South Sea Sinner   212
Southern Pacific Railway   2
Sparks, Ned   133
speakeasies   108
Spicy Adventures and Weird
    Menace   204
Sponable, Earl   73
Spreckles, Kay   146
spy film   222
Spy Swatter   182
Squaw Man, The   16, 23, 38, 49
St. John, Al   35
Stage Door Canteen   191
Stagecoach   144, 162, 165, 172
Stalin, Joseph   92, 93, 199
Stanford University   3
Stanford, Leland   2, 3
Stanislavski   96
Stanislavski, Konstantin   96
Stanislavski's Method   96, 202
Stanwyck, Barbara   124, 127, 207
Star Spangled Rhythm   183
Stars Over America (campaign)   190
State Cinema School (Russia)   93
State of the Union   155
states rights exhibitors   67

Steamboat Willie   71
Stein, Gertrude   97
Stein, Jules   191, 192
Steinbeck, John   165, 170
Sterling, Ford   28
Stevens, George (director)   150, 210
Stevenson, Robert Louis   87
Stewart, Anita   59
Stewart, Jimmy, also Stewart,
    James   122, 127, 162, 164, 185, 188
stock market crash, October 1929   31,
    48, 84, 105, 142
stock ticker   5
Stoker, Bram   87
Stone, Hayden   66
Stone, John (writer)   141
Storm Over Asia   94
Story of G.I. Joe, The   196, 197
Strand, Mark   19
Strand, The (first movie palace)   19
Strasberg, Lee   202, 203, 204
Streetcar Named Desire, A   203
Streetcar Named Desire, A (play)   202,
    209
Strictly Dishonorable (play)   177
Stride Soviet   95
Strike   92
Strindberg   96
Strong Boy   142
Strong Man, The   124
Struggle, The   26
stunt movies   135
Sturges, Preston   127, 177, 178
Submarine   78
Suddenly Last Summer   158
Sullivan, Margaret   122
Sullivan's Travels   127, 178
Summer Stock   131
Sun Also Rises, The   161
Sunrise   48, 88, 142
Sunset Boulevard   206, 207, 208, 214
Sunshine Sammy (short films)   118
Surrealism   97, 111
Susan Lenox, Her Fall and Rise   139
Suspicion   150
Swain, Mack   29
Swanson, Gloria   39, 66, 67, 82
Sweet Smell of Success   208
Sweet, Blanch   16
Swing Time   130

Switzer, Carl Alfalfa   119
Tabu   88
Tales of A Dog   119
talkies, also talking pictures   77, 78
Tally, Thomas   23
Talmadge, Norna   84
Taming of the Shrew   81
Tarkington, Booth   174
Tarzan (film series)   136
Tarzan the Fearless   136
Taylor, Elizabeth   212
Taylor, William Desmond (director)   33,
    37
Technicolor   166
Technicolor corporation   71
Technicolor process   134
Teddington Studios   159
telephone   5
television, invention of   84
Temple, Shirley   64, 131, 119, 143
Ten Commandments, The   146
Test Pilot   155
Testament of Dr. Mabuse, The   88
Texas Rangers, The   139
Thalberg, Irving   46, 58, 59, 60, 61, 62,
    113, 146, 154, 155
Thanhouser Company   68
That Lady in Ermine   122
Them Thar Hills   118
Theory of Quantum Physics   97
They Were Expendable   162
They Won't Forget   138
Thicker Than Water   118
Thief of Baghdad, The   53
Thin Man, The (series)   147, 148
Third Man, The   208, 221
Third Reich   89
Thirty Seconds Over Tokyo   194
This Day and Age   136
Thomas, Billie Buckwheat   119
Thomas, J. Parnell (Chairman,
    HUAC)   201, 202
Thomas, Olive   52
Thompson, Fred   66
Three Bad Men   141
Three Little Pigs, The   167
Three Musketeers, The   53, 166
Three Nightingales, The   111
three-color, three-strip process (System
    Three)   167

three-strip cameras   167
three-strip Technicolor process   160, 165
Throop College of Technology   123
Tillie's Punctured Romance   29
Time Magazine   197
Time Out For Lessons   119
To Be Or Not To Be   122, 195
To Catch A Thief   151
Toast of New York, The   149
Today We Live   126
Todd Boarding School   171
Toland, Gregg   166, 170, 172, 173, 197
Tone, Franchot   202
Too Much, Too Soon   161
Top Hat   130
Topper   134, 149
Touch of Evil   208
Tracy, Spencer   137, 138, 153, 154, 155,
    156, 158, 215
Traffic in Souls   69
Trail of the Lonesome Pine, The   167
Tree Grows in Brooklyn, A   215
Trespasser, The   82
Triangle Studios   59
Triangle, also Triangle Films, also
    Triangle Film Corp   22, 30, 56, 57,
    68
Tribute to a Bad Man   155
Tri-Ergon sound system   73
Trip to the Moon, A   9, 10, 133
Tri-State Motion Picture Company   124
Triumph of the Will   188
Truckline Café (play)   209
True Grit   158, 162
Truman Administration   192
Truman, Harry S. (Vice President)   199
Trumbo, Dalton   201
Tsar Nicholas II   90
Tucker, George   69
Tunisian Victory   189
Turpin, Ben   30
Twain, Mark   52
Twentieth Century   126, 127
Twentieth Century Fox Corporation, also
    Twentieth Century Fox   62, 63, 72,
    90, 161, 170, 174, 184, 185, 189, 204,
    211, 214, 215
*Twenty Thousand Leagues Under The
    Sea*   133
Two Color Kodachrome system   166

two-color additive system (System
    One)   166
two-color subtractive system (System
    Two)   166, 167
Tzara, Tristan   97
U.S. Marine Corp   185
UFA Studios (Universum Film AG)   85,
    86, 89, 132
Un Chien Andalou   97, 98
Unaccustomed As We Are   117
Unchanging Sea, The   16
Unholy Three, The   83
Uniformed Entertainment Units   191
Union Pacific   166
United Artists (UA)   23, 24, 26, 53, 102,
    151, 180, 181, 184, 216
United Artists/Goldwyn   68
United Services Organization
    (USO)   190
United States Justice Department   184
Universal, also Universal Pictures, also
    Universal Films   46, 61, 68, 71, 80,
    81, 115, 152, 184, 212, 214, 216
Universal City   46, 55, 140
Universal headquarters   60
Universal studios   12, 132, 135, 140,
    141, 143, 177
Universal Weekly (newsreel)   69
Universum Film AG (UFA Studios)   85
Unseen Enemy, An   17
Up the River   154
USO   153
V For Victory   182
Valentino, Rudolph   39, 117
Vallee, Rudee   131
Vamp (poem)   47
Vampire, The (poem)   47
Van Dyke, W.S. (director)   78, 147, 148
Van Runkel, Samuel   60
Veidt, Conrad   86, 87
Venice Film Festival   218, 219
Verdoux, Monsieur   43
Verne, Jules   133
Vertov, Dziga (spinning top)   91, 95, 96
Vidor, King   139, 165
Vietnam War   44, 163, 187
Villa, Pancho   62
Virginia City   160
Virginian, The   151
Visconti, Luchino   218

Vitagraph   11, 65, 74, 75
Vitagraph Broadway Review   128
Vitagraph Concert, The   74
Vitagraph studios   32, 59, 117
Vitaphone   80
Vitaphone sound technology   75, 76
Vitascope company   9
Vitascope projection system   11
Volstead Act   34
von Sternberg, Joseph (director)   39, 138
von Strondheim, Erich   60, 61, 82, 100
vote-counting machine, patent   5
Wagner   89
Wagon Master, The   80
Wake Island   193
Wake of the Bounty   159
Walk East On Beacon!   204
Walk, Don't Run   151
Wall Street crash, October 1929   110
Wallis, Hal   195, 196
Walsh, Raoul (director)   20, 79, 141, 159, 161, 162, 208
Walt Disney Studios   71
Wanger, Walter   180
War Activities Committee (WAC)   182
War Bonds   190
War Comes to America   188
War of the Worlds (radio program)   171
Warfield, David   58
Warner Brothers, also Warner   20, 25, 57, 62, 63, 64, 65, 66, 74, 75, 76, 77, 78, 79, 80, 109, 111, 120, 125, 128, 129, 138, 139, 140, 146, 148, 149, 152, 153, 155, 159, 160, 161, 175, 182, 184, 187, 191, 192, 194, 195, 216
Warner, Albert   64, 65
Warner, Benjamin   64
Warner, Harry   63, 64, 65, 74
Warner, Jack   37, 64, 65, 74, 125, 139, 159, 180, 181, 201
Warner, Mrs. Jack   159
Warner, Pearl   64
Warner, Sam   64, 65, 74, 77
Warrens of Virginia, The (play)   51
Warrior's Husband, The   157
Watch on the Rhine   195
Way Down East   24
Way of All Flesh, The   88
Way Out West   118
Wayne, General Anthony   161

Wayne, John   68, 69, 143, 144, 158, 161, 162, 163, 165, 210
Weary River   81
Wedding Present   149
Wedgewood, Thomas   1
Wee Willie Winkie   143
weird tales   204
Weismuller, Johnny   136
Welcome Comedians (series)   125
Welles, Orson   43, 113, 170, 171, 172, 173, 174, 175, 208, 213, 222
Wellman, William   109, 185
Wells, H.G.   132, 171
West, Billy   70, 117
West, Mae   139, 149
Westbrook   200
Western Electric Company   74, 75, 80
westerns   135, 204
Westinghouse   74
Whale, James (director)   132, 133
What Ever Happened to Baby Jane?   153
What Happened to Mary (film series)   135
When You're In Love   149
Where The Sidewalk Ends   208
White Front Theater   45
White Heat   208
White Shadows of the South Seas   78
White Ship, The   218
White telephone films (Italy)   218
White, Pearl   135
Whiteman, Paul   213
Whitney, John Hay Jock   167, 182
Whoopee   50, 128
Why We Fight (series)   188
Wiene, Robert   86
Wilder, Billy   122
Wilder, Billy   206, 207, 208, 210, 213
Wilder, Thornton   215
Wilhelm, Kaiser   64
Williams, Tennessee   202, 208, 209, 215
Wilson, Fireworks   20
Wilson, Dooley   196
Wilson, Woodrow   21
Winchell, Walter   200
Wings   151
Winkler, Margaret   71
Winning of Barbara Worth, The   151
Winning Your Wings   189

Winters, Shelly   211, 212
Wise, Robert   155, 173, 174
Wizard of Oz, The   131, 165, 167, 179
Woman of the Species, The   16
Woman of the Year   155, 158
Women's Christian Temperance   108
Wood, John S.   202
Works Progress Administration
    (WPA)   171
World War I   190
World War II   182, 197, 199, 200
Wright Brothers   65
Wuthering Heights   166, 190
Wyler, William   166, 174, 190, 197, 208
Wyman, Jane   50
Yale Drama School   202
Yalta   199
Yank in the RAF, A   181
Yankee Doodle Dandy   183
Yates, Herbert J.   68
You Bet Your Life   114
You Can't Cheat an Honest Man   115
You Can't Take It With You   127
Young Men's Christian Association
    (YMCA)   107
Young Mr. Lincoln   166
Young, Loretta   145, 146, 154
Yukon Patrol   195
Zanuck, Darryl   62, 63, 64, 161, 170,
    174, 175, 189
Zavattini, Cesare   218, 220
Ziegfeld Follies   114
Ziegfeld Girl   185
Ziegfeld, Florenz   79
Zinneman, Fred   210
Zoetrope   2
Zola   100
Zoopraxiscope   4
Zukor, Adolph   11, 12, 18, 22, 23, 25,
    30, 36, 37, 38, 39, 48, 49, 52, 57, 58,
    66, 76, 106